Unworking Choreography

D1611089

Oxford Studies in Dance Theory

MARK FRANKO, Series Editor

French Moves: The Cultural Politics of le hip hop
Felicia McCarren

Watching Weimar Dance
Kate Elswit

Poetics of Dance: Body, Image, and Space in the Historical Avant-Gardes
Gabriele Brandstetter

Dance as Text: Ideologies of the Baroque Body, Second Edition
Mark Franko

Choreographies of 21st Century Wars
Edited by Gay Morris and Jens Richard Giersdorf

*Ungoverning Dance: Contemporary European Theatre Dance
and the Commons*
Ramsay Burt

Unworking Choreography: The Notion of the Work in Dance
Frédéric Pouillaude

Unworking Choreography

The Notion of the Work in Dance

Frédéric Pouillaude

Translated by Anna Pakes

OXFORD
UNIVERSITY PRESS

OXFORD
UNIVERSITY PRESS

Oxford University Press is a department of the University of Oxford. It furthers
the University's objective of excellence in research, scholarship, and education
by publishing worldwide. Oxford is a registered trade mark of Oxford University
Press in the UK and certain other countries.

Published in the United States of America by Oxford University Press
198 Madison Avenue, New York, NY 10016, United States of America.

© Oxford University Press 2017
Originally published in French as *Le désœuvrement chorégraphqiue. Étude sur la notion
d'œuvre en danse* by (c) Librairie Philosophique J. Vrin, Paris, 2009. http://www.vrin.fr

This translation has been made possible by the financial support of the Institut Universitaire
de France, the Prix 2013 de la traduction du Salon du livre et de la revue d'art - Festival
de l'histoire de l'art à Fontainebleau, and the Centre National du Livre.

Library of Congress Cataloging-in-Publication Data
Names: Pouillaude, Frédéric, 1978– author.
Title: Unworking choreography : the notion of the work in dance / Frédéric
Pouillaude; translated by Anna Pakes.
Other titles: Désœuvrement chorégraphqiue. English
Description: New York, NY: Oxford University Press, 2017. |
Series: Oxford studies in dance theory | Translation of: Le désœuvrement chorégraphqiue. |
Includes bibliographical references and index.
Identifiers: LCCN 2016036117 | ISBN 9780199314652 (paperback) |
ISBN 9780199314645 (cloth) | ISBN 9780190649968 (Oxford scholarship online)
Subjects: LCSH: Dance—Aesthetics. | Dance—Philosophy. |
BISAC: PERFORMING ARTS / Dance / Notation. | PHILOSOPHY / Mind & Body. |
MUSIC / Genres & Styles / Dance.
Classification: LCC GV1588.3 .P6813 2017 | DDC 792.8—dc23
LC record available at https://lccn.loc.gov/2016036117

9 8 7 6 5 4 3 2 1

Paperback printed by Webcom Inc., Canada
Hardback printed by Bridgeport National Bindery, Inc., United States of America

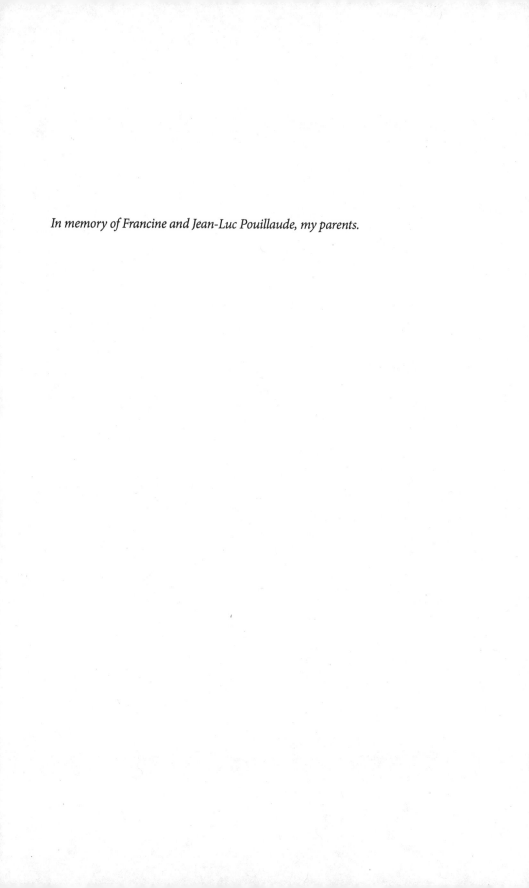

In memory of Francine and Jean-Luc Pouillaude, my parents.

CONTENTS

PREFACE TO THE ENGLISH TRANSLATION

I am honored to see *Le désœuvrement chorégraphique* translated into English and published in the Oxford Studies in Dance Theory series. The original French manuscript was almost complete by the end of 2006, and the book was published in 2009. Given that this translation appears more than ten years after the manuscript's completion, one wonders if the person writing these lines is the same person who wrote the book. In this preface, I would like to introduce the reader to the book's main argument, retracing the intellectual and biographical process of its genesis; I would also like to examine what has changed in dance philosophy in the last ten years, including some things that challenge my thesis and other things that could be updated or addressed in different ways.

In 2002, I was studying philosophy at the École Normale Supérieure in Paris, preparing to begin a PhD. I was also a dancer, with training in ballet and a commitment to contemporary dance. I was convinced at the time (as I am even now) that the only way philosophy could move forward, after the end of metaphysics and the general obsolescence of speculative discourse, was to become engaged with empirical, historical subject matter, which in turn implied a need for real and extraphilosophical expertise (as in the case of Georges Canguilhem with medicine, Jean-Toussaint Desanti with mathematics, or Michel Foucault with social history). I was also convinced that the traditional (or "Continental") discipline of history of philosophy was not the way forward for contemporary thought. My personal background had made me a kind of expert in one empirical field, namely, dance, to which I therefore decided to devote my PhD research.

Two methodological problems quickly emerged. The first concerned philosophical discourse: there were (and still are) very few philosophical texts about dance, and the few that existed (or now exist) were really not very satisfying, such that I always remained somewhat confused and stuck for answers when asked about the philosophical corpus on which I based my work. The second

problem concerned dance itself: if my PhD was to be about dance, it should logically have focused on selected major choreographic works from dance history,
used as a basis for aesthetic and philosophical analysis. But these choreographic
works were not accessible to the academic community to which I belonged, at
least not in the same way as paintings or novels. They were not "stable," self-
identical objects, accessible to anyone at any moment. Every time I mentioned
a title—for example, *Giselle* or Maguy Marin's *May B.*—not only could I not be
sure that my interlocutor had a clear idea of the objects I was referring to but,
mostly, I could not even indicate where he or she might directly access these
works. As a result, each time I was asked about the artistic corpus on which my
work was based, I also found it difficult to answer the question—not because
the artworks did not exist but because their stability and accessibility were not
very clear.

These were the two methodological problems I faced. Instead of sweeping
them under the carpet, I decided to make them the explicit object of my research,
in a reflexive gesture quite typical of philosophy. My research really began when
I figured out a possible link between the two problems, between the lack of
philosophical literature on dance and the fragile status of choreographic works.

To understand that link, one needs a clearer sense of the philosophical literature on dance that does exist. Dance has disappeared *twice* from philosophy.
First *literally*, with Kant's aesthetics and the *Critique of the Power of Judgment*
(2000 [1790]), which simply expels dance from the system of the fine arts. The
birth of aesthetics as a systematic, philosophical discipline (which Kant's work
emblematically represents) is also the moment when dance paradoxically disappears as a legitimate object of philosophical study. This literal absence of
dance within the various systems of the fine arts was reinforced by the work of
the great nineteenth-century German philosophers—by Hegel, Schelling, and
Schopenhauer.

But dance also disappeared a second time, not *literally* but *transcendentally*,
through the various ways in which it was philosophically re-evaluated. After its
exclusion by Kant, dance could only become an object for philosophical inquiry
outside of the system of the fine arts, even outside aesthetics. The process began
with Nietzsche, continued with Paul Valéry and Erwin Straus, and concludes
(or, at least, so I hope) with Alain Badiou. In the work of each of these thinkers,
Dance (the first letter becomes capitalized) is never considered positively as a
real, empirical art form, with authors, works, venues, and specific dates, but
rather as a private bodily experience that is simultaneously infra- and supra-
artistic: *infra-artistic* in the sense that it is a subjective experience that does not
aim to produce or communicate anything, and *supra-artistic* insofar as it is considered the origin or condition of possibility of all the arts (as Badiou claims,
"Dance is not an art because it is the sign of the possibility of art as inscribed in

the body"; 2005 [1998], 69). Not only do these thinkers never mention specific choreographic works in their texts, they also describe dance in a way that suggests Dance has nothing to do with producing or showing dance *works*: dancing, they suggest, consists mainly in expending time and energy, in the present, in the solipsism and hedonism of kinesthesia; dancing becomes a kind of orgasmic ecstasy without product or the possibility of transmission. Furthermore, in less descriptive and more conceptual perspective, Dance is ultimately denied status as a real art and instead given an odd transcendental status as origin or condition of possibility of all other art forms. This transcendental status might appear to be a positive re-evaluation of dance's status. Yet my claim is that, by elevating Dance to the dignity of origin, this paradoxical re-evaluation only makes choreographic works disappear once again. This philosophical image of Dance (the second way in which works disappear) can be summarized in the claim that, for philosophers, dance is merely "absence of the work" [*l'absence d'œuvre*] or "worklessness," adapting Michel Foucault's claim about madness.

This philosophical notion of *absence of the work* helped me to take the next step in my research. I was now able to connect my two methodological problems, namely, the paucity of philosophical literature on dance and the ontological weakness of dance itself. If so many philosophers were spontaneously inclined to describe dance as unproductive practice (as *absence of the work*), this could not be pure chance; it must have something to do with dance itself and its complicated relationship with the notion of the work. Of course, these philosophers were literally wrong: choreographic works do exist. We can cite authors and titles. And dance is in fact an art form alongside others, with its own history, schools, trends, and so on. Nonetheless, choreographic works do not seem as ontologically robust, easily identifiable or stable as (say) paintings or novels. As a performing art, dance generates moving objects that have always been difficult to identify across time and space, and a feature of whose being is their disappearance. Thus, the "absence of the work" in the philosophical discourse on dance could be interpreted as a direct consequence or speculative effect of the more fundamental, internal fragility specific to choreographic works. I then needed to modify my terminology only slightly to confront my topic head-on. Instead of "absence of the work," I proposed the term *désœuvrement* (translated here as "unworking") to describe the various ways in which dance history and practices have continually challenged the notion of the work. Hence my general title, *Le désœuvrement chorégraphique*, or *Unworking Choreography*. The French word *désœuvrement* also has a moral meaning in the way it is commonly used to designate a state of idleness or inactivity. My title thus rested on an implicit pun that is very hard to translate, evoking both the common meaning (idleness) and the more etymological, artificial sense of a process by which a work (*œuvre*) is exposed to its own undoing: a process of unworking.

Some further explanation is needed to specify the direction of the argument in part I, which aims to guide the reader from *absence of the work* to *unworking*, from the abstraction of a philosophical image to the reality of dance practices and products. This movement is first and foremost dialectical. If my criticisms of Paul Valéry, Erwin Straus, and Alain Badiou are strong and I denounce the abstract image of dance as orgasmic or ecstatic experience, I nonetheless try to extract and retain some elements of truth from their arguments. But those elements of truth (centrally, choreographic works' ontological weakness) are not known to the writers themselves, who may be right, but for reasons and in a sense of which they remain unaware. I hope that my dialectical strategy can be discerned in the simultaneous distance and proximity between the two expressions, between *absence of the work* and *unworking*, between an abstract, static fact (on the one hand) and a dynamic and concrete process (on the other). Secondly, these philosophical discourses demand to be taken seriously. They do not deserve commentary and deconstruction merely as philosophical bloopers on dance. They really do grasp something about dance—something related to the unproductive core of dancing itself—recalling how constitutive of dancing the notions of presence, expenditure, and auto-affection really are. I must admit here that, even as I was clear that these discourses had to be critiqued and deconstructed, I also found them both fascinating and perennially true, at a different level. These writers' descriptions of dancing perfectly matched my own past experiences, my own memories of sweating and expending energy, my own fantasy of dance as an intensified present. My borrowings from Bataille and Blanchot helped me to accept this "accursed share" in the form of a naive image of dancing that, at that time, was also my own. Bataille's notion of "negativity without employ" allowed me to associate the unproductive core of dancing with a general and rather gloomy anthropology: human nature as itself negativity without employ, as a general process of unworking. Blanchot's application of the notion to literature showed me how this choreographic negativity could be at work in every art, and even in one barely involved with performance, namely, literature. With Bataille and Blanchot, I had the conceptual tools to take philosophical discourses on dance seriously and could retain something of them to assist my next move. Thirdly, even if the *absence of the work* can be amplified to become a universal dimension of general anthropology (as in Bataille), I still draw a clear distinction between the descriptions of dancing provided by these texts and the idea of dance having transcendental status (Dance not as art but as origin or condition of possibility), which remains, in my view, absurd (especially in Badiou's version). There is no transcendental Art, there is no *Ur-Art* or *Arche-Art*. There are only empirical art forms, with manifold cross-medium influences and complex histories.

I turn now to "unworking" itself—to the concrete ways in which choreographic practices challenge the very idea of the work. If we want to examine the capacity of dance to produce works, we need to conceptualize clearly what a work is. I propose two essential features: *publicity*, that is, the fact of being shown publicly and addressed to an audience; and *durability*. As regards *publicity*, the point to acknowledge is that a work cannot exist "in one's head," in either the brain or the mind. An artwork is never merely a private object: it is neither a sensation nor a thought. There must be some mechanism by which the work can be experienced as a public object, as a shareable entity, addressed by one person to another. In the case of dance, the mechanism that overrides the privacy of kinesthesia is traditionally called "the stage" (*scène* in French). I therefore needed to examine how the Western stage has functioned as a "publicity operator," that is, as one of the conditions of work-making. As regards *durability*, the Western concept of the artwork seems to imply not just that the work is public but also that it can be self-identical across time and space. In line with this conception, a desire for works is always also (albeit implicitly) a desire to transcend the limitations of time and of death, to leave something behind after one's own disappearance: a desire for durability, in other words. I therefore needed to examine how dance remains: both how it can be repeated and how it is preserved and transmitted. With these two conceptual conditions (publicity and durability), I had two clearly defined fields to investigate, two fields where the notion of *unworking choreography* could be developed.

The first of these conditions is explored in part II. It is debatable whether what we call "the stage" or "live performance" really is an adequate structure for presenting artworks. Indeed, the phenomenon of live performance (which is what I really mean by "stage" [*scène*]) has always been subject to two connected extra-artistic tendencies: it is either elevated to the rank of ritual or demoted to the role of mere entertainment [*divertissement*]. At practically every point in their history, theatrical dance practices have been particularly vulnerable to these two ways to disappear from the realm of art: either they become religious or political ritual (think of Greek tragedy or French *Ballet de cour*) or, in contrast, they are conceived and employed as mere entertainment, as providing pleasant, even delightful, events that still have nothing to do with art. These two tendencies to disappear from the domain of art constitute what I called the "heteronomy of the stage": that is, the fact that theatrical space is always torn between ritual and entertainment and is certainly not the best site on which to present (aesthetically) autonomous artworks that are free from extra-aesthetic (religious, political, or entertainment) functions.

Two comments are pertinent here: one concerns ritual, the other entertainment or *divertissement*. First, dance modernity did not negate the choreographic dependence on ritual—quite the opposite. Just think of Duncan's or Laban's fascination with the (religious or political) ritual potential of dance. Think also of Mallarmé and Artaud, whose writings strongly associate dance modernity with a desire for new rituals, better suited to the modern spirit of the late nineteenth and early twentieth centuries. This modern focus on the dance-ritual connection is also, for all these writers and choreographers, a way of rejecting the function to entertain traditionally associated with dance. Second, note that the French word for "entertainment" is *divertissement*, a word that also has a special, technical sense, referring to the choreographic intermissions or interludes (*divertissements chorégraphiques*) within operas. For many years, dance appeared on the stage only as a minor, diverting element of a major, serious opera. The general heteronomy of the stage (based on the double vanishing point of ritual and entertainment) is further reinforced by dance's minor status and dependency within the field of performing arts. My question, then, was twofold. When and how did dance achieve, historically and artistically, an autonomous status within that field? And when and how was the stage (the theater, or performance) able to liberate itself from both ritual and entertainment? My answer was twofold as well: the acknowledgment of dance as an autonomous performing art happens very late, both artistically and institutionally, and remains fragile; meanwhile, the autonomy of the stage is also very precarious, with the performing event always capable of turning itself back into ritual or entertainment. This twofold answer points to the first concrete meaning of the term "unworking," the first issue dance encounters in its process of work-making.

Moving now to the second problem, that of durability, discussed in part III: What "survives" of a dance performance once it has taken place? What can remain? Ordinarily, a performance remains by being repeated, or (as some analytic philosophers say) re-instantiated. Repetition requires that the identity of the work be established. The easiest and most common way of establishing and preserving the identity of a temporal work is notation or writing, a method employed in both music and theater. I therefore had to examine the problem of dance notation—what might be described as the failure of notation systems in dance history. When I speak of "failure," I do not mean that in dance such systems are not adequate to their objects or that there is some ineffable feature of dance (a choreographic *je ne sais quoi*) that cannot be captured in writing. I mean simply that dance notation systems have never really been integrated with dance practices, except at very few historical moments: even now, very few dancers or choreographers can write, or even read, a notation score in (for example) Labanotation or Benesh. This lack of practical integration explains why dances survive in the way they do, through person-to-person transmission. Choreographic works are repeated from one season to another, from one generation to another, but this repetition is almost always devoid of written mediation and remains based on the continuity of the oral tradition, grounded on personal transmission and teaching.

This seems an odd mode of existence for an artwork. Nelson Goodman's ontology of art helped me to describe this oddity more precisely. In *Languages of Art*, Goodman distinguishes two kinds of artworks, or rather two regimes of artwork identity: the autographic and the allographic. By "autographic work," he means a singular material object, which can be counterfeited and whose identity rests on its material history of production (like a painting or a sculpture, for instance). By "allographic work," he means an ideal object, susceptible of multiple instantiations, which cannot be counterfeited and whose identity (resting on a distinction between essential and contingent features) is independent of any history of production, as in the case of a symphony or a novel (at least, in Goodman's view). Drawing on that distinction, I had a clear thesis to defend: choreographic works are neither autographic nor allographic. They are not autographic because they can be repeated: they do not usually consist in a singular event, which would be the performing equivalent of what Goodman calls an autographic object; they possess a general identity, which rests on a distinction between essential and contingent features, and that distinction is precisely what makes repetition possible. But nor are they allographic because that general identity cannot be accessed from an external and anonymous perspective—like that of the written score—but remains dependent on the work's material history of production and transmission. Finally, I had discovered a precise description of the ontological peculiarity of choreographic works, as neither autographic nor allographic. And this argument was also a refutation of Goodman, who does not really consider the possibility of a third term between the autographic and the allographic, whereas in my view choreographic works offer perfect examples of such a third term.

This technical description of the ontological oddity of choreographic works corresponds precisely with the second sense of the term "unworking": the special way in which dance confronts the issue of durability without any substantial system of writing. I only had to develop the manifold consequences of this simple fact (repetition without writing), which led me to various topics like the diverse structures of oral transmission, the role played by archives and documentary sources in dance re-enactments, and the important issue of the status of video recordings. These consequences are also developed in part IV, devoted to the notion of "dance technique."

One last comment before moving on to update the discussion in this book. I mentioned how Bataille had helped me accept my own naive attachment to presence and liveness, reconceptualized as expenditure, nonproductivity, and negativity without employ. These notions perfectly matched my youthful romanticism and the gloominess toward which I was perhaps too easily inclined. Certainly, I would not address these issues in the same way today. Nonetheless, even at that time, there was a strong counterweight to that romanticism of presence and expenditure, another important influence without which this book would have never been finished, namely Jacques Derrida. When I began to work on the problem of dance notation, I was reading the three major books published by Derrida in 1967: *Of Grammatology, Voice and Phenomenon*, and *Writing and Difference*, which quickly became close companions of my own research. Derrida—an astute reader of texts—not only helped me to deconstruct the writings I was discussing (Valéry and Straus, but also Mallarmé and Artaud) but principally gave me the conceptual tools to critique my own fantasy of presence, providing the necessary counterweight to Bataille's influence. No, there is no such thing as pure presence. Presence is always penetrated by repetition and conceptuality, and there is no singularity that is not always already permeated and contaminated with some otherness and exteriority. Even in death there can be no total consumption of the present that leaves no remains or traces. Derrida's concept of "arche-writing" became for me the term for this ineluctable penetration of presence, also fully at work in dance practices and dance history. Mao Zedong said that one has to walk on two legs: so I did, with Bataille as one leg and Derrida as the other, trying to find a precarious balance between presence and trace. Sometimes I limped a little, sometimes I ran pretty fluently.

I would now like to explore what in the book could be updated and those features that make it clearly a product of its time, the first decade of the twenty-first century.

First of all, if I were to write the book again today, I would certainly not say that philosophy has never addressed the question of choreographic works. For some years now, dance has been a legitimate object for analytic aesthetics, and the ontological problem of work identity is one of the main concerns of that approach. One could cite, as examples, Graham McFee's *The Philosophical Aesthetics of Dance* (2011) or David Davies's *Philosophy of the Performing Arts* (also 2011). Nevertheless, these philosophical approaches address the problem in such an abstract and ahistorical way that choreographic works and practices seem, once again, to disappear, in favor of a merely logical puzzle linked to the status of ideal entities: If choreographic works are ideal entities, in what sense do they exist? Should we be Platonists or Nominalists? And so on. In this regard, note how it is almost always the same work title—*Swan Lake*—that is cited as an example of the logical puzzle, as if dance history had produced only one work, and despite the fact that almost any other work could be referenced instead. Discussing *Swan Lake*, these philosophers never mention the quite complex history of the work, nor the equally complex history of its transmission, so that *Swan Lake* seems to become a mere label, an emblem of the ontological problem of work identity. Such abstraction is not inevitable. Anna Pakes's *Choreography Invisible: The Disappearing Work of Dance* (forthcoming) brilliantly demonstrates that analytic aesthetics can combine conceptual rigor with empirical knowledge and attention to history and practices. I hope that my own ontological approach manifests the same kind of empirical engagement.

Secondly, if I were to write the book again, I would give greater prominence to relevant Anglo-American literature. For example, the reader might wonder what relation there is between my own concept of *unworking choreography* and Peggy Phelan's notion of performance as *disappearance*. I must confess that I discovered Phelan's *Unmarked: The Politics of Performance* (1993) very late, at a time when my book was almost complete. Ten years later, I would suggest that Phelan's statement seems to me both excessive and naive: excessive because it emphasizes only one aspect of performance (its disappearing presence), and naive because this disappearance is not in itself a way to resist capitalism, commodification, and reification. A counterweight is needed to consider all those elements that exceed the vanishing present of performance. As shown by Rebecca Schneider in *Performing Remains* (2011), attention to what remains of performance is also a way to resist a new kind of capitalism, a "performing capitalism," a capitalism of the perpetual event and the forever new.

When I completed the manuscript in 2006, André Lepecki's *Exhausting Dance* (2006) was not yet published. Nevertheless, I had already had the opportunity to discover a clear convergence of objects and method by reading Lepecki's essay on dance notation, "Inscribing Dance" (2004). This convergence was extended when, as guest editor for the *Drama Review*, Lepecki invited me to submit an article for a special issue on dance and philosophy. This became "*Scène* and Contemporaneity," translated by Noémie Solomon (Pouillaude 2007), the text being also (in a slightly different version) the start of this book's first conclusion. The connections between *Exhausting Dance* and *Unworking Choreography* are important but mainly due to a powerful choreographic zeitgeist and a common immersion in the same field of references.

The Anglo-American reader will be aware of other omissions too. For instance, Sally Banes's (1987) statement about modern dance is cited without any real engagement with the historical debate between Banes and Susan Manning concerning modernity, modernism, and postmodernism (Manning 1988, 1989; Banes 1989). Equally, some pages consider the relation between dance and labor without specifically making use of Mark Franko's book *The Work of Dance* (2002). There has been some slight updating of the references for this translation. But seriously considering the whole field of Anglo-American dance studies would have implied writing a different book. For better or for worse, *Unworking Choreography* preserves its unavoidable flavor of provincial "Frenchness."

Thirdly, this book clearly belongs to its time and place. The final chapters ("The Reflexive Labor of Performance" and "The Memorial Labor of the Work") can be read as a philosophical description of two major trends in European choreography of the early 2000s: on the one hand, the reflexive investigation of performance as a medium through what has been called "conceptual dance"; and, on the other hand, the performed activation of dance history and memory onstage in the work of artists like Dominique Brun, the Carnets Bagouet, Latifa Laâbissi, the Quatuor Knust, Olga de Soto, or Mark Tompkins. My own research was clearly connected to the second of these trends and was involved in a more general movement that (perhaps in reaction to the topos of ephemerality) focused on memory, history, archive, documentary trace, transmission, and re-enactment as fundamental issues for dance studies. But this focus on history could not hide what was occurring simultaneously, often in the work of the very same artists, in the complete redefinition of what a dance event could be, displayed and developed by artists such as Xavier Le Roy, Jérôme Bel, and Laurent Pichaud. The current situation of dance and contemporary choreography is now very different—it has other issues and concerns. If the final chapters of this book can be read as historical documents on European choreography, I do hope that the conceptual and philosophical framework leading up to them has some more general, transferable significance. Again, I have tried to walk on two legs, balancing between the universality of the concept and the historical inscription of the critic.

This translation has been made possible by the support of the following institutions: the Institut Universitaire de France, the Festival d'histoire de l'art de Fontainebleau, and the Centre National du Livre. I warmly thank them. I would like also to express my profound gratitude to Mark Franko and Norman Hirschy from Oxford University Press for their continuous support and advice throughout the translation process. My final thanks go to Anna Pakes. Translating Le désœuvrement chorégraphique into English required a high level of competence in French, philosophy, and dance. Fulfilling all these requirements, Anna Pakes was certainly a rare pearl, perhaps unique for the job. I profoundly thank her for the amazing work she accomplished and the brilliant solutions she proposed.

Frédéric Pouillaude
Paris, June 20, 2016

TRANSLATOR'S PREFACE

Frédéric Pouillaude's fascinating book poses a number of issues for the translator: here I will offer a rationale for solutions proposed to the most pressing issues, drawing the reader's attention to problems of transfer in the general approach and specific concepts or terminology employed.

The first issue to note is the particular registers of philosophical writing employed here, which draw largely on "Continental," and particularly French, philosophy, although reference is made to an impressive range of traditions and authors, from Plato to Immanuel Kant, Friedrich Nietzsche to Nelson Goodman, Gérard Genette to Maurice Blanchot. The work of these philosophers will be more or less well known to the readership of the English translation. Poststructuralist thought's influence on Anglo-American dance and performance studies (indeed, on the humanities in general) has no doubt accustomed English readers to relevant modes of discourse, at least to some extent. Yet most such readers probably remain less familiar with twentieth-century French philosophy and literature than the book's original audience. Nonetheless, I have kept explanatory glosses and footnotes to a minimum, assuming that Pouillaude's detailed explication of certain authors' positions to some extent speaks for itself and not wishing to overload the text with extensive editorial interference. Of course, thinking one's way into the philosophical apparatus employed here implies not just a degree of background knowledge but also an understanding of the typical modes of exposition and argument of that apparatus. French philosophical writing tends toward abstract conceptualization, manifest linguistically in frequent nominalization, that is, the use (even coinage) of abstract nouns and noun structures where verbal or adjectival phrases might be more natural in English. Where possible, I have tried to soften the English presentation of abstract concepts (for example, "ritual" for "ritualité" in part II, chapter 2), while retaining others that seemed difficult to naturalize without distorting or diluting Pouillaude's argument (for example, "empiricity" as employed in part II, chapter 1).

The second key translation issue concerns particular items of vocabulary: key terms in Pouillaude's discussion that do not have exact equivalents in English. Sometimes, apparent equivalents convey the denotative content clearly but have different connotations. Thus, the French word *désœuvrement* figures in the book's title and is the central organizing concept of the argument. It might be rendered by "unworking" or "worklessness," the former implying an ongoing process where the latter suggests a state of being. The French word carries both meanings, however, and (as Pouillaude indicates in his preface) can also denote the personal characteristic "idleness," unlike either English alternative. In discussion with the author, I have mostly opted for "unworking" in this translation, to designate a process that dance undergoes on multiple fronts (as Pouillaude himself eloquently explains in the new preface and conclusions). Occasionally "worklessness" seemed more appropriate (particularly when Blanchot's work was referenced, since Susan Hanson often takes this option in the English translation of his work). After either English word, the French *désœuvrement* is typically included here in square brackets to remind the reader of its range of meanings in the original language.

Similar issues apply in the case of the French word *divertissement*, which can mean "diversion," "entertainment," and/or "choreographic interlude." Pouillaude's argument makes explicit play of this polysemy, which none of the possible English equivalents has to the same extent. I have therefore typically retained the French word here (sometimes using "entertainment" instead where this seemed more appropriate to the context). *Divertissement* should be familiar (at least in its technical sense) to dance specialists, although they may need to bear in mind the broader range of meanings too. Also problematic for the translator is the French word *spectacle* (the key topic of part II, chapter 2), which could be rendered as "show," "spectacle," or "performance," although none of these options quite captures the range of meaning of the French word. "Show" carries strong connotations of light entertainment (stronger than *spectacle* in French, which is more frequently used in art dance contexts that the English "show"), while "performance" refers more to a process than a social institution (the historical/conceptual development of the spectacle *as institution* being Pouillaude's focus). I have tended to use the English "spectacle," despite its possible emphasis on (extravagant use of) the trappings of the stage (the French word being somewhat more neutral). I hope the context will make clear that the English "spectacle" is also intended more neutrally here, to mean something closer to its French cognate.

The third point to note is my approach to citations from other writers included in Pouillaude's text. Where possible, I have cited the published English translations of those cited texts originally written in other languages (French, but also German and ancient Greek). Most have been translated only once, but in some cases there are two or more translations from which to choose. Aristotle's *Poetics* in particular (discussed in depth in part II, chapter 3) is available in numerous English editions. Here I reference mainly Stephen Halliwell's translation, partly because of its wide availability but also because it respects the same chapter divisions as the French translation (by Dupont-Roc and Lallot) employed by Pouillaude. There are, however, some discrepancies in the different translators' interpretations of the Greek text and their approaches to dealing with inconsistencies. Where these affect the argument of this book directly, I have amended or supplemented the cited translation, adding explanatory footnotes. The close textual analysis of Stéphane Mallarmé's prose works (part II, chapter 1) also poses particular translation issues. Mallarmé's prose, like his poetry, fully exploits the syntactical and lexical resources of the French language, such that it is impossible to convey the same wealth of meaning with the same economy when translating into other languages. Again, I have chosen to cite a translation (by Barbara Johnson) that is widely available and has the advantage of rendering into English the *Divagations* in their entirety. Discrepancies between Johnson's translation and Pouillaude's reading of Mallarmé are again highlighted in footnotes, with the translated citations amended as necessary.

There are also citations from some French (particularly historical) texts that have not (to my knowledge) been translated into English (for example, the treatises by Louis de Cahusac and Claude-François Ménéstrier). I offer my own translations of these quotations, but the reader should bear in mind that I am not a seventeenth- or eighteenth-century specialist. Those who are might reasonably question the vocabulary choice and register of my translations: as they stand, they are approximations intended to serve Pouillaude's reading and argument, rather than attempts to produce definitive renderings of the texts as such. Note that both translated texts and historical texts with later editions are referenced here by publication year of their translated/modern version, followed by the original publication date in square brackets the first time the text is cited. The bibliography gives both the year of the edition and the original publication year, as well as the original title where appropriate.

I dedicate my work on this translation to the memory of Carol Clark (1940–2015), Fellow and Emeritus Fellow in French at Balliol College, Oxford. Without her support and encouragement early in my career as a linguist and dance specialist, I would never have been in a position to take on the challenge.

ACKNOWLEDGMENTS

Thanks first of all to Catherine Kintzler, who has been present through the different stages of this research—its moments of doubt, enthusiasm, and renunciation.

Thanks to Bernard Sève, who, throughout these years of research and writing, has been a constant partner in conversation. What you are about read would quite simply not have existed without him.

Thanks to all those friends, colleagues, dancers, choreographers, and philosophers who at various moments took the time to read my work and offer encouragement, particularly Lluis Ayet, Alain Badiou, Renaud Barbaras, Anne Bossière, Dominique Brun, Jacqueline Challet-Haas, Axelle Chassagnette, Véronique Fabbri, Barbara Formis, François Frimat, Gérard Genette, Valérie Gérard, Claude Imbert, André Lepecki, Jacqueline Lichtenstein, Mathilde Monnier, Bernard Pautrat, Dominique Pradelle, Jacques Rancière, Maël Renouard, Philippe Sabot, Noémie Solomon, Christophe Wavelet, Francis Wolff, and Pierre Zaoui.

Thanks to three very dear friends whose availability, reading, and unstinting support in the final months of editing enabled me to complete the book: Jacques-Olivier Bégot, Laetitia Doat, and Stéphane Legrand. Thanks, finally, to Noémie Coquet, for everything.

It is rare not to feel passionate about a topic of study that one has oneself chosen. I was afraid of this while writing this book and, to guard against excess, I reminded myself a thousand times of the ridiculous pretensions of the different tutors in Molière's *Bourgeois Gentilhomme.*

Thus I declare before beginning that I do not believe Dance to be the most excellent thing there is. I am convinced that there are in the world more important things even than the fine arts.

LOUIS DE CAHUSAC
La danse ancienne et moderne, ou Traité historique de la danse

INTRODUCTION

Initially, this was intended to be a philosophical study of dance, centered particularly on what is known as "contemporary" dance. But it turned out to be a different kind of book. It can be read as an explanation of why that first project failed. On which body of work could the first project have focused? Which stable, shared objects were available for interpretation and analysis aimed at an academic community that is well known to be essentially based on a culture of writing and preservation? There is no library of movement, no place where choreographic works are preserved, self-identical and accessible to all. This is a fact—a mere fact, but with huge implications.

The first implication is the incapacity of philosophy and aesthetics to conceptualize choreographic practice in line with a shared regime of the artwork. Dance always seems to spring from another space, at once more frivolous and more fundamental, which is always at one remove from the project of the artwork. I analyze this absence of the work, as it is brought to light abstractly by philosophy, in part I. This forms the real and substantial introduction to this book.

I then explore another related but distinct concept: that of *unworking* [*désoeuvrement*]. Philosophical writings on dance align the practice of movement with pure absence of production, with the experiences of energy expenditure and auto-affection. I argue that this philosophical trope (designated here by the *absence of the work*) cannot but mirror discursively the fragility proper to choreographic "works", a fragility that I call attention to and problematize here as *unworking* [*désoeuvrement*].

Two features will serve to define the concept of the work: publicity and durability. I will try to determine the extent to which choreographic objects can be described as *works* in virtue of one or other of these features. That discussion is in two distinct parts. I explore how far, in terms of these features, describing dance in "operal" terms is problematic, even impossible. In short, I am interested in how far *unworking* operates, or rather "dis-operates", within the very production of the dance work. Ultimately, I try to envisage how the work might be relayed through the perpetuation of practices and techniques, as examined in part IV.

Finally (since this is a short, even terse, introduction), I will say a few words about my method. Starting from empirical reality—as described in the literature or as lived—my method nonetheless aims to be *philosophical*, attempting to maintain a simultaneously close and distant relation to the objects analyzed, and avoiding discourse that speculates "from on high." Several teachers helped me develop this approach (in books and in life), including Georges Canguilhem, Michel Foucault, and Jean-Toussaint Desanti. Moreover, I here attempt a number of detailed critical readings, in the exegeses of the work of Valéry, Straus, Mallarmé, and Artaud, respectively. Jacques Derrida is the one who taught me how to read. Such are the sources of my (absence of) method.

PART I

Philosophy of Dance
and the Absenting of Works

The philosopher exults. No outside world!

PAUL VALÉRY
Philosophy of the Dance

Chapter 1

On Transcendental Absenting

Clearly, philosophy has paid little attention to dance. Less clearly, this paucity of commentary takes a range of specific forms that beg articulation. Historically, the few existing scraps of philosophical discussion of dance appear scattered around a glaring blank space, like a central, inaugural void. Absences are datable, just like births and deaths. The absence of dance from philosophy coincided precisely with the birth of aesthetics. This was the moment when a new kind of discourse about art and the beautiful was established, when a new discipline was formed that reorganized the disparate empirical realities of practices and works according to the architectonics of the concept (a system of the fine arts that classified and hierarchized). It was also the moment when dance was excluded, positioned beyond classification, and ultimately marginalized as an art form. I will argue that this central void operates like a caesura, determining a "before" and an "after," and weighing in systematic fashion on the discourse that follows.

Only a few decades before the publication of Kant's *Critique of the Power of Judgment* (2000 [1790]), dance still seemed acceptable as an object of theoretical inquiry. Its status as such was in large part linked to the nature of the discourses that engaged with it: these hold themselves apart from the systems about to be developed, leaving open the question of what is and is not art, and by what criteria; they operate in relative indifference to the strict organization of practices. The Abbé Dubos's *Critical Reflections on Poetry, Painting and Music* (1748 [1733]),[1] which in their very proximity to the age of aesthetics are paradigmatic of an antecedent discursive regime, speak extensively of dance, particularly of ancient

---

1. First published in Paris in 1719 as *Réflexions critiques sur la poésie et la peinture*, Dubos's treatise was substantially reworked and republished in 1733. Thomas Nugent's English translation appeared in 1748.

pantomime and its possible revival by the "moderns." These *Reflections* were extended and reworked throughout the central decades of the eighteenth century by writers such as Condillac,[2] Diderot, and Rousseau, as well as Cahusac[3] and Noverre.[4]

However, the theoretical excitement around dance was suddenly interrupted by the birth of aesthetics. Kant's *Critique of the Power of Judgment* includes only two very brief comments on dance. Hegel's *Lectures on Fine Art* (1975 [1826]) and Schelling's *Philosophy of Art* (1845 [1802–3]) legitimate and radicalize this relative silence by reducing the number of references to nil. Philosophy began to accept as art only those forms subjected to scrutiny in terms of essence, and only once they had been inscribed in a System that could regulate and conceptually generate the distinctions between them, determining their relative importance—stage-managing their entrances and exits. And from this point on, dance was purely and simply absent. Dance was not simply only rarely mentioned. It was actually expunged from the classificatory system. Architecture, sculpture, painting, music, and poetry were all ranked among the true arts. But not dance. About dance there was at most the occasional remark in passing.

This primary, "literal" absenting of dance engendered a second. Once excluded from classification as an art, dance could only return to philosophy in terms of a very particular conceptual regime, one quite different from that governing empirical art practices: according to this *transcendental* regime, dance simultaneously far exceeds and falls well short of a recognized art form, and the site where it might enter into discourse is already mapped out in advance. If dance was absent from the great aesthetic systems, this was ultimately because the clothes cut for it at the turn of the eighteenth into the nineteenth century were simultaneously too small and too big to fit. Dolled up for the fashion parade of the fine arts, dance remained badly dressed in attire at once too baggy and too tight. Dance belonged in another space, both more marginal and more fundamental, which existed alongside and beyond what was normally practiced in the name of "art." The logic of this space points to the already intersecting

2. Etienne Bonnot de Condillac's *Essai sur l'origine des connaissances humanies* was first published in Amsterdam in 1746. The first English translation, also by Thomas Nugent, appeared in 1756. Condillac's essay explores the origin of language and the problem of "language of action" (*langage d'action*) (2001 [1746]).

3. Louis de Cahusac published *La danse ancienne et modern, ou Traité historique de la danse* in 1754. The treatise has yet to be translated into English.

4. The first edition of Jean-Georges Noverre's *Lettres sur la danse et sur les ballets* was published in Lyon in 1760, and the book was revised in numerous subsequent editions. Cyril Beaumont's English translation, *Letters on Dancing and Ballets*, appeared in 1930 (referenced here as Noverre 1930).

ideas of the "anthropological" roots of dance and its possible elevation to the plane of the transcendental, that is, the conceptual realm of origins and conditions of possibility that is supposed to ground empirical practices idealistically. A universal practice, present prior to any division of domains and art objects, dance would become the transcendental moment of all art, by virtue of its *infra-artistic* character—because (and this is how it will come to be described) dance is not an art in itself but rather the anthropological site where each art becomes possible.

Arguably, this elevation of dance to a transcendental sphere has been just another way to absent dance. The literal exclusion of dance is extended by refusing it the trappings that ground the empirical reality of every other art: artists' names, titles of works, places and dates, and, more generally, a history. This indicates a necessary connection between the transcendental absenting of dance and the *absence of the work*, a connection that this first part of my book seeks to retrace.

For the moment, I return to the inaugural void—the initial moment where, simultaneously, dance vanished and aesthetics was born. This void opens up in the gap between two texts, more specifically in the gap between §14 and §51 of Kant's *Critique of the Power of Judgment*. The "elucidation by means of examples" in §14 mentions dance to illustrate the distinction between *play* and *shape*:

> All forms of the objects of the senses (of the outer as well as, mediately, the inner) is either shape [*Gestalt*] or play [*Spiel*]: in the latter case, either play of shapes [*Spiel der Gestalten*] (in space, mime and dance), or mere play of sensations [*Spiel der Empfindungen*] (in time). (Kant 2000 [1790], 110)

This contrast between *play* and *shape* takes up the traditional division between time-based and spatially configured arts but also prefigures Kant's own distinction, made in §51, between music (an art of the play of sensations in time) and the pictorial arts (the art of shapes in space).[5] Dance, however, cuts across that division and immediately upsets the general scheme based upon it. Dance is play but is also distinguished by its deployment of shapes. But this already moves dance beyond art form status by positioning it precisely at the point where two fundamental genres intersect. There is only temporal play and spatial shapes. Yet dance is a *play* of *shapes* and must therefore be understood as articulating

---

5. In Guyer and Matthews's translation (Kant 2000), the term "pictorial arts" ("*bildenden Künste*") encompasses architecture, sculpture, and painting. Architecture and sculpture are termed "plastic arts" (the arts of "sensible truth") and represent one kind of pictorial art; painting (the art of sensory appearance) is another. See §51 of the *Critique of the Power of Judgment*.

space and time, as an intersection of the pictorial arts and music. This peculiar status of being both art-kind and hybrid is never discussed again in Kant's text. Moreover, in §51 ("On the division of the beautiful arts"), when it comes to determining his classification, dance simply disappears while Kant's system continues to be based largely on the play-shape (*Spiel-Gestalt*) opposition.

The classification proposed in §51 depends on "the analogy of art with the kind of expression that people use in speaking in order to communicate to each other," through word, gesture, and tone (Kant 2000, 198). These three expressive modes are rooted in spontaneous human expression and allow a tripartite division of the fine arts into (1) the arts of speech, (2) pictorial arts ("*bildenden Künste*"), and (3) the art of the beautiful play of sensations.[6] Since dance is an "art of the play of shapes in space" (and, by definition, also in time), it might be expected to reappear in Kant's account of either the second or third of these categories: dance might be classed as a pictorial art, insofar as the latter originates in expressive gesture, or it might be an art of play, following the line taken in §14. But dance fails to reappear. Architecture, sculpture, painting, and landscape gardening all take their place in the category of pictorial art (even though this derives from gesture!). Music and the art of colors are ranked as arts of the play of sensations. But dance is nowhere. Even though a clearly defined space seems to be carved out for and to demand it, dance is ultimately omitted by Kant. The omission is explicable in several ways. For one thing, dance had a distinctly minor status, its productions never quite managing to escape the horizon of festivity and entertainment. For another, aesthetics was relatively uninterested in the stage and performance generally: if theater occupied an important position, this was centrally as a form of poetry, created to be read more than to be seen. Finally, the choreographic work lacks permanence and stability across time; its evanescence makes it hardly tractable as an object of analysis. But whatever the reasons, the fact remains that dance was purely and simply absent at the very moment when the first philosophical system of fine art was established as a thoroughgoing aesthetics.[7]

6. Kant himself acknowledges the frankly provisional character of his classification, which is merely an attempt at establishing such: "The reader will not judge of this outline for a possible division of the beautiful arts as if it were a deliberate theory. It is only one of the several experiments that still can and should be attempted" (2000, 198). See Nancy (1996 [1994]) and Escoubas (1986) for further discussion of this section.

7. The absence of dance is all the more difficult to understand given that Kant's proposed classification in §51 (into arts, respectively, of word, gesture, and tone) is largely borrowed from the work of Batteux (2015 [1746], pt. III, sec. III, chap. 1). Batteux's classification organized the field in terms of three arts: poetry, dance, and music. Kant takes up Batteux's principle but eliminates the deductions he makes from it and (to the detriment of dance) transforms the arts of gesture into arts of plastic shape without any explicit justification.

Dance returns, however, even within Kant's text. All divisions, once established, demand reconnection: once the arts have been distinguished from one another taxonomically, their possible synthesis in the form of a single work, or "combination [...] in one and the same product," becomes imaginable. Only here can the empirical reality of dance make a return (§52):

> Rhetoric can be combined with a painterly presentation of its subjects as well as objects in a play; poetry with music in song; this, in turn, with a painterly (theatrical) presentation in an opera; the play of the sensations in a piece of music with the play of shapes [*Spiel der Gestalten*] in dance, etc. (Kant 2000, 203)

Excluded from the list of pure art forms, dance can return only as an element in combination, being already a union of the pictorial and the musical. Moreover, dance is destined to return in this way only by virtue of its hybrid status as a *play* of *shapes*, at the intersection of space and time. Hence it becomes clear that dance can find a place only on the stage, the space that belongs to the combined arts and where the dream of a unification of all the arts has existed since time immemorial.[8]

Hegel and Schelling, meanwhile, retain nothing of §52 of the Third Critique but everything of §51. They reiterate and extend the absence inaugurated by Kant. Hegel's *Lectures on Fine Art* include no discussion of dance, except minimally in passing; similarly Schelling's *Philosophy of Art*.

Having made the case for this void and its function as a caesura, I turn now to examining the discourse scattered here and there around it. From antiquity to the Enlightenment, one finds a host of writings about dance, deriving from disparate and often hybrid textual genres: pedagogical, moral, theological, poetic, hygienic, technical, and semiological texts, for example. Thus in Plato an orthopedics of movement in Book VII of the *Laws* is accompanied by a theory of Bacchic trance and a taxonomy of dances as dances of war or peace. In Xenophon's *Symposium*, we find the figure of Socrates dancing at a banquet and lauding the hygienic and moral virtues of the practice (see chapters 2, 7, and 9). Plutarch, in Book IX of his *Table-talk*, develops a veritable semiotics of dance based on a tripartite distinction between movements (*phorai*), poses (*schemata*), and the demonstrative (*deixis*). Plotinus reflects on choreographic schemata within the *Enneads* (III and IV). Lucian writes his treatise *The Dance*, which goes on to function as an essential link with Enlightenment discourse. Mersenne, in his *Harmonie universelle* (1636), envisages dance as the revival of the phantasm of universal language. Claude-François Ménestrier gives us a

---

8. On the fundamentally heterogeneous character of the choreographic stage, see Part II of this book.

poetics of the *ballet de cour* in *Des ballets anciens et modernes* (1972 [1682]). And finally, close to the inaugural moment of the void just discussed, we find the dance writings of Dubos (1748 [1733]) and Condillac (2001 [1746]).

From this disparate list, what stands out is that these texts, for all their differences, all assert the possibility of treating dance as a technical and artistic configuration governed by specific rules and purposes. As Gilbert Rouget (1985 [1980]) has shown, even Bacchic dance was always framed by an organizing ritual: in other words, even when dance became explicitly linked to Dionysus, it continued to be understood as a practice and as a technique. There are techniques of possession, techniques of loss of self, of abandon, and so on, described by Plato with great precision.

By contrast, once the central void was established, dance began to be conceptualized as prior to all *techne*, prior to all training, and prior to the domain of the empirical. In short, dance preexisted the yoking of art to technique, occupying what might be called its negative space, and thus excluding itself from history. That dance was banished from the system of the fine arts here clearly functioned as a constraint. Denied status as art, dance could be reassessed only in other spheres. Since the site of its actual existence was barred by the discourse of aesthetics as dance was relegated to a minor role, it became appropriate to look beyond the empirical. One logical route remained open: to elevate dance to the transcendental plane, such that it became simultaneously both much more and much less than an acknowledged art form.

Nietzsche is an essential link in this process, although we need to be sensitive to the various emphases of his writings from different periods. Until *The Gay Science*, dance still functions in Nietzsche's text as a positive referent. It is the practice that accompanies the "Greek musical drama," traces of which can still be found in the sources just cited. In fact it is Nietzsche's training as a philologist that leads him here to write about dance in a manner that moves beyond the great void within Romantic aesthetics. Of course, his discourse on dance is already very complex. Sometimes dance is connected to the Dionysiac (§1 of *The Birth of Tragedy*), sometimes to the Apollonian (§9 of the same work). Yet it still functions as a topic for discussion. In later writings (like *Thus Spoke Zarathustra*), dance becomes something else, namely, essentially a *metaphorical trope*. Its metaphorical status allows it to be assigned a great diversity of functions: dance is the precursor of a truly Dionysiac and simultaneously impossible writing;[9] dance is an anti-Wagnerian and anti-German war machine;[10]

9. See the chapter "On Reading and Writing" from *Thus Spoke Zarathustra* and also Pautrat (1971).

10. See, for example, the essay "Nietzsche contra Wagner" or §368 of *The Gay Science*.

dance is a touchstone that allows idols to be unmasked;[11] dance is a moral code beyond all moral codes; and so on. In short, dance is anything and everything, except the dumb and concrete frivolity of the ballet.

This exclusion from the realm of the concrete has led to a second "absenting" of dance, which I call "transcendental." It is implied in some recent statements, the full implications of which I will develop in what follows. Thus, Alain Badiou suggests:

> Dance is not an art, because it is the sign of the possibility of art as inscribed in the body. (2005 [1998], 69)

Badiou's claim is rooted in the intersection between the writings of Nietzsche and those of Mallarmé. Nietzsche, he suggests, made the mistake of classifying dance as an art in the same category as theater. Mallarmé, meanwhile, had the wisdom to exclude dance from the site of theater, thereby providing himself with the means to think dance according to its own essence.[12] All true, provided one reverses the terms. In fact, it was Nietzsche who expelled dance from the theater and Mallarmé who reinstated it, with his *scribbling at the theater*.[13] But I will let this issue go and focus simply on Badiou's singular formula, that dance is not an art but a condition of art's possibility displayed directly on the body:

> I will say that dance is precisely what shows us that the body is capable of art. It provides us with the exact degree to which, at a given moment, it is capable of it. But to say that the body is capable of art does not mean making "an art of the body." Dance signals towards this artistic capacity of the body without thereby defining a singular art. (2005, 69–70)

---

11. "I would believe only in a god who could dance" (Nietzsche 1968, 153).

12. "We must put forward a provocative but necessary statement: Dance is not an art. Nietzsche's error lies in the belief that there exists a common measure between dance and theater, a measure to be found in their artistic intensity. In his own way, Nietzsche continues to arrange theater and dance within a classification of the arts. Mallarmé, on the contrary, when declaring that the theater is a superior art, does not in any sense wish to affirm the superiority of theater over dance. Of course, Mallarmé does not say that dance is not an art, but we can say it in his place, once we penetrate the genuine meaning of the six principles of dance" (Badiou 2005, 69). I will point out simply that nothing in Mallarmé's text indicates that dance is the implicit term of comparison in the formula "Theater is, by essence, superior" (Mallarmé 2007 [1897], 142–52).

13. See below 69–92 for a more developed argument to this effect. Translator's note: "Crayonné au théâtre," or "Scribbled at the Theater," is the title of one of Mallarmé's prose writings on dance.

If it is unclear whether or not the body is capable of art, then this needs showing or demonstrating, if not proving. Perhaps the body is merely physical
mass, closed to all thought and imagination, absorbed in the sensorimotor
routines that anchor it to the world and chained to the practical activities
on which survival depends. To escape this vision of what it is, the body must
attest to a certain "capacity," namely, that of exhibiting the advent of the arts
as such in a sign external to them. The possibility of art must already be given
to the body, its transcendental dimension already manifest. Dance becomes
the site of that manifestation. And so—this being the price of its elevation to
the transcendental—dance is necessarily excluded from the empirical reality
of the artistic: because it displays a capacity, it cannot count as a specific art
form. The difficulty faced by this argument is how to account for what seems,
despite everything, to be the empirical reality of dance as choreographic *art*.
Badiou resolves this difficulty in his text by attempting to historicize the
transcendental. Dance is not an art but a condition of possibility; but since
it is clear that choreographic art exists and that it has a history, the thesis
must be adapted and a historical trajectory attributed to dance as general
emblem, correlative to the history of truths, and parallel to the history of the
acknowledged arts:

> But since dance is not an art, but only a sign of the capacity of the body *for*
> art, these inventions follow the entire history of truths very closely, including
> the history of those truths taught by the arts proper.
>
> Why is there a history of dance, a history of the exactitude of vertigo?
> Because *the* truth does not exist. If *the* truth existed, there would be a defini-
> tive ecstatic dance, a mystical incantation of the event. Doubtless this is the
> conviction of the whirling dervish. But what there are instead are disparate
> truths, an aleatory multiple of events of thought. Dance appropriates this
> multiplicity within history. (Badiou 2005, 70)

So if dance has a history, if the "mystical incantation of the event" can be evaded,
then this is not because it has empirical reality as an art form with artists, works,
and trends like any other but only because of the historical character of the
transcendental: there is a history of the body's capacity for art, which closely
follows the history of truths and parallels those of the recognized arts. But we
learn nothing of this history. It is postulated but never actually delineated. Alain
Badiou mentions no work titles, artists' names, or specific styles. Historicity
here appears merely as a worthy idea.

This maneuver of raising dance to the transcendental plane in order to say
no more about it is also apparent in the work of other contemporary philosophers. They pursue different lines of argument but evidence the same troubled

relationship with the empirical reality of dance. Thus, according to the French philosopher Renaud Barbaras:

> In other words it is *dance* which for me can be read as the essence of art. [. . .] As Straus explained, dance shows an originary unity of feeling and move-ment, a unity constitutive of both and anterior to all training. Dance sponta-neously gives form to the auditory logic inherent in hearing itself; it displays a kind of creative activity that springs directly from sensory receptivity. Choreographic art itself is, as Straus remarks, merely a specific modelling of a general unity which preexists sensory impressions and movement, and which is mingled with the approach itself. Dance is thus located where the spontaneous creations of sensibility and artistic creation intersect, thereby bringing to light the continuity between them. [. . .] This echoes Valéry's claim in *Philosophy of the Dance* that all the arts can be conceived as particu-lar cases of a general art type that is dance. (1998, 38–39)

Dance can appropriately be seen as the *essence* of art because it manifests an originary unity. In its spontaneous link to sound, dance articulates in a man-ner anterior to all convention and all training. Dance displays the link between sensory receptivity and creative activity in its purest and most general form, a connection on which the whole collection of recognized art forms depends as each renders it specific. As the origin of this connection, dance is anterior to any articulation in specific domains and objects. Dance enables one to speak of Art in the singular, in terms of both essence and origin. But the same diffi-culty presents itself. Alongside *Dance*, the originary art, we find that empirically existing *choreographic art* will not go away. Barbaras resolves this difficulty via a strategy that is the inverse of the one proposed by Alain Badiou. No fusion of the empirical and the transcendental is posited, but rather a clear disjunction: on the one hand appears Dance as an originary unity of feeling and movement, the basis of all the arts; on the other hand is *choreographic art*, a specific articu-lation of that unity without any particular privilege, which shares with the other arts the vagaries of empirical reality and convention. This same conceptual framework anchors the work of Erwin Straus[14] and finds confirmation—albeit in somewhat modified form—in Paul Valéry.

---

14. In *The Primary World of Senses* (the 1963 English translation of *Vom Sinne der Sinne*, first published 1935), Straus argues as follows: "Long before the youngster is taught conventional dance steps, he dances in rings, hops to the hopping movement of a polka, is drawn by the music of a march into the ranks of the marching columns. The dance as an art form is pos-sible only as a specific shaping of this general, antecedently existing unity of sense impressions and movement. The motions of a dance may be as artistic as you please, but that which is

The foregoing discussion also articulates the plan of this book. Today, it appears impossible to speak philosophically about dance without it first being absented and pushed toward the transcendental. But this is neither inevitable nor necessary. It is simply a historical constraint born of the system of the fine arts: since dance is empirically denied status as art, it can be re-evaluated only via the terms of another space. I now need to trace the wider implications of this logic of absenting. Much as the sources cited by Alain Badiou seem inadequate to justify his argument,[15] those mentioned by Renaud Barbaras appear crucial. Valéry and Straus in their work of the 1930s exemplify better than anyone the incapacity to treat dance as an art form and the temptation to see it rather as an originary source, a general condition of possibility, in which arts in general find their common emblem. And since we are now concerned with a "transcendental aesthetics"—the only kind of aesthetics that is possible in the dance case, it seems—this should be tackled in relation to its a priori forms: first in terms of *time*, through the work of Valéry; and secondly in terms of *space*, through the writings of Straus. In the process, a very simple truth is revealed: dance hybridizes space and time, thus proposing something akin to a unitary reading of the "aesthetic," as much in line with the first as with the third of Kant's Critiques.

artistic, invented, and teachable in it is always only a particular instance of that universal which is the nonartistic, uninvented, and unlearned original unity of music and movement" (1963 [1935], 233).

15. I have already suggested that Mallarmé is an antidote to, rather than a proponent of, the transcendental absenting of dance. As regards Nietzsche, I maintain that dance is not an *object* of his discourse but functions rather as an *operator*. Nietzsche says nothing *about* dance, although he manages to say much *through* reference to it.

Chapter 2

A Time with No Outside
(Valéry and *Jouissance*)

Three texts form the core of Paul Valéry's writings about dance: a poetic-Socratic dialogue entitled "Dance and the Soul" (1957, 27–62 [1921]); a paper entitled "Philosophy of the Dance," originally presented at a dance performance (1964, 197–211 [1936]); and a short chapter called "The Dance" in *Degas, Dance, Drawing* (1960a, 13–18 [1936]). Fifteen years separate "Dance and the Soul" (1921) from the other two texts (1936). The former still clearly bears the imprint of Stéphane Mallarmé's influence,[1] whereas the latter seem rather decisively to distance themselves from it. Moreover, the poetic and dialogic form of "Dance and the Soul" allows multiple theses to be advanced simultaneously, and intuitions to be articulated, without offering robust arguments in support. The other two texts, meanwhile, are more discursive and demonstrative. In what follows, I discuss mainly "Philosophy of the Dance" and "The Dance" because of the nature of the texts themselves as much as the particular claims they advance. I refer to "Dance and the Soul" essentially to confirm or complement insights drawn from the other two essays.

The two later texts are written in a very particular style, characterized by a combination of frivolity and grandiloquence. This style is immediately

---

1. In a letter to Louis Séchan (August 1930), thanking him for sending a copy of his book *La danse grec antique* (1930), Valéry acknowledges the burden of Mallarmé's legacy when writing "Dance and the Soul": "I never intended to write on dance, having never thought seriously about it. I also judged—and still do—that Mallarmé had exhausted the subject insofar as it is relevant to literature. On the basis of this conviction, I initially refused the commission from the *Revue Musicale*. Other factors led to my decision to accept. What Mallarmé had so eloquently written has since become a singular condition of my work, to be neither ignored nor embraced. I took up the challenge of presenting, among the various ways the three characters in my dialogue interpret the dance, the view expressed in the claims and incomparable stylistic demonstration of Mallarmé's *Divagations*" (1951, 191).

apparent on their surface but also operates at a deeper level. And it does not take the form that one might expect, namely, a serious (philosophical) mode of writing employed to discuss a trivial theme (dance). Rather, the mode of writing throughout accepts its own frivolity in discussing what it nonetheless claims is the most serious of topics. The frivolous mode seems to be generated by an excess of feigned gravitas. Valéry clearly takes pleasure in overplaying the philosophical tone, in ramping up his usual rhetoric and thereby nullifying its force in the comedy of its own seriousness. This is partly evident in the titles he selects: the French title of "The Dance" is "De la danse," strongly evocative of the titles of Latin texts and scholastic treatises; "Philosophy of the Dance," meanwhile, appears rather pompous as the designation of a text that is barely ten pages long and is ultimately merely an occasion piece. It seems hardly plausible that Valéry was so weighed down by heavy intellect that he chose such titles naively. Most likely, then, these are in fact deeply ironic texts, adopting a feigned seriousness to reproduce the typical moves of philosophical method, offering a reflexive and deadpan presentation of the philosopher's strategies in the mode of pastiche. This is suggested by a number of remarks, made as the text unfolds, that thematize in its very artifice the philosophical method here employed:

> Quite a bit of philosophy, you may think . . . and I admit that I've given you rather too much of it. But when one is not a dancer; when one would be at a loss not only to perform, but even to explain, the slightest step [. . .] there's no help but in a certain amount of philosophy—in other words, *one approaches the matter from far off, in the hope that distance will dispel the difficulties.* [. . .] [The philosopher] goes about [his task] in his own fashion. . . . The fashion of a philosopher. Everyone knows how his dance begins. . . . His first faint step is a *question* [. . .] He plays his game, beginning with its usual beginning. And there he is, asking himself: "What then is the dance?" [. . .] That is what my philosopher has come to: he stands hesitant on the forbidding threshold that separates a question from an answer, obsessed by the memory of St. Augustine, dreaming in his penumbra of the great saint's perplexity: "What is time? But what is the dance?" But, he tells himself, the dance after all is merely a form of time, the creation of a kind of time, or of a very distinct and singular species of time. Already he is less worried: he has wedded two difficulties to each other. (1964, 201–3, my emphasis)

I will postpone until later in the chapter detailed discussion of this marriage of Dance and Time. Presented as a contingent connection, generated by the philosopher's disquiet and the inevitable Augustinian echo it produces, the theme appears as a way to illuminate the general terrain of the inquiry rather than shining a spotlight on its present concern. But at least making that connection dispels to some extent the philosopher's anxiety. The marriage of Dance and Time—to which I will return later—is the core of what Valéry has to say about dance. For now, note that philosophy is here defined as a discourse that approaches its topic from the outside, distanced from empirical support, familiarity, or complicity with its subject matter. The philosopher is, indeed, at a loss to explain the slightest step. And so the only viable option is to dispel the object and its difficulties in distance, letting it dissolve in a discursive configuration governed from afar by other principles. This is what makes philosophy frivolous. It is a kind of utterance contingent on suspending all practical knowledge, which can rely only on the dialectical veins of language. Philosophy can make certain characteristic moves, certain well-worn gestures, indeed has its typical, indefinitely repeatable, ways of beginning its own dance. Valéry, with his customary lucidity, recognizes this frivolity and accepts it, inevitably in the mode of pastiche.[2]

Yet once the discussion turns to dance itself—or, more accurately, to the status of dance—the frivolous tone abruptly vanishes, ceding place to a seriousness bordering on grandiloquence. Given a topic ordinarily conceived as light and trivial, the task becomes its rehabilitation, necessary if philosophers are to discuss it. This task of rehabilitation shapes the opening of "Philosophy of the Dance," as well as the essay's close:

> Let me begin at once by telling you without preamble that to my mind the dance is not merely an exercise, an entertainment, an ornamental art, or sometimes a social activity; it is a *serious* matter and in certain of its aspects most *venerable*. (1964, 197, my emphasis)

> I wanted to show you how this art, far from being a futile amusement, far from being a specialty confined to putting on a show now and then for the amusement of the eyes that contemplate it or the bodies that take part in it, is quite simply *a poetry that encompasses the action of living creatures in its entirety*. (210, emphasis in original)

2. "Dance and the Soul" is a dialogue between Socrates, Eryximachus, and Phaedrus at the conclusion of an overabundant feast, so already presents an explicit pastiche of Plato's *Symposium*, the idea of beauty emerging through the light, naked grace of the dancing bodies that seek to charm and solicit the well fed guests. Valéry in some ways is merely rewriting the *Symposium* in a way that does not exclude dancers and musicians from the philosophical gathering. This is a symposium in which music and dance do not seduce the soul from the path of virtue, but rather become, in their material presence, spiritual catalysts for the dialectical investigation of Beauty. The dialogue is also reminiscent of Xenophon's *Symposium*, in which the dancers open and close the dialogue, Socrates praising the benefits of dancing as an activity and acknowledging that he himself practices it.

Again, I will postpone discussion of the final part of this quotation—the enig-matic "poetry that encompasses [. . .] action [. . .] in its entirety"—and note here its point of contrast: dance as futile entertainment, putting on a show for the amusement of the eyes, in other words everything that (from one perspec-tive) constitutes the empirical reality of dance as art, as a practice producing shareable objects presented via the stage. Indeed, the rehabilitation of dance takes place on the ruins of the stage and theatrical spectacle. As stage produc-tion, dance remains inescapably minor, bordering circus, the fairground, and its fire-eaters. Dance can only be considered serious if distanced from, and rooted elsewhere than, actual practice. The seriousness attributed to the object thereby follows the same path as the explicit frivolity of the discourse, placing empirical reality in parentheses, if not forgetting or denying it entirely. Valéry never mentions the title of any dance work or the name of any dance artist. Neither does he acknowledge that dance is usually presented onstage, within the horizon of theatrical spectacle. And this double denial is directly linked to the tone he adopts, to the strange combination of frivolity and seriousness it implies. The object's seriousness is achieved at the expense of its empirical real-ity, and the frivolous mode of discourse that overplays its own philosophical character merely legitimates that denial at another level. A different, converse approach would have been possible: adopting an unashamedly serious mode of discourse about a perfectly trivial object. I want to claim, provisionally, that this other approach is exactly the one taken by Mallarmé in his prose texts "Scribbled at the Theater."[3]

Valéry's position in this regard is surprising on a number of counts. These texts appear still largely dominated by the influence of Mallarmé, yet also strik-ingly committed to dismanteling that heritage. For Mallarmé, dance could not be dissociated from the horizon of the stage, yet Valéry forces the two apart. This perspective on dance is not linked to disinterest in spectacle itself but rather to a disjunctive operation that places spectacle on one side and dance on another. Valéry is, like his mentor, fascinated by the theater, similarly aware of its political and religious stakes. That fascination is explicitly articulated in his essay "Mes théâtres"[4] and in the daily writing practice of his Notebooks, which include a fairly large number of entries revealing a well-developed and highly personal theory of the stage.[5] What is more, Valéry's interest developed beyond

3. See below, 69–92.

4. Originally published in *Les dernières nouvelles* on September 19, 1942, and reprinted in Valéry (1977).

5. See the multivolume CNRS edition of Valéry's *Cahiers*, and particularly VI, 150 and 508; IX, 659; XIV, 776; XV, 164 and 187; XVI, 648; XVII, 426 and 758; XIX, 11–2; XX, 510–11; XXII,

the merely theoretical. He wrote two lyric plays: *Amphion* (1931) with music by Honegger and choreography by Massine, for Ida Rubenstein and her ballet company; and *Sémiramis* (1934) with largely the same team of collaborators (Fokine replacing Massine as choreographer). Valéry thus took the plunge into stage production which Mallarmé never did.[6] The product of Mallarmé's fascination with the theater was his mad dream of *The Book* (*Le Livre*), intended precisely to replace the splendor and ritual of the stage with writing. But Valéry's interest pushed him toward actual involvement, and into a role as librettist and occasional collaborator of the Ballets Rubinstein, with all the attendant risk of disappointment.[7]

So Valéry knows full well that dance takes place in the theater and that its presence there is far from negligible. If frequenting the Opéra was not enough to convince him of this, Mallarmé's authority should have been. Valéry also knows that there are specific ballets and choreographers, because he collaborates in/with some of them.[8] And the idea of "spectacle" is extremely important to him, as abundantly demonstrated in the private practice of the Notebooks. Yet when he speaks and writes *publicly* about dance, he seems constrained to forget all of this, and only to treat dance as it exists beyond the stage, in an enigmatic space. Perhaps the disjunction can best be explained once again by invoking the double tone of his writings about dance: the seriousness with which dance is rehabilitated, combined with the frivolity of the philosophical as such. Dance can only escape its minor status by extracting itself from insignificant spectacle. And that suits a *philosophical* discourse that would never stoop to considering the empirical reality of dance.

496; XXIII, 901–22; XXIV, 11–12, 16, 315, and 565; XXIX, 672. An English translation of the *Cahiers* is available in five thematically organized volumes (Valéry 2000–2010).

6. *Amphion* was premiered at the Paris Opéra on June 23, 1931, and *Sémiramis* also at the Paris Opéra on May 11, 1934. English translations of both play texts are available in Valéry (1960b).

7. See the letter to Sully Peyre (1933), in which Valéry justifies the publication of *Amphion* in the following terms: "I published this text—perhaps mistakenly. I was unfortunately unable to impose my views—which were really very simple—and I was forced to endure a Russian ballet when I had conceived the work as a kind of religious ceremony. Indiscipline, incoherence and fantasy reigned" (Valéry 1951, 209–10).

8. Another notable collaboration was Valéry's preface-writing for Serge Lifar (see Cocteau, Lifar, and Valéry 1943; Lifar 1946). The *Cahiers* reveal that Valéry also conceived a ballet project for Lifar in 1941 with the provisional title of "Harmoniques" or "Figures" (see the CNRS edition of the *Cahiers*, XXIV, p. 95): "I am looking for a theme for a ballet for Lifar—(quite a business). I cannot currently think of anything suitable. My theme of 'Souls' is too difficult to be treated in flight. I am thinking of quite a rigorous frame on which I might weave a subject. Harmonics. Figures." I am indebted to Laurenti (1973) for this information and the other facts about Valéry's theatrical involvement.

Valéry, then, is primarily concerned with philosophy itself. Hence his characterization of the object as *essence*, his beginning the reflection with the inevitable "What is . . . ?" questions. "What, then, is Dance?" asks our philosopher. "Dance" (in general), that is: not "ballet" or "social dance" or "flamenco" (though he is supposed to say something about the latter),[9] nor the minuet, nor the farandole. No: "What is Dance?" as singular and timeless essence, situated beyond all particular manifestations, hidden behind the empirical veneer of various actual gestures and positioned as their foundation. Conventionally, philosophy calls the attempt to articulate an essence a *definition*. And Valéry is indeed concerned with definition here, seeking to understand all dance in its community of *essence*. There are two main types of definition, once mere nominal definitions have been set aside. The first proceeds by combining and successively restricting classes of things: as Plato would say, through a series of dichotomies or, as Aristotle would argue, by articulating genus and differentia. I will refer to this as *taxonomic* definition: it involves identifying the correct category within a global classification system. The other type of definition is not concerned with classification and aims simply to show the provenance of the thing in question, the ground of its being. Here the aim is to illuminate essence by returning to origins, and the assumption is made that those origins determine essence. I will call this *genetic* definition. At the risk of bending the texts somewhat, we can say "The Dance" develops a *taxonomic* definition, while "Philosophy of the Dance" is concerned with *genetic* definition.

TAXONOMIC DEFINITION, OR WHY DANCING IS NOT WALKING

"The Dance" begins with what looks like a definition in proper Aristotelian form, giving both the genus and the differentia of dance as a species: "Dance is an art based on all those human movements which can be *consciously willed*" (Valéry 1960a, 13). This definition is obviously problematic, particularly the differentia proposed, which are at once too inclusive and too restrictive. The category of "consciously willed movements" excludes the dancing in those contexts where the will seems to be in abeyance: some sacred dances, "primitive" dances, even social dances, for example, attest to the ancient connection between dance and ecstasy or trance. Valéry is well aware of this connection: after all, he describes dance elsewhere as a form of somnambulism.[10] So the differentia of his definition are too

---

9. Valéry's paper preceded a performance by the great flamenco dancer La Argentina.

10. He does call it "artificial somnambulism" (1964, 205) but seems to struggle to account for the nature of that artificiality, as I discuss below.

restrictive. But it is also self-evident that many non-dance movements fall into the category of consciously willed movement. The differentia are therefore also too inclusive. Perhaps, though, the differentia are actually articulated in the word "art," which forms the first element of the definition. Despite the way the syntax appears, the second element would then constitute the genus (consciously con-trolled movements) and the first the differentia (art).[11] On this reading, dance is defined as the collection of consciously willed movements, whose proper function is to present themselves as art. Assuming that the first objection (that the condi-tion is too restrictive) can be set aside, the whole text of "The Dance" is still needed to explain and justify this interpretation of Valéry's definition.

Supposing that "consciously willed movements" are indeed the genus, the next step is to make a further distinction, isolating a first of the differentia, according to whether the aims and ends of a movement are or are not external to it. Among consciously willed actions, there are some whose telos is always projected outside of the movement as such, taking the form of an object to be grasped or a place to be reached.[12] Such movements are always already complete, already accom-plished in the representation of the goal that animates them.[13] There are, how-ever, also movements that embody their own ends, that have neither term nor object and therefore no development or pre-envisaged conclusion.[14] The jumps and gambols of children and the leaping of animals offer paradigm examples of this kind of movement. Although such movements are still some distance from dance, they are nonetheless closer to it. Indeed, a first temporal condition for something being dance emerges here as a necessary. The word "end" is ambigu-ous, such that an activity without telos should also be understood as un-*ending*. Being their own ends, these movements are properly unlimited, only achieving completion through some external modification that brings them to a halt:

> They can only cease with the intervention of something foreign to their motive, their character, and their kind. (1960a, 14)

---

11. If the genus is "art of human movement" and the differentia that those movements are "consciously willed," that would imply that there is an "art of movement not consciously willed," which is difficult to conceive except as dance in one of its possible manifestations.

12. "Most of our conscious movements have some exterior aim in view; they are directed at a place or an object, or toward modifying a perception or a sensation at some particular point" (1960a, 13).

13. "[The movement's] achievement involves its extinction; it could not have been either con-ceived or carried out without the prompting and the presence of the idea of an event which was its aim and end" (1960a, 14).

14. "But there are other movements whose evolution cannot be prompted or determined, moti-vated or fulfilled, by any exterior object" (1960a, 14).

This temporal condition aligns with a certain economy of effort. Practical movements are economical in representing an end that completes them in advance. But gratuitous movements can aim only at complete release, the end of which is continuously deferred and only occurs with the advent of a contingent external event:

> Far from being conditioned by the economy of effort, they seem on the contrary to aim directly at *squandering* it. (1960a, 14, my emphasis)

Goal-directed or practical movement is contrasted with energy-squandering or gratuitous movement, through their respective relationship to time. And this becomes a frequently reiterated motif in the discussion of dance. Because Dance belongs to the second type of movement, its very nature is in-*finite*. It can only ever be the indefinite perpetuation of a state of being, seeking only its own prolongation. Thus, in "Philosophy of the Dance":

> [Dance] moves in a self-contained realm of its own and implies no reason, no tendency toward completion. A formula for pure dance should include nothing to suggest that it has an end. (1964, 206)

In other words, the expenditure of energy within dance opens a new relationship to time, which moves beyond the finite teleology of practical action. And this in-*finite* temporality with no outside is where Dance deploys its force. There is, however, more to be said about the dichotomy between practical and gratuitous movement. Dance can hardly be identified simply with the class of energy-squandering movements and is surely not equivalent to the physical restlessness of the animal releasing its superfluous energy. A second condition is needed to define dance as such, identifying a new movement kind within the category of gratuitous movements:

> But this expenditure of energy exists in one particularly remarkable form, which consists of ordering and organizing the movements that release it. (1960a, 15)

Such is the essence of dance, which consists in *giving some form to release*, ordering superfluous energy, and constructing rhythms and figures from the shapeless force of our vitality. And this condition articulates precisely the meaning of the term "art" in the second interpretation of Valéry's definition discussed earlier. Art is both use-less and gratuitous,[15] or so it appears on reading

---

15. "The most evident characteristic of a work of art may be termed uselessness" ("The Idea of Art," in Valéry 1964, 71).

movements of release according to the terms of Valéry's definition. The release or squandering of energy occurs in the absence of practical goals and is the origin of art. But art also accompanies and counterbalances this primary lack of utility, configuring, elaborating, and refining that which lacks purpose and which exceeds practical life. This makes dance an art of human movement on two distinct counts: its affiliation with the domain of the useless and its power of organization. Dance is thereby positioned at the root of an ambiguity present in every art. It reveals a constitutive and contradictory dual requirement on anything called "art": that it be *simultaneously* release of energy opening to the domain of nonutility, *and* configuring force which can transform that expenditure of energy into an object.

Anticipating my later discussion, I would argue that this is the tension at the heart of the *work*, as distinct from both product and nonentity. The work's particular status in this respect—its condition of impossibility, perhaps—has been thought and rethought in various ways from Kant to Blanchot. The same theme emerges in Kant's theory of Genius as in Blanchot's claims about the work's *absence*. Only in the proof of its own impossibility can the work (if it really is *work* and not product or object) discover what guarantees its existence. There are no rules of art, according to Kant, only Genius acting in a complete absence of precepts.[16] There is no work to speak of, according to Blanchot, only the work's *absence* as condition and sign of the residues that contingently remain.[17] Quite simply, the very existence of works, their reassuring stability and concreteity in the form of objects, masks the fundamental impossibility that conditions them at source. It obscures the connection to pure release that simultaneously prevents and demands their existence. Dance, meanwhile, produces few objects and so reveals that central tension in its raw state. Dance is an art from before there was art, from before art was absorbed into works, and which challenges the work's very conditions of possibility. Dance, in short, is a transcendental art.

GENETIC DEFINITION: FROM ENERGETIC EXCESS TO THE POETRY OF ACTION IN ITS ENTIRETY

Another way to define dance, as explained earlier, is to trace its origins, showing whence it derives and how its essence is determined by derivation from those origins. The taxonomic definition given in Valéry's essay "The Dance" could also be read in these terms. Dance is born of certain privileged bodily states, states of release and energetic expenditure, in which the body ceases to be merely the

---

16. Kant (2000), §43.

17. Blanchot (1993 [1969]), especially 422–34 ("The Absence of the Book"). For discussion, see below 53–64.

organon of action and becomes itself the focus through movement without end or object. Dance, then, would be a more complex or organized manifestation of this originary ground, from which it never really detaches. "Philosophy of the Dance" presents a genetic account of this kind.

Dance develops—or, more accurately, can be *deduced*—from nothing less than life itself, in all its generality. This deduction has two key implications: firstly, that Dance is already incipient in life itself, as though analytically contained within it; and secondly, that Dance nonetheless detaches sufficiently to differentiate itself from life in general:

> The dance is an art *derived* from life itself, since it is *nothing more nor less* than the action of the whole human body; but an action transposed into a world, into a kind of *space-time*, which is no longer quite the same as that of *everyday* life. (1964, 198, my emphasis)

The first theme supporting this deduction can be understood in terms of restrictive identification. Dance "is *nothing more nor less*...." Dance, like life itself, is defined by an absence of specification and of technical supplement. There is no tool for dancing, in the same way as there is (at least from a certain perspective) no tool for living. In both cases, there is no privileged domain in which activity is concentrated or specialized. In both, what is given is simply "the action of the whole human body" in all its fullness and bareness. Working the vein of life in general, caught in the same seam that exists prior to all technical specification, Dance merely prolongs our most basic gestures. Yet Dance is also given as other, being completely detached from the world of practical movement and the space-time of praxis, where anticipation of a goal always already signals the movement's completion. Dance, then, seems in a relation of pure contradiction with life itself. It is both vital growth, spontaneous behavior of the body, *and* a subversion of the connection with utility. Note, however, that when Dance detaches, it detaches from life already specified and constrained, from life appropriately described as *practical*. Is there, then, another order of life—life as such, in its bare state—above and beyond the practical? So it would seem. And this *bare form of life*, from which Dance is supposed to derive, is characterized by Valéry as an overabundance or surplus of energies and sensations that we do know how to use:

> Man perceived that he possessed more vigor, more suppleness, more articular and muscular possibilities, than he needed to satisfy the needs of his existence. [...] We have, then, too much energy for our needs [...] we can perform a multitude of acts that have no chance of being utilized in the indispensable, or important, operations of life. (1964, 198)

Here a second theme comes into play. If dance is deduced from life itself, this is probably because it shares the same generality, the same absence of technical specification. But equally (and more fundamentally) it is because life directly demands dance, being as it is merely a surplus waiting to be spent. Dance is therefore simultaneously the immediate consequence and the derived development of this excess characterizing every living being (man's distinguishing feature being his awareness of such). It is an "immediate" consequence because it occupies the same terrain and releases its superfluity in unmediated fashion. It is a "derived" development because it remains an *art* form, implying a minimum of artifice and contingency, which redirects and reconfigures the abundance of vital energy for its own benefit. Dance is an art deduced from life itself. This deduction—or the origin—of Dance exposes a specifically human ambivalence in its raw state. Man is at once a living being anchored in his environment and an animal distinctive enough to prize nonutility.[18] Man finds in Dance the image of this ambivalence, the point of conversion where nature pours its energy into artifice, and where the living being escapes itself by inventing new configurations, both arbitrary and useless, yet inscribed in the movement of life itself. This is the process that Valéry's deduction invites us to consider, in the form of a paradox. Dance is as close as it can be to life, being composed of the same impulses, but also furthest from it, being always already escape and essential rupture. Dance is a kind of second nature that nonetheless constantly attests to the first:

> This second nature is what is farthest removed from the first, but they must be so like as to be mistaken the one for the other. (1957, 37)

This paradox—a play of proximity and distance—can ultimately be articulated in terms of a fictive chronology, in the mode proper to genetic definition:

> I have tried to communicate a rather abstract idea of the dance and to represent it above all as an action that *derives* from ordinary, useful action, but *breaks away* from it, and finally *opposes* it. (1964, 207)

Yet it soon becomes clear that this genealogy far exceeds its object. Discernible here is the germ of an anthropological thesis about the possibility or origin of art in general. Dance is the moment where man tips into nonutility in order to refine it. It is absolutely general, prior to the specification of any particular

---

18. "Man is the singular animal who watches himself live, puts a value on himself, and identifies this value with the importance he attaches to useless perceptions and acts without vital physical consequence" (1964, 200).

domain or object, and prior to any determination by technique. This is why there is much more to Dance than is ordinarily assumed: it is not so much futile entertainment, or the vulgar activity of putting on a show, but nothing less than a manifestation of the general possibility of art within life itself. This genetic—or diachronic—elevation of Dance to the transcendental plane (as it becomes the point of origin of all art) must have a synchronic counterpart. One can show how these origins are still at work in the present of each art form: each art becomes merely a particular embodiment of a general idea of Dance, understood as a transcendental art, that is, an originary Art preceding the empirical diversification of the various art forms:

> But this very general formulation (and that is why I have adopted it today) covers far more than the dance in the strict sense. All action which does not tend toward utility and which on the other hand can be trained, perfected, developed, may be subsumed under this simplified notion of the dance, and consequently, *all the arts can be considered as particular examples of this general idea.* (1964, 207–8)

Again here a link is posited between expenditure and ordering, nonutility and perfection, a link already operating in the taxonomic definition. If "art" is defined synthetically as the *perfecting of the use-less,* Dance then becomes its general emblem. The different arts merely shape that emblem according to various modes of perception, materials, and techniques. But a second theme also emerges here, if the same passage is reconsidered:

> [. . .] *all the arts can be considered as particular examples of this general idea,* since by definition all the arts imply an element of action, the *action which produces,* or else manifests, the *work.*
>
> A *poem,* for example, is *action,* because a poem exists only at the moment of being spoken; then it is *in actu.* This act, like the dance, has no other purpose than to create a state of mind; it imposes its own laws; it, too, creates a time and a measurement of time which are appropriate and essential to it: we cannot distinguish it from its form of time. To recite poetry is to enter into a verbal dance. (1964, 208)

It becomes clear, then, that Dance models not the entirely of each art but only its *actuality* or *present.* This actuality is not that of the completed work but resides rather in its margins. To articulate the thought in more conventional terms: this actuality resides in both the action that produces the work and the action that manifests it. In each case, if the various arts derive from Dance, this is because activating the work obliges one to step beyond the fixity of its substance, dance around it in order to make it stand up. The *work* is only possible in virtue of that which is most foreign to it, the action which *unworks* it. There is, then, necessary recourse to *the act*, a necessary detour via actualization of that thing that would otherwise remain merely virtual, dispersed in dreams of a future work or in half-dead traces of a past one. And this leads us to see in dance the *living present* of every art.

This twofold account of transcendental absence (both diachronic and synchronic) makes it possible to understand the enigmatic formula thrown out by Valéry: dance as a "poetry that encompasses the action of living creatures in its entirety," enabling its putative escape from the vain frivolity of spectacle. From a diachronic perspective, Dance represents the moment where vital action is poeticized, where nonutility is shaped and refined, in other words, the moment from which all art derives. From the synchronic perspective, Dance reveals what every true poem is: not a collection of textual traces but rather something beyond the concrecity of the work, namely, the indefinite reactivation of a state of being. As is well known, for Valéry the poem only exists to be read, to be reactivated in the living present of its utterance. Also well known is his view that the poem in itself is infinite, always capable of being set in motion again, never finding its end, except (as in Dance) by contingent external event.[19] And this connection between Dance and the Poem again implies a particular relation to time and the present.

DESCRIBING "DANCING": THE BODY LOST WITHIN ITSELF

That relationship is also at stake on another level of Valéry's text, through a rather different thesis that emerges on the periphery of his definitions and deductions. Writing is assigned a task that far exceeds the necessarily artificial delineation of the dance concept. Beyond taxonomy and abstract derivation, the writing seeks to demonstrate and reveal—intuitively and through the evidence of the senses—dance itself, and thus to represent a little of its real flesh. Valéry, then, is perhaps more empiricist than he might at first have seemed.

Once again, it is important to note just what Valéry describes. "A dancer who dances"—that seems perfectly straightforward. And yet, aside from the sociological fact that, in the 1930s, this generally implies a woman dancing, the idea is wholly abstract. Valéry does not describe a particular ballet, or even a particular dancer dancing a specific role from the repertoire. He describes merely "a dancer who dances," as if this description functioned indeterminately and

---

19. And that is precisely why dance, in its contrast with walking, can serve as the model for poetry in its contrast with prose. See Valéry (1954).

generically such that whatever and however someone dances, more or less the same effect is ultimately produced. Indeed, it is not even dance as such being described here but only "dancing," that is, dance conceived as subjective experience rather than product, a lived experience essentially hidden from view. For it seems clear, as far as Valéry is concerned, that no-thing ever detaches itself from the dancer, no-thing is really shown, except perhaps movement as indexical sign of a wholly private experience, which it is his task somehow to describe.

The wholly private experience of "dancing" consists in an experience of *detachment* or (to use a term already suggested)[20] of *escape*. The dancing body is an "escaped" body. It has extracted itself from the everyday world of work and of practical action. It constructs its own, wholly immanent domain, where movements generate themselves, according to their own rules. Negatively, then, detachment is understood as rupture and opposition, in the manner of Valéry's genetic definition:

> This *detachment* from the environment, this *absence* of aim, this *negation* of explicable movement [. . .] all these features are radically *opposed* to those that characterize our action in the practical world and our relations with it. (1964, 206, my emphasis)

More positively—and here Valéry's description enters the frame—detachment is understood as self-enclosure and construction, more accurately as a constructive self-enclosure. Multiple passages can be cited in support:

> [The philosopher] observes that the dancing body seems unaware of its surroundings. [. . .] Yes, the dancing body seems unaware of everything else, it seems to know nothing of its surroundings. It seems to hearken to itself and only to itself [. . .] For the dancer is in another world; no longer the world that takes color from our gaze, but one that she weaves with her steps and builds with her gestures. (1964, 204–5)

Seeing nothing of what surrounds her, the dancer retreats into her own world. Despite her apparently frenetic relationship to space, the dancer's movements have no outside, so she simply folds back in on herself, imprisons herself within a body that, in the absolute horizon of her present, eliminates all exteriority. This self-enclosure can also be understood as unmediated reflexivity. A sphere of pure interiority, the dancer hearkens to herself and to herself alone. She spends her *time* hearkening only to herself. Or, rather, she makes that hearkening the

---

20. See the letter to Séchan cited at the beginning of the chapter: "Dance is the very type of that which escapes" (Valéry 1951, 191).

very foundation of time, effectively time's a priori form. Intimate attention is the environment and the very condition of the duration she generates. If the terms are inverted, the proximity to Kant, Bergson, and Husserl becomes clear.

"Quite a bit of philosophy, you may think. . . ." And yes, "I admit that I've given you rather too much of it." Yet this articulation of self-reflection and time, revealed by dance suspending the world, is eminently philosophical. More specifically, we are presented with an image of consciousness through the body. There is a striking parallel between corporeality that is dancing and thought that is thinking itself.[21] The shared movement of the phenomenological *epochē* underwrites *both* a consciousness that, in order better to attain certainty, refuses to assent to the world, *and* a body that extracts itself from the everyday game of utility in order to revel in its own being. In each case, exteriority is bracketed. And out of the suspension, the same immanence is born: whether in consciousness or corporeality, the same sphere is established where nothing is given except the self focused in on itself in time. One can only imagine the delight of the philosopher as he finds himself on familiar ground:

> The philosopher exults. No outside world! For the dancer there is no outside. . . . Nothing exists beyond the system she sets up by her acts—one is reminded of the diametrically contrary and no less closed system constituted by our sleep, whose exactly opposite law is the abolition of all acts, total abstention from action. (1964, 205)

But what a strange kind of *epochē* this is—a corporeal *epochē* vacillating between dream and the cogito, conceived as an acute form of attention that nonetheless maintains a strange connection with sleep and the absence of consciousness.[22] A "sphere of lucid, passionate life" (1964, 197), dance shows a body that is at once self-absorbed and extremely lucid: it is perfectly "alienated" insofar as its participation in another world can be understood as a form of bewitchment or possession, and perfectly "liberated" insofar as its activity depends on a loosening movement that returns the body to itself, allowing it to escape the heteronomy of practical gesture. The body has a strange power to play or to oscillate

21. To some extent, this parallel is the explicit theme of "Dance and the Soul," as suggested by its very title: "And the body, which is that which is: see it here unable to contain itself in extension!—Where is it to put itself?—Where become?—This *One* wishes to play at being *All*. It wishes to play at the universality of the soul! It wishes to atone for its identity by the number of its acts! Being a thing, it bursts into events! [. . .] so the body which is there wishes to attain to an entire possession of itself, and to a point of glory that is supernatural" (1957, 57).

22. "A dream, a dream, but a dream interpenetrated with symmetries, all order, acts, and sequences!" (1957, 35).

subtly between listening lucidly to itself and trance-like automatism. At this point in Valéry's text the idea of somnambulism inevitably appears:

> He sees the dance as an *artificial somnambulism*, a group of sensations which make themselves a dwelling place where certain muscular themes follow one another in an order which creates a special kind of time that is absolutely its own. (1964, 205–6, my emphasis)

But it is important to consider what makes this somnambulism *artificial*, to understand how it is always *constructed* or *established*, distinguishing itself from a state of being merely engulfed by sleep. Valéry offers little help here, indicating only that construction occurs *in* and *through* time. The dancer establishes her own time; she constructs sensations of duration that are wholly her own. But she only ever operates on herself. Closed to any outside, her "work" is only an *inner life* with some slight modifications:

> An inner life, indeed, but one consisting entirely in sensations of time and energy which respond to one another and form a kind of closed circle of resonance. (1964, 207)

Imprisoned in her (self-)enclosure, a sphere of pure auto-affection, the dancer knows only time. Through the sensations that she enables herself to experience through this self-enclosure, she merely reproduces the original articulation of Self and time and replays, amplifies, and refines the intensely intimate pulse of that process often called "inner life." At the risk of paradox, then, the consequence which follows is that the dancer knows nothing of space. This consequence is fully accepted by Valéry, notably in "The Dance":

> Space, as we have said, is only the background to movements of this kind; *it does not contain their object*. In this case it is Time which plays the dominating role. . . . (1960a, 15)

Dance, folded and refolded in on itself, is ultimately purely indifferent to space.
    This is not an inevitable consequence. The dancer's self-absorption is briefly disrupted, and there is a moment when another object than herself appears for the dancer. Here I must reiterate a quotation deliberately cut short earlier in the chapter:

> He observes that the dancing body seems unaware of its surroundings. It seems to be concerned only with itself and *one other object*, a very important one, from which it breaks free, to which it returns, but only to gather the wherewithal for another flight. . . .

That object is the *earth*, the *ground*, the *solid place*, the plane on which everyday life plods along, the plane of walking, the prose of human movement. (1964, 204–5, my emphasis)

The earth, or the ground, is this *other object* that reveals the exteriority of space. It enables a vision of dance as a rather different kind of *construction*: a construction of space, of places, of directions, and so on, and not merely of intimate duration. But the ground's exteriority is denied once again a moment later in Valéry's text. The ground supports exteriority in walking, or the prose of movement. But in the poetry of dance, it is immediately integrated with the intimacy of sensation and transformed into a mere feeling of *weight*, a set of experiences of the pull of gravity, through which the dancer constructs her enclosure. This poetic metamorphosis of the ground into *ponderous* sensation is clear from the simple, ever-present fact that Valéry's dancer always has her eyes shut:

She is entirely in her closed eyes, and quite alone with her soul, in the bosom of the most intimate attention. . . . (1957, 40)

Cloistered behind those closed eyes, the dancer is only concerned with space as weight. Like a spontaneous black hole, she absorbs the ground; she lightens it, transforming the ground into a lived experience with no outside, aligned with pure unextended sensation and in denial of place. This is no longer really space, then, but merely a ground interlaced with time.[23]

Pause a moment longer to reflect on the dancer's *closed eyes*. Through them, the global apparatus of the descriptive mode adopted by Valéry is betrayed. It is revealed as a simultaneously very simple and very complex mode of looking, typically known as "voyeurism." Valéry watches the dancer dance. His eyes are glued to her, even. But the dancer closes her eyes, her attention directed inward toward intimate sensation; she is engulfed by a body that no longer sees. She is not dancing *for* Valéry. Rather, she abandons herself, passively allowing herself to be watched, knowing herself to be elsewhere. There is no hint here of communication addressed *to* someone, nor even of any latent discourse intended by an "I" for a "you." Nothing emerges that might be the product of such an intention directed toward another. The dancer says nothing, and to no one. And in place of this nonexistent discourse there remains an impoverished and very general phenomenon,

---

23. "First she seems, with her steps charged with spirit, to efface from the earth all follow, all fatigue. . . . And see, she is fashioning a dwelling for herself, a little above things—as though making herself a nest within her white arms. . . . But at this moment would you not say that she is spinning with her feet an indefinable carpet of sensations? . . . She crosses, she uncrosses, she weaves the warp of the earth with the woof of duration" (1957, 42). Also: "How [the body] furiously, joyously destroys the very place upon which it is" (56).

clearly not made *to be seen*: the pleasure of a body's self-absorption, "the pure and immediate violence of extreme felicity" (1957, 55).[24] This impoverished pleasure conditions also the descriptions' generality (whatever the dance, the same phenomenon is always in play) and the mechanism on which they depend (voyeurism). The phenomenon addresses itself to no one and yet provokes in the other an irresistible desire to see it, to stare at what is not intended to be seen, and is only revealed because a particular condition is fulfilled: that one can watch without oneself being seen. That is the second function performed by the dancer's *closed eyes*. Not only do they ensure the self-enclosure of jouissance, they bear the imprint of he who looks, the imprint of the voyeur's gaze.

It is clear, then, that interest in dance becomes pure fascination with the woman's sex. This equation of the two is characteristic of Valéry but also very commonplace. And the woman's sex is understood in terms of the maritime metaphor of the Medusa that sums up the nature of the gaze, with its intertwining of closed and open eyes, enlaced in Valéry's discourse. A sham relationship is thus established, based on the impoverished logic of desire and prostitution:

No woman dancer, inflamed, exalted by the rhythm, the toxic force of her own overwrought energy, and by her consciousness of the ardent change of desire in the eyes of her audience, ever expressed the imperious oblation of sex, or mimed the challenging urge to prostitution, like the great Medusa, transforming herself into an erotic phantasm, with an undulating shudder passing through the scalloped flounces of all her skirts, which she lifts and lowers with a strange and shameless insistence; and then, suddenly flinging back all her shivering finery, her robes of severed lips, inverts and exposes herself, laid furiously open. (1960a, 18)

From the serious aim of rehabilitating dance to the solitary excitement of pornography there runs a single continuous thread: stage and theater are forgotten, and with them the site where a dancer addresses herself to the person watching. The site is forgotten where, by virtue of this very address, a third object can emerge: a *work*, or (failing that) a *meaning* of some kind.

---

24. Recall, in passing, that "Dance and the Soul" ends with a "little death," Athikté fainting in paroxysms of pleasure and returning gradually to life: "*Phaedrus*: She turns, she turns. . . . She is falling! *Socrates*: She has fallen! *Phaedrus*: She is dead. . . [. . .] *Phaedrus*: What did she say? *Socrates*: She said something for herself alone. *Eryximachus*: She said: 'How well I feel!' [. . .] *Socrates*: Whence do you return? *Athitké*: Refuge, refuge, O my refuge, O Whirlwind! I was in thee, O movement—outside all things . . ." (1957, 60–62).

Chapter 3

A Space with No Place
(Straus and Ecstasy)

Erwin Straus is clearly interested in dance because of its indissoluble connection with music. It is not that Straus thinks music more important than choreography—rather, the connection is a necessary presupposition of his thought. I have already explained how, in *The Primary World of Senses*, dance is used as an example to support Straus's thesis about the phenomenological unity of *sensing* and *moving*: as an immediate response to music, dance demonstrates how sensations are necessarily prolonged by action of the body and never entirely passive; dance therefore merely manifests a unity that extends far beyond dance itself. I also explained how this argument implies making a clear distinction between dance and the art of choreography, and that this distinction (particularly in the way it figures in the work of Renaud Barbaras) gives rise to what I have called "transcendental absenting." Prior to any empirical artistic reality, dance reveals—through the articulation with sound—a form of creative activity at the heart of sensuous receptivity as such. On this view, then, dance represents the point of origin of all art, its condition of possibility.[1]

The argument crucially depends on the link between music and dance, so it seems important to be sure that they are indeed indissolubly connected. Barbaras treats this as self-evident. Yet Straus seems more tentative. At least, he judged it necessary five years before *The Primary World of Senses* to publish a long article on the subject, seeking to demonstrate that dance effectively operates under the condition of music and that a silent dance is an absurdity, if not an impossibility.[2] And however strange it seems given that music is primarily

---

1. See above, 10–12.

2. "Die Formen des Raümlichen. Ihre Bedeutung für die Motorik und Wahrnehmung," in *Der Nervenartz* 3, book 11, pp. 633–56 (Berlin: Springer, 1930). English translation by Erling Eng, "The Forms of Spatiality," in *Phenomenological Psychology: The Selected Papers of Erwin Straus* (Straus 1966, 3–37 [1930]).

an art of time, the crux of Straus's argument is a particular thesis about lived *space*. Thus, if music is dance's condition of possibility, this is in virtue of the particular spatial structure that only music can establish, and without which danced movement cannot happen.

Before I turn to Straus's text itself, I will try (somewhat tangentially) to highlight what is at stake conceptually in the argument. More specifically, I will approach from a distance the idea of choreographic space or, rather, of the dancing space that it mobilizes. The space of dancing can be understood in two different ways.

Dancing arguably—as Valéry sought to show at some length—suspends the practical relationship with space, bracketing the whole system of directions and everyday orientations as they are given in the context of the surrounding world.[3] When I dance, I escape the striated space of praxis and the different vectors mapped out by the objects that typically surround me; I thus gain access to a *smooth* space, with no pregiven directions, dominated by the solitary presence of the body to itself. But to dance is also to construct new spaces that are more complex and better mastered, to invent for the body useless directions and improbable orientations, and to establish them as a movement vocabulary: the dancing space, then, rather than a smooth or virgin space, is archi-striated, being constructed around contingent spatial discontinuities and fleeting motor distinctions, without which there could be no shared choreographic practices.

The vacillation between these two ways of understanding the space of dancing probably stems from the practice itself. All conventional dance establishes a vocabulary: steps, directions, and other discrete units that can be shared and reiterated by others. But this vocabulary is always fragile and transitory. In contrast with the discontinuous notes of music, it is not inscribed in a form external to the subject like a musical instrument, which embodies in its very materiality (in the solidity of its wood or its strings, in the keys of a flute or piano) the shared categories (notes, scales, and so on) that make collective practice possible. There is no instrument for dancing. The vocabulary—if that is the appropriate term—can only be inscribed in the body that dances, in a kind of trace that is obscure and veiled. Consequently, the discontinuous movements of dance must be perpetually re-enacted. In dance, there is no striated space except under condition of continuously re-experiencing smooth space. Contemporary improvisation practices, which eschew all preexisting vocabulary and demand the continuous reinvention of movement, merely push that condition to its extreme.[4]

3. "In that world acts have no outward aim; there is no object to grasp, to attain, to repulse or run away from, no object which puts a precise end to an action and gives movements first an *outward direction* and *co-ordination*, then a clear and definite conclusion" (Valéry 1964, 205, my emphasis).

4. On the issue of discontinuous notes, their establishment, and their properly choreographic fragility, see below, 267–72.

By focusing on this tension between smooth and striated space, borrowing very freely from Deleuze and Guattari (who themselves borrow very freely from Pierre Boulez), it becomes possible not only to interrogate the nature of choreographic space but also to illuminate at a more fundamental level the complex and specific relationship between dance and historicity.[5] There can be no history of smooth or pure space. The smooth is simply the eternal rebirth of the self in a pure presence without memory. The striated is the hallmark of history and contingency, that fissure in presence through which emerges the possibility of repetition and sharing in collective practice.

Within the framework of this tension, I will argue that Straus assigns dance very definitely to the domain of smooth space. Music is dance's condition of possibility because it establishes the only space that could be adequate to dancing: an acoustic space, both homogeneous and nebulous, in which the directionality of praxis is obliterated. This acoustic space of dance contrasts with the optical space of directed and purposeful movement. The optical space, Straus tells us, is "historical": in it, I live the history of my practical existence, made up of memories and anticipations, of places to reach and tasks to accomplish. The acoustic space, meanwhile, is "presentic"; in it, I am concerned only with my own body, in a kind of present without term, without past or project, where spatiality ceases to be directional. Dance, as an extension of music, enables this "presentic" relation to space, which Straus calls "ecstasy" or "becoming one." But ecstasy is only really apparent in dances "which are not yet dances," such as children's dances, social dances, or "primitive" dances. Paradoxically, only those dances that are neither expert nor constructed can be conceived as *real dances*. They are the only dances not perverted by a directional and discontinuous relationship with space—by steps, directions, and all the historical and technical baggage condemning learned dances to the status of mere supplementary avatars of the optical space of expertise.

---

5. See Deleuze and Guattari (2004 [1980], 523–51). Schematically, Deleuze and Guattari's contrast between the *striated* and the *smooth* subsumes the contrast between metrical and vectorial space; the first is *static* and the second *nomadic* (at the risk of further over-simplying their view). The contrast I am drawing is very different. By *striated* space, I mean all space whose directional character is historically established. This establishment of *directions* stems either from the personal history of the subject within his environment, or from the collective history of practices and institutions. "Striated space," then, can refer to the way in which I orient myself within my neighborhood—the grocery store is here, over there is the newsagents, a little further up is the subway station—as much as to spaces that are more obviously "technical" and "artificial," such as those instituted by work, dance or sport. "Smooth space" refers by contrast to any attempt to free oneself from the institutional, to rediscover a relationship to space which is unmarked by any exterior determination, or any predefined orientation: this is, so to speak, a *bare* space. It is this latter type of space to which music and dance, according to Straus, give access, in the mode of *ecstasy*.

With and in critique of this text, I wish simply to re-establish the claims of the conventional, the directional, and the discrete. I want to affirm against Straus's primitivism that there is no "primitive" dance, arguing that dances labeled thus are generally exceptionally complex rhythmically and directionally, and that even the most childish dance is saturated with concepts and motor categories borrowed from the realm of the social. In short, I want to affirm that there is no originary dance, nor is there a pure, unadulterated body. However simple they may be, there are only "conventional dances." However raw and inarticulate they may sometimes seem, there are only "historical bodies."

But this effort to rehabilitate the conventional and the discrete (the converse of the rehabilitation discussed earlier)[6] would remain naive, or at least purely external, were I unable to discover the traces of its own necessity within the very text under scrutiny.[7] One might object that Straus and I are simply not discussing the same thing: that Straus is trying to reveal through dance a core element of *experience*, an invariant phenomenon that always to greater or lesser extent affects the dancing subject; in opposition to this experiential core or the *ecstasy* always at least latent in dancing, I posit the merely historical and social codes of its practice, meanwhile. From this perspective, I simply reiterate the contrast between structure and event, code and experience, rather than really confronting that dichotomy. I have two lines of response to this objection.

Firstly, Straus's incapacity to think through conventional dances and the complexity of the spaces they construct is, in my view, directly linked to the blind spot in his argument. Indeed, the blind spot is twofold. It concerns, on the one hand, the notion of *motor learning*, which Straus discusses in some detail, but which surprisingly disappears as a theme as soon as he begins to discuss dance. And, on the other hand (and this for me is the more important point), it concerns the concept of *lived space* in its link with orientation. Paradoxically, in Straus's work, lived space is never constructed on the basis of the body itself as a center of orientation and movement. Rather, it derives from preexisting psychological structures, assigned to the different fields of sensation, within which the body moves in various ways: the optical space of movements that are directed and purposeful, the acoustic space of danced movements, and so on. It is space, in its predetermined psychological and sensory structures, which makes the body move, not the body that, as a center of orientation, constructs space. This way

6. See above 11–12, 15–16.

7. The traces of its own impossibility, similarly. But this is another topic. I will say merely that I do not at all intend to dismiss Straus or Valéry; indeed, they will remain present—in relation to the *absence of the work*—in the argument of the following chapters. However (and this is precisely the strategy I want to adopt), their presence operates at a wholly other level than the one they intended to reach: the empirical level of *works* and their paradoxical existence.

of understanding lived space neglects the neutral level of subjective orientation, establishing an absolute division between the psychological structures of optical space and those of acoustic space. This is certainly not inevitable. Other contrasting ways of understanding that space are possible, notably that developed by Husserl, particularly in his manuscripts from the 1930s.[8] If, like Husserl, one makes subjective orientation and its cardinal directions (right/left, up/down, before/behind) the constitutive core of lived space, practical movement and danced movement can be articulated in a wholly different way. This also confers a very different status on the directions deployed in dance. Indeed, this is the conceptualization at the root of the descriptive analytics developed by Rudolf Laban.[9] Graphic description of movement becomes possible because there exists a shared directional base, common to movement in dance and in work or everyday life. Based on the system of directions, notation's condition of possibility is its own universality. Notation is only possible when supported by a conception of "lived" space indifferent to the psychological determinations of movement (as practical/gratuitous, historical/presentic, and so on) and accepting of the idea that movements made in different contexts can be equivalent, even though they may be experienced subjectively in very diverse ways. Hence, in the final analysis, the possibility or otherwise of thinking the directional and discrete character of choreographic space stems from a more general philosophical problem—that of lived space—and from the decisions one takes about it. Either, as in Husserl (and in some ways also in Kant), orientation and the cardinal directions it implies are made the very principle of space as experienced by the subject. Or, as in Straus (and somewhat differently in Heidegger, who is critical of Kant on this issue),[10] orientation from the body itself and its directions (up/down, right/left, before/behind) become pure abstractions, for which can be substituted the concrete determination of a psychological or existential order: the "historical" relation of praxis, the "presentic" relation of ecstasy, or, in the case of Heidegger, the relationship with the tool and its conjuncture. This is the blind spot in Straus's discourse, the decisive move made but never mentioned.

Secondly, my attempt to "rehabilitate" the directional and the discrete remains conscious of how fragile choreographic discontinuities and efforts to

8. Essentially, manuscripts D17, D18 (May 1934), and D12 IV (1931). See also §41 of *Ideas II* (Husserl 1989).

9. Rudolf Laban is generally considered by dance historians to be the "founding father" of German modern dance. He was also the inventor of a notation system (Labanotation) that is still in use today. On his life, work, and thought, see Launay (1997); Hodgson and Preston-Dunlop (1990); Preston-Dunlop (1998); and Maletic (1987). On the links between Laban and the Nazi regime from 1933 to 1936, see Guilbert (2000).

10. See Heidegger (1962), §22 and §23.

establish a vocabulary are. The repertories of movements established in dance rarely extend beyond the generations that develop them. When they do, they seem capable of persisting only by virtue of the opaque and veiled logic of oral transmission. Thus dance seems continuously to confront the smooth and virgin space assigned to it by Straus: it is as if, each time, it must begin again from *bare experience*, as if it can have no structure except under the permanent condition of its eventfulness or, to use Straus's term, of its *ecstasy*.

Straus admits at the beginning of his essay that his study of lived spatiality is rooted in "a [. . .] remote and, I might say, contingent event":

> In the years just following World War I, many attempts were made to create new forms in the art of the dance. It was then the fashion to talk about "absolute dance." Dance was no longer to pine away in the bonds of musical invention but was to be freed of the tyranny of music. But, after actually observing such muffled dances without accompaniment, it became evident that the tie between music and the dance was by no means accidental. In its absolute form, dance had not lost the ground from under its feet, to be sure, but *it had lost the space that is idiomatic for dance*. Evidently, there is an essential connection that ties the movement of the dancer to the music and *to the spatial structure produced by the music*—a tie that cannot be set aside arbitrarily. (1966, 3, my emphasis)

The task, then, is to explain the failure of "absolute dance." And the explanation offered takes the form of a two-stranded thesis: (1) there is an essential connection between music and dance, and (2) this connection is spatial. As Straus says, dance needs music—and attempts at "absolutization" are doomed from the start—because dance alone cannot create the appropriate spatial structure but must return to music to do so. But note what else the citation implies. It suggests, first and foremost, that philosophical reflection is in some way dependent on history and the empirical—a contingent dependence, perhaps, but nonetheless real. Straus acknowledges that the reflection developed in his text was provoked by a specific form of artistic experiment, a phenomenon that is datable historically, which (to be specific) emerged during the early years of the Weimar Republic: so-called absolute dance and its supposed failure. He writes as though he knows of the phenomenon at first hand, or at least in some other way than through hearsay. Yet the term remains strangely unattributed, anonymous, and abstract. Moreover, as the argument continues, the term simply disappears: despite being at the root of the problem, the notion is not revisited. Rather, other empirical examples are substituted: the minuet, the waltz, children's dances, or what Straus calls "primitive" dances. The "new forms in the art of the dance" created in 1920s Germany are the text's point of departure but immediately obscured—the empirical *impetus* that need never be mentioned again nor its implications for the argument explained. The failure of these new dance forms is presented as self-evident. Moreover, they are described as a "remote and [...] accidental event," leading the reader naturally to surmise that they no longer exist.

Let's try to pull those experiments out of their anonymity. Two names immediately spring to mind: Rudolf Laban and Mary Wigman.[11] The "free dance" promoted by these artists from the end of the First World War was conceived from the beginning as independent of music. They were interested in discovering the immanent musicality of bodily movement, a musicality distinct from the body's capacity immediately to visualize accompanying music. Music, they claimed, might even become completely superfluous, if only the theater would stop demanding it create decorative or affective atmosphere. To explain the break with music, it is useful to recall Wigman's initial training with the father of Eurhythmics, Emile Jaques-Dalcroze. His teaching was focused on learning about rhythm and music through bodily movement. Within this frame, the only function of dance was to project bodily the rhythms and structures of the music, as given externally in the process of listening. For Wigman, the encounter with Laban signaled a definitive break with this conception of dance, allowing her to discover the possibility of a musicality intrinsic to movement, on which the whole tradition of "modern dance" was then built.[12]

Laban and Wigman founded their respective schools and theaters at the beginning of the 1920s. By 1930 (the publication date of Straus's text), they already had considerable reputations. In fact, by then Laban was no less than ballet director of the Berlin Opera. It is difficult to say for sure whether Straus knew of the work of these dance artists as he was writing. But given that he seems to have been interested in dance from the 1920s onward, it seems hardly likely that he could be entirely ignorant of them. This makes the anonymity of the experiments as he describes them, and particularly his claim that the experiments were stillborn, significant. His neglect of the empirical—or at least the tendency to drown it in abstraction—becomes the condition of possibility of his discourse: without claiming at the start that the whole experiment of "absolute

11. If Laban is generally considered the father figure in the family of German modern dance, Wigman is the mother. The artistic trajectory of both closely follows the institutionalization of modern dance in Germany, initially under the Weimar government and then, in more chaotic fashion and at the cost of undeniable compromises, under the Nazi regime. On the life and work of Mary Wigman, see Launay (1997) and Wigman (1966 [1963]). For a fictional depiction of the period of "absolute dance" under Weimar, see the very fine, funny, indeed bitingly satirical *Sodome et Berlin* by Yvon Goll (1989).

12. In fact, the story is rather more complex. But at least this is generally how modern dance narrates the myth of its own birth. On the teaching of Jaques-Dalcroze, see Jaques-Dalcroze (1967 [1921]).

dance" was a failure (a view apparently contradicted by the subsequent history of German dance), Straus's text would simply lose its own rationale. There would be no need to uncover the enigmatic spatial structure that explains why dance cannot survive without music. Or, rather, in an effort to rescue the text via a more complex reading, one would need to show that it aims, through the discussion of music and dance, at something well beyond the question of how they are related, seeking to illuminate a *structure of shared experience* that subsumes music and dance under a single category, leaving open the question of their order of priority and their empirical connection. I think this is just the kind of structure that Straus explores, through the two concepts of *intoxication* and *ecstasy*: a structure to which both music and dance give access, each perhaps independently of the other, although in a more immediate and intense fashion when they are conjoined. I take up this argument again in a moment.

For now, I focus on the more straightforward reading of Straus's text. What he wants to show is that music opens a space for dance, outside of which the latter cannot exist. But he still needs first to demonstrate that sound really is given as *spatial*. This idea seems to contradict common usage:

> A widely accepted view in psychology [is] that a spatial order is connate only
> for the optical, tactile, and kinesthetic spheres. (1966, 4)[13]

The rationale for this accepted view is twofold. Firstly, it is not easy to transfer to the domain of sound the conventional way of conceptualizing space as geometrical, that is, as empty, homogeneous, and three-dimensional. According to Straus, this conceptualization is anchored in practical activity and governs the sensory field of vision. Straus maintains, meanwhile, that lived space in general is not constituted by the optico-practical spatiality from which geometrical space derives. Other modes of spatiality also need to be considered, he says. Secondly, various psychophysical experiments have shown that it is only temporal delay in binaural hearing that enables the localization of sound. Auditory sensations themselves have no "original spatial character" because their sources are only localized through an implicit comparative judgment concerning the time at which the sound reaches our ears. To this Straus responds that we do not in fact perceive isolated stimuli affecting the ears, but rather concrete sounds that appear to us from the beginning to have a precise origin.[14]

13. Note in passing the sidelining of the kinesthetic. The "spatial order" of kinesthesia is not sufficient to ground choreographic space. Dance can only find its true space in a spatiality at once proper and alien to dance itself (since borrowed from music).

14. Moreover, it seems that the problem of localization and implicit judgment affects sight as much as hearing: think of the role played by binocular vision in depth perception.

But this risks leading one into error, Straus suggests. More fundamentally, the issue of localization should be set to one side. Localizing the source of sound itself remains an optico-practical issue. It conceives sound as the mere index of the thing that produces it, a thing that must have a determinate location within optical space. If the aim is to reveal a properly sonic spatiality, the starting point should be a "pure case" where sound is given in a way ultimately unconnected to the question of its origin. Only musical tones present such a case:

> It is in the tones of music that the spatiality of sound is most fully actualized. Hence, in making our comparison, we must start from the tone and then show how, in noises that indicate the presence or closeness of an object, the purely spatial character of tone is changed through the tone's function of "pointing to something." (1966, 7)

This already indicates the (entirely negative) specificity of sound in relation to the visual. If sound really is pure sound—that is, musical tone—then its specificity is no longer to "refer to something," no longer to disappear behind the constitution of the transcendent object, but rather to be "pure self-presence [*reines Eigendasein*]":

> While color and form—optical givens in the broadest sense of the term—constitute the object, sound, both as tone and noise, merely points to the object and only indicates it. The sound that detaches itself from the sound source can take on a pure and autonomous existence [*reines Eigendasein*]; but this possibility if fulfilled solely in the tones of music, while noise retains the character of indicating and pointing to. (1966, 8)[15]

This quality of "pure self-presence," by which musical tone is distinguished from noise still trapped in the structure of referral, is the key to acoustic spatiality. Noise still indicates, albeit vaguely and indeterminately, the direction of its source. Musical tone, meanwhile, cancels all direction, fills space, homogenizes it, renders it completely nebulous and open:

> Even though we may describe the direction of the sound source as indeterminate, we still maintain that it is determinable—i.e., we state that it must be in this direction, that direction, or a third direction. But the tone itself does not extend in a single direction; rather, it approaches us, penetrating, filling,

---

15. Likewise, Straus argues: "In music alone tone reaches a purely autonomous existence" (1966, 9).

and *homogenizing*[16] space. Thus, the tone is not confined to a single spatial position. This lack of *topical* determination accounts for the denial of any original *spatiality* in the acoustical sphere. (1966, 7)

Acoustic space, then, presents a spatiality without direction or place, a homogenized spatiality. Straus remarks in a footnote that the precise character of acoustic homogeneity still needs thinking through and that it should certainly not be confounded with the static homogeneity of Euclidian space. The stakes of this distinction are high. If Euclidian space is itself homogeneous, it is legitimate to ask what aspect of space needs homogenizing. In anticipation of a later argument, I would suggest that optico-practical space is at issue here, conceptualized as heterogeneous, saturated with various locations and constituted by practical and vital orientation. In short, optico-practical space is like the *striated* space of praxis that music must render smooth by suppressing any local determination. Besides, the lack of localization generated by music can be connected to the structure of presence evident in tone. Given as "pure self-presence," tone simultaneously cancels out the question of its own location and the *distance* of the transcendental object, which is only ever given through its *indices*. A pure present is never *here* or *over there*. Rather, like sound, it is at once everywhere and nowhere

So why is music the condition of possibility of dance? This still needs explaining. Initially, the claim is simply asserted via a clear distinction between purposeful movements and danced movements:

Forms of movement such as marching and dancing are possible only with music, the music founding the structure of space within which the dancing movement can occur. Optical space is the space of directed, measured, and purposive movement; acoustical space is the space of dance. Purposive movement and dance cannot be understood as different combinations of the same elements. They are two entirely different basic forms of movement, related to two different modes of the spatial. (1966, 20)

There are, then, purposeful movements directed toward certain goals, places, or objects, which forget themselves in that for which they reach. But there are also other movements that do not, and these are called "danced" movements. Having no purpose, their particularity is to make us "experience ourselves" or to "experience [...] not the action but our vital doing" (1966, 22). Such auto-affection is possible, Straus argues, only on condition of abandoning the

---

16. My emphasis. Other italicized words in this citation are emphasized in the original.

directional relationship with space. What properly characterizes danced movements is being directed toward nothing, toward nowhere, toward no line or
particular point in space. The claim should be taken quite literally: the absence
of direction is not merely an absence of telos for action (which would simply reiterate in different words the idea that dancing consists in moving for no
reason); it is a more radical abolition of the directional relation to space, an
abolition of orientation. Danced movements are not really dance except at the
moment when they cease to be *oriented*. Straus finds proof of this absence of
direction and orientation in the particular importance that movements of the
torso (or trunk) have in dance:[17]

> We must begin with the negative statement that all these trunk move-
> ments—the turning and bowing, lowering and raising, inclining and
> rocking—are not particularly functional for *advancing in a straight line*.
> They do not help to keep the body *in one direction*, but, rather, they force
> it *out of a straight line*. Not only is this true for the movements of the
> trunk, but it also applies to all other dance steps, just as it applies, in the
> last analysis, to the movement of the dance as a whole.
>
> *The dance is not related to any particular direction*; we do not dance to
> get from one point to another in space. Among primitive peoples, there are
> many dances in which *no change of place occurs*. Since the dance is *not goal
> directed*, it must also lack reference to distance. Walking, we move *through*
> space, from one point to another; dancing, we move *within* space. In walk-
> ing we leave a certain distance behind; we traverse space. The dance, on the
> contrary, is *non-directed and non-limited movement*. (1966, 23–24)[18]

Yet it is difficult to understand why Straus argues that movements of the torso
cannot be oriented in a particular direction. I can perfectly well lean back, with
my upper body at forty-five degrees, on an approximate diagonal. Indeed, this
movement is termed an "arch" in the vocabulary of American modern dance. I
can equally lean my torso forward, at ninety degrees, or to the side, and so on,
each time aiming at a precise direction. These doubts are confirmed by what

---

17. Again, it is difficult to believe that he is not thinking of modern dance!

18. My emphasis, except on the words "through" and "within." In a paper entitled "Lived
Movement" given at the Sorbonne on December 12, 1935, Straus very clearly reasserts the nondirectional character of dance, which he claims follows directly from music: "As long as we
do not resist these motor tendencies evoked by the music, we move in a way that is neither
determined by nor directed to a goal. [. . .] In optical space, we are always directed from one
place to another, and movements without direction are impossible. Dance, on the other hand,
is a rhythmic movement requiring *no precise direction* in space" (Straus 1966, 56, my emphasis).

Straus says concerning a lack of change of place (something held to be notori-
ously "primitive"). I do not automatically cease to move my body in determinate directions just because I remain on the spot. I can perfectly well lift my
right leg to ninety degrees, straight in front, behind, or on the diagonal (still
spatial directions), without changing place. It thus becomes clear that Straus
means something rather particular by the word "direction": not the cardinal
directions that originate in the own body and that have a value independently
of any context (front/back, up/down, right/left), but certain spatial vectors that
practical space always already delineates for me (such and such an object to
grasp, a particular place to reach, a given fellow human being to love, and so
on). In this sense, a direction is not an orientation in space but a goal to attain.
So, in saying that dance is nondirectional, Straus is ultimately merely reiterating
its absence of finality, ignoring all those elements of dance that can effectively
remain oriented and directed. I will develop this conclusion after outlining a
further supporting argument in what follows.

If dance has no spatial limits—no place or goal to reach—then it has no temporal limits either. Having nothing to realize, dance has no reason to end. At
this level, the theme of ecstasy comes into play, and simultaneously the idea that
art, theater, and convention distort it:

> Wherever the dance has not been shaped by social conventions or aesthetic
> intentions, it is free of temporal limits and terminates in exhaustion or
> ecstasy. [. . .] Walking, however, is measured, directed, numbered. Measure
> and number are originally alien to dance movement, which is free of refer-
> ence to direction or limit. Measure and number invade the dance when it is
> naïvely or artistically stylized or when the dance movement is subordinated
> to pantomimic representation. (1966, 24)

Note first that, in the state of ecstasy, dance completes itself without finding an *end*: ecstasy is not a telos for dance. If it were, the structure of doing
would be restored in its very excess. As a presentic relation to space that
suspends "subject-object tension," ecstasy should rather be conceived as ani-
mating the whole process of dancing from the beginning, as Straus clearly
indicates: "The dissolution of the subject-object tension [*Die Aufhebung der
Sujekt-Objekt-Spannung*], culminating in ecstasy, is not the aim of the dance;
rather, the very experience of dancing originally arises within it" (1966, 31).
Hence his exclusion of any stylized or theatrical (pantomimic) dance—his
exclusion, in short, of all artistic dance. The process of creating a dance form
that subordinates movement to number and measure (even though these are
ancient attributes of dance) is entirely self-defeating. It produces merely the
caricature of an ecstasy seeking to *master itself*. Dance suspends the division

between subject and object; and, as the body returns to itself and simultaneously expands to the dimensions of the world, dance bears witness to a complete
lack of differentiation between inside and outside. Yet theater and stylization
restore the exteriority of an object for the subject either to master (that subject's own body) or to represent (the story contained in a libretto), transforming ecstasy into one practice among others, capable of being perfected and
managed.

Note, moreover, that dance "is one of the primary human creations like language, clothing, ornamentation, and using tools" (1966, 25). It thereby seems to
depend on nature and culture combined: dance is universal, like a fact of nature,
yet also distinguished, as a phenomenon of culture, by its various local manifestations and forms. But (and here is its real distinguishing feature) a given form
or technical specification can in the long term only distort it.[19] In contrast with
other natural-cultural phenomena like language, clothing, or decoration, dance
depends on an ecstatic relation to the present and resists elaboration:

> Dance originates in a kind of immediate experience poles apart from the
> theoretical knowledge—from purposive, planned and calculating action
> and the technical control of things [...] the tension between subject and
> object, between I and world, is dissolved in the immediate experience of
> dancing [...]. (1966, 25–26)

> The reduction of subject-object tension as it develops throughout the dance,
> perhaps even to ecstasy, is not experienced as the subject's dissolution, but
> as his "merging with." Hence, the dancer requires a partner, either an indi-
> vidual or a group; that is also why he needs music, which bestows its own
> movement on space so that the dancer can participate in it. (32)

The ecstasy that dance enables thus consists in a "becoming one." The subject
is not dissolved but rather enters into pathic communication with an outside
that instantly ceases to be external: it *ec-stasies*. And in this outside (partner,
group, ultimately the world itself) the subject simultaneously finds and loses

---

19. Conventional dances, trapped in the historical movement of culture and learning, are
always at one remove from their own essence or nature—or so a passage I already cited from
The Primary World of Senses very clearly states, with a view to establishing the unity of sensing and moving. Here is the passage again: "Long before the youngster is taught conventional
dance steps, he dances in rings, hops to the hopping movement of a polka, is drawn by the
music of a march into the ranks of the marching columns. The dance as an art form is possible
only as a specific shaping of this general, antecedently existing unity of sense impressions and
movement. The motions of a dance may be as artistic as you please, but that which is artistic,
invented, and teachable in it is always only a particular instance of that universal which is the
nonartistic, uninvented, and unlearned original unity of music and movement" (1963, 233).

itself (these being essentially the same process), in line with a regime of the inseparable, the One.

The question remains unanswered, however: Why does dance in its ecstasy need music? Why must its space first be homogenized and set in motion? Here, Straus's understanding of the term "lived space" becomes important. Lived space is not organized in terms of the subject's perspective or cardinal directions. It is not *constituted* by the own body but depends rather on preexisting psychological structures, which are imposed on it and which make it move in various ways:

> Experienced movement is never related to empty Euclidian space but always to a space with its own characteristic structure and articulation. This articulation is not determined by a system of directions—right-left, over-under, before-behind—anchored in the live body; it is independent of such a system. (1966, 33)

Independently of a system centered on the body, concrete psychological and sensory structures impose themselves on the subject: optical space, where one acts; acoustic space, where one dances; and so on. And because these structures do not depend on subjective orientation and direction, it is clear why *lived directions* within optico-practical space are actually always external to the subject, caught up in a system of reference related neither to the own body nor to geography but rather to the historical traces of our action in the world. For example, I take the subway to get myself to work. Even when I sit facing backward, I always have the feeling of going forward, of moving toward the "thither" where I work. And, reciprocally, as I travel home, even when I sit facing forward, I always have the feeling of going backward, of coming *back*, of returning to the distinct "thither" that is my home. In other words, practical space is not oriented according to abstract directions of the own body but in terms of privileged and external reference points that our personal history has always already traced.

> The way thither and the way hither are not determined by the cardinal directions. When we ride in an automobile from home to our place of work the way thither remains just that, even if we sit with our back toward the direction in which we are going. What is to our rear preserves the character of "forward." In the corresponding case, with conditions reversed, what lies before us preserves its character of re-turn.
>
> In other words, the space in which we live is a historical space. (1966, 34)

This makes it clear what music is supposed to homogenize. The historical space of doing is anything but homogeneous: it is saturated with privileged places, with "hither" and "thither," routine and vital orientations, concrete and symbolic directions (home, the workplace, the diner, and so on). Music offers to clear, homogenize, and render smooth this heterogeneous spatiality of the *Umwelt*,[20] making possible the disoriented movements of dance. And it also becomes clear why this homogenization leads to an ecstatic relation to the present. The historical space of doing only ever positions us at one remove from ourselves—in the memory of past actions, in anticipation of tasks yet to be accomplished—configuring for us a history where our own present will always be hidden from view. But, once space has been "flattened," once the heterogeneity of practical directions has been suspended, once the "pure self-presence" of music and of dance has been opened up, we accede to a spatiality without history, without future or past, without anything that would separate us from ourselves or from the world:

> We achieve our goals, realise our life history, in optical space. In acoustical space, on the other hand, we live only in the present, forgetting past and future; we accomplish nothing concrete, and we experience only the union between ourselves and our surroundings. (1966, 56)

> Historical action is suspended while dancing; the dancer is lifted from the stream of historical becoming. The dancer's experience is a mode of being present that does not point to any future end and is, thus, spatially and temporally unlimited. The dancer's movement is a nondirectional motility that resonates to the autonomous movement of the space by which it is pathically induced. Space filled with tone and homogenized by a single pervading movement—and in this the homogeneity of the acoustical mode of the spatial differs from that of empty metrical space—has itself a presentic character. (35)

The whole system is thus mapped out. The homogeneity of acoustic space is distinguished from Euclidian homogeneity in virtue of its "presentic" character, built on the ruins of "historical" space where our purposeful actions would normally play themselves out. Along comes dance, ringing in unison with this

20. On the heterogeneity of the *Umwelt*, elaborated this time at the animal level, see *The Primary World of Senses*: "The mobility of animals fully corresponds to their nonhomogeneous space, a space filled with a varied distribution of goods. If everything necessary for sustenance were uniformly distributed, then mobility in such a homogeneous space would be without purpose [...] The space of animal movement is not simply and only a field of gravity, but a field of action with zoomorphic configuration. It is divided into value regions, into sections which present themselves as hospitable and friendly or inhospitable and hostile [...] The environment [*Umwelt*] of the animal is charged with appetitive vectors" (1963, 231–32).

musicalized space, where nothing is now held at a distance, where everything is affectively there, without division: present.

Since this is how the argument seems to work, I will now attempt the more complex reading of Straus's text proposed earlier. I will seek the hypothetical shared concept that would subsume both dance and music while leaving open the question of their relation. This concept is identified by Straus himself and termed "intoxication." In the chapter of *The Primary World of Senses* devoted to distinguishing sensing from perceiving, Straus suggests that the sensory world is to the perceptual world what landscape is to geography.[21] To clarify the analogy, Straus resorts to the categories already set out in his 1930 essay:[22]

> In the landscape we cease to be historical beings, i.e. beings objectifiable to themselves. We are dreaming in broad daylight with our eyes wide open. We are beyond the reach of both the objective world and ourselves. Just the opposite way lies walking, self-reflection, perception. [...] The contrast between geography and landscape, which is here indicated, has been describe elsewhere by me [in "The Forms of Spatiality"] as the difference between optical and acoustical space as opposed to the space of the dance and directed movement. (1963, 322–33)

The analogy operates, then, on two fronts: sensing is to perceiving what landscape is to geography, and landscape is to geography what the acoustic space of dance is to the optical space of goal-directed movement. The consequence is an emergent generic term, common to dance and music: the space of *sensing* understood as a pathic communication with the world, and contrasted with gnostic representation of *perception*. A very beautiful passage follows about the link between music and landscape or, to be more precise, about music as a point equidistant between mathematical structure (Bach) and pure presentic landscape (the songs of birds and the music-making of gypsies): "Music lies in the middle between both extremes; to all the arts it is in this respect the most exactly central" (1963, 324). But Straus does not seem entirely satisfied here with his mention of either dance or music. It seems that a deeper structure is in play, shared by both: a structure that would in fact account for their shared *space*, for this *community* of space that is demonstrated by *landscape*

21. In Straus (1963), part IV: G, "The Difference between Sensing and Perceiving," 316–30: "The space of the sensory world stands to that of perception as the landscape to geography" (317).

22. "The Forms of Spatiality" is cited in two key respects in *The Primary World of Senses*: firstly, to support the thesis of the originary unity of feeling and moving (the passage from p. 233 already cited above, 43, fn.19); and secondly to maintain the distinction between feeling and perceiving (375–84), the passage that I discuss here.

and *sensing*; a structure until now obscured by talk of conditions and the conditioned. This is why things should be described as they really are and why Straus
needs to "once more recall the intoxicated addict":

> Let us once more recall the intoxicated addict. They all long for the space
> of landscape; they find their fulfilment in the dionysiac lingering by their
> dreams, intoxications, ecstasies, by turning from the bright waking world of
> the day to the night, to sleep and to that music of which the gypsy is the mas-
> ter. The tavern [*Kabarett*] is the sympathetic landscape space of the drinker,
> his center of life. (1963, 324)

Straus's point thus becomes clear. The disoriented and workless space of dance
under the condition of music—the space where nothing needs accomplish-
ing because everything is already in a state of self-plenitude—is ultimately just
another form of intoxication. And this intoxication groups together spaces as
diverse as landscape, the concert hall and the dance floor. Music, our relationship with landscape, and dance each restores that unity with the world that is
obliterated by action. And, ultimately, this restoration matters to Straus more
than the diverse means by which it is achieved. Intoxication is not the ordinary drunkenness that interrupts everyday life in marginal moments of self-
indulgence, ending with a hangover the next morning. Intoxication is not
the excessive but drearily commonplace experience we think it is. Rather, it
is the condition that permanently accompanies the continuous, subterranean
life of *sensing*, alongside the waking clarity of *perceiving*. This life of sensing
and pathic communication is ordinarily obscured by our preoccupation with
purposeful gesture. But there is a location where it comes to the fore, a location whose very name designates a particular union of dance and music in the
shared experience of intoxication. That location is *cabaret*: the venue of choice
for the Berlin avant-garde of the early 1930s, a space where people drink, sing,
and dance all at once. Cabaret is the decadent, urban substitute for *sensing* itself,
its latter-day restoration in toxic artificiality. Dance participates in cabaret, just
as music does, but without either being subordinated to the other: the main
business here is *drinking*. And so Straus seems ultimately to conceptualize two
different forms of dance, a before and an after: namely, a primitive dance that is
organized by the beat of the music, and an artificial dance requiring the toxicity
of drink. The same notion underlies each form of dance, a notion never articulated but still omnipresent: namely, what Nietzsche termed the "dionysiac."

There is one last thread of the internal critique of Straus's text to tie off. That
thread has two strands. The first might be formulated as follows: Straus is unable
to conceive of the simple fact that sometimes it is possible to *learn* to dance. Of
course I do not mean that one cannot dance without training. That is clearly not

the case. But in some instances, dances are learned. And "learning" in this context has a particular meaning: it implies dismembering the infinite continuum of possible body movements, establishing some stable points and discrete entities which are fixed and repeatable. Straus says something similar about motor learning in general, and notably about what it takes to play an instrument:

> Voluntary movement is not simply the repletion of a chance movement. If it were, such a thing as *expertise* would not be possible: dexterity, sports, musical instruments could not be learned. The learning of movements follows an inner systematics. It involves a gradual differentiation of movements *and* sensory data, a dividing up of the sensory field, the formation of constants, the focused organisation of individual movements within this region, something which in its turn furthers a differentiation of movements and an assimilative grasp of their extent [. . .] It is not individual movements which are learned via the principle of "trial and error," but rather the articulation of self-movement and the movement of the limbs in relation to the visible, audible and tangible objects in their spatial arrangement. (1963, 256–57)

However, as soon as the discussion turns to dance, there is no mention of the possibility of learning, of the differentiation of bodily movements that any technique demands. The critique of this text can thus adopt the classic strategy of using Straus against Straus, contrasting the disoriented motility of dance with the directed and discrete motility of technical learning to show that there is probably but a short step from one to the other. Bergson might be invoked as a point of contrast, given the focus of his interest in dance as a preeminent case of motor learning.[23] But there is a deeper theme in Straus's text that explains the disjunction. The examples of learning given in *The Primary World of Senses* are all organized around a prior articulation of the external domain. Movements regulate themselves "in relation to the visible, audible and tangible objects in their spatial arrangement." The musician's movement depends on the preestablished sets of discontinuous notes and scales, as well as on the material discontinuities of the musical instrument that embodies those categories. Conversely, dance does not depend on any such thing. The rationale for effacing the potential technicity of dance is discovered in the simple fact that dance is a technique without object. I analyze this effacement in detail later.[24] For now, it supports my provisional hypothesis about the fragility of choreographic vocabulary.

23. See, for example, Bergson (2007 [1919]), part VI ("Intellectual Effort"), 174–77.

24. See below, 267–72.

The second strand consists in identifying a blind spot in Straus's text, a point where a philosophical decision is made on which everything else depends, but which is not explicitly formulated. This point turns on the concept of *lived space*. I reiterate my earlier argument. On the one hand, lived space can be conceived as organized by preexisting psychological and sensory structures, as it is in Straus and his claims about the optical space of purposeful movement, the acoustic space of dance movement, and so on. This treats the fact of subjective orientation according to the directions of the own body as a pure abstraction that says nothing of the *lived experience* accompanying the movement. This position enables a distinction to be drawn between danced movement and practical movement but simultaneously renders it impossible precisely to describe the movement itself. In other words, attachment to the lived (or to what one believes is lived) here entails descriptive silence. On the other hand, orientation and the directionality anchored in the own body can—as in Kant, Husserl, and Laban—be conceived as the very principle of spatiality. This is an abstract conception, to be sure. We never actually move in terms of the cardinal directions of front/back, right/left, up/down in any absolute sense. Even in dancing, movement is always relative to concrete locations, to points of spatial support. However, this second account of spatiality enables something like a universal, shareable descriptive analytics of movement. Laban attempts to develop just that through his notation system. The upshot is that the whole thrust of Straus's argument is based on a single issue that he never articulates: on a particular decision he takes about the nature of lived space (as either concrete or abstract) and, even more radically, on a decision about how the very term "lived" should be understood. The "lived" is either a subjective domain that can be shared through an externalized description or an intimate and wholly private experience that can only distantly be evoked, since we know that it can never be fully captured by language.

To conclude this discussion, let's try to take a step back. Straus's text should also be understood as a product of its historical context. As such, it can be read alongside Curt Sachs's *World History of the Dance*, published in 1933.[25] Ethnologist and historian of dance and music, Sachs shares Straus's vision of dance in terms of ecstasy and the primitive. True dances, which testify to the ancient connection between trance and the sacred, are only evident among peoples whose geographical and cultural distance from ourselves promises to bring us closer to humanity's origins: among "primitives," in other words. Conversely, proximate dances labeled "artistic" can only ever be the distant

---

25. Originally published in German as *Eine Weltgeschichte des Tanzes*, an English translation appeared in 1937. As discussed later, Marcel Mauss has nothing but praise for this book in his famous essay "Techniques of the Body."

degradation, or belated dilution, of a power that surpasses them and predates all artifice.[26] Dance has no real *history* except in the mode of ethnography of ecstasy, or a taxonomical summary of the various modalities of trance. This Sachs accomplishes with great depth and erudition. But the cost is a complete lack of interest in *choreographic* history as such. Among the four-hundred-odd pages of *World History of the Dance*, only about forty are devoted to "spectacular" or "theatrical" dance.

This connection between Straus and Sachs is, I think, more than a simple coincidence of date and place. Aside from whatever contingent positions each adopts, their writings express the same epochal motif: a configuration of thought that, between the wars, leads to a conception of dance as simultaneously much more and much less than an art form. Dance becomes a mirror in which man sees the reflection of his own origins. Dance is at once the disorganized movements of the child responding to the sound of some music; an ecstatic experience in which the whole world seems given in its pristine state; and a form of inchoate stuttering ignorant of all artifice. It exceeds in all respects the conventional understanding of "art."[27] And in this very excess, dance also offers the hope of another kind of art, which is both new and very ancient. Laban and Wigman are caught in this cultural moment just like Sachs, Straus, and Valéry. Modern dance, at least in its early days, conceived of itself as a return to origins. Through improvisation, and at one remove from the theater stage (compromised by its association with ballet forms subject to extensive critique), modern dance promised to reactualize the primitive ecstasy governing all dance.

Confronting this historical configuration, and by way of accentuating the distance that renders it strange from a contemporary perspective, it seems that our own era rejects precisely that separation of the ecstatic and the theatrical, the primitive and the artificial. One should remember, with André Schaeffner (1947), Michel Leiris (1958), and Gilbert Rouget (1985), that there is no ecstasy

---

26. The introduction to Sachs's book is very clear on this point, particularly in the following passage: "But when, in higher cultures, it becomes art in the narrower sense, when it becomes a spectacle, when it seeks to influence men rather than spirits, then its universal power is broken" (Sachs 1937, 6). Later he claims, even more radically, "The history of the creative dance takes place in prehistory" (62).

27. Sachs articulates this exceptionally clearly: "The dance is the mother of the arts [...] The word art does not altogether express this idea. Indeed, one almost fears to use the word, for its present-day significance, exaggerated and at the same time circumscribed, is not sufficient to explain what the dance in all its richness really is. The dance breaks down the distinctions of body and soul, of abandoned expression of the emotions and controlled behavior, of social life and the expression of individuality, of play, religion, battle, and drama—all the distinctions that a more advanced civilization has established [...] there is no 'art' which includes so much" (1937, 3–4).

without ritual, without a constraining theatrical framework with very specific, strict rules. The primitive, far from representing what lies beyond theater and artifice, demonstrates by contrast how they are inexorably maintained, even in its false appearance of excess. Ecstasy is no antidote to convention: it does not fulfill as desired the fantasy of pure presence but rather proves that presence is always already shaped by the ritual that informs it, the theater that distances it or the convention that regulates it and opens it to repetition.

However, despite rejecting its premises today, we must concede an element of truth in the overarching vision of Valéry and Straus. If dance seems predisposed toward a discourse of *jouissance* or ecstasy, this is not simply in virtue of a metaphysics of presence or a grand fantasy of origins. It also (and more straightforwardly) stems from the eminently *fragile* character of dance's artifice, wedded as it is to the unstable memory of the bodies that incarnate it, beyond the support of any concrete object such as an instrument, or a memory trace external to the subject. Thus, one is obliged more or less continuously to return to *smooth* space, to rediscover in bare experience the principles of artificiality as such, or, perhaps, always to *repeat* that which was never *known*.

- So you do not believe in ecstasy, or in presence, or in any aspect of life that escapes conceptualization and reiteration.
- No. Or rather, I believe in them so firmly that it seems impossible to speak of them. *Jouissance* is the point where language stops.
- So you are a mystic.
- Yes, but in a distinctly negative vein.

Chapter 4

The Absence of the Work

Presence, Expenditure, Auto-affection

The time has come to tie up some threads of my argument. I begin that process by addressing a possible objection.

Perhaps all I have done so far is to reiterate a well-worn criticism (itself somewhat abstract) of philosophy's tendency toward abstraction. Perhaps my critique of the work of Alain Badiou, Renaud Barbaras, Paul Valéry, and Erwin Straus rests on the flimsy basis that there are no titles of works or names of artists in their writings. Perhaps I merely sing in tune with the self-satisfied empiricist, who holds to be null and void any discourse not grounded in concrete actuality. Is there any particular consequence for dance to be drawn alongside the general repudiation of philosophy's abstraction? After all, when he writes about painting, Kant is just as miserly with proper names. A merely general critique would be too easy and would fall flat: thinking that I had identified a real shortcoming, I would in fact have simply reiterated a feeble truth—namely, that philosophical discourse generally is "abstract," disguising what, in empirical actuality, conditions its validity.

So I need to show that the abstraction here is something more than a habit of philosophical language in general, something other than merely a mode of discourse, and that it already indicates the particularity of the object under discussion. The abstraction needs connecting to that object itself, as though it would map that object's very contours. The notion of "transcendental absenting" is already a step down the path toward making this connection. Works are not absented because of any ordinary neglect or general indifference but because of a more particularized structure through which absence becomes a condition of discourse. If one can only speak of dance once it has been understood as transcending its artistic reality—dancing being not an art form but rather (at once) a condition of possibility, a general emblem and an originary source—we must expect the traces of its actuality to disappear. I now need to explore this process of absenting in more radical terms.

More specifically, I need to move from *absenting* as a mere tendency of discourse to the *absence of the work* as an explicit determination of what dance is. It is not just works that are absented; rather, the object of inquiry itself, understood in terms of the twin notions of expenditure and auto-affection, is identified with the absence of the work. *Presence* (from the self to itself in the intimacy of an unstinting present) becomes the generic term allowing conversion of the negative as such (absence of the work) to a positive (*jouissance* or ecstasy).

The texts on which I have commented suggest indeed that dance is characterized by its failure to produce any-thing. As pure release, divorced from all exteriority, dance disappears in the very moment of appearing. And in this moment, dance seems capable of transcending the closure of the subject who lives it. By definition, expenditure of energy goes beyond a concern with mere survival, annihilation being the horizon it both approaches and shuns. Meanwhile, auto-affection excludes any kind of sharing. The body is reduced to purely listening to itself, only ever producing "internal" or "kinesthetic" sensations that are necessarily hidden from others and divorced from the shared world of objectification: in dancing, I auto-affect without sharing anything with anyone, except perhaps a visual image to which I myself can never have full access. On the basis of these twin characteristics—expenditure as indifference to the residues of action and auto-affection as negation of relation to the other—dance can be conceptualized as essentially an *absence of works*.

Through this negative determination, the anticipated definition of "the *work*" also emerges. An experience becomes a *work* once it is extracted from the subject in whom it was born and survives that subject's disappearance. Inverting those twin characteristics (auto-affection and expenditure), two distinct dimensions of the work follow: (1) the work as a public and sharable object, offered to the judgment of the other; and (2) the work as a resistant object, capable of surviving the death of its initial protagonists. The first dimension merely postulates the public character of the object, its exteriority to the subject—it is no longer an intimate sensation but an object given in the form of otherness and displayed to a multiplicity of points of view. The second dimension is more demanding and posits the survival of the object itself beyond the experience or the process. This engages a theory of the work as an object that persists through time, as developed particularly by Hannah Arendt in *The Human Condition*. The work, as reification, guarantees the durability of the human world. The work configures and stabilizes the artifice that constitutes it, ensuring its own continuity, even permanence, despite the transience of the individuals responsible for its creation. The work thus counterbalances the cyclical movement of biological rhythms that the working process merely reproduces alongside its construction of the world:

> Because of their outstanding permanence, works of art are the most intensely worldly of all tangible things [. . .] Nowhere else does the sheer durability of the world of things appear in such purity and clarity, nowhere else therefore does this thing-world reveal itself so spectacularly as the non-mortal home for mortal beings. (Arendt 1998 [1958], 167–68)

> The reality and reliability of the human world rest primarily on the fact that we are surrounded by things more permanent than the activity by which they were produced, and potentially even more permanent than the lives of their authors. Human life, in so far as it is world-building, is engaged in a constant process of reification, and the degree of worldliness of produced things, which all together form the human artifice, depends upon their greater or lesser permanence in the world itself. (95–96)

Concomitantly—and returning to the first dimension—the work is that which guarantees the *commonality* of the world, that through which a *third object* emerges alongside multiple perspectives, and which establishes the possibility of sharing between subjects. The process of interpreting a work probably never ends. Interpreters may never be in complete agreement about its true meaning. Nonetheless, the work constitutes for everyone an external, shared object. It resists the intimacy of thought and of sensation, resists the "myth of interiority." The work is always given from *outside*, not in one's mind, still less in one's proprioceptive experience. According to the two dimensions just described, the work so determined seems thus to align with one of the possible definitions of the *object* in general, understood as self-identity and exteriority in relation to the subject.[1]

But dance—or rather the experience of "dancing"—transcends this twofold determination. In the name of what is lived and of presence, dance refuses to reify experience. Being a movement of release, dance cannot inscribe lived experience by anticipating an object or a product. And since it depends entirely on the intimacy of the present, dance cannot deliver experience to exteriority and abandon it to the infinite drift of interpretation by another. Expenditure and auto-affection gesture toward a horizon of presence that specifically precludes the possibility of the work, or the survival of experience in a time external to the

1. I will return to this minimal determination of the work as *object* later in the chapter but see also below 197–214.

subject. The vocabulary of *jouissance* and of ecstasy merely obscures once again what has already been precluded, making that absence positive.

This generates a surprising insight. What has thus far been defined as plenitude, as a saturated experience without lack, suddenly takes on the features of negativity. In the movement from *jouissance* to the absence of the work (synonymous as they may be), our conception of dance is inverted. More precisely, it becomes indeterminate in a constant vacillation between the more and the less. I must reconsider that conception and slightly modify its contours, in line with the two determining notions of auto-affection and expenditure.

In the experience of the dancer, kinesthesis delivers a kind of auto-affection through which the subject turns in on itself. The intimate attention described by Valéry represents a moment of immediate and foundational reflexivity, inaugurating in the body a relation of the self to itself that reflexive consciousness merely extends.[2] Pushed to the extreme, this corporeal image of reflection opens onto a pure and simple negation of exteriority: as we saw earlier, the dancer knows nothing of what surrounds her. It can even be claimed that she has no outside. The dancer's experience thereby seems to present something like an excessive and pathological model of motor consciousness, where the external world is obliterated in favor of pure corporeal reflexivity. I should probably make this conception more nuanced, given that not all dance is introverted, cloistered in the intimacy of the dancer's closed eyes. There are dances that directly confront the exteriority of space: filling it, crossing it, "eating it up," as is sometimes claimed. And dancers do this consciously, with eyes wide open: kinesthetic melodies then become mere background, the bass line of a construction playing itself out elsewhere.[3] However, the image of dance offered by Valéry reveals the general basis of dance in negativity (its obliteration of exteriority) under the banner of the idea of auto-affection.

---

2. The operation of engendering reflexive consciousness through motor consciousness has a long history, the milestones of which are identified in Gabriel Madinier's (1938) study of movement and consciousness in French philosophy from Condillac to Bergson. The notion of effort derived from the work of Maine de Biran holds a privileged position within this history; see Henry (1975 [1965]). As concerns extensions of the link between consciousness and motility post-Bergson, essential reference points are the work of Merleau-Ponty and the later Husserl (notably Ideas II and III, where the own body and surrounding spatiality are constituted only on the basis of kinesthesis and originary movement).

3. This contrast between types of dances is extended in the rather fragile yet operational taxonomy of Curt Sachs. He classifies dances according to two main categories: "introvert" and "extravert." I distance myself from Sachs, however, as soon as he begins to interpret this contrast along gender lines (introverted dances as essentially feminine, extraverted dances as masculine).

Moreover, kinesthesis promises to establish a sensory apparatus particular to dance. In the same way as the identity of music or painting seems founded on the specificity and the homogeneity of a given sensory modality (respectively, hearing and vision), so dance seems to discover its distinctive sense in kinesthesis. A particular physiological configuration of the organs and the senses seems in some way to validate, on the basis of facts of nature, the identity of a given artistic practice. If each art relies on a particular sense, dance relies on the kinesthetic. But the idea of the kinesthetic, deriving from late nineteenth-century psychology, remains largely uninterrogated. It seems obvious that the motor and postural information received by the body form a unitary perceptual structure, a sense, equal in status to vision, hearing, and touch. Yet the supposed unity of the kinesthetic sense is largely refuted by contemporary advances in neuroscience and cognitive science. What appears phenomenologically to be a single sense is actually scattered and heterogeneous, constituted by a multiplicity of captors (in the muscles, joints, and so on) and diverse mechanisms (the vestibular system, the role of the cerebellum, the neural anticipation of motor commands, and so on).[4] This seems to overturn the very idea of a single sense modality, inviting in turn a still more radical general re-evaluation of that idea in relation to the other sensory fields.

Finally, kinesthetic auto-affection raises the question of its capacity to be shared with others. The audible and the visible presuppose an unmediated, shared sense experience, via their general reference to something external to the subject. By contrast, the purely proprioceptive character of kinesthesis folds the sensory back in on itself and keeps the experience hidden from others. When I sing, I affect both myself and the other through the same sensory modality: the audible is in principle shareable. When I dance, by contrast, I am concerned only with solitary auto-affection, which the other cannot access except in the form of a visual image largely hidden from me. The same sensory modality is not employed in the processes of dancing and watching someone dance: despite some overlap, the two experiences remain distinct, not to say hermetically sealed in relation to one another. At the end of the nineteenth century (and notably in the work of Theodor Lipps), the notion of *empathy* both drew attention to and promised to resolve this problem in psychophysiological terms. "Kinesthetic empathy" became a way to describe a common experience that remains difficult to explain: namely, the fact of never perceiving the other's movements merely as visual images but always also as the stirring of movement in one's own body. Accordingly, the other who is confronted with my

---

4. Berthoz (2000 [1997]) offers a detailed description of these mechanisms and their heterogeneity. See also the work of Jeannerod (1997). For a more philosophical treatment of the issues, see Petit (1997).

movements is no longer thrown back on his own stillness but perceives somatically and virtually the motion that he sees. Contemporary cognitive science has recently advanced hypotheses about the neural basis of this empathic perception of movement.[5] The stakes of this discussion are of course high. Resting on intermodal sense perception, "kinesthetic empathy" would imply a philosophical redefinition of what is ordinarily considered a single sense (the visual seems to be always already kinesthetic and vice versa). And by revealing the physiological basis of my relation to the other, it would also imply a different account of intersubjectivity.[6] These issues are clearly well beyond the scope of my concerns here. Yet they seem indissociable from the potential "spectacularization" and exposure of choreographic experience, which alone seem capable of allowing dance to escape the absence of the work.[7]

I leave these issues aside for the time being to focus on my second theme: that of *expenditure*. By extracting my body from the heteronomy of action, expenditure seems to return me to myself. But this return can only be fully understood through the element of violence and pure negativity that constitutes it. The meaning of "expenditure" must be taken seriously in this context, without fear of lingering on a kind of physiology of sweat. We need to acknowledge the liter of water that we lose while dancing, the pools that gather as sweat drips on the floor around us. We need to recognize the steam room of the body in its exertion, the accelerated pulse of the blood as it beats in the temples, neck, and thighs. We need to acknowledge breathlessness, the heaving of the ribcage as the lungs gasp for air; to reveal the vertiginous exhaustion (less an obstacle to overcome and more a condition of dancing) and articulate the basis of pure violence—without object other than ourselves—in which it is rooted. We must speak of the intensification of time that expenditure produces and reveal these thickly experienced moments—which seem to both last an eternity and be over in an instant—where *jouissance* is only ever experienced within a horizon of self-annihilation.[8] In short, we need to take seriously the simple notion of moving *for nothing*.

5. I am thinking particularly of the idea of "mirror neurons" developed by Rizzolatti et al. (1996) in their work on macaque monkeys, and also of the notion of "shared presentations" developed in Jeannerod (1997). For a general discussion of contemporary work on empathy, see Berthoz and Jorland (2004).

6. On this issue, see the recent work of Jean-Luc Petit (for example, Petit in Berthoz and Jorland 2004, 123–47). He seeks a philosophical redefinition of the notion of intersubjectivity based on contemporary advances in neurophysiology.

7. See below, 122–23.

8. If this description seems too lyrical and subjective, too immersed in a poorly concealed primitivism or a morbid fascination with trance, then think of all the dances of exhaustion and

Negativity is indeed at issue here: more precisely, a form of negation that goes beyond the traditional (Hegelian) idea of the negative as *work process*. The negation that invests itself in the world, that denies the natural element of human being in order better to master it, thus always recuperating in the end the fruits of loss (this being the economic sense of the *Aufhebung*),[9] contrasts with a "negation without reserve" or rather "without employ"—a negation that might already (in anticipation) be termed *workless*:

> Man is the being that does not exhaust his negativity in action. Thus when all is finished, when the "doing" (by which man also makes himself) is done, when, therefore, man has nothing left to do, he must, as Georges Bataille expresses it with the most simple profundity, exist in a state of "negativity without employ." [...] One might well say that man has at his disposal a capacity for dying that greatly and in a sense infinitely surpasses what he must have to enter into death, and that out of this excess of death he has admirably known how to make for himself a power. Through this power, denying nature, he has constructed the world, he has put himself to work, he has become a producer, a self-producer. Nonetheless, a strange thing, this is not enough: at every moment he is left as it were with a part of dying that he is unable to invest in activity. Most often he does not know this, he hasn't the time. But should he come to sense this surplus of nothing-ness, this unemployable vacancy [...] then he must respond to another exigency—no longer that of producing but of spending, no longer that of succeeding but of failing, no longer that of turning out works and speaking usefully but of speaking in vain and reducing himself to worklessness: an exigency whose limit is given in the "interior experience." (Blanchot 1993, 205–6)[10]

annihilation produced by the classical Western tradition: notably *Giselle*, where the heroine exhausts herself in madness at the end of act 1, and where the prince flirts with death in the act 2 variation at the end of a diagonal of double *tours en l'air*. In each case, the possibility of mim-ing madness and death is based on an actual physical excess, real rather than pretend exhaus-tion and a form of negation that has nothing to do with mime.

9. Derrida demonstrates this in his commentary on Bataille, in the chapter "From Restricted to General Economy: A Hegelianism without Reserve," from Derrida (2001 [1967]).

10. Blanchot here appears to be commenting on Bataille's 1937 letter to Kojève, which states: "If action ('doing') is—as Hegel says—negativity, the question poses itself of knowing if the nega-tivity of someone who has 'nothing left to do' disappears or persists in a state of 'unemployed negativity.' Personally, I can only decide in one sense, being myself precisely this 'unemployed negativity' (I could not define myself in a more precise fashion)" (Letter to X, Instructor of a Class on Hegel ... , reproduced in translation in Bataille 2011 [1965], 111). Thanks to Jacques-Olivier Bégot for the reference.

Blanchot's commentary on Bataille already presents a particular rereading of the contrast between dance and labor. Valéry and Straus continuously affirm that dance is the absolute other of labor: governed by no external end, dance's use of the body does not defer the moment of *jouissance* but immediately offers the subject the fruits of expenditure. But the contrast between labor and dance is not equivalent to the contrast between emptiness and fullness, or the negative and the positive. Beneath the veneer of *jouissance* and ecstasy a different regime of negativity is established. Hegelian negativity—always arrested and spiritualized, always internalized in a future reward and externalized in the work of the world—is contrasted with a negativity without remainder, employ, or use, which Bataille summarizes with the notion of expenditure (Bataille 1985 [1933], 116–29). Dance is one of its possible forms, indeed enters the frame precisely at the moment "when man has nothing left to do," when he is forced to exist in a state of "unemployable vacancy": when *worklessness* becomes the very site and condition of his activity.

In fact, dance is not diametrically opposed to labor (a negativity that always delivers a surplus) but to the work. We should give the lie to the often-made claim that dance is the absolute other of labor, reactivating the distinction already borrowed from Arendt between work and labor. From certain points of view, the movements of labor share with dance a constitutive lack of productivity: caught in the eternal cycle of consumption and renewal of needs, inscribed in an unending process of life continuously reproducing and dying, those movements have the sterility of life itself when contrasted with the human world of *works*. The vital determination of labor requires that it be clearly dissociated from the permanence of objects in the human world. And this dissociation is evident in all modern thought about labor, in all thought that moves beyond artisanal models of production. This is clear in Arendt's discussion of Marx:

> Unlike the productivity of work, which adds new objects to the human artifice, the productivity of labor power [*Arbeitskraft*] produces objects only incidentally and is primarily concerned with the means of its own reproduction; since its power is not exhausted when its own reproduction has been secured, it can be used for the reproduction of more than one life process, but it never "produces" anything but life. (1998, 88)

> Unlike working, whose end has come when the object is finished, ready to be added to the common world of things, *laboring* always moves in the same circle, which is prescribed by the biological process of the living organism and the end of its "toil and trouble" comes only with the death of this organism. (98)

Marx's consistent naturalism discovered "labor power" as the specifically human mode of the life force which is as capable of creating a "surplus" as nature itself. Since he was almost exclusively interested in this process itself, the process of the "productive forces of society," in whose life, as in the life of every animal species, production and consumption always strike a balance, the question of a separate existence of worldly things, whose durability will survive and withstand the devouring processes of life, does not occur to him at all. (108)

Once the notion of producing things has been abandoned, to be substituted by a concept of "force" indifferent to the nature of objects ("force" whose "productivity" resides simply in the fact that, once its renewal is assured, a surplus emerges), the idea of labor is necessarily dissociated from that of the work. Less a production of things and more an infinite cycle of renewal of its own force, labor is estranged from the durable configuration of the world, from the human elaboration of works. A paradoxical intimacy with dance is thus established— to which I return later—relevant to "primitive"[11] labor as well as factory labor in its compartmentalization and separation from an (alienated) end. Force's indifference to things implies treating labor in terms of pure bodily movements, of wholly local and delimited expenditures of energy, infinitely distanced from the object that is ultimately produced. The movements of labor can then be understood as kinds of dance—peculiar, alienated dances, to be sure, but which deploy their own patterns and rhythms just like other dances. And it is this autonomization of movement on which ergonomics and the modern science of work are based at the end of the nineteenth century.[12] This modernity (which reaches beyond artisanal models to an idea of the primitive) thus generates an intimacy with choreography, as Charlie Chaplin clearly understood in his film *Modern Times* and which Laban put into practice when he became a consultant for industry while in exile in England.[13]

To sum up, auto-affection and expenditure represent the failure of the concept of the work, firstly by precluding the transformation of experience in something external offered to the judgment of the other, and secondly by rendering

11. On this issue, see the debate between Guillaume Ferrero ("Les forms primitives du travail", 1896) and Karl Bücher (*Arbeit und Rythmus*, 1896) concerning the paradoxical productivity of primitive man. Bücher maintains that this is directly linked to the "rhythmic symbiosis" that primitive peoples put into practice and to the songs that always accompany work. For a commentary on this debate, see Rabinbach (1990, chap. 6), as well as Arendt (1998, 145–46).

12. On the constitution of this modern science, its link with the notion of *Arbeitskraft*, and the autonomization of the movements on which it rests, see Rabinbach (1990).

13. See the book resulting from Laban's collaboration with the English industrialist F. C. Lawrence (Laban 1947), as well as the work of Mark Franko devoted to the links between dance and labor in America in the 1930s (Franko 2002).

its survival through time impossible. In each case, *presence*—a particular fantasy of presence—grounds negation and absence as such. So, I reiterate my earlier claim: *dance is the absence of the work.*

But I still need to connect this absence to the work itself. The work and the absence of the work are not, in fact, wholly separate and reassuringly distinct. Indeed, one could only believe they were by committing to a definition of the work that aligns with the object pure and simple, or the "thing," as Arendt does when taking the lead from artisanal production. If we are to understand the real specificity of the work—that by which the process known as "art" is distinguished from mere production of objects—then, it seems, absence must become an internal condition of the work itself, so to speak the very bounds of its possibility. That would lead to those philosophical sources that I have until now deliberately obscured: Foucault and Blanchot. Foucault's slogan, which I applied to dance earlier in the chapter, is well known: *madness is the absence of the work.* Equally, we know that the work is the last defense against dissolution, the site that still attests to the community of a language capable of struggling against the void and imprisonment: *where there is a work, there is no madness.* And yet, the work is only meaningful when it depends on the madness it battles; it emerges only from the experience of its own absence, a center by which it is constantly decentered, a core that simultaneously precludes and demands its possibility:

> Madness is the absolute break with the work of art; it forms the constitutive moment of abolition, which dissolves in time the truth of the work of art; it draws the exterior edge, the line of dissolution, the contour against the void. Artaud's *oeuvre* experiences its own absence in madness, but that experience, the fresh courage of that ordeal, all those words hurled against a fundamental absence of language, all that space of physical suffering and terror which surrounds or rather coincides with the void—that is the work of art itself: the sheer cliff over the abyss of the work's absence. (Foucault 2001 [1961], 273)

Blanchot extends the thought in these terms:

> "Madness" is the absence of work, while the artist is one who is preeminently destined to a work—but also one whose concern for the work engages him in the experience of that which in advance always ruins the work and always draws it into the empty depths of worklessness [*désoeuvrement*], where nothing is ever made of being. (1993, 200)

> The act of writing is related to the absence of the work, but is invested in the Work as book. The madness of writing—*this insane game*—is the relation of writing: a relation established not between the writing and production of the

book but, through the book's production, between the act of writing and the absence of the work.

To write is to produce the absence of the work (worklessness, unworking [*désoeuvrement*]). Or again: writing is the absence of the work as it *produces itself* through the work, traversing it throughout. Writing as unworking (in the active sense of the word) is the insane game, the indeterminacy that lies between reason and unreason. (424)

Through the book, the disquiet—the energy—of writing seeks to rest in and accrue to the work (*ergon*); but the absence of the work always from the outset calls upon it to respond to the detour of the outside where what is affirmed no longer finds its measure in a relation of unity. (426)

Perhaps this thematic of madness and the absence of the work merely radicalizes and exhausts an already well-worn trope: the Kantian idea of Genius. If, with Foucault and Blanchot, the specificity of art can only be conceived on the basis of the work's absence, this is probably because the work has long been conceptualized in terms of a secret tension by which it is opposed to itself: the work cannot be straightforwardly aligned with the fabrication of objects or participate in the reassuring structure of finality proper to the fabricator (since this is a finality without the representation of an end); nor can it be generated from a prototype (since this is creation without concept). Drawing Kant beyond himself, it appears that the traditional definition of the fine arts is nothing less than a tacit affirmation of their impossibility. Foucault and Blanchot merely articulate what is already implicit in the Kantian project, completing that image in all its monstrous consequences: art is the practice whose condition of possibility is impossibility itself, and which is founded on the negation of its own products.

Dance is no stranger to this process. The negativity without employ, which has characterized dance throughout this chapter, is discernible in the energy opposed to the *ergon*, in the anxiety of the act that refuses subsumption in the work. And since the work only ever depends on such negativity—because there is only ever a work on condition of worklessness—it becomes easier to understand (or at least possible to understand differently) how dance has often and readily served as the transcendental dimension of all art. Dance, like the various modes of its rehabilitation and elevation by philosophical discourse, is only ever the work's infinite lament for its own absence, for that center that is always hidden and dissolved in the reassuring traces of the object.

- You linger in the transcendental.
- Escaping its closure is difficult. And it seems that critique always shuts itself up in the truth of the discourse it challenges.
- What should we do, then, other than exit this domain?

- Let's exit. Let's broach those works that dance has been producing all along. And let's recognize from the start that the same difficulty will re-emerge in the process. Escaping the transcendental plane and its *absence of the work*, we will inevitably confront *choreographic unworking*, encountering in turn the diverse concrete modalities in which dance negotiates the impossibility of its "making works."

PART II

The Work (1)

The Stage and Signification

The stage is the obvious focus of pleasures taken in common, so, all things considered, it is also the majestic opening to the mystery whose grandeur one is in the world to envisage, the same thing that a citizen, having an inkling of it, expects from the State: to compensate him for his social diminishment. [. . .]

Dance alone, because of its twirls, along with mime appears to me to necessitate a real space, or stage.

STÉPHANE MALLARMÉ
Of Genre and the Moderns

Then, through an exchange of which her smile seems to hold the secret, she hastily delivers up, through the ultimate veil that always remains, the nudity of your concepts, and writes your vision silently like a Sign, which she is.

STÉPHANE MALLARMÉ
Ballets

The discussion in part I suggested one condition on which dance can escape the absence of the work: namely, if there is some structure that enables dance experience to be transformed into a public and shareable object, addressed to an audience. Traditionally, this structure is known as the stage [*scène*]. And thanks to the stage, the solipsism of auto-affection is inherently disrupted. Here, display is no longer accidental as in the case of voyeurism; rather, it governs the event as such. And however abstract or enigmatic the object presented may be, we cannot help but see it as conveying some meaning—albeit vague or obscure—which an "I" addresses to a "you." We might, then, reformulate this first condition as follows: dance only escapes the absence of the work by generating meaning, addressed to the other only via the institutional structure of "the stage." This condition weighs on dance but must also begin to constrain discourse itself. Most often, works are absented because two phenomena are forgotten: the stage structure that is the environment and condition of existence of choreographic work, but which is generally devalued on the grounds of the frivolity of spectacle and entertainment; and the possibility of gestural or choreographic signification, capable of transcending the solipsistic experience of movement, a generally obscure, unattributed signification. Part II examines this first condition of work-making, analyzed in terms of the stage and meaning (the structure of address and its possible content).

A second condition has also emerged: that the object be capable of survival and transmission through time. That the object be public and addressed to an audience are necessary but not sufficient criteria. To be a choreographic work, properly speaking, the object must also be durable: that is, capable of transcending the limits of time and of people, and able to escape the restricted presence of experience. I postpone discussion of this second condition until part III.

Returning to the first condition—that the object be public and addressed to an audience—a number of difficulties present themselves. For a start, it is not obvious that the show or spectacle [*spectacle*] is an adequate structure of presentation for the work. Indeed, spectacle seems to constantly oscillate between two vanishing points or modes of excess in relation to aesthetics, which suspend the horizon of both the work and its presentation: namely, *ritual* and entertainment [*divertissement*]. In both, what happens matters less than the fact that it happens; the object proposed matters less than the occurring event. It then becomes a question of examining those different historical and conceptual moments when the spectacle becomes autonomous, transformed into a pure space of display that is liberated from community ritual and its function to entertain: when and on what conditions does spectacle become merely an aesthetic medium of presentation? And assuming that spectacle does at some point have this autonomy (or neutrality), we still need to investigate the conditions of dance autonomy within this wider structure: When and on what conditions does dance become dominant through the whole spectacle's duration, itself developing a proposition not delegated to the other art forms? This twofold problem of autonomy (of the spectacle in relation to ritual and *divertissement*; of dance in relation to the other spectacular media) is the focus of the second chapter of part II, "Spectacle, Ritual, *Divertissement*."

Another difficulty appears that anticipates and prepares the ground for the discussion of durability or survival. If the stage and signification are actually minimal conditions of the work, they nonetheless risk being overturned in an immediate aporia or condition of impossibility when applied to dance. The scenic event as such is precisely the nonrepeatable part of the work. As singular actualization, it escapes the ideality of repetition that grounds the identity of temporal works. So if dance exists nowhere but the stage, its capacity for work-making risks being compromised, at the very least. Also (although this is probably a version of the same problem), gestural signification seems difficult to align with the ideality (or repeatability) of verbal signification. Only rarely is a movement's meaning detachable from its singular actualization, from its context of performance. Gestural signification, then, presents an example of meaning that is always immanent: it cannot be detached from its relation to its bearer, remaining embroiled in the sensible matter whereby it is conveyed. This is meaning that always shirks ideality and repeatability. The tension between the event's singularity and the ideal conditions of its repeatability is the topic of the third chapter of part II, "Presence, Ideality, Signification."

These two central chapters, which explore the conditions under which dance both opens on, and closes down, the horizon of the work, are framed by two chapters offering close textual analyses. The first is devoted to Mallarmé and seeks to give a proper name to my book's shift in perspective. In his writings on dance, Mallarmé has the very unusual distinction of naming dance works, dancers, and venues. And I think this "empiricity" of his discourse is directly linked to the problematic I identify here. On the one hand, Mallarmé's interest in dance depends on an undeniable fascination for the political and religious implications of the stage. On the other hand, ballet always functions in Mallarmé as a dumb and frivolous model for what will become his great Book: as the *public ritual of the Idea*, no less. This heralds a new regime of the sign. My other analysis focuses on Artaud, taking up these two threads and tying them together in the form of an aporia. The work of Artaud calls repeatedly for two things: the establishment of a truly independent scenic event, dissociated from any governing antecedent text, and detached from the repeatability of language; and the establishment of a kind of *infra*-verbal signification, which passes via the absolute ritualization of gestures and postures, and which depends upon a form of arche-writing and therefore of repeatable ideality.

The tension between presence and ideality, between the event and its repeatability, is pertinent to the arts of the stage in general. Yet it is obscured—or, rather, domesticated—by a clear distinction made by theatrical and musical traditions: the distinction between the work and its production [*mise en scène*], between the notated text and its interpretation. Artaud's "Theatre of Cruelty" dissolves that distinction, allowing the tension to appear once again, violently and unavoidably. And so, I argue, do choreographic works.

Chapter 1

Mallarmé: Deciphering the Stage

To begin, I wish to draw out some minimal or superficial effects of Mallarmé's writings on dance, and of his other prose texts that mention dance tangentially. The first thing to note is that, as the title suggests, these texts are *scribbled at the theater* and only ever envisage dance within the horizon of the stage, even if the latter is ultimately presented as a perverse and banal location.[1] There is no primitive dance in Mallarmé, then. But nor is there dance detached from the gaze that establishes it as such. Hence, there is nothing that ever escapes the conventional artifice of theatrical spectacle.

The horizon of the stage dictates the very status of Mallarmé's texts as "the exercise of a backward glance" (Mallarmé 2007, 131).[2] The writings grouped under the title *Scribbled at the Theater*, collected and published in 1897 as part of *Divagations*, are essentially the product of Mallarmé's theatrical chronicles, which were first published through 1887 as "Notes sur le théâtre" in the *Revue Indépendante*. Their status as chronicles generates, within the very matter of the texts themselves, the rarely noted characteristic that I will call "empiricity," which is evidenced in their singular tendency to gaily deploy proper names: La Cornalba, La Zucchi, Mauri, La Laus, *Viviane, The Two Pigeons*, Eden Theater, but also Loïe Fuller and the Paris Opéra, all feature here. The first four are half-forgotten dancers; the Eden Theater foundered even in Mallarmé's own

---

1. "A banality always floats between the danced spectacle and you" (Mallarmé 2007, 136).

2. Translator's note: I cite here Barbara Johnson's translation of Mallarmé's *Divagations* (Mallarmé 2007 [1897]), the only publication to offer English versions of all the prose texts in the original collection. Mallarmé's prose (like his poetry) poses formidable difficulties for the translator, and interpretations differ between those who have attempted the task. See Mallarmé (2001) for alternative translations by Mary Ann Caws and Rosemary Lloyd of some of the texts cited here. In what follows, the phrases in square brackets have occasionally been substituted for parts of Johnson's translation where her rendering seems inappropriate in the context of Pouillaude's argument.

lifetime; and nothing survives of *Viviane* except two posters, by some miracle still preserved in the library of the Paris Opéra. Yet the poet writes the names into his text with the jubilant assurance that his writing will survive. Only *The Two Pigeons* and Loïe Fuller swim against the general tide of oblivion, and still vaguely speak to the contemporary reader.

EMPIRICAL PLACES AND NAMES

I will attempt to isolate some features of this empiricity and give flesh once more to the various ghosts it displays, starting with a place—the Eden Theater as described in the text *Parenthesis*:

> There was once a theater, the only one I willingly went to, the Eden, signifi-
> cant of today's state, with its godlike Italian resurrection of dances offered for
> our vulgar pleasure. (Mallarmé 2007, 153)

Despite its (very evocative) name and the importance Mallarmé accords it (confiding in the reader that it is the only theater to which he went willingly), this location hardly seems to have interested commentators on Mallarmé's work. Yet it is the unique focus of *Parenthesis*, both as a theater for dance and (as we will see) as a notorious site of Wagnerian performance. I will, then, spend a few words on the subject of "this singular local spot" (154).

The Eden Theater opened in January 1883 at 7 Rue Boudreau in the 9th *arrondissement*. Its proprietors aimed to give Paris a grand theater, capable of rivaling the Opéra by presenting big *ballets féeries* imported from Italy and orchestrated by the choreographer Luigi Manzotti. The theater's proportions and luxury were most impressive. The stage space itself was larger than the Opéra's, and the auditorium could seat sixteen hundred. Manzotti's *Excelsior* was presented on opening night, with music by Romualdo Marenco. The dancer Elena Cornalba enjoyed her first Paris triumph and was the marvel of the city. Yet it seems that Parisians were most struck by a more trivial thing that evening, namely, the theater's chandelier. Thus, the press of the time comments:

> Note the quite new model of chandelier, with a huge bulb of colored glass at
> its center. . . . It weighs 7,000 kilograms! We hope, for the sake of the audi-
> ence in the stalls, that it is properly attached.

> And did we mention the colossal weight of the chandelier? Seven thou-
> sand kilograms![3]

3. From the Paris Opéra library's press cuttings for "Éden-théâtre," from unidentified publications.

The chandelier is an important image within Mallarmé's poetry. Offering an infinite play of reflections, diffracting the object into multiple facets and instantaneous relations, the chandelier effects exactly what the poem should also achieve. But this diffraction of objects into an infinite number of provisional metaphors also describes the achievement of the dancer. At least, that is what Mallarmé would have us believe, as he concludes the longest passage on dance in *Scribbled at the Theater* with this image:

> Sole principle! And just as the chandelier [*le lustre*] shines, that is, by itself, and exhibits at once our adamantine look, a dramatic work shows a succession of exteriors of an act without any moment's having any reality, and what happens is, finally, nothing at all.
>
> Old-style Melodrama, occupying the stage together with Dance, under the reign of the poet, satisfies this law. (2007, 120–21)[4]

The chandelier thus designates a common feature of the stage space, encompassing dance, theater, and melodrama: the instantaneous superficiality of reflections, as perceived by the virgin and multiple (or "adamantine") gaze of the spectator. Within this space, nothing ultimately happens, bar the display of a series of exteriorities, which vanish as soon as they appear: "it being understood that everything [. . .] is, as art itself would want it, in the theater, *fictional or [momentary]*" (120).[5] This principle of fiction or instantaneity governs the stage in general. But it comes to light in *Scribbled at the Theater* thanks to two simultaneous discoveries: that of dance (the primary object of the formulation) and that of the chandelier (the principle means of the formulation), empirically united in a common place: the Eden Theater at 7 Rue Boudreau.

The first section of *Parenthesis* is devoted to the task of evoking the Eden Theater as a site of dance. Here, we find the chandelier ("the glow of false electric skies bathed the modern crowd" [153]), as well as the "irremissible lassitude, mute with all that isn't first illuminated by the spirit" (153). We also find here luxurious baubles and rustling costumes, linked to expert group choreography.[6] And finally, there is the dubious morality conventionally associated

---

4. And a few lines further on in the same text: "Moved, the perpetual suspension of a tear that can never be completely formed or fall (*le lustre* again) shines in thousands of gazes" (Mallarmé 2007, 121). See also *Catholicism*: "No one, unless he hangs, as his vision, the heavy *lustre*, evoker of multiple motifs, will cast light here" (245).

5. Translator's note: Johnson translates *momentané* as "outside time," more appropriately rendered here as "momentary" (see also Mallarmé 2001, 104).

6. "Sometimes, I thought, when the conductor lifted his baton, it was the tap of an old-time fairy's magic wand, transforming a multicolor crowd gradually into a glittering, garrulous

with dance.[7] Yet the Eden's life as a theater was not limited to presenting cho-reographic *féeries* imported from Italy. Opera was also sometimes shown there. Indeed, on May 3, 1887, Charles Lamoureux (who had already been using the theater for two years prior to present a series of concerts under his name) pro-duced Wagner's *Lohengrin* at the Eden:

> In the absence of a ballet expiring in luxurious tiredness, this singular local spot, for two years already, has enthroned the purified symphony via the Sunday vesper bells [. . .] by creating a whole art, the most comprehensive of our time, such that through the omnipotence of a still-archaic total genius it landed and planted itself among us, validating the origins of a rival race: it was *Lohengrin*, by Richard Wagner. (154)[8]

The event provoked furor. "Young patriots," still smarting at the memory of the Franco-Prussian war of 1870–71, demonstrated in the Rue Boudreau and even threw stones at the theater. Mallarmé objects to this misplaced chauvinism, protesting against it through the whole of the second half of *Parenthesis*.[9]

The Eden, then, has twofold significance: as a site for the Italian *ballet fée-rie* (*Viviane*, created in October 1886 and amply described in Mallarmé's text *Ballets*), but also for the apparently radically dissimilar phenomenon of the Wagnerian *Gesamtkunstwerk*. While Nietzsche, a few years earlier, based some of his thinking on dance (and notably Italian dance) in the attempt to exorcise the burden of the Wagnerian system, the Eden seems rather to imag-ine a hypothetical meeting of the two phenomena through a simple conjunc-tion of site. The very construction of Mallarmé's *Parenthesis* around the single

sorcerer, a rare and charming effect; but all of this and of the light shed on the masses' move-ments according to their subtle leaders . . ." (153).

7. "For prostitution in this place—and that was an aesthetic sign—in front of the satiety of frills and nudity, swore off even the puerile extravagance of plumes, trains, or makeup, and only triumphed in the underhanded and brutal fact of its presence among uncomprehended wonders" (153–54).

8. More accurately speaking, this was a reintroduction of Wagner's work. Lamoureux's 1887 production of *Lohengrin* at the Eden was the first time Wagner had been performed in Paris since the 1870 Franco-Prussian War. His operas had been presented previously, notably *Tannhäuser* at the Paris Opéra in 1860. But this did not go well, precisely because of the Opéra's requirement that there be an element of dance, which gave rise to a new version of the bac-chanale in *Tannhäuser*.

9. For example: "Never has the elite, concerned to worship properly something splendid, received a worse slap in the face than that given by the mob demanding, with or without the government, that such a masterpiece, panicked itself by itself, be suppressed" (154).

unifying focus on a single location (the Eden), merely accentuates this, making an improbable and yet demonstrable connection. This is a kind of *coincidentia oppositorum:* on one hand, we find the most frivolous of entertainments, made of tinselly decor, scantily clad dancing legs, and stupid plots, immediately consigned to oblivion; on the other hand is an artwork that aims at recapitulating the whole history of the Western stage, reconnecting the arts and making the theater the site of a new community among men. What relation is there between these two? None, perhaps, aside from their location, henceforth described as a *stage* (which is already significant, because every stage implies, even unconsciously, a politics of the audience and a division between art forms). Or perhaps there is a more developed relation than this, in that Mallarmé's discussion of dance can only really be understood in terms of the conflict whereby he opposes Wagner. Within the generalized contest[10] pitting music against poetry in imagining future, quasi-religious festivals (a contest that Mallarmé's text on Wagner pushes to its limit),[11] ballet seems to be beside the point—too minor and too stupid to aspire to any civic or political efficacy. Yet precisely in virtue of its minor status, ballet represents for Mallarmé something of a line of flight. Being definitively outside the contest, dance can in fact function as a model of writing, once theatrical pretentions have been abandoned and integrally repatriated within the poet's great dream of The Book.

But this moves too quickly, and I should instead continue my detailed account of names and empirical markers. Mallarmé does not just name places (the Eden, but also the Opéra Garnier and, for different reasons, the Palais du Trocadéro),[12] but also dancers, whose surnames are elevated by the addition of the definite article to the quasi-essentiality of the commonly recognized:

> La Cornalba enthrals me—she dances as though unclothed. (129)

> The claims of the ones who occupy an ideal function—La Zucchi, La Cornalba, La Laus—setting aside with a kick of the leg the banal conflict, new, enthusiastic, and designated by a supreme foot above the venalities of the surrounding atmosphere, higher even than the stars painted on the ceiling. (154)

La Cornalba has the honor of appearing right at the start of the text *Ballets* and, together with La Zucchi and La Laus, at the end of that section of *Parenthesis*

10. Or *agôn*, as Philippe Lacoue-Labarthe calls it in the chapter devoted to Mallarmé in his *Musica Ficta: Figures of Wagner* (1994 [1991], 41–84).

11. See *Richard Wagner: The Reverie of a French Poet*, in Mallarmé (2007, 106–16).

12. See *The Same*, in Mallarmé (2007, 251).

devoted to dance. Trained at La Scala in Milan, Elena Cornalba came to Paris in 1883 to appear in the inaugural performance at the Eden Theater. She returned in 1886 to dance the principal role in *Viviane* (in which capacity she is mentioned in *Ballets*). She danced for Petipa in St. Petersburg between 1887 and 1889, then worked in London until 1895.[13] Virginia Zucchi also arrived in Paris in 1883 to dance *Sieba*, also at the Eden. She made her debut in St. Petersburg in 1885 and, notably, danced in Petipa's version of *La Fille Mal Gardée*. Finally, she choreographed the bacchanale from *Tannhäuser* at Bayreuth in 1891, repeating fifteen years after the Eden performance that astonishing conjunction of Italian dance with Wagner's work. It seems we no longer know anything about La Laus, except (thanks to an extract from the *Journal Amusant* reproduced in my appendix) that she played the role of Queen Geneviève in *Viviane*.

To these "ones who occupy an ideal function" is added a fourth, product of the Paris Opéra and mentioned in *Ballets*: "the marvelous Mademoiselle Mauri, an unparalleled virtuoso, who sums up, with her incomparable divination, an animality both earthy and pure" (132). Of Spanish origin, Rosita Maury toured the great European stages until she was discovered by Gounod in 1878, who encouraged the Paris Opéra to engage her. She remained at the Opéra for the rest of her career (and perhaps by giving her the title "Mademoiselle," Mallarmé signals the gap in status between the Eden Theater and the Opéra dancers), where she created roles in *La Korrigane* (1880) and *The Two Pigeons* (1886) by Louis Mérante. It is in connection with the latter work that she is mentioned in *Ballets*. She also seems to have posed several times for the painter Manet.[14]

Alongside these four names, Loïe Fuller must also be mentioned, of course. Two prose texts by Mallarmé, *Another Study of Dance* and *The Only One Would Have to Be as Fluid as the Sorcerer*, are explicitly devoted to her:

> About Loïe Fuller, insofar as she spreads around her the fabrics she then brings back to her person, through the actions of dance, everything has been said, in articles, some of which are poems. (135)

"Everything has been said" about Loïe Fuller, and about her abandoning fixed decor in favour of a costume that could make its own music and dance. Her name is still widely known today, and biographies abound, to which I refer the reader for further information.[15]

---

13. See the article "Cornalba," in Le Moal (1999).

14. See the article "Maury," in Le Moal (1999).

15. See, for example, the very well-researched biography by Giovanni Lista (1994).

So much for the ghosts of people and the invocation of their names. There are also other ghosts, less easy to grasp, inscribed in Mallarmé's text in the form of work-titles: those of the ballets themselves. Note that the text called *Ballets* is not about dance (as is too often claimed) but about something both distinct from and connected to dance, namely, "ballet." And Mallarmé in fact writes not of Ballet but of *ballets*, and of two in particular: *Viviane* at the Eden, and *The Two Pigeons* at the Opéra. It is only in the context of these two works that Mallarmé makes his most famous statement on dance: that the dancer is not a woman dancing, for the juxtaposed reasons that she is not a woman (but a metaphor) and that she is not dancing (but writing). For the moment, consider simply the way in which these work-titles appear:

> And the haughty, incoherent lack of signification that shines in the alphabet of Night will consent to spell out the word VIVIANE, the enticing name both of the fairy and of the poem, stitched into the stellar surface on a blue backdrop. (129)

> The dance is all wings: after all, it's about birds; departures in the forever and returns like a well-aimed and vibrating arrow. Anyone who studies the show called *The Two Pigeons*, will see, by virtue of its subject, an obligatory series of Ballet's fundamental motifs. (130–31)

Those passages describing each ballet remain incomprehensible if the minimal plots they enact are not borne in mind,[16] particularly since Mallarmé here interrogates the conditions under which the story set out in a ballet's program can be translated or transposed into the corporeal, mute writing that is dance, along with the element of defeat or "trickery" that this process implies.[17] I will therefore try to give some idea of each of these works.

Choreographed by Louis Mérante, to a scenario by Henri Régnier and music by André Messager, *The Two Pigeons* premiered on October 18, 1886, at the Paris Opéra. Rosita Maury danced the principal role of Gourouli, a young girl abandoned by her fiancé, Pepio, who has left her to join the adventurous life of the Bohemians. Gourouli follows her fiancé to the camp, seduces him once more, and brings him back home. Mérante seems to have taken particular care over the group choreography, attempting to rival Manzotti's corps de ballet performing simultaneously at the Eden. Having disappeared from the repertoire

---

16. *Viviane* is described in the paragraphs from "The whole memory—no! not the whole!—of the show at the Eden . . ." (129) to "being only an emblem, never Someone . . ." (130). *The Two Pigeons* is discussed from "After a legend, a Fable . . ." (130) to "an impatience of plumes toward the idea" (132).

17. ". . . the transposition to the Ballet, not without trickery, of the Fable . . ." (132).

for many years, the ballet was restaged in 1978 by the school of the Paris Opéra Ballet, following which it has been regularly reperformed.

Vivane is a more complicated case. No French dance dictionary includes an entry on it. All we know is that the ballet was premiered at the Eden Theater on October 28, 1886, just ten days after *The Two Pigeons*, and was performed sixty-six times. Edmond Gondinet's scenario, as well as the musical score by Raoul Pugno and Clément Lippacher, seems to have disappeared. The only documentation I have managed to find consists of two posters,[18] one engraving taken from the *Monde Illustré*, and two series of illustrations in the *Journal Amusant* retracing the story of the ballet (about the fairy Viviane and Queen Genièvre arguing over the love of Maël).[19] These are reprinted in the appendix (figures 1 to 5).

What is gained by fleshing out the various ghosts that Mallarmé scatters through his text, but which are always passed over by critical commentary that does not pause to consider them? In some respects, not very much. We know that the Eden Theater had a big chandelier, that Zucchi choreographed the bacchanale from *Tannhäuser* in 1891, and that the ballet *Viviane* told the story of a fairy whose name was written "in the folio of the sky" like a starry spell book. But for anyone who has read even a little Mallarmé, this is already interesting.

Yet this seven-ton chandelier, these half-forgotten Italian or Spanish dancers, and these engravings from the *Journal Amusant*, retracing a ballet that no one now knows anything about, seem a long way from the great poem of the Absolute that Mallarmé was supposed to write. They seem a long way from the absolutely pure purity, which both demands and simultaneously precludes the writing of the poet's great Book. But Mallarmé clearly thought it relevant to write of these diverse curios—places, objects, people, as small and insignificant as they are—and that is already pertinent. The fact should inform our reading, as Jacques Rancière suggests in his commentary, to which my own interpretation owes much.[20]

The multiple names in the texts that I am discussing must in part be linked to the writings' status as theatrical chronicles. The texts collected as *Scribbled at the Theater* are derived from the "Notes on the Theater," published in the

---

18. Library of the Paris Opéra-BNF, posters 276 (Chéret) and 277 (anonymous).

19. Library of the Paris Opéra, press cuttings for *Viviane* from *Le Monde Illustré* (no date) and the *Journal Amusant* (no date).

20. See Rancière (2011): "To the transcription of the great drama of the Absolute, Mallarmé visibly preferred the attentive gaze grasping the splendour of a decorative object, of a rustling robe or a fairground attraction. He enjoyed the 'dietary' task of reporting on World Expositions as he also did the spectacle of pantomimes and fireworks, or the dream of revamping popular melodrama" (xvi). See also Rancière's critique of Badiou's reading of Mallarmé in "Alain Badiou's Inaesthetics: The Torsions of Modernism" (Rancière 2009 [2004], 63–87, specifically 74–78).

Revue Indépendante in 1887, and clearly retain traces of their earlier mode—an account of what went on, which obliges one to name and identify what one has seen.[21]

However, the liberality with which names are welcomed within the poetic text is also linked to a deeper issue. The text can embrace anything—even the most trivial details—ultimately because the poem no longer has an attributed object, in fact no longer has any object at all. The poem's function is to establish the Idea, but this Idea does not involve reference to any superior object. Rather, it involves putting some aspects or reflections of existence into superficial and instantaneous relation with one another, aspects that are in themselves indifferent but become transfigured by the way the poet's negligent reverie collects them together:

> Nature has taken place; it can't be added to [...] The one available act, forever and alone, is to understand the relations, in the meantime, few or many: according to some interior state that one wishes to extend, in order to simplify the world [...]
>
> Some such occupation suffices, to compare aspects and count their numbers as it touches our intelligence, so often brushed aside: arousing, like a décor, the ambiguity of a few beautiful figures, at the intersections. (187–88)

And this establishment of the Idea is not just an issue for literature, immediately shut up in the closed world of the poem. For Mallarmé, it has a particular religious and social function, described as a "consecration" or "proof." It is important at the turn of the century to dream, on the ruins of Christianity, that something like "a consecration results, which is the proof of our treasures" (120). It is necessary for "Man and his authentic stay on earth [to] exchange a reciprocity of proofs" (112). The Idea is nothing less than the new name given to this process. And since the Idea does not care about objects, but rather depends entirely on superficial and fleeting relationships of certain aspects, multiple and scattered like the reflections of the chandelier, every object and every event, however trivial, can be an opportunity for its establishment. Hence the occasional verse that Mallarmé writes on sweet wrappers. Hence his interest in fairground attractions, dancing bears, and fireworks. Hence, also, the paradoxical empiricity of our texts and the entire array of impure names (trashy theaters, stupid ballets, and illiterate dancers) from which they are woven. Empiricity is just the flip side of the Idea—precarious and without object—that Mallarmé seeks to establish.

---

21. Mallarmé is, moreover, hardly the dupe of this mode of account writing: "I rarely went to the theater: from which fact perhaps derives the chimerical exactitude of these remarks" (see *Bibliographie* in Mallarmé 1998–2003, 1562).

Excepting that the poetic consecration of ideality seems to divide in two in the case of the stage and its ballet. To be more precise, in the object that serves as its pretext, that consecration encounters a model or concomitant of its own process. The structure of the stage, as a "communion, or part of one in all and all in one" (246), presents the very image of a ritual of the future, embodies the dream of new, communal festivities that can substitute the civic and atheistic rite of the Idea for moribund Catholicism. Moreover, among the various occupants of the stage, the ballet—as frivolous and stupid as it is possible to be—seems to be the only art (in contrast with theater or music) to present a regime of signification pertinent to establishing the Idea. Ballet escapes the *agôn* between the major scenic arts: because it cares nothing for the Idea, it is exactly the right art form to present a model of writing adequate to it.

THE POLITICS AND RELIGION OF THE STAGE

Scribbled at the Theater opens with a very "peculiar notion of the public," expressed through the image of a hole and of hunger, which also represents the people in general:

> the magnificent hole or hunger or anticipation dug every night as the sun is setting—the opening of a Chimera's maw, carefully frustrated by the current social system. (118)

The term "public" is ascribed to the people as they figure here, imagined as a gigantic hunger that, while it waits for something unknown, seeks illusion and diversion. The city, emblem of the Industrial Revolution and the social system's frustrations, can only be sustained if it remains a site of perpetual distractions, which can artificially satisfy expectation. A society of the spectacle, perhaps. But the connection between city and people through the regime of diversion or entertainment [*divertissement*] also enables the emergence of new (distinctive and minor) theatrical forces, as the traditional regime of Art is suspended:

> In the course of this kind of interregnum for Art, the sovereign, in which our era lingers, a genius must discern—but what? if not the unexplained but invading flood of exact theatrical forces: mime, juggling, dance, and simple acrobatics. This doesn't prevent people from coming to, living in, and going about in the city—a phenomenon that only hides, apparently, an intention to go occasionally to a show. (144)

Attentive to these shifts, Mallarmé discerns in them an ancient need, at once political and religious. The spectacle is something more than mere diversion or entertainment [*divertissement*]. This derivative that appeases the Chimera's hunger already experiments with a form of minimal community. The stage space gathers together multiple individuals and unites them around the focal point of the pleasures it proffers. A politics (of the stage) re-emerges in the very place that seemed to offer only compensatory escape. And this politics has a religious dimension, insofar as what binds one individual to another is given in the form of cultural pomp, on the model of the Mass, no less. The need for spectacle thus becomes at once civic and sacred:

> The stage is the obvious focus of pleasures taken in common, so, all things considered, it is also the majestic opening to the mystery whose grandeur one is in the world to envisage, the same thing that a citizen, having an inkling of it, expects from the State: to compensate him for his social diminishment. (144)

> Our communion, or part of one in all and all in one, thus, withdrawn from the barbarous food that designates the sacrament—in the consecration of the host, however, the prototype of ceremonials, is affirmed, despite its differences from a tradition of art, the Mass. (246)

Among Mallarmé's three texts collected under the title *Services*, there is one called *The Same* that explicitly examines the Mass as the prototype of ceremony. It reveals the impossibility of political community, or rather the State, being based on itself alone. The contractual model of a union of individual interests will always be compromised by the enormity of the sacrifices it demands. The State can only be accepted when it is anchored in cult and ceremony. In other words, the State *owes us* pomp:

> The State, because of unexplained (and therefore demanding faith) sacrifices required of the individual, [owes us pomp]: it's improbable, in fact, that we should be, with respect to the absolute, the same little men we ordinarily appear to be. (249)

> When the old religious vice, so glorious, which was to divert toward the incomprehensible sentiments that were natural, in order to give them a solemn grandeur, is diluted in the waves of the obvious and the plain-to-see, it will nevertheless remain true, that devotion to one's country, for example, if it is to find its backing elsewhere than on the battlefield, needs a religion, is of the order of piety. (251)

Mallarmé here discerns a problem that, in some respects, exercises the whole nineteenth century. After monarchy's collapse and growing disaffection with the church, how can new religious celebrations and forms of worship be developed to reassert an experience of communion? How can the Republic—a regime of reason—become something to which citizens feel intensely and instinctively that they belong? How can it be celebrated in holidays, choirs, or processions? Both Henri de Saint-Simon and Auguste Comte asked the same question, as did the German idealists in what has been called their "most ancient programme,"[22] and more vividly also the leaders of the French Revolution.[23]

But, as the century draws to a close, it seems that the Republic has still not succeeded in producing its own form of worship and its own myths. Indeed, it seems inherently to lack ambition in this direction and currently addresses itself only to "the same little men we ordinarily appear to be" (249). In short, Mallarmé confronts an epoch devoid of ceremony. Only the stage, which brings together the various arts and diverse individuals, still offers the hope of festivals to come. But that epoch in fact cares nothing for the stage:

> The stage, our only magnificence, to which the participation of diverse arts sealed by poetry contributes, according to me, a religious or official charac-
> ter, if one of these words has a meaning, I note that the century now ending couldn't care less about them, thus understood; that miraculous assembly of everything needed for the divine, except for human clairvoyance, will end up being for nothing. (143)

There does, however, appear to be a model for this "miraculous assembly" or "participation of diverse arts sealed by poetry." Or at least there is one way in which they are realized empirically, and Mallarmé must engage with it: the work of Wagner. That work is all the more powerful because music is declared, at the turn of the century, to be the "last plenary human religion" (239). In contrast to theater—whose communication halts in the figure of the character, and which, in relation to the Absolute, merely returns us to "the same little men we ordinarily appear to be"—music secures a perfect reciprocity of the stage and the auditorium via a form of communication without object:

> The miracle of music is this penetration, in reciprocity, of the myth and the house, topped by the sparkling of arabesques and golds, which trace the blockage of the pit, the vacant space, facing the stage, the absence of anyone, where the audience parts and which characters can't cross. (245–46)

---

22. See Rancière: "At the century's dawn, Hegel, Höderlin and Schelling committed this idea to paper in a rough draft. It was to be the 'first systematic programme of German Idealism': that is, the creation of a new religion and a new mythology for the people, on the very basis of that new philosophy which internalizes and radicalizes the political revolution. The idea was left abandoned in draft form but not forgotten within the very rigours of speculative philosophy" (2011, 28).

23. As articulated, for example, in Robespierre's report on national celebrations.

The orchestra floats and fills in, and the action in progress does not seem
isolated or foreign to the spectator, who is no longer just a witness: but,
from each seat, through tortures or gleams, one is each by turns, circularly,
the hero—who is pained at not being able to reach himself without storms
of sounds or of emotions displaced onto his body or onto our invisible
surges. (246)

This purification of the stage—a "thorough washing of the Temple, accomplished
[...] by the orchestra, pouring out its floods of glory and sadness" (153)—
establishes transparent and circular communication, inaugurating a hero without shape or content in the form of each one of us. But this purity is also a weakness. Music probably serves as a model for the poem, by presenting an image of
speech released from the brutality of reference, subtracted from the "denomina-
tive and representative function" (210). Music escapes the "universal *reporting*"
(210) in which language ordinarily consists. In this sense, it dominates the poem.
However, music is also too quick to do away with meaning in noisy sonorities.
The orchestral flood remains "vain, unless language, dipping and soaring on the
purifying wings of song, gives it meaning" (189). The spirit must "[regain], with
a lesser sonority, signification: none of the mental ways to exalt a symphony will
be left out—just rarefied from the fact of thought, that's all" (228–29). To return
thought to music—that is what Poetry aims to accomplish.[24]

Is this not exactly what Wagner's work achieves? In its fusion of myth and symphony, its union of musical, verbal, and visual means, do we not discover "the
most comprehensive art of our time" (154)? Probably. But in this alliance, music
seems to have lost precisely that quality which gave it an exceptional position
within ancient theater. The empty, purely allegorical circulation proposed by the
orchestra is effaced by the massive figure of the Hero. The concert's communication without object is returned to ordinary games of recognition and communal
participation. And all this because the solution proposed was too hurried:

The mere addition of an orchestra completely changes things, annulling the
former theater's very principle, and it is as strictly allegorical that the theater
now is experienced; the stage, empty, abstract, and impersonal, now needs,

---

24. Hence the constant demand that poetry rival, or even supplant, music: "Does this mean
that the traditional writer of verse, he who works with the humble and sacred artifices of language alone, will try, crowned somehow by those very constraints, to compete?" (160). Or, "I
call for the restitution, to impartial silence, in order to help the mind repatriate, of the whole
[...] apparatus; minus the tumult of sonorities, still transfusible into dream" (189). On this
general struggle between music and poetry, see Rancière (2011, 35–38); Lacoue-Labarthe
(1994, 41–84).

in order to come alive with plausibility, the life-giving flood dispensed by Music. (109)

He alone did this.

To take first only the most urgent thing: he reconciled a whole intact tradition, just about to fall into decadence, with the virginal, occult energy surging up from his scores. Outside of some sterile perspicacity or suicide, this creator's gift for assimilation was so life-filled that, of the two elements of beauty that exclude each other, or at least remain unknown to each other, personal drama and ideal music, he brought about the Hymen. Yes, with the help of a harmonious compromise, calling forth a specific phase of theater, which corresponds, as if it were a surprise, to the fundamental character of his race! (109–10)

As Jacques Rancière notes, the political consequences of this hurried solution are significant. This "fraudulent compromise between music and representation [. . .] turns the abstract poetic type into a national hero; it transforms communion 'through the vacant space' into the people's real presence to itself, invited to the celebration of community origin" (2011, 40).

Here, Mallarmé can only break ranks, invoking a specifically "French spirit" that is "strictly imaginative and abstract" and "rejects [. . .] any existing Legend" (111). Kings and heroes are dead. There is no way back. To offer the people (amplified by the orchestral flood) the image of a primitive community, albeit immersed once more in mythical sources, is to sell them a lie. The age of industry cares nothing for Siegfried and Brünnhilde.[25] More fundamentally, the very connection between fiction and political community needs rethinking for the times, beyond questions of representation. The foundational myth, which transforms the scenic act into a fallacious mirror of community, should be counteracted by "the Fable—virgin of anything: place, time or known characters," which simply mobilizes "the sense which is latent in everyone's striving." The national Hero, in whom the anonymous power of the crowd is arrested, should be replaced by the "type without a prior designation," who embodies in a multiplicity of aspects and gestures "all our dreams of places or paradises" (111–12). The Fable and the Type do not require or represent any kind of belonging; they merely deploy the very structure of the stage, as a "fictive focal point of the eyes of a crowd" (112). Only through this abstract symbolism of the Fable and the Type, this emptying of representation, can the stage become the site for a modern celebration in which "Man and his authentic stay on earth exchange a reciprocity of proofs" (112).

---

25. "Exposition, Transfer of Powers, etc. Can I see you in it, Brünnhilde, or what would you do there, Siegfried!?" (111).

But this critique of Wagner also declares that it is impossible effectively to realize the Fable or the Ode onstage. The festivals of the future will only ever take place within the Book, as the poet folds into the intimacy of his mental theater. This establishes a logic of supplementation [*suppléance*]—of theater by writing, of stages by pages:

> A book in our hand, if it pronounces some august idea, takes the place of all theaters, not through the oblivion it causes but by imperiously recalling them, on the contrary [. . .] a spirit, hiding among the pages, defying a whole civilization that neglects to build for his dream, so that they will take place, the prodigious Hall and the Stage. (168)

> Anyone who has really looked at nature contains inside himself a theater inherent to the mind, a summary of types and correspondences; just as any volume confronts them, opening up its parallel pages. [. . .] With two pages and their lines of verse, and the accompaniment of my whole self, I supply the world! Or at least I perceive, discreetly, its drama. (161)

As Derrida remarks in his vertiginous commentary on Mallarmé's text *Mimique*,[26] this supplementation or addition [*suppléance*]—far from denying the externality of the stage through the internal resumption of reading—extends and repeats the spacing of the stage, through a regime of the page and the trace. Poetic writing is not a vicarious experience of the real presence or the live speech celebrated on the boards of the stage. Rather, it repeats (in the parallel opening of pages and the juxtaposition of blanks and black) the distancing effected by the theater, the strictly graphic and allegorical force of the stage.[27]

But aside from spacing, ceremonial and ritual are also to be repeated here. Mallarmé's project of the Book involves a *public ritual* of the Idea. Of course this ritual is effected in absence, outside of the stage, but it must nonetheless be realized according to rules and strict protocols, as revealed in Jacques Scherer's (1957) presentation of the various fragments that Mallarmé devoted to the Book. The need for ritual, which persists alongside the absenting of writing, probably

---

26. See "The Double Session," in Derrida (1981 [1972], 173–286).

27. "Here, supplementarity is not, as it apparently or consciously is in Rousseau, a unilateral movement which, falling from inside to out, loses in space both the life and the warmth of the spoken word; it is the excess of a signifier which, in its own inside, makes up (for) space and repeats the fact of opening. The book, then, no longer repairs, but rather repeats, the process of spacing, along with what plays, loses, and wins itself in it [. . .] Far from replacing the stage or substituting a perfectly mastered interiority for the slipping away of space, this *suppléance* [addition/representation] implacably retains and repeats the theatrical stage within the book" (Derrida 1981, 234–35).

suggests some revision of detail to Derrida's interpretation and implies inter-rogating whether it is possible completely to eliminate presence in the actual-ization of the Book. If the Book is understood as ritual, it must be given—one way or another—in the form of a present event. Even so, it remains true that the festivals of which Mallarmé dreams will only ever be realized on the page.

There is one model for this scriptural ritual, which exists beyond the page, on the boards of the stage itself: namely, ballet. As an immediate deployment of emblems, ballet presents a simultaneously naive and exact image of the ritual of the Idea, which will ultimately be consigned to the Book. And it does so more easily on account of its minor status, through which it escapes the contest of the major arts and fails to presume to any priestly function. As an analphabetical form of writing and reading, of traces to be deciphered, ballet represents for Mallarmé a sort of line of flight, which draws on the stage itself the path that the Book and its process of supplementation [suppléance] will take.

THE RITUAL (BEYOND PLAY) OF THE IDEA

Recall that Mallarmé's reverie on Richard Wagner begins with an omission, set-ting aside what might have competed—absurdly and ureasonably—with the great Wagner:

> If we leave out the many glances at the extraordinary but unfinished splen-dor of sculptural figuration and concentrate on its one successful outgrowth, Dance, capable of translating, in the perfection of its rendition, the fleeting and the sudden up to the Idea—such a vision comprehends all, absolutely all, of the Spectacle of the future. (107–8)

Both the fact that dance is singled out and the prophetic tone in which it is said to comprehend the whole spectacle of the future have often been treated as ironic.[28] Yet this omission and bracketing is the basis for Mallarmé's discussion of Wagner. It revisits—without appearing to—the secret tension revealed by the Eden Theater's improbable confrontation of *Viviane* and the *Gesamtkunstwerk*. What elements of ballet's summary writing allow it to represent the ritual of the Idea, even better than the work of Wagner?

Mallarmé always describes dance from the position of spectator. Whereas Valéry focuses on the hidden and private inside of corporeal experience, fan-tasized via the unseen gaze of the voyeur, Mallarmé seems by contrast to be committed to pure surface. He never asks about the intimate experience of the

28. See, for example, Lacoue-Labarthe (1994, 46).

dancer, in which he does not seem remotely interested. Caught by the gaze of the spectator, the dancer is pure and immediate visibility, leaving nothing to be unveiled. There is no enigmatic inside (whether of experience or character) to be discovered under the transparent tulle: the dancer is "as though unclothed."[29] Nothing to see under these skirts! The dancer has no inside. And the "near-nudity" of the dancer, this surface visibility, also functions as an emptying of representation and theatricality. It offers the mind "a pleasant debauchery," liberating the stage from "people in robes or suits and famous words" (129).

. So, there is nothing to bring to light within the visible, except what the spectator's gaze fleetingly assembles, on the surface, in its "floating reverie." Indeed Mallarmé always describes choreographic spectacle in terms of what lies between the visible phenomenon proposed and the spectator's welcoming gaze. To be more precise, he envisages a kind of "commerce" between writing and reading, which links the illiterate dancer to the poet-spectator. This commerce is established against ballet's background of general poverty, which directly solicits the viewer: "The ballet gives but little: it's an imaginative genre" (120). The ballet is poor because it has little meaning and no story—or only a story imposed from outside by the etic and misleading tutelage of the *livret*. Ballet's poverty directly demands the spectator's imagination. Without it, total boredom results. Mallarmé proposes a sort of method or training in viewing:

> The only imaginative training consists, during the ordinary hours of attending Dance without any particular aim, in patiently and passively asking oneself about each step, each strange attitude, these [*pointes*] and *taquetés*, these *allongés* or *ballons*, "What could this mean?" or, even better, from inspiration, to read it. For sure, one would operate fully in the midst of reverie, but appropriate. (133–34)

This is also a method of reading and deciphering not in terms of the general continuity afforded by a clear narrative or plot but rather in terms of reverie's immediate and inspired instantaneity, which transforms each step into a metaphor, is always at one remove, inherently subjective and yet somehow adequate.

29. "La Cornalba enthrals me—she dances as though unclothed" (129), an image echoed at the end of the same text with mention of "the ultimate veil that always remains" (134). This "near-nudity" characteristic of the dancer needs attentive explication, as does this visibility that, in the very moment of its exposition, is also a means of concealment. In the text *The Only One Would Have to Be as Fluid as the Sorcerer*, for example, Mallarmé writes of Loïe Fuller: "Yes, the suspension of Dance, the contradictory fear of seeing too much and not enough, requires a transparent extension" (138). And, in the same text, and on the subject of *coryphées* in ballet, he says: "The *central near-nudity*, except for a brief halo of skirts, either to cushion the fall or to lift up the points, shows merely her legs" (139, my emphasis).

One must willingly float without preconceived aim, passively deciphering movements according to "poetic instinct." The dancer does not, then, inscribe a general signifier; rather, she directly inscribes the vision of the spectator. The dancer *is* a Sign. But what she is a sign *of* cannot be determined in advance, nor translated, because the establishment of the sign as sign remains strictly contemporaneous with its reading by the floating gaze. The "near-nudity" of the dancer thus unites with the mental near-nudity of the spectator:

> Then, through an exchange of which her smile seems to hold the secret, she hastily delivers up, through the ultimate veil that always remains, the nudity of your concepts, and writes your vision silently like a Sign, which she is. (134)

The dancer becomes a sign through a kind of commerce. She offers an empty form as a gift to the gaze, presenting pure surface deprived of immediately recognizable elements and always clothed in an "ultimate veil." Conversely, this gaze itself tends to be stripped bare. Thrown back by the failure of recognition onto its own conceptual nudity, the gaze can only really dream. And in this in-between movement of visibility and the gaze—where clothing and nudity continually swap roles—some isolated signs ultimately emerge:

> When a sign of scattered beauty is isolated for the eye—flower, wave, cloud, jewel, etc.—if our only way of knowing it is to juxtapose it with our spiritual nudity so we can feel that it is analogous, and adapt it in some exquisite confusion of ourselves with this fluttering form—even if it's through a rite, the utterance of the Idea. Doesn't the dancer seem to be half the element in question, half humanity eager to melt into it, floating in reverie? (120)

This is exactly what is envisaged by the ritual of the Idea: the instantaneous juxtaposition of a factual form and a suggested figure; the precarious assemblage, effaced as soon as it is effected, of a *symbol* or *metaphor* that links the gaze and the visible, escaping both. The dancer is the direct instrument of this ritual, which enables a renewed celebration of our stay on earth:

> so much so that the figurative representation of earthly props by Dance contains a test of their aesthetic merit, and a consecration results, which is the proof of our treasures. (120)

Dance can realize the sacrament of our treasures because the "near-nudity" of the dancers' legs reveals "with a significance other than personal, [...] a direct instrument of the idea" (139). And recall that Zucchi, Cornalba, and Laus are the "ones who occupy an ideal function" (154), while Mademoiselle Mauri "simulates an impatience of plumes toward the idea" (132).

The purely emblematic and impersonal character of the dancer follows from this ideal, indeed sacred, function: "the dancer [is] only an emblem, never Someone . . ." (130) (although it is worth emphasizing in passing that this does not mean she is anonymous). The emblem is instantaneous representation: it cancels out the possibility of a "someone," suppresses the temporal interiority of the individual, whether that individual is fictional (a character) or real (the woman who dances). The emblem also gestures toward the purely graphic dimension of signification. An emblem is only ever an assemblage, in the simultaneity of space, of various traced signs. Mallarmé's most famous statement about dance follows from this twofold nature of the emblem (the fact that it both denies the person and makes meaning graphic):

> *The dancer is not a woman dancing*, for these juxtaposed reasons: that *she is not a woman*, but a metaphor summing up one of the elementary aspects of our form: knife, goblet, flower, etc., and that *she is not dancing*, but suggesting, through the miracle of bends and leaps, a kind of corporal writing, what it would take pages of prose, dialogue, and description to express, if it were transcribed: a poem independent of any scribal apparatus. (130)

The metaphor retains the very essence of the dancer: movement. She displaces meaning (*metaphora*), assembling under the spectator's gaze a fugitive symbol: a juxtaposition of aspects that immediately vanishes. None of this should be puzzling, given the analysis above. Yet the second half of Mallarmé's statement does seem problematic. Why is the dancer *not dancing*? Why must one claim that she *writes*? And what exactly is a "poem independent of any scribal apparatus"?

Alain Badiou, commenting on these texts, voices a similar concern: "This second statement is just as paradoxical as the first ('The dancer does not dance'), since the poem is by definition a trace, an inscription, especially in its Mallarméan conception. Consequently, the poem 'set free of any scribe's apparatus' is precisely the poem unburdened of the poem, the poem subtracted from itself" (Badiou 2005, 65–66). To this, I would respond with Jacques Rancière that "with Mallarmé the poem is always worded and laid out, not as the trace of an already transpired event, but as the very act of a tracing: the deployment of an appearing and of a disappearing which is laid out in analogy with the 'subject' of the poem [. . .] A consequence follows from this [. . .] This consequence is precisely the possibility that the poem can be 'set free of any scribe's apparatus,' that it may consist in the way in which the legs of the illiterate dancer translate, without knowing it, the reverie of the spectator who

lays a flower 'at her feet,' " (Rancière 2009, 76). Mallarmé himself clearly delineates the nature of choreographic *writing*. He calls it "a hieroglyphic language"
(Mallarmé 2007, 139),[30] associating with religious ritual the spatiality of a trace
rigorously estranged from the voice. What is written in dance is not an imitation of temporally deployed speech but rather the spaced inscription of an
emblem, an instantaneous grapheme. This hieroglyphic image of dance will
recur later in this book. It is a feature of seventeenth- and eighteenth-century
discourse as well as figuring in the work of Artaud, for example. What interests
me for the moment is the way in which the image demands that we rethink the
connection between space and ideality. Dance seems to be the only art directly
constrained to space. Lacking notation, and resisting preservation in archives,
dance is the only art form that requires a real space, or the stage. And this,
moreover, differentiates it from theater:

> Dance alone, because of its twirls, along with mime, appears to me to neces-
> sitate a real space.
>   At the limit, a piece of paper suffices to evoke every play: with the help of
> his multiple personality, everyone can act it in his head, which is not the case
> with pirouettes. (Mallarmé 2007, 145)

This spatial requirement seems to imply that dance lacks ideality. Dance
lacks the self-identity of the word, so necessitates externalization in singular, real events. Since it does not have the powers of repetition and survival
associated with the word and writing, dance must be given each time in real
action. And this lack of ideality is what emerges from Badiou's articulation of
the requirement for space and the absence of naming in dance: dance is the
image of thought before this thought has received a name, and can therefore
only be enacted in the exteriority of a real space. Conversely, as soon as there is
nominal fixation (as in theater), temporal interiority is all that is required, and
one can dispense with space: naming can speak for itself alone in the intimacy
of speech (or of a reading that conforms to speech) (Badiou 2005, 61). But this
is merely "vulgar" ideality, understood in terms of verbal self-identity and an
idea of language as an "easy and representational currency."[31] If the dance's
spatial requirement is read rather in terms of the hieroglyph (that is, independently of the alphabetical model that subordinates graphic inscription to the

30. " . . . the name of Dance—which is, if you will, a hieroglyphic language" (Mallarmé 2007, 139).

31. Translator's note: The phrase "numéraire facile et representative" is Mallarmé's (Mallarmé
1998–2003, 857–58).

temporality of the spoken word), then space is revealed as the very condition of writing. Writing, as a spacing of thought, no doubt forfeits the interiority of meaning for the exteriority of the page. But it also enables, by virtue of this spacing, a new, properly Mallarméan play of ideality: a play of traces and of fleeting juxtapositions, assemblages that vanish as soon as they are formed. This is why dance, which is really hierogylphics, can be conceived as writing adequate to the Idea.

But that remains to be seen. Dance, after all, is not just dance. It is also "ballet," which always alters dance in one way or another:

> Theater always alters, from a special or literary point of view, the arts it appropriates: music cannot participate without losing some of its depth and darkness; neither can song, which ceases to be a solitary lightning-bolt; and, strictly speaking, neither can one recognize in Ballet the name of Dance— which is, if you will, a hieroglyphic language. (139)

> [One must avoid] even suggesting [to theater] what might possibly replace him (for the new vision of the idea would just be, for him, another costume: he would put it on in order to deny it, just as the acrobatic trick is already starting to show through in the Ballet) [. . .]. (143)

And it is indeed in terms of alteration and travesty that Mallarmé confronts the two actual ballets he discusses: *Viviane* and *The Two Pigeons*. Ballet reclothes the new vision of the Idea, and the near-nudity of the dancer, with the tawdry old cloaks of narrative and decor. When Mallarmé writes empirically about what he actually sees, it almost always proves a disappointment (Loïe Fuller excepted). In the show at the Eden Theater, "the charm of the book doesn't pass into the representation" (129). Worse still, *Viviane* bypasses the ideal choreographic theme presented by the *livret:* that inscription "in the folio of the sky" of the fairy's name (see the central image of the first series of engravings from the *Journal Amusant*, appendix, figure 4). Instead of watching the name write itself, in the action or movement of the dance and its ensembles, Mallarmé sees it fixed by its inscription on the cardboard decor:

> For the whole chorus of dancers will not, grouped around the *star* (could it be better named!), dance the ideal dance of the constellations. Not at all!
> [. . .] everything that is, in effect, Poetry, or Nature animated, comes out of a text to fix itself in maneuvers of cardboard and the dazzling motionlessness of chiffon, fire, and ash. Thus, in the order of the action, I saw a magic circle drawn by something other than the continual turns or the bends of the fairy herself; etc. (129–30)

Dance offered the hope of a moving, corporeal writing, in line with the near-nudity of what is deployed without words. But what do we get in its place? Good old, solid decor, and its ordinary games of recognition. We thus pass by the "law that dictates that the primary subject of dance, which lies beyond its frame, be a synthesis—constantly moving everywhere—of the attitudes of each group."[32] *The Two Pigeons* hardly fares any better. Only the prelude succeeds in charming Mallarmé: it effects a complex game of translation and retranslation of the *livret*, "according to which human characters and manners are transferred to simple animals" (130), and cleanly discerns the relation between "flight and the choreography of dance moves" (132). But as for the rest:

> I'll stop trying to raise myself up to any consideration suggested by the Ballet, to aid me to reach the paradise of all spirituality, because after this innocent little prelude, nothing takes place, except the perfection of the dancers' skills, that deserves the exercise of a backward glance, nothing. . . . It would be tedious to put one's finger on the precise type of inanity that grows out of such a graceful beginning. (131)

The final kiss, "completely indifferent to art," is saved only by the poet's own extravagance, which allows him to see in this action the very object of Dance itself, as a "mysterious sacred interpretation."[33] Only Loïe Fuller seems to escape criticism: she manages to maintain the empty and pure space of the stage. By dispensing with decor in favor of a simple musicalized costume, and abandoning any identifiable story, she returns to ballet "a spatial virginity undreamed of":

> Opaque vehicles, intrusive cardboard—to the scrap heap! Here we find given back to Ballet the atmosphere or nothingness, visions no sooner known than scattered, just their limpid evocation. The stage is freed for any fiction, cleared and instated by the play of a veil with attitudes and gestures; the site, all movement, becomes the very pure result. (136–37)

What should we think of Mallarmé's criticism here? Just that it returns us to exactly my point of departure: the empiricity of these texts and their object. The very nature of theatrical spectacle, insofar as it is empirically given, is to

---

32. Translator's note: The citation is from Rosemary Lloyd and Mary Caws's translation of Mallarmé's text *Ballets* (Mallarmé 2001, 109), which better matches (Pouillaude's interpretation of) the original French. The remaining citations are from Johnson's translation (Mallarmé 2007).

33. "But to let oneself fantasize like that is to be summoned by the sound of a flute to remember how ridiculous one's visionary state is to the average banal contemporary that one must, after all, represent, to show one's respect for the Opéra's seats" (132).

be disappointing, to bypass the essence or image that it might have realized. A few singular experiences or moments of illumination—like the dance of Loïe Fuller—emerge from this general background of disappointment. And if Mallarmé does not usually like what he sees, this also guarantees the empiricity of his discourse.

Do I need to say that I find Badiou's reading of Mallarmé problematic? I do not think Mallarmé expels dance from the site of theater, nor that he considers dance the sign of the possibility of art inscribed in the body. We are not concerned here with originary or transcendental art.[34] Dance is an art like any other, with actual places, artists, and spectators, all things that can be described and named, with the inevitable degree of impurity that implies. And even when Mallarmé manages to give dance a privileged status (as an adequate model of the writing of the Idea), that status is immediately circumscribed by the reality of spectacle—its distinct and all too empirical disappointments.[35]

The fascination with disappointing empiricity paradoxically brings us back to the idea of "unworking." I thought I had found in Mallarmé's texts a path toward the choreographic work, which would counterbalance the absenting charted in the first part of my book. Scribbling at the theater and writing an attentive account of dance signification, Mallarmé seemed to offer the antidote to the view of his disciple Paul Valéry. He gives us spectacle, not voyeurism. He gives us signification, not masturbation. Yet this reading has reached a real impasse. For one thing, those themes that make Mallarmé attentive to spectacle can also be reinterpreted as suspending the work, at every level. Spectacle fascinates not because it exposes authored artistic objects to the spectator's judgment but rather because it connects two phenomena equally opposed to the making of works: the ritualism of future quasi-religious festivities and the frivolity

34. I note in passing that Badiou's reading depends on a very shaky philological hypothesis. He develops the idea of transcendental absenting on the basis of the slogan "Theater is, by essence, superior" (in *Of Genre and the Moderns*; Mallarmé 2007, 142–52). Dance is very ancient but still inferior to theater because it escapes the ordinary classification of the arts and becomes a kind of art before art. However, the word "superior" in Mallarmé's slogan may well be an absolute comparative, which does not explicitly invoke a second, contrasting term. The first version of Mallarmé's text in the *Revue Indépendante* (January 1, 1887) seems to confirm this because it includes the slogan without any anterior reference point. The theater is superior in itself, absolutely, without reference to dance. If this is right, then Badiou's hypothesis simply collapses.

35. This critique of Badiou is developed in Rancière (2009). For example: "Dance becomes the manifestation of the simple dispossedness of bodies to welcome the pass of an idea. Thus, instead of Mallarmean analogy, a hierarchy of forms of art is established to shore up the status of art—and above all of the poem—as that which is productive of educative truths. To do so, the Mallarmean corpus must be relieved of all those fans, postal addresses and verses covering sweet-wrappers, which comprise such a large part of it" (77).

of the unworthy object. Mallarmé only ever envisages the stage in terms that exceed the aesthetic: either in terms of the rituals that the stage both recalls and predicts, or in terms of its own unworthiness, the frivolity that Mallarmé takes constant pleasure in pointing out. In my next chapter, I explore this ambivalent status of spectacle, which suspends the possibility of works through the pairing of ritual and *divertissement*. Moreover, the hieroglyphs traced by the dancer only ever make sense in the negligent reverie of the poet, from the point of view of his contemplative gaze. Mallarmé insists on the purely relational character of gestural signification, always caught in between a dynamic image and an inter-preting gaze. But he thereby also suspends the possibility of properly choreo-graphic meaning, of a gestural statement explicitly addressed by an author to an audience. There is no real signification in the ballet, according to Mallarmé. The story in the *livret* (if there is one) has but little to do with what really happens onstage. And in place of this absent statement, the dancer's traces are merely a pretext for the poet's own reverie—the only thing that now establishes mean-ing. This fragility of choreographic signification is the underlying thread of my next two chapters.

Chapter 2

Spectacle, Ritual, *Divertissement*

Genesis and Structure of the Choreographic Stage, I

Spectacle is an ambivalent phenomenon. For one thing, it has long and often been condemned on ethical, political, and religious grounds. From Tertullian to Rousseau, from Saint Augustine to Pascal, spectacle is conceived as diverting the subject from self-fulfilment, distracting him from pursuit of the good and losing him in illusory pleasures. Spectacle seems far removed from what really matters in life, such as love of god or the classless society. I will assume that the basis and general formula for spectacle's depravity can be summed up by the term *divertissement*, understood in its multiple senses of diversion, entertainment, and choreographic interlude.

I will, though, state the following as a kind of counterproposition: that even the most grotesque and obscene spectacle still has a hieratic and ceremonial dimension relating it directly to religious worship. The smallest of spectacles involves the silence of an assembled crowd and the unfolding of some ritual. And this persistence of ritual recalls something of the phenomenon's origins: the early association between spectacle and the sacred in a relation (*religio*) between persons. Do I need to emphasize once more the cultic and Dionysiac basis of Greek tragedy, on which our whole theatrical tradition is based? Or—further afield—the deep theatricality of African and Oceanic rituals, as analyzed by Michel Leiris and André Schaeffner?

This apparently originary association between spectacle and the sacred also motivates the various aspirations toward a new religion based on the stage, aiming to substitute for Christianity and to resolve the social and political problem of the nineteenth century: Wagner and his art work of the future, Mallarmé and the magnificence of the stage (immediately transferred to the Book), but also Valéry in the hopes articulated in his Notebooks, and finally (of course) Artaud. Note in passing that this new religion was not conceived as either purely theatrical or purely sacred but rather fantasized as an eventual synthesis of the two. Spectacle fascinates less by virtue of the unilateral and ancient residue of the Mass than because of the strange and permanent association it makes between puppet and priest. Indeed, the ultimately and truly sacred would be a definite celebratory conjunction of the Mass and the fairground. Sometimes, this vision can be glimpsed in Wagner. It becomes explicit in Mallarmé and is also evident—although in a very different way—in Paul Claudel and Artaud. That other dimension of spectacle by which it escapes the traditional frivolity of *divertissement*, I propose to call "ritual."

These two aspects of spectacle, as distinct as they seem, nonetheless converge on the same capacity, summarized in the ordinary, neutral term "interruption." The *divertissement* interrupts the linearity of time, breaks the continuity of work and days, and introduces a kind of syncope of nonutility into the quotidian. Ritual functions similarly, interrupting the weariness of life by virtue of its form. What we call everyday life is amorphous, untidy, and vague. We never really know what we are doing, or how we do it. Here arises our greatest need for ceremony, here the great virtue of ritual intervenes: for our amorphous lives it substitutes an image of distinct, quintessential existence, which, if nothing else, gives life shape. This shape or form can in principle be only temporary and interruptive. Permanent form is merely a lie promoted by advertising ("Be fit and in form!").

This twofold capacity of the spectacle—understood as both ritual and *divertissement*—I will call "interruption." As we will see, it maintains a very particular connection with dance. But let me briefly anticipate my later argument by adding another element that combines with the interruption of ritual and *divertissement* to constitute the ground, or rather general environment, of spectacle's structure. This I will call "presence," an idea that I explore in the next chapter.[1]

For now, and in the whole of this second chapter, I want to pose the question of the conditions under which dance is inscribed on the Western stage. The question is clearly immeasurably vast, and I will furnish only a few lines of response—hasty characterizations of historical periods and general images—which set out the framework for future research (research that would, in principle, be never-ending). The question is also relatively narrow, since from the perspective of a "world history of dance," it excludes the vast majority of dance facts and practices. From the point of view of general anthropology, the history of choreography as such extends only over a few pages, or so Curt Sachs taught us in his *World History of the Dance*. Choreographic history isolates a relatively recent—and probably distinctively Western—institution against a

---

1. See below, 117–46.

background murmur of millennia of festivals, trance, apotropical rituals, and cures for the possessed. Choreographic spectacle separates dances from their social or religious effects, depriving the participant (henceforth known as the "spectator") of any real involvement with what he sees. This Western invention is what I want to outline, in all the ambivalence of its origins—origins that can be identified as *Greek*.

But first, perhaps it is important to pause to consider for a moment the background murmur, which still makes itself heard in today's social celebrations and nightclubs. Anthropology itself must lead us to spectacle. The image of primitive trance, which is Sachs's constant reference, itself contains the seeds of spectacularization. The body possessed is everything but primitive immediacy: trance is enabled and supported by a host of ritual codes, distinct roles for officiants and assistants, strict modes of spatial and temporal organization. In these, the Western stage discovers its imagined origins and structural equivalence, at least when viewed from an ethnologically distanced perspective. It would be relevant here to cite in its entirety Gilbert Rouget's fictional "Letter on Opera," written on the model of Montesquieu's *Persian Letters*, in which an ethnomusicologist from Benin describes an evening at the opera in the vocabulary of ritual possession.[2] Michel Leiris's (1958) discussion of possession's theatrical dimension within *zar* worship is also pertinent. Nor is this origin only imagined. Greek theater was an extension of the curative rituals of Dionysiac possession.[3] Through trance and possession, dance is therefore the very element of a ritual and religious pre-theater,[4] in which the Western stage finds its own beginnings.

But dances of possession and trance are not the only dances beyond the stage. Another, simpler anthropological starting point presents itself in the form of celebratory social dance. People do not dance only to provoke or cure possession by the gods or (in more contemporary parlance) to push the body into an extreme state. They dance because it is time to dance: because work has ended or because others are also dancing and it is important to join with them in some other bond than those of labor or kinship. A fundamental dimension of dance is its sociability. The common experience of rhythm and music, the

---

2. See Rouget (1985, 241–50).

3. See Roland Barthes on "The Greek Theater": "The link uniting Dionysiac worship to these three genres [dithyramb, satyr play, comedy] is of a more or less physical order: it is possession, or, to be even more precise, it is hysteria (whose 'natural' relation to theatrical practices we are familiar with), of which dance is at once the fulfillment and the release" (Barthes 1991 [1982], 72). On the cultic and Dionysiac origins of the Greek theater, see also Jeanmaire (1951), who is cited by Leiris at the beginning of his study of *zar* theatricality.

4. See Schaeffner's "Rituel et pré-théâtre," in Schaeffner (1947).

contact between bodies, the inevitable games of seduction, the vertiginous effects of collective movement in which each individual identifies with his fellow dancers—all of these phenomena are part of an age-old experience of community, which modernity seeks constantly to reactivate (for better or worse), without ever really managing to. Rousseau's image of social festivity, divorced from the stage and from representation, is an exemplary exaltation of this primary sociability, both affective and corporeal, with dance as one of its essential means.[5] And these festivities where people dance are also an opportunity to express ethnicity, to identify rhythmically and gesturally with a community, identity being the core focus of ethnochoreology, or what used to be called "folklore studies."[6]

As diametrically opposed as festivity and spectacle appear, particularly from a contemporary point of view, it is no less crucial to state how the second derives directly from the first. Dramatic and choreographic representation probably had little meaning in fifth-century B.C.E. Athens outside of its role in celebrating and honoring Dionysus (particularly in the Great Dionysia, which took place in the spring).[7] Equally, the court ballet from the Renaissance to the end of the seventeenth century can only be understood against the general background of princely festivals, celebrating marriage, birth, peace, or war. Such representation is only one part of a larger celebration, which unites a whole raft of other elements, including processions, triumphs, and carousels.

Choreographic spectacle discovers something resembling an origin in these religious or festive dances of Greece and the Renaissance. I propose to call them "rituals." The term implies for me two things: (1) strict codification of the event and (2) belief in its symbolic and social efficacy. The explicitly religious dimension of the event is not a necessary component, although it is often present. In this, I follow contemporary anthropology, which tends increasingly to dissociate the idea of ritual from that of the sacred or the religious. There are profane rituals: social festivities, to the extent that they meet the two criteria of codification and symbolic and/or social efficacy, are one example. One of the

5. Except that dance is practically absent from Rousseau's aesthetic and at best indirectly implied as an element of the social festivity supposed to replace theatrical spectacle: see Rousseau (2004 [1758]), "Letter to d'Alembert on the Theater," 251–352.

6. See Grau and Gore (2005). On the precursors of folklore studies in France, see Guilcher (1963), as well as the early work of Francine Lancelot (2000). I would like to note in passing how moved I was to discover, during an evening homage to Lancelot, her early ethnographic films, focused on French village dances in the early 1960s, which equal or even surpass those of Jean Rouch, at least in some respects. They share a similar resistant otherness and effort to combat imminent disappearance, captured on celluloid for an unknown future audience.

7. "We know that the theatrical performances could take place only three times a year, on the occasion of the festivals in honor of Dionysus. These were, in order of importance; the Great Dionysia, the Lenaean Dionysia, the Rural Dionysia" (Barthes 1991, 69).

characteristics of ritual is to be *interruptive*: it ruptures the linearity of social and work time, to establish another "suspended" time, to adopt the expression used by Barthes in relation to Greek theater.[8]

But the interruptive power of spectacle is not reducible to ritual alone. To be more exact, once disengaged from its political and religious anchors, and transformed into something consumable anytime and anywhere by anonymous subjects, this power tends to assume another name: *divertissement*. A *divertissement* is generally understood as something that interrupts time and distracts the subject from his real preoccupations. The spectacle or show is the privileged emblem of the divertissement structure. I will put to one side the underlying axiology of the pairing ritual/divertissement with which I began this chapter and simply say that one can trace a historical curve from ritual to divertissement, which passes through the secularization of spectacle during the Renaissance and ends with its annulment in the general indifference of commercial entertainment: judged strictly in terms of their functionality (relaxation, suspension of time, escapism), one *divertissement* is as good as any other and is only meaningful to the extent that it is continually and indifferently replaced.

Yet in moving from ritual to divertissement, we actually merely substitute one annulment for another. If we are interested in the spectacle as presentation of a work, ritual and *divertissement* are both vanishing points. In each case, the work is merely a pretext for the event, not its end. What matters for the participants is less the object presented than the eventfulness of its presentation (interruptive, whether it is ritual or entertainment). Then it becomes important to examine the conditions under which the spectacle becomes autonomous (moves beyond ritual involvement or the function to entertain). Only once it has achieved hypothetical autonomy can spectacle become merely an aesthetic medium (disinterested, detached, and so on) for the presentation of a work. And I note right from the start that this autonomy is anything but obvious. Probably in every spectacle there is an element of ritual or entertainment that goes beyond mere aesthetic relation or at least exceeds our canonical image of such.

8. "The Greek theater was an essentially festive theater. The festival which brought it into being was an annual one lasting several days. Now, the formality and the extent of such a ceremony involves [sic] two consequences: first of all, a suspension of time; we know that the Greeks did not observe a weekly day of rest, a notion of Hebrew origin; they left off work only on the occasion of religious festivals, though these were numerous. Associated with the 'loosening' of work time, the theater installed another time, a time of myth and of consciousness, which could be experienced not as leisure but as another life. For this suspended time, by its very duration became a saturated time" (Barthes 1991, 76–77).

It is also important to explore what conditions the autonomy of dance within spectacle. Assuming that spectacle can be autonomous (detached from both ritual community and entertainment function), we still need to show, in order to speak of a *choreographic* work, that dance can be given as principal object and not merely accessory ingredient, itself taking control of the whole stage time. Such autonomy has only rarely existed or, at least, is only very recent. Through the centuries, dance has been integrated with dramatic and operatic works precisely in the form of (what are technically known as) interludes or *divertissements*. The interruption that constitutes the spectacle is thus replayed within the spectacle itself: a small *divertissement* built in to the larger divertissement, dance is interruption through and through. Dance's heteronomy in this respect—its incapacity to sustain itself by itself—is perhaps less a weakness than an index. Via dance, the constitutive heterogeneity of spectacle can be understood: spectacle is always mixed and impure, always collective. The Greeks called it *choreia*, the seventeenth and eighteenth centuries *ballet* or *opera*, and the moderns the *total work of art*.

THE GREEK MODEL: RITUAL AND *CHOREIA*

Returning to our opening question (concerning the conditions under which dance is inscribed on the Western stage), we can obviously look to Greek theater as the practice that unites the two dimensions of ritual just explored: that of religious (in this case Dionysiac) possession, which is the origin of this theater; and that of community festival, which determines its civic and political dimension. Greek theater inaugurates our tradition and represents an exact conjunction of ritual and spectacle; it is the tipping point from which representation starts to become autonomous.[9] As we will see, dance is an integral element within this process or, more accurately, is conceived from the beginning as indissociable from it. As *orchestra* rather than *skene*, the site of Greek theater is first and foremost the site on which the chorus evolves.

This regime of inseparability made any dramatic work without a danced moment inconceivable. It was given the name *choreia* by the Greeks: an indissoluble union of music, poetry, and dance in a unique form whose emblem was the chorus. And the role of dance within that theater can be characterized according to the different modes of the chorus's intervention. Omnipresent

9. As Louis Séchan notes in his chapter devoted to "dances within public festivals and at the theater": "It is uncontestable that most of the ceremonies involving the dances discussed in this chapter had a religious character. However, the dances themselves were no longer fundamentally ritual actions; rather they had become what we will come to call *spectacle*" (1930, 183).

in the Dionysiac dithyramb (a purely choric form without individual actors), dance accompanied the entrance, interventions, and exit of the chorus in tragedy, comedy, and satyr plays, structured by a principle of alternation between the spoken and the sung-danced. Here already the interruptive character of dance emerges, a phenomenon that—in relation to narrative continuity—recurs again and again through Western history. From the discontinuous structure of the court ballet to the opera divertissement, dance's interruptive character for centuries determined its status on the Western stage, whether linked explicitly or implicitly to its Greek origins. But the status of dance as interlude does not mean that, originally, the choreographic dimension of spectacle was minor or negligible. We know that Aeschylus and Sophocles themselves orchestrated the movements of their choruses, and that Sophocles was even famed for performing a ball dance in *Nausicaa*.[10] Sometimes too the work's lyrical element made up more than half of the verses.[11]

Let us turn now to the ritual element of this theater, focusing on the Great Dionysia of Spring. This annual festival lasted six days and had a strictly defined schedule. The first day, involving processions and sacrifices, was devoted to moving Dionysus's statue from the temple to the theater. Then there were two days of dithyrambic performance, concluding with a further procession, or *komos*. Three days were then spent on dramatic competition: a tetralogy each morning (including three tragedies and a satyr play)[12] and one comedy every afternoon. At the end of these three days, trophies were presented to the winners. There was no theater outside of this clearly defined spatial and temporal framework.[13]

The work in this context, then, has meaning only within the ritual that generates it. One consequence is that the idea of a repertoire—which assumes that the work can repeat itself indefinitely across different times and places—seems entirely alien to this form of theater: each work was performed only once (at least in the fifth century). I suggest that this rigorous eventfulness is directly linked to the work's ritual dimension. More accurately, the possibility of the event's repetition is in inverse proportion to its ritual inscription (I return to this hypothesis when discussing court festivals and ballets). The framework and its rules are the things to be repeated: protocol as well as poetics. The work activates the framework, actualizing it in singular, dated instances, but in turn

10. See Séchan (1930, 187).

11. As in Aeschylus's *The Suppliants*: see Séchan (1930, 188).

12. Only one tragic trilogy has survived intact: Aeschylus's *Oresteia*. The satyr play, which always followed the tragic trilogy, is now almost entirely forgotten: only Sophocles's *Ichneutae* and Euripides's *Cyclops* have come down to us.

13. See Barthes (1991, 74–75).

becoming inseparable from that dated instance.[14] Two further phenomena supported this eventfulness: (1) the politics of choregy, which was about expenditure and prestige and ultimately implied consumption of one-time works (the
wealthy individuals designated as financing these works could not be content
with merely restaging existing dramas); and (2) the inseparability of the text
from other scenic elements (which *choreia* implies), rendering restaging more
difficult. Finally, as Barthes notes, the open-air setting accentuated the work's
inscription in the event, as the imponderable element of weather became a
direct component of its actualization.[15]

Through studying this Greek model, a problematic connection becomes
apparent that makes ritual and *choreia* indices of the same spectacular eventfulness, the same annulment of the "work" understood as part of a stable and
indefinitely repeatable repertoire. This connection will recur in other historical
and conceptual contexts. For now, I draw attention to just two of its implications.
First, we should distinguish between this connection and another apparently
similar one, namely, Walter Benjamin's link between the ritual function of the
artwork and the nature of its appearance in the *here and now*.[16] Benjamin's thesis depends on an idea of the object's authenticity that pertains above all to the
visual arts and applies only problematically to the performing arts.[17] Secondly,
the heterogeneous and unitary nature of the spectacle that the Greeks called
choreia, which precludes isolating a particular field (text, music, and so on) as
the foundation of the object's identity, is also characteristic of the structure of
today's dance spectacles. An alliance of music, dance, text, lights, costumes, and
scenography, the "choreographic" object exists only in the eventful encounter
of the different media that constitute it, as I will show in the next chapter.

---

14. Or rather we need *only one work*, always the same, inherently absorbing ritual. Commenting
on Gautier's remark ("There should be only one vaudeville—it would be changed somewhat
from time to time"), Mallarmé mischievously imagines this unique ritual work in terms of both
Greek and Wagnerian *tetralogy*: "Replace 'vaudeville' by 'mystery', that is, a tetralogy itself multiple unfolding parallel to the cycle of the seasons, and insist that the text be as incorruptible as
the law: there, you have it! Almost." (Mallarmé 2007, 143).

15. See Barthes: "In the open air, the spectacle cannot be a habit, it is vulnerable, hence irreplaceable: the spectator's immersion in the complex polyphony of the open air (shifting sun,
rising wind, flying birds, noises of the city) restores to the drama the singularity of an event. The
open air cannot have the same image-repertoire as the dark theater: the latter is one of evasion;
the former, of participation" (1991, 79).

16. See "The Work of Art in the Age of Mechanical Reproduction," in Benjamin (1992 [1936]).

17. See below, 120–21.

THE AGE OF REASON: FROM ONE *DIVERTISSEMENT* TO THE NEXT

By periodically reiterating its interdiction against sacred dances (a prohibition thereby revealed as only partially effective), the Christian West has associated dance (almost) inextricably with the frivolous and profane space of the *divertissement*. This association has a history, even an aesthetic, that I need to retrace. To this purpose, I will distinguish three modes of connection, moving from the vaguest and most general sense of the term "divertissement" to the most technical and determinate.

The first mode of connection is *anthropologico-fantasmagoric*. This consists in maintaining that dance is man's most primitive and natural diversion, the most intuitive way for him to interrupt the routine of work and of the day-to-day, expending his energy in the pure and simple joy of uselessness. This reiterates the quite commonplace association (already identified in the work of Straus) between dance and the primitive. The idea is probably a retrospective construction of the nineteenth century, as the entry on "divertissement" in Pierre Larousse's *Grand dictionnaire universel du XIXe siècle* suggests, through its striking claims about "negro" dancing:

> The use of divertissements is found amongst all peoples, but varies according to their nature, spirit and degree of civilization. Dance is the most natural of man's diversions, seen in even the most primitive nations: the savage gambols around his idol and around the captive he will burn to produce food, like King David dancing before his ark [. . .] We know that dance is the favored diversion of negros. By dancing, slaves could forget the miseries by which they were burdened, as slave traders were well aware: when they descried long lines of these unfortunates lost in nostalgic reverie, they would force them to dance, with lashes of the whip, to dispel any idea of suicide that might take hold among their slaves.[18]

To treat dance as a *primitive* diversion, deploying the negro argument (which characterizes a race as perennially jiggling even under the whip), undoes the connection between dance and the sacred both exposed and rejected by the age of reason. For the seventeenth and eighteenth centuries, any primitive element of dance was based not on its immediate power to divert but on its unacceptable but ever-latent connection with the sacred. The first dances—those of the Egyptians, the Jews, the Greeks—were religious dances. Traces were still discernible in some liturgies (particularly Spanish and Portuguese) where they

---

18. See the entry for "Divertissement," in Larousse (1866–77).

continued to be tolerated (more or less).[19] And, for the age of reason, it was precisely the potentially sacred character of dance that appeared as a primitive trait. To counteract primitive religiosity, another space for dance must be invented, leaving the sacred free of choreographic contamination. This space was called the *divertissement*:

> The dance which *today* represents the diversion of the peoples, and of personnages of quality was in its *origin* a kind of mystery and ceremony. (Ménéstrier 1972 [1682], preface, my emphasis)

The *divertissement* is not primitive. Rather, it derives from a profane space, cultivated at the end of the Renaissance from the seedbed of princely festivals.

This leads to our second mode of connection between dance and the profane space of the *divertissement*, which might be termed *historico-political*. This relates to the development of the court ballet as princely diversion. The court ballet is born at the end of the sixteenth century with *Paradis d'amour* (1572), a ballet created to celebrate the marriage of Marguerite de Valois and Henri de Navarre (the beautiful Margot and the future Henri IV), and with the *Ballet comique de la Reine* (1581), celebrating the wedding of the Duc de Joyeuse, which established for several decades a model of artistic fusion. The *divertissement* thereby assumes a more determinate significance than previously: it no longer concerns mere relaxation or rupture in the continuity of work and days but rather a true spectacle that establishes a distinction between performers and spectators—except insofar as the dancers are generally the princely nobility, so that it is never clear whether the real *divertissement* consists in dancing or being its spectator.[20] That ambivalence was only resolved in the final days

19. See Claude-François Ménéstrier (1972 [1682]): "There are ceremonies among the most holy which admit [ballets] in Spain and in Portugal, in Churches and in the most serious and grave of processions. They were once even a significant element in the Acts of Religion between Jews and Christians, as well as among the infidels." As regards Western traces of earlier religious and ritual dance, the Sicilian tarantella also springs to mind, a practice that is more troubling because it directly reactivates the idea of possession and curative ritual. See Rouget (1985) and Martino (1966).

20. Pierre Larousse, an inexhaustible source of information, also acknowledges this ambivalence, developing a strange imaginary geography: "The Orientals, who avoid any violent exercise, have people paid to dance in their place; almés and bayadères perform gracious dances in their presence while they plunge into ecstatic reverie: they enjoy themselves but it is others who move. This explains the naively satirical question of the Turk who, attending a ball of the nobility where the dancers exerted themselves vigorously altogether, asked if these people were paid to give themselves so much trouble" (see Larousse 1866–77, entry on "Divertissement," already cited). This makes Oriental laziness the origin of dance spectacularization. The West,

of the court ballet, when Louis XIV bade farewell to the stage in 1670, in the appropriately named *Divertissement royal*.

The idea of the *divertissement* allows dance to enter a profane space that is indifferent to religion. Theoreticians and defenders of the court ballet—many of them, notably, Jesuit—continually reiterate this fact, in argument against Protestants and Jansenists:

> We no longer perform Acts of Religion as dances like those of the Jews or the infidels. We content ourselves rather with honest *divertissements* which train the body to noble action and well-being. These become public celebrations which, often through ingenious allegories, represent events that contribute to the happiness of the State, allowing the people to taste all the sweetness and charm of pleasure and diversion, to which they become more receptive. (Ménéstrier 1972, preface)

In his preface to *Des ballets anciens et modernes selon les règles du théâtre* [*Ancient and modern ballets, according to the rules of Theater*], Claude-François Ménéstrier sketches the historical curve by which dance swings from religious ritual to mere *divertissement*. One moves from the liturgical dances of the Jews and the first Christians (still visible in Spain and in Portugal) to the ballet as honest diversion, where religious indifference combines with an embedded political function.

However, as mention of the political dimension of the court ballet suggests, ritual is not simply abandoned when *divertissement* becomes profane. Rather, the court ballet displays a weakened ritual dimension in its capacity as princely festivity. Ballet only takes place on celebratory occasions to mark a determinate political event (a marriage, diplomatic agreement, or peace treaty, for example). Again here the idea of a repertoire of ballets appears entirely incongruous. Court ballets are never restaged, if only for lack of the requisite financial resources. They may well be given several times and in several different locations in the course of a single night (the final performance in the public square at around four o'clock in the morning). But then they disappear without return, once the events that gave them substance have passed.[21] It is not the work as stable object that matters here but the festive framework within which the ballet is performed and which it partially activates. If ballets are repeated, this is not

meanwhile, remains undecided about whether it is more diverting to dance or to watch others dancing, maintaining the ambivalence between ball and ballet, between nightclub and the town theater.

21. On this ritual eventfulness of the court ballet, see Prunières (1914).

repetition of an object but of a ritual. In this, the court ballet (albeit secularized) is a direct descendent of Greek theater.

Moreover, one can only properly understand the invention of the court ballet at the end of the Renaissance in terms of its relation to the Greek *choreia*. That relation may be mythical but is no less real for that. The form needs recontextualizing within the experiments of Antoine de Baïf's Académie de Poésie et de Musique. This academy sought to re-establish "both the kind of poetry and the measure and rule of music anciently used by the Greeks and Romans."[22] It was concerned with rediscovering the connection between music and measured verse, on a model of strict equivalence between the temporalities of music, poetry, and (presumably) dance. The ancient *choreia* would thus be restored, "starting from the following basic principle: equivalent duration of steps and notes, which Baïf thought could translate in plastic terms the most varied musical rhythms of Greek meter, harmonizing the dancers' gestures and steps with the singing of the choruses. This would be the means to effect that admirable union of poetry, music and dance that the Greeks once practiced in their tragedy" (Prunières 1914, 65).

This fusion of the arts is explicitly at stake in the *Ballet comique de la Reine* (1581),[23] where it takes on a distinctly political function. At once princely festival and harmonious meeting of the arts, the ballet aimed to represent the harmony of the body politic, in counterpoint to the reality of the wars of religion, the memory of which was still raw.[24] Sometimes cruel irony accompanied the process, as in the case of *Paradis d'amour*, given approximately ten years earlier, in celebration of the marriage of Marguerite de Valois and Henri de Navarre, and which preceded the Saint Bartholomew's Day Massacre by just a few days. In this ballet, errant knights make an assault on paradise (represented by Henri de Navarre and his Huguenot companions) in order to ravish a group of nymphs. Three gentlemen intervene (played by Charles IX and his brothers) to defend the nymphs and send the rebels to hell. At the very moment when nuptials were intended to celebrate an illusory reconciliation between Catholics and Protestants, the ballet offered a direct representation of religious conflict without real political reconciliation. Some (including Agrippa d'Aubigné) even saw the massacre prefigured in the ballet (see Yates 1988, 256). Whether or not this is right, *Paradis d'amour* exemplifies the political dimension of the

22. See the *Lettres patentes établissant l'Académie de poésie et de musique*, November 1570, cited by Yates (1988 [1947], 21), and reprinted in full (in French) in appendix 1 of the same volume (319–22).

23. See the preface to the *Balet comique de la Reine* (Beaujoyeulx 1982 [1582]).

24. For a detailed analysis of the ballet, see Franko (1993, chapter 2), and Yates (1988, chapter 9).

court ballet, indissociable from its inscription in the festive event. This political dimension (most often linked to self-glorification) reaches its pinnacle under Louis XIV[25] and persists until the demise of the court ballet.

Two events are generally thought to mark that demise: (1) Louis XIV's retirement from the stage in 1670, from which point the ballet was gradually transformed into a purely professional affair; and (2) Jean-Baptiste Lully acquiring the privilege of the Académie Royale de Musique, giving him exclusive rights to mount musico-theatrical performances, which confirmed the triumph of the tragedy-ballet in 1672 (one year before the death of Molière).[26] But more fundamentally, the court ballet's demise seems to me to be linked to the problematic I identified earlier: that of ballet's autonomy in relation to ritual and festive inscription. I would suggest that ballet becomes autonomous by following theater and music, and, more specifically, by integrating with them. This is evident first in Molière's *comedy-ballet*, then in Lully's *tragedy-ballet*. The comedy-ballet marks the emergence of double performance, which prefigures the spectacle that we know today. The premiere of the spectacle was reserved— as royal entertainment—for the court, but the work was then also performed (or reperformed) multiple times at an explicitly public location: the theater of the Palais-Royal, which was returned to the control of Lully on Molière's death. This regime of double performance (first at court, then in town) in some ways makes the transition between princely *divertissement* (where the work merely celebrates a datable political event in which all participate) and autonomous spectacle understood as the performance of a repeatable work (where a work is addressed by an author to an anonymous paying public). The comedy-ballet disappears more or less with Molière. Dance participates in this movement toward autonomy and breaks with the old court *divertissement* only by integrating with the French opera of Lully and its innumerable poetic subspecies. But it thereby deprives itself of autonomy: gaily interrupting the narrative continuity of lyric works, dance is henceforth labeled choreographic *divertissement*.

This leads us to our third mode of connection between dance and the *divertissement*, which might be called an *aesthetico-poetic* mode. Here, the term

25. The most striking example of self-glorification is probably the *Ballet de la Nuit* (1653)—a fully realized model of the court ballet, according to Ménéstrier—where Louis XIV embodies for the first time the figure of the Sun King. In the period prior to Louis XIV's reign, one might look to the *Ballet de la prospérité des armes de France*, commissioned by Richelieu in 1641. For a general discussion of the link between spectacle and politics under Louis XIV, see Apostolidès (1981).

26. This is the date given in Christout (1967, 189). For a study of the court ballet prior to the reign of Louis XIV, see McGowan (1963).

"divertissement" no longer refers to the general space of spectacle but rather designates the particular modality of dance interventions in opera. In the general *divertissement* of lyric drama, a second *divertissement* is needed—a second interruption punching a hole in the continuity of action and of meaning for the sake of pure sensory pleasure. The *divertissement*, in short, needs to divert itself. Its interruption must in turn be interrupted or suspended, taking a deep breath so that its regular breathing can more easily return to normal. Dance fulfills this function of *divertissement* and interruption twice over.

Recall the definition of *divertissement* given by Louis de Cahusac in Diderot and d'Alembert's *Encyclopedia*:

> This name is given more particularly to dances and songs that are introduced episodically between the acts of an opera.[27]

The place of dance within theatrical institutions has for centuries been marked by its status as interlude or mere episode. The primary function of a ballet troupe within a municipal opera company is to perform choreographic *divertissements* during operas. And these *divertissements* are themselves conceived as extrinsic to the work, as effects created by the particular production that are variable from one staging to another. The function of the ballet master is not to create works or even fragments of works but merely to compose choreographic interludes during seasons of operatic performance.

Even as it reiterates the discontinuous structure of Greek theater and the court ballet,[28] this notion of *divertissement* irrevocably hierarchizes the different elements of spectacle: song and music are charged with ensuring the continuity of the drama, dance is charged with furnishing agreeable and diverting interludes. The position of the chorus within Greek theater made it impossible to see dance as a marginal element. The court ballet, meanwhile, was structured entirely around choreographic *entrées*, in relation to which speech and song functioned merely as connective links. But late seventeenth- and eighteenth-century opera invented, by contrast, a strict hierarchy within the very melting pot of different media, which condemned dance to purely minor status.

27. See the article on "Divertissement" in the *Encyclopédia*, vol. IV, p. 1069.

28. The connection is made explicit by Cahusac (2004 [1754]), in the second part, book III, chapter 5 on the "Establishment of the French Opera" (pp. 197–205). The most plausible contemporary development of this kind of discontinuous structure (whether it is conceived hierarchically or not) is musical comedy and the film musical (in both Hollywood and Bollywood). In this regard, the long-term history of the Greek *choreia*'s wanderings—and of the serially interruptive dimension of dance in relation to narrative—is yet to be written.

Two historical developments generally signal dance's emergence from this state. The first paradoxically involved maximal integration of dance with opera, through the theory of the "divertissement in action" proposed by Cahusac:

> We have a habit of seeing dance, in the lyric theater, merely as an isolated pleasure. It is however indispensable that it always be intimately linked to the principal action, that it form a single whole with that action, that it be chained to the exposition, the plot and its denouement. (2004 [1754], 237)

Integration of *divertissement* with action depended on an essentially psychological and naturalist theory of gestural signification. The dancing body was conceptualized as *speaking* the natural language of affect. Since that body's universal gestures could reveal the passions of the characters, it should participate directly in the development of the action. This proposed reform of the choreographic *divertissement* then made possible an even more significant shift: the development of the *ballet d'action*, which was autonomous with respect to sung text and occupied the entirety of the work's stage time. This revolution—the second movement toward autonomy, largely prefigured by Cahusac—has been generally attributed to Jean-Georges Noverre: he is supposed to be the first to have presented, under the name of *ballet d'action*, dance spectacles that were independent of any lyrical framework and developed continuous dramatic action without the aid of song or speech. In fact, this revolution was anticipated as early as 1717 by John Weaver in England and by Franz Hilverding in Vienna from the end of the 1730s. Nonetheless, it is with Noverre that the idea of a fully autonomous dance spectacle gets discursively established. The *Lettres sur la danse, et sur les ballets* (1760) are the theoretical and ideological accompaniment of this revolution: to establish for dance the right to appear alone onstage, as an independent object of artistic appreciation, is to demonstrate its subordination to the general principle of imitation. In some respects, this seems like a suspension of the *choreia*, which until this moment has been the obligatory point of reference for all theoreticians. But the autonomy thus acquired proved only intermittent—forcefully claimed but rarely obtained. The majority of choreographic production continued to be danced *divertissements* within opera, right up to the beginning of the twentieth century. These were not works but arrangements of steps inserted into other works and modified across performances and seasons. And their arrangers were not choreographers (or, as Lifar claimed, *choré-auteurs*) but only and always "ballet masters."[29]

29. Nor is the job of the "ballet master," who is charged with choreographing *divertissements* from one season to another, a phenomenon confined to a distant age that we have now left

Here I would like to digress for a moment to note that the notion of "divertissement" signals dance's minority status within the fine arts more generally.
This status is linked in the eighteenth century to a recurrent doubt concerning
the capacity of dance to make sense, imitate, or represent. At each turn, dance
risks collapsing into meaninglessness, into a merely skillful and virtuosic play
of movement lacking any significance. Only by proving that it represents can
dance acquire status as a true art from. This is explained by Jacques Rancière:

> Insofar as it is seen as the mere accomplishment of a religious or therapeutic
> ritual, dance is not an art. But nor is it if it consists merely in the exercise of
> a corporeal virtuosity. Something else is required if it is to be counted as an
> art. This "something else" was, until Stendhal's time, called a *story* [*histoire*].
> For the theoreticians of poetry in the eighteenth century, knowing whether
> or not the art of dance was one of the fine arts involved answering a simple
> question: does dance tell a story? Is it a *mimesis*? (2009, 6–7)

In the age of reason, then, a theory of the ballet had two functions to fulfill: first,
it had to provide historical and philosophical evidence of the capacity of gesture
to make sense; and second, it had to regulate practice such that choreographic
reality could meet the requirements of the aesthetic norm. Despite the differences between theoretical models, these twin functions are articulated as much
by the theorists of the seventeenth as of the eighteenth century, as much in
Ménéstrier and Michel de Pure (1668) as in Cahusac and Noverre.

The imperative of imitation or representation also implies regulating discontinuity or interruption. Such is the case with Cahusac's "divertissement en
action," as much as with the court ballet. Only by imitating something can the
divertissement or *entrées* be integrated into the whole work. But the mode of
signification or representation is modified from one century to the next. The
court ballet imitates in allegorico-analytic mode. The different *entrées* are given
meaning and linked together by their connection to the overarching subject
of the ballet. What does the poet do when he composes a ballet? He first gives
himself a subject, like "the weariness of the day," to take an example from
Michel de Pure.[30] The subject must first be decomposed into a specific number

---

far behind. Dominique Dupuy, dancer and modern choreographer who began his career after
World War II, was ballet master for two years at the Opera House in Mulhouse, and his job was
to produce dances (forgotten as soon as they were performed) for operas. He described his role
as that of "choreographer by the kilometer" (personal communication).

30. "Les fatigues de la journée," described in book II, chapter 9, section 2 "Du sujet," and section 6 "Des entrées" (Pure 1668).

of emblematic figures that will give rise to different *entrées*, each representing various possible ways to become weary during the course of a day. There is no need for a narrative connection between these images, since the general link to the subject is all that matters.[31] Thus one might begin with an *entrée* of bakers, then include an *entrée* of courtesans, an *entrée* of peasants, and so on. The ballet displays a series of graphic emblems that the audience enjoys decoding. There are no "emotions" or "characters" here deployed in time, but rather abstract and instantaneous signs that are offered to the acuity of the audience. The court ballet thus connects with the conceptual mode of the coat of arms, the emblem, and the enigma.[32]

A century later, subjects are no longer decomposed into allegorical images. Rather, a continuous dramatic action is represented through gesture. The allegorico-analytic regime of the court ballet is replaced by a dramatico-affective regime, which—established by Cahusac and Noverre—persists throughout the Romantic and Classical ballet.

I had initially intended that this overly succinct presentation of different theories of choreographic signification in the age of reason be accompanied by a detailed study of texts and works. Several issues would have arisen in the course of this study: (1) the importance of examining ancient sources (Plato, Aristotle, Lucien, Xenophon, Plutarch, and Quintilian), who are cited as authorities in the seventeenth and eighteenth centuries and who become the very site of conflicts between theoreticians; (2) the way these treatises are inscribed within wider theoretical frameworks, which synchronically exceed the treatises' concerns but allow them to be better specified diachronically (one cannot understand the poetics of Ménéstrier without reconstructing more generally the space of taxonomy; equally, one cannot understand Cahusac and Noverre without relating them to the problematic of action language as it develops in French philosophy of the eighteenth century); (3) the need to demonstrate, by taking a historical

---

31. "I have not here forgotten a distinction between the *entrées* of a ballet and the scenes of a dramatic poem. In the latter, the scenes must be linked to one another, while in the former it is sufficient that they are linked to the subject. That which ends need have nothing to do with that which begins after it has finished" (241).

32. Note that Ménéstrier planned to write "in one or several volumes" a work entitled *La philosophie des images qui traite des spectacles, de l'histoire, et de l'usage des devises, hieroglyphes, blasons, etc. [A philosophy of images in spectacles, history, and the use of heraldic devices, hieroglyphs, arms, etc.]* for which a royal privilege was granted in 1679. His *Des ballets anciens et modernes* was intended to be just one part of this great work. Note also that the text on ballet ends with a description of different society games based on the recognition of allegorical images and the decoding of enigmas, through which Ménéstrier's work connects back to Renaissance writings, particularly Alciat's *Emblemata* (1531).

detour, the emergence of a twofold linguistic paradigm underlying theories of gestural signification, treated as either gesture-of-writing or gesture-of-speech. I renounced the project for reasons of economy and coherence, but I hope to be able to bring it to fruition in future research and writing, provisionally entitled *La mimique et l'hiéroglyphe* [*Mimesis and Hieroglyphics*].[33]

To resume: my question concerned spectacle's movement toward autonomy and away from ritual inscription, as well as the movement of dance toward autonomy within spectacle. My answer to this dual question is this: the court *divertissement* invents against ancient tradition a purely profane space, making possible (in opposition to certain strands of religious authority) the exposure of dance practices. However, this profane space does not imply complete elimination of ritual elements. The court ballet remains inseparable from a shared festive event, which provides the pretext for the ballet and determines its character and rationale as a ritual where the division between participants and spectators is not clear. Only in the middle of the seventeenth century do theater and opera become autonomous in the sense of producing repeatable works, presented to an anonymous public, according to the principle of double performance (at court and in town). Dance participates in this movement toward autonomy only by integration and "heteronomization": it then becomes known as choreographic *divertissement*, or joyful and contingent interlude within the main theatrical or operatic work. Only in the middle of the eighteenth century, with Noverre (although his name is just a marker), is a properly autonomous dance spectacle invented. And this autonomy is only fully realized at the end of the nineteenth and beginning of the twentieth century. Even then, it requires some qualification because there continue to be *divertissements* within comic operas right up until the 1950s, and this shapes the natural horizon of dance within French theatrical and operatic institutions.[34]

The persistence of the danced *divertissement* within opera has played a role in the law's failure to acknowledge choreographic works. Until the law of 1957 (article L.112-2 of the code on intellectual property), choreographic works had no legal status and were recognized only in jurisprudence, where the distinction between "divertissement" and "ballet d'action" remained crucial: a choreographer could not claim authorship of a work unless it was a "ballet d'action"

---

33. See also below, 128–32 and 181–90.

34. If a criterion or index of autonomy is ballet's capacity to occupy a whole evening in the theater, then autonomy is certainly intermittent during the nineteenth and twentieth centuries. It emerges at particular historical moments (with the Romantic ballet, the works of Petipa, and Diaghilev's Ballets Russes) and is effaced again at regular intervals. Thus in 1930, it again seems revolutionary to want to devote an entire evening to dance at the Paris Opéra (see Guest 2006, 85).

and not a "divertissement." Such were the terms of the judgment passed by the Tribunal de la Seine, February 10, 1911, in the case of Madame Veuve Catulle Mendès and Monsieur Reynaldo Hahn (representing librettist and composer) versus Madame Stitch (choreographer), concerning ownership of a ballet called *La Fête chez Thérèse*. The judgment rested on the aesthetic notion of the "ballet d'action" in recognizing the autonomous existence of the choreography, but was still overthrown on appeal in favor of librettist and composer, on the grounds that choreography is only ever the scenic adaptation of a preexisting (literary or musical) work.[35] Moreover, the autonomy established by the law of 1957 remained quite fragile for some time. Jean Cocteau, for example, was twice recognized (in 1958 and 1962) as sole and unique author of *Jeune homme et la mort* (1946), a ballet that belongs to Roland Petit, at least from the choreographic point of view.

This all seems, once again, to confirm the *unworking* of choreography.

MODERNITY: THE HOPE OF NEW RITUALS

Paradoxically, dance modernity did not develop from a reassertion of the work but rather in opposition to the "diverting" dance prevalent in theaters, through reactivation of ritual. As we have already glimpsed, the most ancient is also the most modern. Modern dance reacted against the dance *divertissement* within opera and against ballet not by rendering dance representation autonomous but rather by leaving it behind and experimenting with new forms of collective and participatory dance, beyond the stage. Among the founders of this modern dance movement, Laban probably best represents the desire for extratheatrical regeneration.

Laban developed his interest in movement out of nostalgia for a kind of festive culture, encountered during his childhood in Austro-Hungary but displaced by urban and industrial modernity:

I saw the last vestiges of religious dances in Europe [. . .] When I was a child, peasant dances, religious processions, court ceremonials and similar movement manifestations were still alive in my home country [. . .] For someone with eyes and ears for this kind of beauty, it was impossible to miss the great importance of movement in life. (Laban 1951)

---

35. See the *Annales de la propriété industrielle*, 1911, art. 4948, p. 290, and the *Gazette du Palais*, 1911, vol. 1, p. 193. Thanks to Isabelle Meunier, jurist at the SACD, for her invaluable analysis during my seminar "Memoire et identité des oeuvres chorégraphiques," at the Département Danse, Universty of Paris VIII. Thanks also to Anne Branchereau, also from the juridical service of the SACD, for having communicated the precise references to this case.

His first choreographic experiments within the utopian community of Monte Verita (in Ascona) between 1913 and 1917 directly expressed this aim of spiritual and social regeneration through movement: for example, the "cere- mony" given on August 18, 1917 at Ascona, *Sang an die Sonne*, which began at 6:00 p.m. and concluded the following morning at sunrise. Events of this type did not involve making a work or spectacle so much as inventing for the age of the war machine new rites that could offer the social body a form of participa- tory communion. And of course Laban's fame was initially based on his ability to orchestrate the movement of massed dancers in the suspended time of the festival and the rite: for example, his organization of the Munich carnival from 1912 to 1914, and his pageant for crafts and trades [*Fetzug des Handwerkes und der Gewerbe*] in Vienna in 1929, which brought together more than twenty thousand participants. Here again, setting the social body in motion remains alien to the project of creating a work. It is closer to what today might be called (rather alarmingly) "event management"—except that in the early twentieth century the process still has political and religious dimensions that have not yet been completely dismantled by global capitalism.

This kinetic understanding of the crowd was linked to Laban's invention (or rediscovery) of a form of choreography that he called the "movement-choir" (*Bewegungschor*):

> The question arose of what name we should give our activities [...] It was decidedly community dance but not professional dance or social dance in the traditional sense. [...] Then from somewhere a voice said: "Really, we are a movement-choir." This designation met with unanimous approval, though we had no idea that this newly-coined word would spread so widely in such a short time. (Laban 1975, 156)

The movement-choir created a shared motor experience, unburdened of any spectacular aim. This was a community ritual, divorced from exhibition as it was from repetition:

> These plays differed in many ways from the new dances which originated in the circle of our professional dancers. They were really quite different from what had so far been called dance. The movements were simpler and the basic ideas of the plays were not show or stage biased. [...] Audiences were excluded for the time being, except for the occasional chance visitor. (Laban 1975, 155)

And when Laban was promoted to specifically theatrical roles at the beginning of the 1930s (in particular, to the post of ballet master at the Berlin Opera, which he held from 1930 to 1934), this was not so that he could rediscover the closed world of the theater but rather because he could introduce to the fictional and isolated stage space some of the elements of ritual and participation already developed outside of theatrical spectacle. His notable success with the Nazi regime probably stemmed from this. In 1934, he became director of the German dance scene (*Deutsche Tanzbühne*) within the Ministry of Propaganda and devised the opening and closing ceremonies for the 1936 Olympic Games, before his self-imposed exile in 1937.[36]

I will not linger on this Nazification of choreographic modernity. Others have already explored the phenomenon, and I refer the reader to their work.[37] But I do want to examine the extent to which a desire for new rituals was shared across the field of early modern dance, in terms of a dual reference to ancient Greece and Wagner. There are two figures who exemplify this connection: Isadora Duncan and Émile Jaques-Dalcroze.[38]

Both were clearly exercised by a desire to reactivate the Greek *choreia*. It is significant that Louis Séchan ends his book on the dance of ancient Greece by commenting on them.[39] Paradoxically, even while she was forging an essentially solo career, Isadora Duncan offered a rationale for the invention of her dance based on new experimentation with the tragic chorus:

> To unite the arts around the Chorus, to give back to the dance its place as the Chorus, that is the ideal. When I have danced I have tried always to be the Chorus: I have been the Chorus of young girls hailing the return of the fleet, I have been the Chorus dancing the Pyrrhic Dance, or the Bacchic; I have never once danced a solo. The dance, again joined with poetry and with music, must become once more the tragic Chorus. That is its only and its true end. That is the only way for it to become again an art. (Duncan 1969 [1928], 96)

36. See Launay (1997, 15–16); Guilbert (2000, 221–31).

37. Aside from the work of Guilbert (2000), see Kant and Karina (2003 [1996]); Launay (1999); and Manning (1993).

38. The reference to Wagner is probably less obvious in Laban than in either Duncan or Dalcroze. Yet note that when he established his first school in Ascona, Laban decided to call it the Schule für Tanz-Ton-Wort, thus taking up the trinity amply developed by Wagner in his theoretical writings. Moreover, Laban himself choreographed the bacchanale from *Tannhäuser* at Bayreuth in 1930 and 1931.

39. See Séchan (1930, chapter 9), "Rhythmique et plastique de Jaques-Dalcroze," and chapter 11, "Isadora Duncan"; chapter 10 is devoted to a commentary on Valéry's "Dance and the Soul," primarily directed against André Levinson's text *Paul Valéry, philosophe de la danse* (1927).

The reference to Greece—a model for both fusion of the arts and rediscov-ered ritual—is united with a committed Wagnerism. Even though Wagner was always suspicious of dance (especially following his experience in France at the Paris Opéra), he still saw it as the very emblem of the regeneration of theatrical space, springing from Greek roots. If Wagner's own choreographic creations were essentially limited to the bacchanale in *Tannhäuser*, dance nonetheless occupied an absolutely central place within his theoretical writings, where it is envisaged as reactivating the tragic chorus and the trinity of the *choreia*.[40] This means that Duncanism is therefore also Wagnerism:

> Wagner is more than an artist: he is the glorious far-seeing prophet, liberator
> of the art of the future. It is he who will give birth to the new union of the
> arts, the rebirth of the theatre, tragedy and the dance as one.
>
> He was the first to conceive of the dance as born of music. This is my con-
> ception of the dance also, and for it I strive in the work of my school. For in
> the depths of every musical theme of Wagner, dances will be found: monu-
> mental sculpture, movement which only demands release and life. (Duncan
> 1969, 105)

This dual reference to Greece and to Wagner induces in Duncan a clear antago-nism toward the theatrical structure of ballet. Duncan was indeed a "creature of the stage," accumulating performances and European tours. But she never con-ceived theatrical experience except as ceremony, which she called a "concert" or a "recital." And contemporary spectators did indeed perceive her performances through a ritual lens. Thus Legrand-Chabrier, in the program for her appear-ance at the Théâtre du Châtelet on November 18, 1911, asks:

> What will happen when the curtain falls? The end of a performance, I see it,
> I desire it: it is a dancing procession in the street.[41]

Jaques-Dalcroze similarly exceeds the structure of spectacle, through dual ref-erence to Greece and Wagner. And it is notable that his chapter titled "Rhythm

---

40. See "The Art-Work of the Future" (chapter 2, §2): "The arts of *Dance*, of *Tone*, and *Poetry*: thus call themselves the three primeval sisters whom we see at once entwine their mea-sures [. . .]" (Wagner 1993 [1849], 95). These three sisters are later described as "those three most sweet Hellenic sisters" (99), which confirms (if such were needed) that Wagner is con-cerned with reactivating the Greek model. On Wagner's ambivalent relationship with dance, see §3 of the same chapter and its concluding formula: "O glorious dance! O shameful dance!" (110). Thanks to Jacques-Olivier Bégot for these references. See also Coeuroy (1921).

41. Cited by Doat (2006).

and Gesture in Musical Drama" ends by expressing a desire to reactivate popular ceremonies and to set crowds in motion according to a common rhythm.[42]

The Second World War probably marked the end of these aspirations and their impasses. From that point on, modern and then contemporary dance seems to have developed (or rather affirmed itself) within cultural institutions only by integrating with the theatrical structures of ballet. What appeared in France of the 1980s as a contemporary dance "explosion" or boom aligned practice with a canonical, uninterrogated conception of the work as an object presented by an author to an audience through the (supposedly neutral) medium of the theater structure. No more community ceremony, no more new ritual. Rather (and perhaps more simply) the development of stable, authored art objects for exposure to the critical and commercial judgment of an art world. Although these objects were presented as events, they were both signed and repeatable, implying a core identity that was fixed. Laurence Louppe describes very well how the 1980s involved affirmation of both the work and the author in dance:

> During the 1980s in France, we witnessed an inflated use of the notion of *oeuvre* [. . .] linked to another equally nebulous idea—that of "*auteur*." And this, surprisingly, at the moment when the authorial activity of the choreographer was becoming reduced to putting together purely spectacular ingredients as a substitute for the deep work that made the artist of the "*grande modernité*" an inventor of a body, a technique and an aesthetic, and who organised all these factors in a coherent language. While everywhere else the notion of author had been complicated or contested, we witnessed choreography, on the contrary, take hold of this notion enthusiastically and make a banner of it. (Louppe 2010 [1997], 233)

We should probably understand this latter-day affirmation of the work and the author as a reaction to the long-standing subordinate status of dance within theatrical and cultural institutions. It appears like the explicit negation of a model of choreographic *divertissement*, which for centuries had blocked the possibility of the work and authorial authority in dance. The belated nature of the shift would explain why there was little critical interrogation of these ideas:

> The misfortunes and the heavy responsibility that weigh on the activity of the dancer mean that the notion of *oeuvre* in dance is still too precious to be made the object of the slightest intellectual restriction. It is too precise, in .

---

42. Jaques-Dalcroze (1967 [1921], 127–31).

any case, to be able to confront with impunity the kinds of desacralisation staged by the art and thought of the century. (234)

However, by a strange dialectical turn, the concepts of the work and the author that enable choreographic objects to be understood in terms beyond mere diversion or entertainment ultimately bend to the demands of an economy of the spectacle, today based on the figure of the choreographer and the recogniz-able stability of his creations.[43] To produce and tour choreographic works, with named authors and titles, is to offer theater programmers a guarantee that the dance will be the *same*, stable, and identifiable, and to forget the always collec-tive and moving character of spectacular performance. I will return to this idea of the choreographic work as "standard," as it was promoted in France during the 1980s, and further examine below the different ways in which it is being critically questioned.[44]

43. "It is uncertain whether the concept of *auteur* carried over to choreography has freed the dance creator from the economic and ideological pressures of the modes of production [...] On the contrary, the notion of choreographic *auteur* upholds a certain over-valuation of cho-reographic signature, and, even more, of a tag that signals (more than signs) the importance of a label: the name of the choreographer and her/his presence justifying only to itself the function-ing of a company" (Louppe 2010, 234).

44. See below, 293–99.

Chapter 3

Presence, Ideality, Signification

Genesis and Structure of the Choreographic Stage, II

In the preceding chapter, I attempted to trace the historical genesis of the choreographic spectacle. My account was too rapid, inevitably incomplete,[1] and probably too dialectical, yet it seems to me to outline the appropriate framework for future research into the foundations of the spectacle as institution, via the issues of aesthetic autonomy and the tendency of the ritual/divertissement pairing to cancel out such autonomy. Leaving these questions aside, I now propose to explore different territory. I will pretend that the idea of "spectacle" has always existed, as if we could bracket the historical detail of its emergence and development. I will adopt the position of a historically naive contemporary who believes that there is an essence of spectacle simply waiting to be uncovered. I will proceed in line with the fiction of the concept, by eidetic variation and the testing of limits. I start from a few examples of "spectacles," some of which might be considered frankly marginal in relation to the core concept: a football match, a bullfight, a concert, a theatrical performance, and a liturgical ceremony. I then pose and try to answer a very simple question from this historically naive position: In virtue of what common element are these different events called "spectacles," literally or metaphorically?

THE TIME OF THE PRESENT

Note first that all the events just mentioned depend on a *site* being delimited, either explicitly or implicitly: football has its stadia, bullfighting has its arenas,

---

1. It included nothing, for example, on Roman theater in which dance and pantomime (*saltatio*) had a very important role. On this issue, see Dupont (1986).

tragedy has its theaters, music its concert halls, and religion its temples and churches. So "spectacle" perhaps means, first and foremost, "that which delimits a site in order to host an event." But we should acknowledge that the site does not always preexist the event. Rather, we should think of the event itself creating the site. The event's exceptional and noteworthy (festive?) character transforms mere location by tracing a circle that properly constitutes the spectacular site. This is particularly clear in the context of street theater: without any architectural intervention, such theater transforms the purely transitory location of the street—a prime example of a non-site, given that nothing is supposed to happen there because everyone is only passing through—and delimits by the force of the event itself something like a purely immaterial site. Architecture, with its theaters, churches, and stadia, ultimately only supports and protects the delimitation of the spectacular site: it inscribes the latter materially and durably, sheltering and determining the site but never really constructing it as such. Rather, architecture seems only ever really to be an extension of the event.

If the site does not necessarily preexist the event, ultimately this is because its delimitation has less to do with space than with temporal modulation. The Anglo-Saxon notion of *performance*, which is in some respects equivalent to the French *spectacle*, already sets us on this path. The term "performance" insists on the fact that a spectacle only ever occurs in action, in the present, remaining impossible to detach from the time in which it is inscribed. Its reproducibility via video or other types of recording is illusory. Only what has already passed can ever be reproduced. Spectacle is reproducible only on the condition of transforming the present of the event into an atemporal object, into a collection of sedimented facts that are now mere traces of a past; because they can always be reactivated, they have seemingly passed out of time. "In theater people perform, but in film they *have* performed," claimed Louis Jouvet (cited by Gouhier 1989, 65). And this is why film is never performance, properly speaking. It lacks that effect of "presence" that makes every spectacle a singular event—that inscription in the present that alone constitutes the site and makes us think, "Here and now, at this hour and in this place, something is happening which I will never be able to find in an identical way anywhere else." The site, then, is constituted not by space or architecture but rather by this "full time" of presence, a time that is all the more intense because it is bound soon to disappear, and all the more active because each moment it reinvents itself in play and in risk. In using the term "presence," I do not intend any theological or theophanic horizon. I aim only to highlight the element of risk and the unexpected that is proper to all present action. To "perform" in the present is always to confront the possibility of something going wrong—playing a wrong note, falling over, or forgetting one's lines.[2] The prevalence of "events" and ephemeral "happenings" in the United States during the 1960s and 1970s presents an almost too perfect example of this phenomenon of "performance" and of the eventfulness proper to all spectacle. That phenomenon is raised to full self-consciousness and radicalized through the period's preference for the ephemeral event over the identical work, multiple becomings over the finished product, and the fact of happening rather than the thing that happens.

Yet in claiming that spectacle, as event, always implies the delimitation of a site, have I not highlighted a condition that exceeds my object of inquiry? One might object that political revolutions, demonstrations, and natural disasters all also delimit sites. We still need, it seems, to understand what is proper to the site of *spectacle* and to articulate a second requirement. Here, I should state what perhaps seems tautological: that there is spectacle only at the moment when there are spectators. As long as there are only participants—that is, subjects caught up and engaged in the event—there is no gaze to create the site as a spectacle. Instead, as the Stoics argued, subjects are preoccupied with rising to the occasion, acting authentically, or perhaps just (as is most often the case) with seeking a way out. If there are only participants, there is never a gratuitous and disengaged pure gaze to transform the event into a spectacle.[3]

But what exactly does it mean to be a spectator, to be this pure gaze that is somehow outside the event even while it constitutes the very spectacularity of the site? I claim that to be a spectator is fundamentally, in the strongest sense

2. This characterization of spectacle in terms of the effect of "presence" may appear naive to readers of Derrida: it may seem that I am applying to the spectacular field a fantasy of presence that, according to Derrida, governs the whole of Western metaphysics. Derrida himself has shown how this fantasy continues to operate secretly even in as apparently subversive a theatrical project as Antonin Artaud's: desiring a theater freed of all text and all repetition, Artaud could only invoke pure and absolute presence ; see "The Theater of Cruelty and the Closure of Representation," in Derrida (2001, 292–316). I have two lines of response. First, from the textual point of view, I think that Artaud's theater is less exercised by this fantasy than Derrida would have us believe: Artaud also expresses a desire for hieratic writing, fixation, and repetition, which far exceeds the presence of the singular event (see also below, 147). Second, my own work begins with the effect of spectacular presence precisely in order to better interrogate, ultimately, the conditions of repetition of this presence: I want to examine how far this presence, if it is to be repeated, must always already be imprinted with a conceptual framework, with an *arche-writing* (see below, 161).

3. This is why, among all the examples I highlighted earlier, liturgical ceremony is a kind of limit or intermediary case. The dimension of scopic fascination that, in certain respects, assimilates the Mass to spectacle does not detract from the fact that participants are never conceived as spectators but always as active agents within the ritual. Ritual, insofar as it always involves a form of participation, represents an asymptotic limit of spectacle.

of the term, *to be bored*. I can be a spectator only from the moment that I am inherently and profoundly workless, without urgent tasks demanding my attention and without immediate engagement. To be a spectator, then, is precisely to put oneself in a state of vacancy, to take temporary leave of life. What most conventional spectacles do, it seems to me, is construct this state of vacancy and boredom in advance. The disposition of seats, the lowering of the house lights, and the social conventions that prevent me from being too noisy together make up a set of bodily constraints whose only goal is to plunge me into a preparatory state with all the hallmarks of the most intense and profound boredom: I am not allowed to move, sneeze, or speak, and my body is thus reduced to merely eyes and ears. I become focused only on empty temporality, a pure flow that no action, however minimal, can fill. Calling it "empty temporality" does not imply that our experience of time is diminished or made less important. On the contrary, empty temporality is actually a refined and thickened time, an experience in which time is no longer reduced to the abstract and external framework of everyday actions (of what in French is appropriately called *emploi du temps* [occupation]), but which instead is experienced for and by itself, as an empty passage into boredom.

The spectacular connection between time and boredom tends to summon up the Pascalian image of the *divertissement*. But note how a spectacle is not a *divertissement* like any other—it is not merely a means to escape oneself and one's own vacuity by busying oneself as much as possible. The spectacle has the peculiarity of reproducing at its core the structure that conditions it. To "simple" *divertissements* or *diversions* (all the games and tasks into which I throw myself to escape boredom), the spectacle adds something like a *divertissement* doubled over: it makes boredom the very condition of its efficacy. The spectacle is that strange form of *divertissement* that integrates what it is intended to combat, constructing boredom and making it one of its own prerequisites and essential motivations. Only because there is already (absolute) boredom can the counteracting fascination be complete. The event of spectacle recuperates for its own benefit the "thick time" into which the spectator is plunged. A time of boredom is transformed, through the fascinated gaze of the spectator, into a time of presence and eventfulness: one might say that it becomes "aura."

I need to qualify my apparently careless use of this loaded term. Walter Benjamin explored how the "auratic" dimension of the work of art was linked directly to its presence in the here and now; or, in other words, to the unique presence of its manifestation. Clearly, spectacle bathes essentially in a particular kind of aura, which is in part precisely the aura of *presence*. Yet two qualifications apply. Firstly, the "aura" of works of visual art (which are what really interests Benjamin) rests in large measure on their exceeding the here and now. The "aura" is the immediate manifestation of something distant. The surviving work of visual art implies a whole horizon of other places and times, of stories and travels, which are summarized in the immediately given present of the here and now.[4] This is not the case with the "aura" of spectacle, which is "without distance," inherently present and incapable of surviving outside of this presence. Secondly, the "aura" of the work of visual art is consequent on a certain ritual value conferred on its "authenticity." The inscription of the object in the here and now guarantees its numerical identity, and thence the foundation of its authenticity. We know how, according to Benjamin, the mechanical reproduction of works is supposed to make us abandon criteria of authenticity, leading to a decline of the ritual relationship they implied.[5] Here, I wish to note simply that the presence of spectacle in the here and now relates less to the numerical identity of an "authentic" object than to the conditions of possibility and efficacy of its very existence. The "aura" of spectacle has little to do with questions of authenticity: that aura already exists "in series," is reproduced from one place to another, from one evening to another. Presence in the here and now becomes generalized, referring less to the haecceity of a thing and more to the existential environment of a repeatable event. In part III, I examine how this repeatability still does not enable mechanical reproduction. For now, the important point is that spectacle's aura should be distinguished from the fetishism of authentic objects. If ritual value can be attached to this aura (as the title of the preceding chapter suggested), that value is still of a particular character, which I argue is wholly distinct from the value of the aura discussed by Benjamin.

A spectacle, then, is the encounter between full time and empty time, active time (which risks and invents itself in play) and bored time (where nothing is given but the emptiness of pure duration). Diametrically opposed as these two temporalities seem, each represents an intensified experience of the present; each generates raw time that cannot be reduced to the clock's objective progression; each allows a glimpse of the theoretically unthinkable phenomenon of *the present*, only rarely offered in everyday experience which always already projects outward toward tasks to be accomplished. This is why I claim that spectacle, as a conjuncture of event and boredom, furnishes an unparalleled experience of temporality.

4. "We define the aura [. . .] as the unique phenomenon of a distance, however close it may be" (Benjamin 1992, 216).

5. "The instant the criterion of authenticity ceases to be applicable to artistic production, the total function of art is reversed. Instead of being based on ritual, it begins to be based on another practice—politics" (Benjamin 1992, 218).

It might be objected that the encounter between the full time of the event and the empty time of boredom can only be fortuitous and secondary. Perhaps the event only becomes spectacular contingently and its true purpose resides elsewhere, as in the case of football: here, it is not—or not centrally—a question of producing spectacle but rather of winning the game. If there are spectators, these are not directly entailed by the event: to some extent, they are merely tolerated. The two orders of temporality, then, remain estranged from one another or merely juxtaposed: something happens—something with its own purposes and rules—but people also come to watch, without that fact altering (at least in theory) anything about the event itself. If this is indeed a spectacle, it is not yet an "art of spectacle." For there to be an "art of spectacle," there needs to be a conscious and essential relation between the two orders of temporality: the empty time into which spectators are plunged must be the explicit object of an artistic process, and the thick time of boredom must become the very material to be shaped and formed.

The arts of spectacle are thus "time-based arts," in two distinguishable senses of the term. Firstly, spectacle exists only in the time of presence, or in the actuality of play and boredom. Secondly, the action proper to spectacle (by which it properly becomes art) is understood as a form-ing of temporality, or as the creation of a particular rhythm that inhabits and configures the thickened yet slack time of boredom. With this dual interpretation of the expression "time-based arts," the gap between presence and writing already becomes apparent. The time of presence—the environment and material of performance—seems inevitably exposed to the necessity of form-ing, by which it is both anticipated and exceeded, and to rehearsal [*répétitions*].

This provisional definition of spectacle implies two sets of questions. The first relates to the encounter between the two modes of temporality and their recovery—in short, to the connection (or lack of connection) between stage and auditorium. If the link between performance and boredom depends on a form of reciprocal but asymmetrical intentionality (what takes place on the stage is *directed to* the auditorium, while the whole auditorium is *oriented toward* the stage) and depends only on this tenuous connection, then we are also concerned here with rupture and opposition. There is no community of experience—no possible sharing—between the bored bodies in the auditorium and the performing bodies onstage. Dance spectacle makes that disjunction even more radical. In quantitative terms, the onstage performers typically move more than in other types of spectacle, so that it seems likely the audience will feel all the more cruelly the constraint of being seated. In qualitative (or essential) terms, and in contrast to words or sounds, the auto-affection of kinesthesis is shared only by virtue of mobilizing an intermodal sensory apparatus (moving from the visual toward the kinesthetic), which is difficult to assign.

Here we find, even within the structure of the stage, the aporia of auto-affection that I highlighted at the end of part I.[6] I explored how the notion of *empathy* was able to make the psychological connection (or the missing link) between kinesthetic experience and mere visual perception. The same notion recurs in relation to choreography, through what, in the 1930s, the American critic John Martin terms "metakinesis" (Martin 1965b [1933], 13–16). "Metakinesis" refers to the physiological and emotional process enabling spectators to project themselves "kinesthetically" into the bodies of the dancers, to be *moved* by the movements displayed.[7] Once again, I leave questions raised by such ideas unresolved.

The second set of questions raised by my provisional definition of spectacle concerns how the spectacular event—the present encounter of two modes of temporality—can be overtaken or surpassed. Two types of transcendence may contribute to the event being obscured: the transcendence of the prior work, which the spectacle merely actualizes; and the transcendence of the actions displayed, which the spectacle merely represents in a limited way. What we call "the theatrical tradition" is, in some respects, merely the constant conjunction of these two ways to obscure the event, in line with a common structure of "representation." On the stage of transcendence, the event's present ceases to matter in and of itself; it becomes only a secondary and derivative moment, surpassed by the atemporal work being actualized and by the generality of the actions displayed; it is merely a sensible representation of an ideal entity that exceeds the event in all respects. Following Derrida's commentary on Artaud, we can call this stage of representation *theological*:

> The stage is theological for as long as its structure, following the entirety of tradition, comports the following elements: an author-creator who, absent and from afar, is armed with a text and keeps watch over, assembles, regulates the time or the meaning of representation, letting this latter *represent* him as concerns what is called the content of his thoughts, his intentions, his ideas. He lets representation represent him through representatives, directors or actors, enslaved interpreters who represent characters who, primarily through what they say, more or less directly represent the thought of the "creator" [...] This general structure in which each agency is linked to all the others by representation, in which the irrepresentability of the living present is dissimulated or dissolved, suppressed or deported within the inifinite chain of representations—this structure has never been modified. (Derrida 2001 [1967], 296–97)

6. See above, 57–58.

7. See also Franko (2002) on "Metakinetic Interpellations," 59–84.

I argue that the impetus behind this structure of representation can be located in a particular theoretical gesture: namely, Aristotle's exclusion of *opsis* and *hypokrisis* from poetics. I also argue that Artaud's project, as outlined in *Theater and Its Double*, can be understood as a simple reversal of this structure, perhaps as yet unachieved. I develop the arguments in more detail later in this chapter and in the rest of part II.[8]

REPRESENTATION AND ITS TRANSCENDENCE

For the moment, I focus on this double transcendence to explore how dance seems to elude it, more or less. Aristotle's *Poetics* shows how spectacle has been conceived from the very beginning of the Western theatrical tradition as merely the sensible actualization of a preexisting work. As we will see, what matters to this tradition is not the experience of spectacle so much as the dramatic text to which it refers—not the immanent temporality of the event so much as the transcendent logic of dramatic action. The discrediting of spectacle in favor of the performed work is also evident in the model of *arts à deux temps* (or two-stage arts) proposed by Henri Gouhier (1989). Paradoxically, this model accentuates by its own logic the secondary status of spectacle, even while it aims to re-evaluate the latter's importance, critiquing Aristotle in particular. The idea of a "two-stage art" is based on a roughly Platonist model, which contrasts the initial stage of the written work (wholly identical to itself in the heaven of ideal objects) with a second stage that actualizes the work in sensory spectacle. The notated work always encompasses infinite possibilities, linked to the abstract generality of notation. That work presents itself as an infinite resource of meanings, always open to interpretation without ever compromising its self-identity. The work's singular actualization in a given spectacle, then, will always be conceived as an impoverishment and particularization, if not a degradation, of the idea. The spectacle is conceived as a secondary and superficial stage, drawing its power and its reality only from the external work on which it necessarily depends. But this seems to imply a manifest abstraction whereby the theatrical or musical work is conceived outside of its own temporality, in the image that the text and notation retrospectively project of a self-identical, complete object whose moments are all set out simultaneously in the space of the page. Could it not be argued, following Plato's *Phaedrus*, that what is written is mere likeness, and hence secondary and derivative moment? And that the spectacle, far from being an impoverishing particularization, simply restores the work to its proper temporality—to the time of performance and the event—outside of which the

8. See also below, 134 and 147.

work is mere abstraction, just a collection of traces scattered on paper?[9] From this perspective, the model of "two-stage arts," in its essential logic, inverts the order, putting first what should perhaps come second, and conceives the relation of spectacle to work on a basic model of conceptual subordination.[10]

In light of this model of "two-stage arts," which governed (and still governs) the aesthetics of theater, it becomes easier to understand the attitude and strategy of Artaud: if spectacle (as event and as ritual) is conceived as primary, the task becomes that of creating a pure spectacle, inventing a theater of immanence (of the event) which is no longer overtaken by the depth of a text governing that spectacle from the outside; the task becomes that of creating a spectacle that refers only to itself and delivers the raw time of presence proper to the spectacular event. I argue that the event's autonomy in this regard—here merely projected or imagined—is ultimately connected to two ordinary conditions of the dance spectacle.

Firstly, operas and plays are defined in terms of just one of their elements (or two in the case of opera, namely, music and text) and can as a result generate multiple productions. But dance spectacle (particularly contemporary dance spectacle) does not seem to focus in on one element as the guarantor of its identity. Choreography and music are not separated from the apparently secondary elements of scenography, costumes, or lighting. In dance spectacle, it seems, everything participates in defining the work. One consequence is that to speak of (for example) *Rhapsody in Blue* by Odile Duboc is not merely to refer to Duboc's choreography and Gershwin's music, but also to Dominique Fabrègue's costumes, Yves Le Jeune's scenography, and Françoise Michel's lighting. The

9. Yet a different interpretation of the *Phaedrus* is also possible. Plato's critique of writing is governed by his rejection of ideality made corporeal, of any ideality inscribed outside of the living intimacy of the soul. In some respects, the theatrical critique of the text that I propose rests on an exactly converse notion: the body's refusal to be subjected to ideality and to be constrained by the general identity of what is consigned to the text. On this point, see below, 147, and also Derrida's commentary on Artaud: "Artaud's disgust with nontheatrical writing has the same sense. What inspires this disgust is not, as in the *Phaedrus*, the gesture of the body, the sensory and mnemonic, the hypomnesiac mark exterior to the inscription of truth in the soul, but, on the contrary, writing as the site of the inscription of truth, the other of the living body, writing as ideality, repetition. Plato criticizes writing as a body; Artaud criticizes it as the erasure of the body, of the living gesture which takes place only once" (Derrida 2001, 312).

10. A parallel critique of Nelson Goodman's concept of the allographic (1976), as it applies to the performing arts, could be developed. Even if the concept of the allographic has a content and criteria that are distinct from those of the "two stage arts," Goodman's division between essential and contingent properties (as well as the distinction between prescription and execution) also makes the spectacular event secondary to the notated text. Here too the spectacle intervenes only to fill the gaps in notation, to actualize and singularize in the sensory realm an ideal object that defines a class of correct performances. See below, 197.

dance spectacle explodes the framework of "two-stage arts" to the extent that it is one of the few performing arts not to absorb and hierarchize the heterogeneous elements of spectacle. Dance does not distill the hybridity proper to all spectacle into a single element that defines the work in a homogeneous way. Watching a dance spectacle is never a case of attending a contingent and secondary production of a preexisting choreographic text but rather of encountering a strange, multiple, and ephemeral alliance in which heterogeneous artistic fields dissolve in a unique event.[11] Diaghilev's Ballets Russes—where Stravinsky, Cocteau, Picasso, and Nijinsky were brought together in a single evening—is probably the paradigm and modern point of origin of this unitary conception of spectacle:[12] this is spectacle conceived not as the actualization of an external, partial work but as the encounter of different artistic fields itself establishing a kind of paradoxical "work." And Vladimir Jankélévitch focuses specifically on the example of the Ballets Russes when seeking to explain the mysterious temporality proper to the concert and the spectacle:

> There are no "works" of the Ballets Russes, but there is, at the juncture of the various arts, a pneumatic work which is paradoxically a work of the moment, which appears and disappears in the course of a single evening, without leaving any trace of itself in the archives except a more or less illusory electromagnetic recording. This instantaneous "work" is the miraculous conjunction of music, choreography and scenography; and it can be termed "semelfactive," in the sense that, even when repeated, it appears each time for the first time, each time for the last time, each time for the first-last time! (1979, 167)[13]

The dance spectacle cannot be absorbed by any score or archive because it resides entirely in the eventful encounter of the fields that constitute it. It can therefore be understood as the paradigm of a mysterious "first-last-time," or raw presence, hidden at the very moment of its exposure. A major portion of

11. This needs qualifying in the case of the classics of the ballet repertoire, which allow some variation in "stage packaging" (scenography, costumes, lighting, and so on) and thus can generate multiple productions. But this is a case where the "choreographic text" that is produced itself remains poorly established, transformed into a multitude of concurrent versions by oral tradition. On this point, see below, 215.

12. I specify "modern" here because in some respects it is merely a rediscovery of the classical Greek conception, as well as its Wagnerian reactivation through the *Gesamtkunstwerk*. Note in passing that Laurence Louppe bases her critique of Goodman's distinction between autographic and allographic on a reference to the *Gesamtkunstwerk* (Louppe 2010, 246).

13. Thanks to Maël Renouard for pointing me to this text.

contemporary creation is underscored by this paradigm of the global spectacle: think, for example, of Angelin Preljocaj (whose reference to the Ballets Russes is explicit), Odile Duboc, Dominique Bagouet, Josef Nadj, and Anne Teresa de Keersmaeker. None of these choreographers (and the list is only indicative) merely produces a choreographic "text"—making dance and only dance—but rather conceives, in parallel with dance, a general spectacular framework. Each produces a spectacle that is in itself a kind of "polyphonic machine," in which the diverse artistic fields form a whole inaccessible outside of the event.

Secondly, moving beyond this argument about the essential heterogeneity of spectacle (by which the work cannot be defined merely in terms of one of its elements and is identified only with the eventful encounter of its various constituting fields), we should note the ambivalent, seemingly secondary status of notation in dance.[14] Even if we assume that the work can be defined merely through the identity of its choreographic "text," we should remember that this "text" is often poorly established and typically purely oral. Choreographic creation has never, or only very rarely, happened on paper. It always passes first through the actualizing bodies of its performers. The work's identity thus seems to depend more on its material history of production and transmission than on any isolation of general features that define a class of correct performances. This is probably only a matter of contingent fact rather than foundational impossibility. In principle, there is nothing to prevent a dance from being created on paper and transmitted only via the intermediary of a text, rather than from performer to performer, as usually happens in both ballet and contemporary dance. Nonetheless, this mode of production and transmission is extremely rare, and that in itself points to how the choreographic work tends to adhere to its context of production and to the singular bodies that gave birth to it. This adherence precludes its straightforward alignment with Goodman's model of allographic works. Choreographic spectacle is neither the mere execution of an ideal and transcendent object, indifferent to the context of its actualization (the allographic), nor a pure autographic improvisation destined to perish in the very moment that it occurs. The work is repeated from one evening to another, even sometimes from one production to another, but its repetition is not at all founded on the transcendence of an ideal and external model. The work remains inscribed in the original context of its production and in the material lineage of its transmissions. This phenomenon of adherence or of inscription is accentuated further by contemporary processes of creation, based on studio improvisation and the fixing of improvised material as distinct phrases or

14. See below, 163.

modules. The choreographic phrase performed onstage is, then, no longer the actualization of an ideal object that is indifferent to its context but rather the repetition or re-experiencing of what happened by chance in the studio. It cannot be the object of any process of objective reiteration.[15]

In light of this two-pronged argument (about the heterogeneity of spectacle and the weakness of notation), the dance spectacle seems to escape work transcendence (which, I note in passing, is also an index of the choreographic work's weakness). The second mode of transcendence, as I have said, consists in the actions represented. More generally, this is the transcendence of signification. Here, it is no longer the relation between work and event that is at issue (our first sense of the term "representation") but the mode in which spectacle gives form to time. I have claimed that what spectacle does—in contrast to those phenomena that are only accidentally spectacular—is to inform and render rhythmic the thick but empty time of spectators. This form-ing can be effected in two ways, either immanently or transcendently. By "transcendent form-ing," I mean any process of temporal organization that might detach from the event itself: that is, any temporal form that could survive independently of the sensory material whereby it is deployed. Narrative or mimetic form-ing (the second sense of the term "representation") presents the paradigm case of this kind of transcendence. Here, I follow Paul Ricœur's analysis (in his discussion of Aristotle, indeed) for whom only "emplotment" succeeds in transforming time into a comprehensible and representable object (1984 [1983], 31–51). Temporal succession becomes a plot [histoire] and thus a logical scheme of coherent action in which time now appears as a framework of a quasi-teleological development. "Emplotment" is a domesticating operation that wrenches time from its state of pure flow, reifies it, and masters it in the logical simultaneity of the narrative. But we need, then, to identify what this domestication implies or requires in order to grasp its spectacular cost. Through narrative form-ing, the event becomes the representation of an absent—or fictional—reality. Because of its generality, the representation cannot but exceed the event. What happens onstage is less valuable in and of itself than as the sign of an action that could have been presented otherwise. This is the principle of transcendence on which theatrical form-ing is based: the story told is always detachable as content from the singular body that embodies it. The theatrical stage is theological—as has already been noted—to the extent that it always signals toward something external with which it is not to be

15. I will develop this two-pronged argument (about the heterogeneity of the spectacle and the weakness of notation) in part III, where I aim to explore the paradoxical immanence of the work in the event, drawing on a more rigorously Goodmanian framework.

confused. It is theological to the extent that its present is constantly overtaken by something *re-presented*.

But this principle of transcendence is not limited only to narrative form-ing. It actually concerns representation (or signification) as such. There is transcendence as soon as the event is given as the signifier of a detachable signified, like the sign of an ideal object that remains self-identical independently of the sensory bodies who manifest it. The court ballet generally does not tell a story. However, the form-ing of time that it effects (in *allegorico-analytic* mode, as we discussed) does not thereby cease to be transcendent or to project us beyond the event. The succession of *entrées* is ordered in the logical and taxonomical space of the tableau, and each has value only as a more or less striking signifier. The real springboard of transcendence is representation in general, relative to which narration is just one example among others. I will call representational transcendence, insofar as it applies to the form-ing of stage time, "Theater-Form."

What, then, would be an example of form-ing that escapes the transcendence of signification? Music, I would suggest. Adopting Hanslick's thesis (itself adopted by Boris de Schloezer and more recently by Bernard Sève),[16] I will argue that music offers a model of immanent meaning, which cannot be detached from the sensible material that deploys it and to which it seems to stick:

> In music, the signified is immanent in the signifier, the content in the form, to the point where, rigorously speaking, music *has* no meaning, but rather *is* a meaning. (Schloezer 1979 [1947], 31)

Musical form-ing does not make the event into a re-presenting: it maintains its own present, stressing and modulating that present from the inside, without reference to anything external. Hence the impossibility of paraphrase and redundancy in music. What has already been said musically cannot be re-said by other means:

> There is no redundancy in music since there are not different ways of saying the same thing musically, because the matter is confounded with the manner [...] There is in music no transcendence of meaning—the idea of redundancy, meanwhile, assumes transcendence (in the least metaphysical sense of that term) of meaning, or perhaps the externality or objectivity of meaning. Musical meaning is, by contrast, purely immanent. (Sève 2002, 237)

16. See Hanslick (1986 [1854]); Schloezer (1979); Sève (2002).

This immanence of meaning, this strict imbrication of the signifier and the signified as applied to the organization of time, I will therefore call (following
Bernard Sève) "Music-Form."[17]

The contrast between Theater-Form and Music-Form is reflected also within
choreographic practices. Historical parallels are evident in the seventeenth century's contrast between "simple dance" and "figured dance," and in the modern
contrast between "abstract" and "narrative" or "expressive" dance. Each of these
contrasts sets up two poles between which dance has continually oscillated
in aesthetic evaluations which at the very least fluctuate through time. If the
theoreticians of the seventeenth and eighteenth centuries saw "figured dance"
(or dance-in-action) as the only possible theatrical dance, they still remained
conscious of the limits of gestural expression and its incapacity to signify in
strictly linguistic mode: that is, to be merely a transparent signifier of an external, ideal object. Hence, the importance of verbalized plots or programs (and
costumes) accompanying the representation, in order to make the represented
object explicit to the audience:

> It is easy to see that the story [Récit] merely supplements the abbreviated,
> imperfect or ambiguous expressions of dance and of steps. Its function is to
> recite what will happen in the action, if it is given in the form of a Prologue,
> or to state what is currently happening or the consequences that will follow if
> that story is spoken in the middle or at the end of the Ballet. It is a borrowed
> vehicle—a charitable and gracious interpreter of the mysteries of Design and
> the secrets of disguise. (Pure 1668, 277)[18]

A century later, when Noverre transfers the task of telling the story and representing to dance alone, his theory of gestural signification is still distinct from

---

17. This reduction of music to strict immanence of meaning should of course immediately be
qualified. Most vocal music, as well as so-called program music, is thereby excluded. "Form-
Music" in fact designates (as the capitalization suggests) a sort of ideal type within music itself,
specifically realized within instrumental music. On the notion of Form-Music, see Sève (2002,
236–44), as well as Sève (1998).

18. See also the anecdote drawn from Saint Augustine (De doctrina christiana, book II, section
25, §38–9) and often invoked by dance theoreticians: "Saint Augustine, speaking of these repre-
sentations, says that one was constrained to put at one side of the stage a man who declaimed in
a loud voice at the beginning of each entrée what was supposed to be represented" (Ménéstrier
1972, 143). Noverre invokes the same anecdote: "Saint Augustine himself, in speaking of ballets, remarked that a man was invariably placed on the edge of the stage, to explain in a loud
voice the action about to be represented. In the reign of Louis XIV, recitatives, dialogues and
monologues equally served as an explanation of the dancing which could not yet speak for
itself" (1930, 51).

the linguistic model. Dance does not make sense because it relies on a lexicon of pregiven gestures but rather because it is linked with the irreplaceable presence of a singular and expressive body.[19] Even if the eighteenth century is wholly oriented toward Theater-Form, then, it remains conscious of the impossibility of assimilating dance to the linguistic model.[20]

Conversely, choreographic modernity places renewed value on "pure dance" and abstraction—on Music-Form, perhaps. But here too things are less than straightforward. On the one hand, the strongest partisans of choreographic abstraction in the 1920s and 1930s come mainly from the academic ballet tradition. Thus André Levinson and Boris de Schloezer are equally opposed to German expressionism, and see the self-centeredness and gratuity of the "ballet blanc" as the route to a modernism in which dance takes control of its own medium, beyond any narrative or expressive aim.[21] On the other hand, following this (Greenbergian) thesis that modernism is autonomy and purity of the medium, it might only be with Cunningham that "modern dance" becomes truly modern. I postpone examining this historico-aesthetic paradox until my conclusion.[22]

This constant oscillation between Music-Form and Theater-Form, between abstraction and expression, between immanence and transcendence, should probably be understood as a tension internal to dance, not mere historical fluctuation. If I had to hazard a theory of gestural signification, it would probably say that gestural meaning is always midway between immanence and transcendence. Husserl demonstrates in the first of his *Logical Investigations* how gestural communication escapes the strict ideality of the signified; he excludes gestures and bodily expression from the field of true signification.[23] Yet gesture still does

19. See below, 181.

20. On this issue, see Franko's analysis of the burlesque in the seventeenth century, which he understands as dance resisting assimilation to text and language (1993, chapter 4).

21. On this issue, see the astonishing article by Boris de Schloezer "Danse et psychologie. Considérations sur la danse classique" (1921) where he applies his own model of musical autonomy to dance, in a simultaneously classical and modernist vein. Oddly, the argument deployed by Schloezer to defend classical ballet presages the work of Merce Cunningham. Meanwhile, André Levinson's writing (notably 1933) make a similar connection between classicism and modernist autonomy, in reaction against German expressionism.

22. See below, 298–99. John Martin's commentary on Wigman questions this idea that German expressionism is excluded from Greenbergian modernism: "With Wigman the dance stands for the first time fully revealed in its own stature; it is not storytelling or pantomime or moving sculpture or design in space or acrobatic virtuosity or musical illustration, but dance alone, an autonomous art exemplifying fully the ideals of modernism in its attainment of abstraction and in its utilization of the resources of its materials efficiently and with authority" (Martin 1965a [1939], 235).

23. See Husserl (2001 [1900/1901]), Investigation One: Expression and Meaning, Chapter 1: Essential Distinctions, §5 "Expressions as meaningful signs. Setting aside of a sense of

not reduce to mere sensory immanence and remains the (vague and impure) origin of signification as such. This is suggested by Merleau-Ponty making gesture the very model of spoken language and expression (1964 [1960], 39–83). Analyzing the ambiguity of gestural signification would imply a whole other project—the conceptual appendage of the historical work I mentioned in my previous chapter.[24]

For now, the ambiguity and nebulousness of gestural signification seem to me to be reproduced on the stage itself, in experiencing the spectacle. The opposition Theater-Form/Music-Form then appears to be canceled out. All dance, even the most "theatrical," maintains an element of strangeness that resists conceptual translatability. It is difficult to tell the summary story of what one sees, and paraphrases seem destined from the start to fail. Conversely, all dance, even the most "abstract," insofar as it displays onstage gendered bodies that are similar to ours, retains an element of nebulous signification, which distinguishes it clearly from musical immateriality. Vague and dreamlike micro-stories are implied by what we see. This strange intermediary status between Music-Form and Theater-Form is, I think, particularly evident in contemporary dance.

In some cases, like the work of Pina Bausch or Josef Nadj, dance behaves like theater, telling little stories and creating identifiable personae, if not characters: in Bausch, the Chosen One from *The Rite of Spring* and the aging diva from *Nur Du*, for example; or Woyzeck and Marie in Nadj's choreographic adaptation of Büchner's text, and the evanescent figures of Mercier and Camier, or of Vladimir and Estragon in his *Le vent dans le sac*. In other contrasting cases, dance becomes pure music, a gratuitous play of movement that refers only to itself and enjoys the immanence of its own action. Merce Cunningham is probably the first to have liberated dance from all forms of transcendence, inventing a spectacle in which events are (so to speak) left to themselves, shorn of any signitive reference and liberated in the self-evidence of their appearance: those events are like mere things that "just are," neither referencing intention nor calling for interpretation. Hence the crucial role played by chance in Cunningham's work, since (in quasi-Nietzschean mode) only chance seems strong enough to liberate becoming, to render to events their total innocence: that is, their immanence and a-signification.

Confronted with this model of musical immanence, relevant to the neoclassicism of William Forsythe as well as to Cunningham, we should not, however,

'expression' not relevant for our purposes," pp. 187–88. For a commentary on this exclusion of gesture from the domain of true signification, see "The Reduction of Indication," in Derrida (2011 [1967], 23–26).

24. See above, 109–10.

assume that the dance-theater of Bausch and Nadj (to take only some well-known and obvious examples) necessarily reproduces the kind of transcendence characteristic of theatrical form-ing. Rather, dance perpetually deconstructs Theater-Form. Only by subversion and diversion does dance become theater. The stories or (more accurately) sketches that emerge in Bausch's work undoubtedly avoid the unity and continuity associated with plot. They are more like slices of life and of the moment than theatrical action developed to its logical conclusion. They unfold, particularly in her last works, an aesthetic of collage: without apparent logical inks, a traveling salesman's meal, a young woman's glamour poses, and an exhausted couple fighting are jumbled together. There is no "character" here to ensure that the spectacle has a semblance of narrative unity. To some extent, character is always surpassed or bypassed, either because the focus is on the most general and codified of social types (the macho, the vamp, the petit-bourgeois, and so on) or because the personae are developed at the level of a quasi-prelinguistic and prepsychological individuation, being riven with gestural affects that cannot be related back to the explicit, solid identity of a self. In Nadj's work, by contrast, there are continual references to literary works (by Büchner, Beckett, Kafka, and so on), which might suggest a surplus of narrativity. Yet an effect of "estrangement" is immediately produced such that, despite the familiarity of the gestures and mime, nothing is straightforwardly recognizable anymore. The viewer is confronted with incomprehensible rituals that, by their form, regularity, and repetition, sketch a meaning obscurely, although it remains impossible to grasp it univocally and transparently: these are quasi-animalistic rituals (and the animal is very important to Nadj) where one glimpses something vaguely or discerns familiar gestures (a particular hand movement, grimace, or expression), only for these to become so distorted, distanced, or repetitive that they are ultimately unrecognizable. And if it is easy to apply to dance the Deleuzian concept of "becoming-animal," this is perhaps because of this effect of "estrangement," because of the unbelievable and irrational worlds we are shown that are simultaneously close and distant, whose bodies refer only from afar to everyday movement without ever wholly abandoning it. It is perhaps because of these worlds that, since they represent nothing, have only to leave themselves be, for the duration the performance, in the slipstream of a single night.

I will make one final comment. I started from the idea that representation exceeds presence, that signification exceeds the event, then considered music as an immanent form-ing of time, not denoting any external reality. Yet it is not obvious that Music-Form, by virtue of music's very immateriality, can preserve the full immanence of the event. Likely music is immanence, but purified and disjointed from the material events that produce it, to such an extent that spectacle—the fact of performance in action—will always be secondary. The spectacle is no longer here a superficial sign (as with Theater-Form) but rather a necessary rite whereby pure music occurs, a rite that the music-loving ear expects to be as discreet as possible. And perhaps, therefore, the presence and immanence of the event are only really maintained in the in-between of *gestural* signification. Dance is confronted, in its form-ing of time, with its own power-lessness with respect to reference: when constructing objects, it cannot count on the substance of the external world. But this powerlessness in signification does not result in an autonomous or meaningless world being constructed, as is the case with music. The material and gendered bodies displayed onstage always remain *of* our world, immediately expressive beyond all decodable sig-nification. From this flows the immanence of what happens onstage. And since this refers neither to the construction of an immaterial beyond nor to the well-known context of objects that populate our surroundings, the space is left free for the events that happen, here and now, on the stage.

A DOUBLE EXCLUSION: ARISTOTLE AND
THE THEATRICAL TRADITION

I began this account of the "Genesis and structure of the choreographic stage" by discussing the model of Greek theater. And I return to this topic in conclusion. Or rather, I return to the reverse side of the topic, to the process that overturns the model and founds our own theatrical tradition. Aristotle's *Poetics* invents, against the model of Greek theater, a division between the work and its body, between repeatable ideality (the word, the concept, or, perhaps, the action schema) and singular scenic reality.[25] We now think of this division as self-evident, but it is introduced by two particular moves in Aristotle's text: (1) the exclusion of *opsis* from Poetry in chapter 6 (*opsis* being spectacle or dramatic enactment, charac-teristic of tragedy as distinct from epic); and (2) the relegation of *skemata tes lexeos* (the gestural and vocal dimension of expression) to the domain of the actor alone (*hypokrisis*) in chapter 19. The essence of tragedy thus becomes the ordered arrangement of actions in a clear story or a mythos ("the very soul of

---

25. Translator's note: Pouillaude's analysis is based on the French translation of Aristotle's *Poetics* by Roselyne Dupont-Roc and Jean Lallot (Aristotle 1980), from which he cites in what follows. There are numerous extant English translations of the *Poetics*: I have chosen to refer-ence mainly Stephen Halliwell's translation (Aristotle 1987a), partly because it uses the same chapter divisions (originally introduced by Renaissance scholars) as the French edition. I also refer occasionally to Richard Janko's translation (Aristotle 1987b) and (at Pouillaude's sugges-tion) replace some phrases with alternative translations more appropriate to his argument, as well as sometimes including transliterated Greek terms in square brackets within the quota-tions. References to the section/line numbers of the original Greek text are also included in square brackets after direct citations, as they are in Pouillaude.

tragedy," Aristotle claims), which can be accessed independently of any scenic representation, by reading alone. This reduction of the work to the story is all the more difficult to comprehend, given that tragedy is certainly something more than discourse. There is decor but (more significantly) also singing and dancing. Aristotle says practically nothing about this choral element. Dance is mentioned in passing in chapter 1, where there is no suggestion of it being a constitutive element of tragedy. Dance disappears from chapter 6, where Aristotle defines tragedy and compiles a list of its several parts. It seems, then, that all the nonverbal elements of poetic art are excluded by omission, in favor of just the story or mythos.

But the exclusion is actually more radical, since the very process of dramatic enactment (*opsis*) is demoted and devalued. The paradox or difficulty thus becomes internal to Aristotle's thinking. Until now, I have merely put Aristotle's thought in tension with what we otherwise know about tragedy. But by excluding *opsis*, Aristotle seems to contradict his own system of analysis. *Opsis* is precisely what enables a distinction to be drawn between tragedy and epic, between direct representation onstage and mere narration. On the one hand, *opsis* constitutes the differentia of tragedy insofar as it is distinct from epic. On the other hand, these differentia appear purely external and contingent, extrinsic to the true art of the poet, which is to arrange beautiful *mythoi*. Throughout his treatise, Aristotle is confronted with this tension, sometimes recalling the exclusion of *opsis*, sometimes reaffirming the fact that tragedy is given in action onstage with flesh-and-blood actors, this being precisely what constitutes its specificity. The same goes for *skhemata tes lexeos*. The singular actualization of speech matters little to the author of the story (chapter 19). But the author also depends on a kind of gestural mime of affects, if his expression is to be complete. It is through mimic incarnation—through gestures (*skhemata*)—that the author discovers the best stylistic figures, the best tropes, or in other words (yet again) the most appropriate stylistic *skhemata*, the ancient Greek term being as richly ambiguous as it is (chapter 17).

We know that the explicit focus of the *Poetics* is the collection of arts that imitate (or represent) partially or essentially through language: epic, tragedy, comedy, and the Dionysian dithyramb. We also know that the Aristotelian text we have inherited under the title of *Poetics* in fact speaks only of tragedy and (more succinctly) of epic. However, a threefold principle of differentiation is established for the arts collectively as early as chapter 1:

> Now epic and tragic poetry, as well as comedy and dithyramb (and most music for the pipe or lyre) are all, taken as a whole, kinds of mimesis. But they differ from one another in three respects: namely, in the *media* or the *objects* or the *mode* of mimesis. (Aristotle 1987a, 31 [47a14–18])

Chapter 1 is principally devoted to the difference between media, chapter 2 to the difference between objects, and chapter 3 to the difference between modes. It is perhaps surprising to see music featuring in chapter 1 ("the arts of the pipe and the lyre") in a list of works clearly linked, from a contemporary perspective, to literary genres. But if tragedy is closer to opera than it is to the theater play, perhaps this is not so surprising. It would mean that music and tragedy are much closer, making Aristotle's list perfectly natural. And Aristotle's argument probably suggests an even deeper solidarity between music and tragedy, linked to the media employed in the different arts. Applying an anachronistic concept that nonetheless appears illuminating here, all of the arts mentioned derive from what have been known since Lessing as arts of *time*: their media of imitation are only deployed in duration. Moreover, Aristotle suggests this when he contrasts music and tragedy, a few lines later, with those arts that imitate by color and figure: arts of space, as we might now call them today. The latter arts have two media: *chroma* and *skhema*. The arts of time, meanwhile, have three: rhythm, language, and melody. And they are differentiated according to the various combinations of these different media that they effect:

> In the case of all the arts mentioned above mimesis is effected in the media of rhythm, language and melody. But these can be employed separately or in combination [...]. (Aristotle 1987a, 31 [47a20–23])

Thus, epic imitates (or represents) by language alone, albeit via poetically regulated and measured language. The piper imitates by rhythm and melody employed simultaneously. And the dancer, by contrast, imitates by rhythm alone, without melody:

> The art of dancing presents mimesis in the medium of rhythm without melody (for dancers, through the rhythms which shape their movements, engage in the mimesis of character, emotions and actions [*dia ton skhematizomenon rhuthmon*]. (Aristotle 1987a, 31 [47a26–28])

In passing I must emphasize the problematic nature of this formula—*dia ton skhematizomenon rhuthmon*—which seems to present a kind of definition of dance. Dance is thus the figuration of a given rhythm. Deriving from the arts of time (via rhythm), dance thereby aligns through figuration those other arts that depend on color [*chroma*] and figure [*skhema*]. The consequence is a kind of classic ambivalence, with dance positioned at the exact intersection of arts of time and arts of space: it is both animated plasticity and spatially deployed rhythm. And this "figurative" (schematic) dimension of dance is intimately embedded in ancient Greek as a language where *skhema* first and foremost means "gesture." I return to this issue below.

If dance imitates by rhythm alone (disposed in figures), comedy, tragedy, and dithyramb for their part have recourse to all three media at once and are distinct from one another according to whether their use is simultaneous or alternating:

> There are some poetic arts which employ all the stated media (that is, rhythm, melody and metre), such as dithyramb, nome, tragedy and comedy: they differ, though, in that some use all throughout, some only in parts. (Aristotle 1987a, 32 [47b24–28])

Comedy and tragedy alternate speech with song and dance. Dithyrambs and nomes use all the media simultaneously. Aristotle actually says little more about this diversity of media, about the constitutive heterogeneity of the stage space. He concentrates as soon as he can on the very soul of the dramatic work—the mythos and the language that allows it to be best expressed.

Turning now to the different objects (and chapter 2), all the imitations so far discussed are imitations of men in action. But these men are necessarily noble or base, or (more accurately) better or worse. Comedy is concerned with depicting men who are worse than us; tragedy depicts men who are better (as does epic). Comedy and tragedy always exaggerate the reality of our lives, either by lowering characters to the comic level or by raising them to the most noble heroism. A determining feature of classical art is identified here: the inadmissibility of any representation that does not transform the real into the essentiality of a type, which does not stand in sharp contrast with the ordinary mediocrity of our lives. Differentiation by media and by object, however, proves insufficiently discriminating. Two different arts can have the same medium and object. Such that a third differentiam is necessary:

> Beside the two already cited, there is a third distinction: namely, the mode in which the various objects are represented. For it is possible to use the same media to offer a mimesis of the same objects in any one of three ways: first, by alternation between narrative and dramatic impersonation (as in Homeric poetry); second, by employing the voice of narrative without variation; third, by a wholly dramatic representation of the agents. (Aristotle 1987a, 33 [48a19–23])

Aristotle seems to have in mind here the possible intersection of epic and tragedy. Both imitate men who are better than us (they share an object); and both have recourse to meter (they share a medium, at least to some extent, given that epic has recourse only to meter whereas tragedy adds song and rhythm). A third principle of differentiation is necessary: that of *mode*. Either one narrates (directly or via the intermediary of reported speech, as in the case of

Homer), or one imitates the actions of characters directly. Epic employs the first of these modes of imitation, namely, narration, whereas tragedy and comedy depend on the second, dramatic mode, which manifests the action of the characters directly on the stage. Aristotle here adopts, even while distancing himself from it, a Platonic distinction that could also serve to differentiate epic and tragedy: the distinction between *diegesis* and *mimesis*, between simple and imitative narrative (*The Republic*, III, 392c–394c). For Aristotle, "mimesis" no longer designates a specific mode of representation (dramatic rather than narrative), but the general space of representation, within which different modes are deployed (narrative imitation versus dramatic imitation).

By combining the differences of object and mode, Aristotle can thus make explicit the system of relations that unites and differentiates the three genres that really interest him: epic, tragedy, and comedy. Tragedy is identical to epic in its object, but distinct in mode. Tragedy is identical to comedy in mode, but distinct in object. Comedy, meanwhile, is distinct in all respects, except in the medium of meter, from epic.

We are thus armed to understand Aristotle's enumeration in chapter 6 of the constitutive elements of tragedy. What must come first, under the heading of mode, is the organization of the spectacle [*o tes opseos kosmos*]. Then, under the heading of media, come the composition of style (*lexis*) and lyric poetry, that is, the arrangement of verse. Finally, under the heading of object, come character (of those who act), thought (the arguments they advance in talking), and plot-structure, which organizes their actions (see Aristotle 1987a, 36–37 [49b31–50]). Tragedy includes thus six (and only six) elements: plot-structure, thought, character, style, lyric poetry, and spectacle. Three elements stem from the object (plot-structure, thought, character). Two stem from the medium (style and lyric poetry). And just one stems from the mode (spectacle).[26] This can be tabulated as follows:

Differentia	Medium	Object	Mode
Element	Lyric poetry Style	Character Plot-structure Thought	Spectacle

26. "So then, tragedy as a whole must have six elements which make it what it is: they are plot-structure, character, style, thought, spectacle, lyric poetry. Two of these are the media, one the mode, and three the objects of the mimesis—and that embraces everything" (Aristotle 1987a, 37 [50a8–15]).

Spectacle is therefore the only element that guarantees the specificity of tragedy in its modal difference to epic. However, it is consistently devalued, even
radically excluded, from the art of poetry, as if tragedy's most distinctive trait is
simultaneously its most external and contingent feature.

In fact, after this enumeration of different constitutive elements, Aristotle
proceeds to a rapid commentary on each. *Opsis* opens and closes that discussion, featuring in two apparently contradictory propositions. On the one hand,
Aristotle tells us that spectacle is a strange element encompassing all the others,
and that this is plausibly because of difference in mode with which it is associated.[27] Tragedy being dramatic enactment and not narration, all its elements must
in some sense pass via the filter of the scenic space and participate in this space
of dramatic enactment. Otherwise, it would no longer be a question of a dramatic
work but rather of a poem or a novel. This view of spectacle as all-encompassing
is, however, immediately overturned when it is positioned as external to tragedy.
Concluding his commentary on the different elements of tragedy, Aristotle argues
that this all-encompassing term *opsis* ultimately has nothing to do with the true
art of the poet:

> Spectacle is emotionally powerful but is the least integral of all to the poet's
> art: for the potential of tragedy *does not depend upon [competition] [agonos]*[28]
> *and actors [hypokriton]*; and, besides, the art of the mask-maker carries more

27. Translator's note: The French translators Dupont-Roc and Lallot give the following translation of lines 50a12–14 of Aristotle's text: "Le spectacle implique tout: caractères, histoire,
expression, chant et pensée également" ["Spectacle encompasses everything: characters, plot,
style, song, and thought"]. English translators, meanwhile, suggest that it is Aristotle's list
(rather than spectacle) that "encompasses everything." Thus Stephen Halliwell translates the
passage as follows: "So then, tragedy as a whole must have six elements which make it what it
is: they are plot structure, character, style, thought, spectacle and lyric poetry. Two of these are
the media, one the mode, and three the objects, of the mimesis—and that embraces everything"
(Aristotle 1987a, 37). Richard Janko suggests: "So tragedy as a whole necessarily has six parts,
according to which tragedy is of a certain sort. These are plot, characters, diction, reasoning,
spectacle and song. The media in which [the poets] make the representation comprise two parts
[i.e., diction and song], the manner in which they make the representation, one [i.e., spectacle],
and the objects which they represent, three [i.e., plot, character, and reasoning]. There are no
others except these" (Aristotle 1987b, 8). The discrepancy between French and English translations probably stems from their authors' decision concerning whether or not to "correct" the
Greek text in order to render it internally consistent. Note that Pouillaude's point here rests on
the interpretation of the French translators and the fact that they opt for "non-intervention"
(Artistotle 1980, 202).

28. Translator's note: I have amended Halliwell's "the potential of tragedy does not depend
upon public performance and actors" to emphasize the competitive dimension of the framework of tragedy, as does Pouillaude.

weight than the poet's as regards the elaboration of visual effects. (Aristotle
1987a, 38–39 [50b16–20], my emphasis)

No competition, then. Tragedy is presented as existing outside the institutional
and religious framework regulating and authorizing representation, outside the
singular competition [âgon] between poets where each must present a tragic
trilogy followed by a satyr play, outside the circumscribed time of the Great
Dionysia. Yet the strict inscription of the work in the ritual time of *opsis* was
marked for the Greeks by the simple fact that it was impossible for a work to
be repeated. Recall that tragedies were only ever performed once. And it is this
fact, this strict eventfulness, that Aristotle here denies. What can the phrase
"does not depend upon public performance and actors" mean other than that
tragedy can be experienced just through impersonal, repeatable reading, in the
reflective ideality of the word? Tragedy is no doubt dramatic enactment, given
in the eventful and visual form of *opsis*. Yet its effects must be able to pass the
test of invisible ideality, of solitary reading. Visual effects and the event are thus
strangers to the art of the poet. They are the concern of another art that is,
in fact, barely an art at all: that of the designer or mask-maker. This trial by
reading is confirmed in another passage, which specifically examines the tragic
effects of *phobos* and *eleos*:

> The effect of fear and pity can arise from theatrical spectacle, but it can also
> arise from the intrinsic structure of events, and it is this which matters more
> and is the task of a superior poet. For the plot-structure ought to be so com-
> posed that, even without seeing a performance, anyone who hears the events
> which occur will experience terror and pity as a result of the outcome; this is
> what someone would feel while hearing the plot of the *Oedipus*. To produce
> this effect through spectacle is not part of the poet's art, and calls for material
> resources [*choregias*]. (Aristotle 1987a, 45 [53b1–8])

If the aim of this passage is to eliminate showy effects—dripping blood, mur-
ders enacted onstage, and so on—it nonetheless remains very problematic in its
insistence on audition and the exclusion of *choregia*. If simply narrating a story
suffices to produce the same effects as dramatic enactment, then what the latter
brings to the table is no longer clear. It is not just showy effects that are eliminated but also (more radically) the performance of the actors themselves, that
visible and singular element of the work. Probably spectacle adds *something*
(production effects or incarnate pathos, visible in the bodies performing, for
example). But once again that addition is said to be external to the art of poetry,
indifferent in relation to the tragic essence of the work that should be judged
by other criteria.

The ambivalent status of *opsis*—as both necessary and external to the work—is evident once again when the respective merits of epic and tragedy are compared in chapter 26. Aristotle here develops two series of apparently contradictory arguments. In the first, he maintains that tragedy is inferior to epic because addressed to a less noble audience. The audience for tragedy is less noble than that for epic because it needs everything to be represented, and things to be effectively imitated or figured in the body itself, in gestures and in speech. The audience for epic, meanwhile, is content with mere narration:

> It is reasonable to consider whether epic or tragic mimesis is the superior. If the superior is the less vulgar, and this is the one addressed to the better kind of spectators, it is unarguable that the art which consists entirely of imper-sonation must be vulgar: for here the performers use a great deal of physical action, as though the audience would not appreciate the point without this emphasis (for instance, with the wheeling motion of bad pipe-players, when portraying a discus, or their hauling around of the chorus-leader, when play-ing Scylla's music). Now, tragedy is of this kind, and the point is similar to the opinion which earlier actors held of their successors: Mynniscus used to call Callippides an "ape," on the grounds of his excesses, and such was also the view held of Pindarus. The relation of the whole art of tragedy to epic is analogous to that between these actors and their predecessors. So people say that epic is for good spectators who require no gestures, while tragedy is for vulgar spectators. Consequently, if tragedy is vulgar, its inferiority would be evident. (Aristotle 1987a, 63–64 [61b26–62a4]).

This is argument by analogy. Tragedy is to epic what contemporary actors—who overact, exaggerate, and gesticulate wildly—are to their apparently more sober and measured predecessors. The dramatic (and non-narrative) nature of tragedy is here directly indexed to the composition of its audience. Tragedy is the way it is because addressed to an audience that needs corporeal figuration (*skhemata*) and spectacle (*opsis*), and for whom narration alone will not suffice. And by virtue of this audience, tragedy is judged inferior to epic on the grounds of a principle presented as self-evident, but which remains unexamined: the idea that imitating everything is wholly vulgar.

In the second series of arguments, however, Aristotle rehabilitates tragedy, presenting two apparently opposed lines of thought. The first aims to show that tragedy is *not* inferior to epic: the earlier attack on corporeal figuration and actors gesticulating does not concern tragedy proper and the art of the tragic poet, but merely the art of the actor (and, through this, the art of the bad actor). The tragic work as such remains exempt from criticism: essentially, it escapes the inevitable corporeal figuration induced by spectacle and play-acting. Why?

Because just reading suffices. One can access the work without *seeing* it, aside from its actualization onstage, in the intimate and ideal theater of reading. So it is not distinct from epic after all:

Besides, tragedy, just like epic, achieves its aim even without enactment [*kinesis*]: for *its qualities become apparent through a reading.* (Aristotle 1987a, 64 [62a12–14], my emphasis)

Once Aristotle has shown that tragedy is not in fact inferior to epic—that tragedy is reproached for something inessential to it, which is the concern rather of spectacle and play-acting—he needs to demonstrate its real superiority, which he does by offering three arguments. Leaving aside the last two (that tragedy is shorter and that its object has more unity than that of epic, which can join together different plots), I will focus on the first of these, showing once again the necessary yet external, almost superfluous, status of *opsis*:

Tragedy possesses all epic's attributes [...] and in addition it has music and spectacle, which produce very vivid pleasures. (Aristotle 1987a, 64 [62a14–18])

Considered independently of spectacle and play-acting, tragedy as such has nothing to envy epic. It can generate, merely through reading, the kind of pleasure with which it is associated: a pleasure involving emotions of fear and pity produced via the organization of the plot. But in addition to this properly tragic pleasure there are other pleasures—probably external and vulgar, but pleasures nonetheless—that are not negligible: pleasures of music (whether sung or instrumental), pleasures of rhythmic and melodic variation in the text, and pleasures of spectacle and of visual effects like decor, costume, gesture, dance, and so on. And this supplementary pleasure must be just that—a supplement, variation, or external addition. If it were an integral element of the tragic work, the latter would be exposed to the already formulated criticisms of gesticulating actors and vulgar corporeal figuration. Structured in this way, tragedy seems to win on all fronts. When spectacle is criticized, it can be pointed out that this has nothing to do with tragedy, which can just as well be read. But when tragedy's superiority over (and specificity in relation to) epic is in question, this supplementary pleasure can be easily invoked: the optical, vocal, and gestural variation that constitutes spectacle. In short, then, chapter 26 merely reiterates in a different way the difficulty formulated in chapter 6.

This tension concerning the status of incarnation or figuration is even found within style (*lexis*). Aristotle distinguishes between two dimensions of style: one that is properly poetic and related to the author, and another that is theatrical and related to the actor. Once again the term *skhema* is used to refer to this other, nonpoetic dimension of style:

> In matters of verbal style, one kind of study concerns figures of speech [*ta skhemata tes lexeos*]. Knowledge of these (for instance, the difference between a command, a prayer, a narrative, a threat, a question, an answer, and so on) belongs to the art of rhetorical delivery [*tes hypokritikes*] and to anyone with such expertise [...] Let this consideration be left for some other enquiry, not for poetry. (Aristotle 1987a, 53 [56b8–19])

"Figures of speech" (*skhemata tes lexeos*) should be understood to mean the incarnate dimension of speech but also, more generally, the fact that speech as singular utterance typically functions like a gesture (or a *skhema*). This gestural dimension of speech (both auditory and visual) is not the concern of poetry but of another art (if indeed it is one)—the art of the actor (*hypokrisis*). Following Dupont-Roc and Lallot, "*Lexis* can be understood as operating at two levels: that of vocal realization where style is effective elocution, and the more abstract level of language where it is formal structuration of phonic materials. At the first level, it is apprehended as figures, *skhemata tes lexeos*, at the second level, it is analyzed into parts, *tes lexeos mere* (Aristotle 1980, 101). The first level is mentioned in chapter 19 only to be rejected as outside the competence of poetry, while the second is discussed in detail in chapter 20.

As Dupont-Roc and Lallot suggest, the relegation of part of style (*lexis*) to the actor's art "is exactly analogue with the exclusion of spectacle (*opsis*) from poetry: the latter is liberated from both the auditory and the visual dimensions of the drama's performance" (Aristotle 1980, 312). But aside from this distinction between the auditory and the visual, there is probably a deeper connection between the two exclusions, especially bearing in mind that *skhema* is precisely the term employed for "gesture." By distancing *opsis*, Aristotle excludes not just the effects stemming directly from *choregia* (decor, costumes, and so on) but also the gestural action of the performers (their *skhemata* or expressive gesticulations, as we saw in chapter 26). In chapter 19, meanwhile, a more specific kind of gesturality is excluded: the gesturality of the voice—that collection of expressive intonations by which actors make sense beyond the mere text—or what we might call the gestures of verbal expression (the *skhemata tes lexeos*). Articulated differently, the general domain of play-acting (*hypokrisis*) must be understood as a collection of gestures, or visual and vocal *skhemata*. The discussion of *opsis* excludes visual *skhemata* (gestures, properly speaking), while the discussion of *lexis* here excludes also vocal *skhemata* (intonations), both of which have the particularity of remaining external to the text's or the work's identity.

But here again, the exclusion is far from straightforward. As in the case of *opsis*, Aristotle seems to want to maintain the possibility of the most external feature becoming the most all-encompassing or necessary. More accurately, the element deliberately set aside and considered extrinsic to the poet's art returns as an internal demand within the most intimate and solitary moment of writing:

> A poet ought to imagine his material to the fullest possible extent while composing his plot-structures and elaborating them in language. By seeing them as vividly as possible in this way—as if present at the very occurrence of the events—he is likely to discover what is appropriate, and least likely to miss contradictions [. . .] So far as possible, [the poet should also bring his plots to completion with gestures]:[29] for, assuming the same natural talent, the most convincing effect comes from those who actually put themselves in the emotions; and the truest impression of distress or anger is given by the person who experiences these feelings. (Aristotle 1987a, 50 [55a24–33])

In saying that plots should be completed with gestures, Aristotle does not mean through the actor's interpretation, but rather in the poet's act of writing. The poet is invited to awaken in himself, as far as possible, the emotions and passions of his characters, through gestures and bodily techniques. It is clear how bodily and gestural imitation might help someone imaginatively to feel relevant affects. But how can gesture be of direct use to writing in helping it complete verbal expression? Answering that question requires establishing a real relationship between the body's attitudes and linguistic expression as such. That relation depends in Greek on a single word, *skhema*, which designates corporeal as well as linguistic figures and makes a strange connection linking choreographic figures and stylistic tropes. In other words, the notion of *skhema* is a vehicle for an idea of a perfect continuity between gesture and language, between body and speech. Figures of style would be like gesticulations of language (*quasi aliquos gestus orationis*, says Cicero in *De Oratore*, III, §222). Equally, gesture would be a kind of mute way to make the body speak.[30] I will return to this *rhetorical* continuity between gesture and figure, between body and language,

---

29. Translator's note: Again, there is discrepancy between Dupont-Roc and Lallot's French translation of the Greek text and that of Halliwell, although Janko's comes closer. The phrase in square brackets here is from Janko's translation. This idea of the poet *completing* his plot or process with gestures is important to Pouillaude's argument below, such that Halliwell's more general "the poet should even include gestures in the process of composition" does not sit well with that argument.

30. For a general analysis of the formula "*ta skhemata tes lexeos*" within Aristotle's works, see Ildefonse (2004).

later. Here, it helps us better understand, via the notion of *skhema*, the strange demand made by Aristotle that the author should gesticulate to discover the best (linguistic and literary) tropes!

Aristotle thus invents and isolates a field of idealities, divorced from the corporeal singularity of what is displayed onstage, despite his apparent concern with theater. He establishes a clear distinction between the repeatable ideality of the work and the theatrically singular (*opsis, hypokrisis*), the very idea of there being an art (or indeed a science) of the latter seeming inconceivable. From this distinction follows the structure, still evident today, between the work and the production, a structure that Artaud seeks to overturn. Yet rejected singularity makes a return at the very core of the *Poetics*, in the moment of composition and writing. The author must imagine the stage and gesticulate a little to complete verbal expression. This points to the ineliminable corporeality of the work, at the very heart of writing.[31]

---

31. This chapter was already complete when I had the good fortune to discover Dupont (2007), which develops a critique of Aristotle quite similar to mine.

Chapter 4

Artaud: Presence and Ritual

Perhaps, then, the essence of the stage is the irreplaceable presence of the present, working against the inevitable pull of representation. And this presence has been suppressed from the beginning, overtaken by that distinctively Western tendency to subordinate it to the word and the text, to the persisting work and the transcendent drama. This essence occasionally emerges in what might be termed—for want of a better expression—"corporeal theater," and should be properly reinstated or liberated. Such, at least, is the thrust of Antonin Artaud's writings, which offer a radical and exemplary articulation of this desire. To wrench the uniqueness of scenic presence from the doubles that constantly haunt it—from those phantoms beyond the stage that ensure its return and make presence itself into a ghost—that is ultimately the ambition expressed throughout *Theatre and Its Double*.[1] This has also been, to some extent, the underlying schema of my argument. Beginning with a "naive" description of the stage and of the different ways in which it has been occluded, I considered dance spectacle as an emblem of presence, of singular uniqueness, divorced from the ideal conditions of repetition.

Now I must modulate this argument, if not invert it. To what extent is the desire for presence destined from the beginning to impossibility and unrealizability? How much does it reproduce, alongside the empiricity of the stage, an *absence of works*, in a process that I call *unworking*? Assuming that this presence—always pure and never redoubled—can be realized, to what extent can it be displayed, via the distancing of the stage, without once again adopting

---

1. First published in French in 1938. Translator's note: The full English translation of *Theatre and Its Double* is reprinted in volume 4 of Artaud's *Collected Works*, trans. Victor Corti (Artaud 1974). An edited selection of these essays was first published in English in 1970 (Artaud 1970), but since that collection does not include some chapters cited here, the *Collected Works* edition (Artaud 1974) is referenced in what follows.

and legitimizing its double, without confirming the ineluctable necessity of representation? In the context of such concerns, Derrida's commentary on Artaud obviously should be discussed.[2] For Derrida, re-presentation is (via a continual reversal of origin and supplement) the very condition of presence, and all attempts to evade its closure would only confront an unmediated contradiction. I begin my discussion with this problematic. And through examining and critiquing Derrida's position, I will ultimately trace a new path for the work—a path that passes via survival and repetition, or via *inscription*, in other words.

THE DIALECTIC OF PRESENCE

I will temporarily take as given the central proposition of Derrida's reading, the hypothesis through which Artaud's whole project should be read and organized. At the core of Artaud's project in *Theatre and Its Double* is a simple determining and motivating force: the haunting of the stage subordinated to repetition, or rather the haunting of *repetition* as such. This can be summarized as a rejection of any theater "that would not be totally exhausted in the *act and present* tense of the stage, that would not coincide with the stage, that could be repeated without it":

> Here we touch upon what seems to be the profound essence of Artaud's project, his historico-metaphysical decision. *Artaud wanted to erase repetition in general.* For him, repetition was evil, and one could doubtless organize an entire reading of his texts around this center. (Derrida 2001, 310)

And this does indeed appear to be the case. An early text springs to mind where Artaud very clearly expresses his rejection of repetition:

> We can no longer subscribe to theatre which repeats itself every night according to the same, ever the same, identical rites. The show we are watching must be unique and give us the impression of being as unexpected and as incapable of being repeated as any act in life, any occurrence whatsoever brought about by events. (Artaud 1971, 18)[3]

Of course this text dates from 1926—and is not, moreover, cited by Derrida— while the texts collected in *Theatre and Its Double* were written between 1931 and

---

2. See "The Theater of Cruelty and the Closure of Representation," in Derrida (2001, 292–316).

3. The quotation is from the essay "The Alfred Jarry Theatre (1926–27 Season)," first published in 1926 and reprinted in vol 2. of the *Collected Works*, cited here.

1936. Nonetheless, the early text already points to the "historico-metaphysical decision" governing Artaud's whole project. The active power of the stage resides in the consummation without return of the present. This defines both the value and the specificity of the stage, as Artaud explicitly states in *Theatre and Its Double*:

> Let us [...] acknowledge that what has already been said no longer needs saying; that an expression twice used is of no value since it does not have two lives. Once spoken, all speech is dead and is only active as it is spoken. Once a form is used it has no more use, bidding man find another form, and *theatre is the only place in the world where a gesture, once made, is never repeated in the same way.* (Artaud 1974, 57, my emphasis)

> And just as masks, once used in magic rituals, are no longer fit for anything but to be put in museums—in the same way, the poetic effectiveness of a text is exhausted—theatre's effectiveness and poetry is exhausted least quickly of all, since it permits the action of movement and spoken things, *never reproduced twice.* (59, my emphasis)

The effective essence of theater depends on the mystery of the "one time only." This essence is always already erased by the Western tradition, suppressed by the text and the word, by the ideality of that which can repeat itself indefinitely. The concept's interiority—a repetition founded in ideality—constantly defers consummation without return, rescuing it from extinction in the mysterious "one time only."[4]

Artaud's whole project stems from this idea: his critique of the text and its primacy within Western theater, but also his revaluation of what is inappropriately named "production" [*mise en scène*] or "spectacle":

> As long as staging remains just a means of presentation, a subordinate way of expressing works, a kind of display interlude without any meaning of its own even in the minds of the boldest producers, it has no value except

---

4. It is striking how Derrida's commentary on these two passages ultimately makes Artaud speak the language of Bataille, in order to apply more effectively the Hegelian line of argument he uses against Bataille in "From Restricted to General Economy: A Hegelianism without Reserve" (Derrida 2001, 317–50): "Dialectics is the movement through which expenditure is reappropriated into presence—it is the economy of repetition [...] Nonrepetition, expenditure that is resolute and without return in the unique time consuming the present, must put an end to fearful discursiveness, to unskirtable ontology, to dialectics [...] In this sense the theater of cruelty would be the art of difference and of expenditure without economy, without reserve, without return, without history. Pure presence as pure difference. Its act must be forgotten, actively forgotten" (311–12)

insofar as it succeeds in hiding behind the works it is intended to serve. And this will continue as long as the principal interest in performed works lies in the script, as long as in theatre—a performing art—literature takes precedence over a kind of performance incorrectly called the show [...]. (Artaud 1974, 80)

We ought to consider staging from the angle of magic and enchantment, not as reflecting a script, the mere projection of actual *doubles* arising from writing, but as the fiery projection of all the objective results of gestures, words, sounds, music or their combinations. (55, my emphasis)

In this way we can repudiate theatre's superstition concerning the script and the author's autocracy [...] Above all, we intend to base theatre on the show. (95)

The single term "text" is thus employed to denote the double transcendence I discussed earlier: the transcendence of the prior work, condemning spectacle to the status of accessory presentation; and the transcendence of articulated language, the touchstone of dramatic mimesis, which condemns the bodies onstage to a role as mere vehicles for represented characters. The notion of "text" fuses the anteriority of the work and the ideality of language. It establishes the primacy of speech within theater—more specifically, the primacy of a speech disengaged from its own body, separated from any connection to gesticulation through sound, which would break the ideal union of word and concept. It is not the word as such that must be suppressed but rather (to borrow Derrida's expression) what makes it "diaphanous," or transparent to its own body and a mere vector of signification. The word will once more be present on the stage, but employed in a way that is both new and archaic. It will become, once again, gesture and expressive cry, will regain the sonic flesh that the transparency of signification can only suppress.[5]

The primacy of the text, insofar as it ensures double transcendence by the work and by signification, can only obliterate the spatial materiality of the stage, and with it the extension and mobility of the bodies displayed there, in their singularity, in configurations irreducible to language and its writing. The stage is first and foremost a site of physical dramaturgy—composed of lights, costumes, and gestures—that the West summarizes and diminishes when it uses the terms "production" [*mise en scène*] and "show" [*spectacle*]. This stage must

---

5. On this new status of the word within the theater of cruelty, see (for example) the essay "Oriental and Western Theatre": "To change the purpose of theatre dialogue is to use it in an actual spatial sense [...] This means handling it as something concrete, disturbing things" (Artaud 1974, 54). See also Derrida (2001, 301–3).

be returned to itself. More specifically, it must be liberated to speak its own language.[6]

The renunciation of text does not imply abandoning *language* as such. The critique of text and dialogue is only meaningful when supported by the invention of *another* language, the establishment of a properly scenic and spatial idiom:

> The idea of a play built right on the stage, encountering production and performance obstacles, *demands the discovery of active language*, both active and anarchic, where the usual limits of feelings and words are transcended. (28, my emphasis).

> This *archetypal theatre language* will be formed around staging not simply viewed as one degree of refraction of the script on stage, but as the starting point for theatrical creation. (71–72, my emphasis)

The stage is built on the intersection between space and time. It is merely a spaced temporality in the movement of certain bodies or, perhaps, a concrete, bodily, rhythmically temporized spatiality. And *gesture* evidently supplies the model—perhaps even the *grammar*—of any distinctive language it might develop on that basis:

> We must use nature's own distinctive language in place of speech [...]
>   This new language's *grammar* is undiscovered as yet. *Gesture* is its substance and mind or, if you like, its alpha and omega. It springs from a NEED for speech rather than preformed speech. But finding a deadlock in speech, it spontaneously returns to gesture. On the way, it touches on a few of the rules of substantial human expression. It is steeped in necessity. It poetically retraces the steps which culminated in the creation of language. (84, my emphasis, capitalization in original)

In opposition to the primacy of "natural language" within the theater—the primacy of that language whose articulation appears wholly unconstructed—another, entirely artificial language must be invented, developed out of what is specific to the stage. But, paradoxically, when gesture is adopted as the model, this language of pure artifice can only be understood as reactivating what lies beyond construction. Anterior to constituted speech is the brute necessity of exchange, which cannot be negotiated—in line with the various primitive stages of the

---

6. "I maintain the stage is a tangible, physical place that needs to be filled and it ought to be allowed to speak its own concrete language [...] The most urgent thing seems to me to decide what this physical language is composed of, this solid, material language by which theatre can be distinguished from words" (Artaud 1974, 25–26).

origin of language—except by marginal means: the body's spontaneous expression in gestures and cries. Much might be said about this reiteration of the problem of the origin of languages, just at the moment when Artaud seeks to establish an artificial language. In some respects, Artaud here seems close to Condillac and the strange connection that the latter draws, in his *Essay on the Origin of Human Knowledge*, between mythic action language and the actual pantomime of ancient Rome and ballet.[7] In short, pantomime reveals through the present of artifice what language was before it was language, before it was stabilized in the properly linguistic conjunction of voice (presence) and phoneme (ideality). A particular model of pantomime seems, moreover, to guide Artaud in his construction of a scenic language, a pantomime that is unsullied by verbal language:

> And I hope I may mention that other aspect of pure theatre language that escapes words, that sign, gesture and posture language with its own ideographic values such as they exist in some undebased mime plays.
>
> By "undebased mime plays" I mean straightforward mime where gestures, instead of standing for words or sentences as in European mime (barely fifty years old) [...] stand for ideas, attitudes of mind, aspects of nature in a tangible potent way, that is to say by always evoking natural things or details [...] (27)

I will need to return to discussing more fully the "ideographic" value of gesture that adapts both a prior (Renaissance and Baroque) and a subsequent (Mallarméan) model to the action language of the seventeenth and eighteenth centuries. This is ultimately singularized by Artaud in his heterodox reactivation of the problem of the origin of languages.

Regardless of this issue—and aside from the strange to and fro between artifice and origin that seems to underwrite scenic language—the desire for *language*, for fixation and codification, remains paradoxical. The stage must be liberated from its doubles and returned to the nudity of the present. However, this does not mean liberation to a state of pure absence of *grammar*: this is not improvisation in the manner of Jacques Copeau.[8] Artaud's frequent insistence on the necessity of language (albeit a distinctive and idiomatic language) indicates that the present of the stage must still be framed by a set of regulations and codes that are the very condition of its efficacy. Perhaps here we are confronted with the distinctive contradiction of the term *mise en scène*. As pure present, the stage [*scène*] is always exposed to the anteriority of its *mise*, to the prior preparation that, through categorial organization, ensures its finish, rhythm,

7. See Condillac (2001 [1746], part 2, section 1, chapters 1 and 4).

8. "My shows have nothing to do with Copeau's improvisations" (Artaud 1974, 83).

and form. If the liberation of presence is only enabled by the prior establishment of a language, then it seems that presence is always already doubled, that it can only henceforth represent an antecedent ideality. This reveals the dialectical knot. Derrida only needs to pull on the threads:

> Artaud kept himself as close as possible to the limit: the possibility and impossibility of pure theater. Presence, in order to be presence and self-presence, has always already begun to represent itself, has always already been penetrated. [...] Underneath this side of the limit, and in the extent to which he wanted to save the purity of a presence without interior difference and without repetition (or, paradoxically amounting to the same thing, the purity of a pure difference), Artaud also desired the impossibility of the theater, wanted to erase the stage [...] (2001, 314–15)

> [Artaud] knew this better than any other: the "grammar" of the theater of cruelty, of which he said that it is "to be found," will always remain the inaccessible limit of a representation which is not repetition, of a re-presentation which is full presence, which does not carry its double within itself as its death, of a present which does not repeat itself, that is, of a present outside time, a nonpresent. The present offers itself as such, appears, presents itself, opens the stage of time or the time of the stage only by harboring its own intestine difference, and only in the interior fold of its original repetition, in representation. (313)

Artaud's project and its supposed failure thus seem merely to actualize an already well-worn dialectical moment: the impossible presence of the "one time only," its necessary retention in the concept which, through subordinating it to absent ideality, is also what ensures its return and its reality. The contradictions of the stage ultimately merely replay the originary scheme of Hegelian dialectic: the deictic paraphernalia of presence—the grammar of the "here" and of the "now"—can only be overturned in an immediate absence of content, in a vacancy of language which simply means that it disappears. Only the deadly power of the concept—of generality or repetition founded in ideality—can bring the phantom presence back to life and guarantee its return [*revenance*]. This was the initial driving force in Hegel's *Phenomenology of the Spirit*, which wrenched "sense certainty" from itself. This is also the scheme that Derrida applies to Artaud (as well as Bataille). If presence is to be real presence, it will always already have been penetrated by the concept:

> Pure expenditure, absolute generosity offering the unicity of the present to death in order to make the present appear as such, has already begun to want to maintain the presence of the present, has already opened the book and memory, the thinking of Being as memory. [...] Such, reduced to its

bloodless framework, is the matrix of the history of thought conceptualizing itself since Hegel.

The possibility of the theater is the obligatory focal point of this thought which reflects tragedy as repetition. (Derrida 2001, 311)

The stage—as presence exposed to the necessity of completion, or to the "before" of its repetition—ultimately merely reflects another theater and another more fundamental drama: the drama of the dialectic, which Hegel himself established as tragic.[9]

THE EFFECTIVENESS OF RITUAL

I now want to raise some doubts about the efficacy of Derrida's reading of Artaud. My first question is this: Is it so certain that Artaud's project is destined to impossibility from the beginning? Can we say without being misleading that the project strives toward its own impossibility, in fact desiring the effacement of what it intends to restore? We shall see.

The model on which Artaud depends in *Theatre and Its Double* is not merely the product of wishful thinking or some stillborn aim. That model is real, and it occupies an actual, concrete stage: it is the Balinese theater, which he discovered during a colonial exhibition in 1931. Balinese theater becomes for Artaud the very proof of the effectiveness of pure theater, the guarantee that an autonomous language of the stage can be established:

> But no one in the West has ever tried to bring this concept of pure theatre to life since we regard it as merely theoretical, whereas the Balinese Theatre offers us an outstanding production that surpasses any likelihood of recourse to words to clarify the most abstract subjects; it has invented a *language* of gestures to be spatially developed, but having no meaning outside it. (1974, 44–45, my emphasis)[10]

> In short the Balinese produce the idea of pure theatre with the greatest exactness, where everything in concept and production is valued and only exists through the degree of its objectification *on stage*. (38, emphasis in original)

The idea of a stage liberated from the text and from dialogue, and returned to the immanence of its own time, does not therefore arise from pure impossibility. It

9. "To think the closure of representation is to think the tragic: not as the representation of fate, but as the fate of representation" (Derrida 2001, 316).

10. Note also that Derrida's commentary hardly ever mentions this model of Balinese dances, even though it occupies an important place in—and several pages of—*Theatre and Its Double*.

has in fact already been realized. Or better still, it was always already real, given with the historical and geographic otherness of the East. Only Western theater history has succeeded in covering over, and ultimately rendering inconceivable, this effective autonomy of the stage.

Yet the model obliges some modification of the image of pure theater. Artaud's descriptions reveal the existence within Balinese theater of a will to hieratic fixation and codification that Derrida's commentary continually seeks to erase. Yes, the Balinese theater is liberated from the written work and from articulated language. But it remains fixed in its slightest details and thus attests to the existence and force of *another* code, derived from the stage itself. This is the proof that Balinese theater furnishes: a proof not of pure presence but rather of internal codification, which enables it to bypass writing and dialogue. Through its very regularity and precision, this codification offers the spectator something like the suggestion of a language, "a language to which we no longer seem to hold the key" (41):

> And by language I do not mean an idiom we fail to catch at first hearing, but precisely that kind of theatrical language foreign to every *spoken* language, where it seems a tremendous stage experience is recaptured, beside which our exclusively dialogue productions seem like so much stammering. (41)

> There is a horde of ritual gestures in it to which we have no key, seeming to obey a very precise, musical indication, with something added that does not usually belong to music and seems to be aimed at encircling thought, hounding it down [...] In fact everything in this theatre is *assessed* with loving, unerring attention to detail. Nothing is left either to chance or individual initiative. (41, my emphasis)

> Everything is just as *ordered* and just as impersonal with them. Not one rippling muscle, not one rolling eye does not seem to belong to a kind of *deliberate accuracy* directing everything, through which everything happens. (42, my emphasis)

This Balinese model of gestural precision and impersonal rigidity, which supports the very idea of language, reveals in Artaud a haunting of the unformed and approximate—of whatever is left unfixed and thus at the mercy of the moment, chance, or initiative—much more than it does a fear of repetition. And this coded precision can be summarized in one word: *ritual*.

My earlier discussion identified two defining features of ritual: (1) strict codification of the event; and (2) the belief in its symbolic and/or social efficacy.[11]

---

11. See above, 96.

I emphasized the second feature at some length. The event thereby seems to evade the indifferent repetition of the work as well as the transcendence of representation. Belief in the event's efficacy means it cannot be reduced merely to the function of representing. The event must become a presence with value by and for itself. In other words, the event is only "effective"—"magic," Artaud would say—because it is given in the irreplaceable singularity of its present. And this dimension of ritual is evident in Artaud, insofar as the ritual element of Balinese theater effects a kind of emptying of representation, an elimination of all the doubles that haunt the stage on which the work or *mimesis* is performed:

> This theatre does away with the playwright to the advantage of what in Western theatre jargon we call the producer. But the latter becomes a kind of organiser of magic, a *master of holy ceremonies* [...]
> There is something of a religious ritual ceremony about them [its productions], in the sense that they eradicate any idea of pretence, a ridiculous imitation of real life, from the spectator's mind. (43–44, my emphasis)

Ritual suspends both the commanding power of the work and the structure of representation. It gives the event a kind of autonomy that is the very condition of its efficacy and that seems to have always been lacking in Western theater. Be that as it may. I developed the point at some length earlier: Artaud merely confirms it. Here I want to revisit the first feature of ritual—its strict codification. This has so far been pushed to the margins of the event, and seen as a feature of the framework rather than the event as such.[12] However, strict codification is at the heart of what Artaud sees in the Balinese theater. The coded formalism of liturgy replaces the approximations of everyday life and the wanderings of subjectivity. The ritual framing of ceremony replaces the nudity of the scenic present. The coded ritual is the condition on which precise gesture becomes a language or, at least, proposes enigmatic signification.

In other words, then, our concept of ritual is dialectical. The belief in its symbolic and social efficacy returns us to the necessity of presence: no ritual can be removed from the effectiveness of the event, or be given in absence. But its codification also points up an internal demand for repetition, or rather repeatability: no ritual lacks rules or codes, which are de facto inscribed in the event within the horizon of its own iteration. To push this contradiction to its extreme, the notion of ritual implies that the event is always strictly *different* and yet also always strictly *the same*. Ritual thus merely radicalizes a tension

12. See above, 99–100.

inherent in all the arts of spectacle, a tension that the division between work and production, between text and interpretation, ordinarily obscures.[13]

Drawing out the implications of the model of Balinese theater, Artaud forcefully articulates this demand for fixation and codification that alone can inscribe the event in the horizon of a language and thereby remove it from the approximation of the present, from loss:

> The show will be *coded* from start to finish, like a language. Thus no moves will be wasted, all obeying a rhythm, every character being typified to the limit, each gesture, feature, and costume to appear as so many shafts of light. (75, my emphasis)

The conditions of this fixation, of coding, must now be explored.

HIEROGLYPHIC (ARCHE-)WRITING

I need to distinguish (perhaps artificially, certainly temporarily) between two questions: the question of the nature of stage language and the question of its possible writing. One implies analyzing the construction of the field of signifying idealities that form the framework of a shared theatrical practice (which might be called a theatrical *language*). The other implies discussion of whether or not it can be notated in traces that are external to the memory of the subject. Derrida has shown how porous this division between language and writing is. As unnotated trace of the categorial and the repeatable, all language can already be conceptualized on the model of inscription, in terms of what Derrida calls arche-writing [*archi-écriture*] (1976 [1967]). I will focus, then, on the idea that Artaud supplies a single term in answer to both questions (the distinction between those questions being ultimately difficult to maintain): he writes of the *hieroglyph*.

In one stroke, the hieroglyph successfully constitutes as language the gestural spatiality of the stage and guarantees the possibility of its notation:

> One could say the spirit of the most ancient hieroglyphics will govern the creation of this pure stage language. (Artaud 1974, 96)

---

13. Midway between ceremony and spectacle, Spanish bull racing presents a good example of this ritual radicalization. Because the *tercios* is strictly codified, the *corrida* is always the same, and the same even across its six iterations during the course of the afternoon. But, because the *toro bravo* represents a double principle of imponderability and consummation, the *corrida* is always different too, always presented in the irreplaceable singularity of its dated event. Thus, I would maintain that the *corrida* radicalizes a contradiction inherent in the arts of performance, but also cancels them out.

Moreover we must find new ways of recording this language [Stage language], whether these ways are similar to musical notation or to some kind of code.

As to ordinary objects, or even the human body, raised to the dignity of signs, we can obviously take our inspiration from hieroglyphic characters not only to transcribe these signs legibly so they can be reproduced at will, but to compose exact symbols on stage that are immediately legible. (72)

The hieroglyph is a kind of writing or, perhaps, a mnemonic. It allows some signs to be noted, inscribed outside of the fluid memory of subjects. It therefore makes it possible to reproduce theatrical language "at will," to repeat the event in another that is *the same* (which already implies a significant modification of Derrida's interpretation). Moreover, the hieroglyph is nonphonetic writing, radically alien to the interiority of the voice. It depends only on the spacing of a trace, only on the deposit of a gesture. Like all ideograms, this writing never returns traced spatiality to the interiority of the voice, such that it becomes for the stage—which depends only on the spacing of several bodies—the very model of language and significance. And the hieroglyph does not just—in keeping with its nature as writing—offer the hope of a notation; it also presents the very model of a corporeal language, through the gesturality that flourishes in it (Mallarmé already taught us this). Added to which, this writing is deliciously hieratic and seems, in its combination of the sacred and the mysterious, the only kind of writing equal to the ritual of the stage.

There are numerous passages about the hieroglyphic construction of the language of the stage. I will point out just a few:

We must take inflection into account here, the particular way a word is pronounced, as well as the visual language of things (audible, sound language aside), also movement, attitudes and gestures, providing their meanings are extended, their features connected even as far as those signs, making a kind of *alphabet* out of those signs. Having become conscious of this spatial language, theatre owes it to itself to organise these shouts, sounds, lights and onomatopoeic language, creating true *hieroglyphs* out of characters and objects, making use of their symbolism and interconnections in relation to every organ and on all levels. (68, my emphasis)

This tension between the alphabet and the hieroglyph, between the asemic writing of the voice and the gestural trace of the idea, continues to be problematic. I will discuss it further below. It remains the case that, given the textual omnipresence of the hieroglyph, alphabetical reference is barely mentioned.[14] The hieroglyph certainly remains the model for signifying gesture, for that significance that is entirely dependent on the mobile spatiality of a body, liberated from vocal interiority. This is what we already know from Balinese theater:

> In fact the strange thing about all these gestures, these angular, sudden, jerky postures, these syncopated inflections formed at the back of the throat, these musical phrases cut short, the sharded flights, rustling branches, hollow drum sounds, robot creaking, animated puppets dancing, is the feeling of a new bodily language no longer based on words but on signs which emerges through the maze of gestures, postures, airborne cries, through their gyrations and turns, leaving not even the smallest area of stage space unused. Those actors with their asymmetrical robes looking like moving *hieroglyphs* [. . .] (38–39, my emphasis)

> This show gives us a wonderful compound of pure stage imagery and a whole new language seems to have been invented in order to make it understood. The actors and costumes form true, living, moving *hieroglyphs*. And these three-dimensional *hieroglyphics* are in turn embellished with a certain number of gestures, strange signs matching some dark prodigious reality we have repressed once and for all here in the West. (44, my emphasis)

All well and good, but a lingering doubt emerges. The omnipresent references to the hieroglyph might be just another route to ineffectiveness, a way of presenting a model for realization that simultaneously cancels out any real possibility. What exactly do we know about hieroglyphs? How do they make sense? Is there meaning to attribute to them that does not depend on the values of a hermeticism that envelops and justifies everything? I think there is. The hieroglyph is not only a fantasy of resolution. It does not merely trace a path that is immediately blocked. It has its effective history in relation to the stage, as both language and notation. This is illustrated by two facts (of which Artaud was probably ignorant, not that this matters to my argument). Firstly, there is

14. Since I am discussing the contrast between alphabet and hieroglyph, I will say in passing how, paradoxically, Derrida does nothing with this hieroglyphic model as it appears in Artaud, other than to refer to the Freudian play of dreams that actually explains very little. Indeed, Derrida's text by its very logic minimizes the will to autonomous inscription revealed by Artaud's project. Once again, we are concerned with a desire for pure presence that cannot but confront its own contradictions. However, everything within Derrida's subsequent work suggests that another development of the idea of hieroglyph would have been possible here. I am thinking particularly of the preface to Warburton's essay on hieroglyphs (in Warburton 1737–41).

evidence that the body can function as hieroglyph on the Western stage, in the "druidic alphabet" that the *Ballet de Monseignuer le Duc de Vendosme* (1610) aimed to reproduce (see appendix, figure 18). And secondly, the numerous scores in Feuillet notation (which I will examine later) show how the graphic inscription of movement can assume the allure of the hieroglyph (see appendix, figure 7).[15] Both cases reveal a synthesis of language and its trace.

My argument depends, in short, on a simple discrepancy. The desire for autonomy of the stage does not mean giving it over to a state of pure abandon. The desire for scenic specificity—in other words, for an autonomous theatrical language—does not strictly equal the haunting of repetition, or a pure fantasy of singular presence. In the theater, the text can be impugned without the desire for *works* thus being excluded. The only constraint is the invention of a new writing, which Artaud acknowledges in magisterial fashion (and that I will examine in detail in part III of this book):

> When I say I will not put on written plays, I mean I will not act plays based on writing or words, rather, in the shows I intend to put on, the predominant part will be physical and could not be determined or written in normal word language [...]
>
> But [...] all this groping, all these experiments and jolts will nevertheless culminate in an *inscribed* composition, every last detail decided on and recorded by means of notation. Instead of taking place in an author's mind, this composition, this creation will take place in nature itself, in real space, and the final result will remain *as meticulous and calculated as any written work*, in addition to having enormous objective wealth. (85, my emphasis)

This brings us back to the work as an object that *survives*. I now need to examine the conditions of that survival, which necessarily involve inscription, although not necessarily inscription on paper.

15. See below, 173.

PART III

The Work (2)

Immanence and Ideality

> Discarded dance-programmes and faded flowers, concert programmes
> or dinner menus: they compose, there is no doubt, a literature all of their
> own, immortal with the immortality of a week or two.
>
> STÉPHANE MALLARMÉ
> *The Latest Fashion* [*La dernière mode*][1]

There seem to be two key dimensions to the concept of the work: the object is
both *public* and *durable*. Part II was focused on examining the first of these
dimensions, exploring the conditions under which dance accedes to the status
of work within the institution of spectacle, and how it comes to be exhibited
as autonomous artistic object. The question of autonomy (of the stage, and of
dance on that stage) brought us back, via an exploration of Artaud's arguments,
to the necessity of inscription and therefore to the question of durability or
survival. This second dimension of the work will be my focus here.

The hieroglyph—already encountered in Mallarmé's writings as well as
among seventeenth- and eighteenth-century theorists—represented for
Artaud the (half-real, half-dreamed) solution simultaneously enabling one to
understand gestural signification and guarantee its inscription. I will begin with
the topic of nonverbal and ideogrammatic inscription of movement, examining

---

1. Mallarmé (2004, 32). Extracts from Mallarmé's writings on fashion in the serial *La
Dernière Mode* also appear in Mallarmé (2001), translated by Patricia Terry and Mary-Ann
Caws.

different choreographic notation systems and their relative failure to withstand the passage of time. From this failure of writing in dance (or, at least, its lack of integration with practice), I will deduce the very particular ontological status of the choreographic work, analyzed in chapter 2. Finally, I will explore the various real modalities of work survival, whether these depend on the oral tradition or on material traces.

Chapter 1

Writing That Says Nothing

It seems clear that *presence* is of central concern in dance—whether it be the presence of the body to itself when executing movement, the presence of dancers in the fragile moment of scenic representation, or the co-presence of performers and choreographer in the shared time of creation. Less clear, and in need of further discussion, is whether this intimate connection between the dancer and presence can fully explain the surprisingly marginal and external character of dance notation— that is, the fact that notation appears to be a mere graphic accessory, leaving traces on paper and allowing fixation and archiving, while the essential core of what it aims to inscribe eludes its grasp.

Although numerous more or less well-developed notation systems have been available in dance since the end of the fifteenth century,[1] it remains a fundamentally oral art form, in which knowledge and dance works seem incapable of being transmitted except from person to person, body to body, via the transparency of present movement. Even choreographic invention and composition are subordinate to the imperative of presence: inconceivable in the abstract and solitary spaces of writing table and page, creation only happens through dialogue with the embodied presence of performers. In fact, unlike music and contrary to the meaning of the very term "choreography," dance-making practice has always been dissociable from the activities of writing and reading. Thus, today's "choreographer" is not someone who *writes* but rather someone who invents, demonstrates, and composes. Nor is the dancer someone who *reads* (a score) but rather someone who makes visible, reproduces, and also participates in invention. A third person *reads* and *writes* dance, namely, the notator.[2] While

1. For a comparative analysis in historical perspective of the different choreographic notation systems, see Ann Hutchinson-Guest (1989).

2. "Notator" is the modern term for the role that used to be more appropriately designated by "choreographer." "Choreographer," in the eighteenth century, did not mean the author of a

the Western musical tradition internalized its notation system to the point where *reading* and *writing* became synonymous with *playing* and *composing*, in dance the responsibility for reading and writing was delegated to this third person, alone conversant with and expert in the graphic system of notation. Musical writing, like literary creation, occurs in a solitary space. The space of choreographic notation has a surprisingly triangular structure, involving as it does three parties: the choreographer who demonstrates and proposes, the dancer who makes visible, and the notator who inscribes.

This functional externality of the notator is particularly evident today and is probably a consequence of a more fundamental externality. All dance practice—at least all *codified* dance—rests, like its notation, on the isolation and identification of discrete, nameable, and repeatable entities: all dance isolates steps, figures, positions; and the codification of a dance vocabulary, however implicit or transitory, is conditional on introducing discontinuities within the ensemble of possible human movements. For there to be dance and a dance vocabulary, the infinite continuum of possible movements must be carved up and distilled to extract identifiable elements: a *dégagé*, a *dévéloppé*, a *saut de basque*, a curve, a contraction, and so on. Graphic notation functions similarly, because the establishment of each sign works simultaneously to dissect, categorially isolate, and divide the continuum. In this way, one might say that all dance depends on a kind of arche-writing in Derrida's sense, a sort of primary articulation that introduces discontinuities within being and functions as a condition of recall and identification. The difficulty in the dance case is that the two forms of writing—the arche-writing of the movement vocabulary and the graphic writing of the notation—have never really been coextensive. The categorial divisions underlying the graphic signs have always remained external to, not superimposable on, the elements isolated by the choreographic vocabulary. More precisely, there has been no match between systems, except at brief historical moments.

---

ballet but the person capable of writing dances down. The author of a ballet, or rather the author of those elements of a ballet that consisted of dance, was then called a "ballet master." The two roles were neither mutually exclusive nor mutually inclusive. At the point where the term "choreographer" began to replace the term "ballet master," losing the purely graphic dimension of the former, a new term was needed that would be capable of accommodating and isolating this element of meaning: hence, the "notator." On the usage of the terms "choreographer" and "ballet master" in the eighteenth century, see Jean-Georges Noverre (1760) and particularly Letter XIII Translator's note: Also Letter XIII, 132–42, in Cyril W. Beaumont's translation, referenced here as Noverre (1930).

Raoul Auger Feuillet's *Chorégraphie* (1700a)[3] marks one, and probably the most striking, such moment. It records and articulates very clearly the vocabulary of *la belle danse*, the genre today known (perhaps inappropriately) as "baroque" dance. The categorial divisions effected by the system graphically reproduced the arche-writing of the style: the notation merely inscribed in signs the elements already isolated in the movement vocabulary. There was thereby every chance that the notation system would become truly integral to the practices it described, because what was spelled out on the page was no different than what was thought and made visible in practice. And, in fact, Feuillet notation was remarkably successful and very widely used. Published in 1700, *Chorégraphie* was reprinted just a year later and regularly republished thereafter. The book was translated into English as early as 1706 and appears to have been the object of a quasi-universal consensus for approximately sixty years.[4] From 1700, a collection of dance scores was included alongside the book's exposition of the notation system, a true repertoire of dances that everyone who knew how to decode the signs might teach himself and perform.[5] The book's success was such that a new collection of dances was published in 1706 (Feuillet 1706b). Ballet masters were thereby encouraged—whether it was a case of fixing or disseminating their work, or protecting their intellectual property—to themselves become "choreographers," noting down and inscribing their dances in pages of notational writing that could be appended to the musical score and to the *livret* text. Consequently, during this brief interval, it seems that dance all but became a real practice of writing and reading. The integration of the notational system with the practices described (the homogeneity of the categories each established) at least made this possible. However, this integration paid the price of a necessarily limited life span. Adhering to a given style allowed the system to become integrated with practice, but simultaneously condemned it to obsolescence as soon as that style itself disappeared,

3. See also the inventory of dances recorded in Feuillet notation compiled by Francine Lancelot (1996). Translator's note: Feuillet's *Chorégraphie* was first translated into English by John Weaver and published in 1706. Citations are from this translation (Feuillet 1706a) unless otherwise specified. See also Ralph (1985).

4. Some improvements and revisions were proposed but without making a significant impact. See, for example, Pierre Rameau (1725) or Goussier's article on "Chorégraphie" in Diderot and d'Alembert's *Encyclopédie*, in which Goussier mentions the notation system developed by a man called Favier. On the system generally, its English translations, and its integration into different dance treatises of the time (notably Tomlinson 1735), see Jean-Noël Laurenti (1991) and Catherine Kintzler (1997b).

5. See Feuillet (1700b).

as it effectively did in the 1750s.[6] This general fact of notation's dependence on a given style partially explains the extraordinary proliferation of dance notation systems that have succeeded one another since the end of the fifteenth century.[7] Each system articulated just one specific movement vocabulary and, because of this, was destined to die with that vocabulary, Feuillet notation being the most striking example of this adherence of system to style.

There remained the possibility—or rather the fantasy—of a truly universal system: that is, a system that would inscribe not one style or another, one vocabulary or another, but all possible movement, in general. Such a system would be capable of accommodating all dance styles but at a cost of remaining necessarily external to practice. The system could not be a system that could transcribe all possible movements except by establishing categorial divisions and elements of its own that were indifferent to the steps, figures, and positions of any given particular vocabulary. From this point on, learning notation's categories became a process external and secondary to the practice of dance itself, dissociated from the ordinary elements on which that practice depended. In short, the figure of the notator emerged. Labanotation,[8] the development of which coincides with the establishment of this notator role, is the perfect example of the universal system's externality. Kinetography—another name for Labanotation—achieved the capacity to accommodate any type of movement, whether choreographic or not. But it could do so only by abandoning all categories local to specific practices, all elements of choreographic arche-writing. It could do so only by establishing its own categories, by operating in pure freedom from and indifference to the "parochial" elements of current practice. The failure of Labanotation is thus the converse of that of Feuillet notation: not the adherence to a given style resulting in the system's imperviousness to history but the inevitable externality of any language with universal pretensions. Together with Benesh notation, Kinetography Laban is one of the two principle notation systems in use today. But that use remains constrained by the regime of externality here discussed. Very few choreographers and dancers

6. On this issue see Noverre (1930, 132–40), Letter XIII, where the author both argues against notation in principle and shows how the Feuillet system has become incapable of accommodating the growing complexity of gesture and movement.

7. Ann Hutchinson-Guest (1989) gives a chronology that identifies no fewer than sixty systems.

8. Rudolf Laban began to develop his movement notation system during the 1920s in Germany. The basic principles gave rise to two publications, Laban (1926) and (1928). The system was continually reworked, with the book *Principles of Dance and Movement Notation* published in 1956. A definitive and exhaustive account of the system can be found in the work of a pupil and collaborator of Laban's, Albrecht Knust (1979), and in Ann Hutchinson-Guest (1961). Jacqueline Challet-Haas (1999) is also pertinent.

know how to read or write a Laban score, and training in notation remains a spe-cialized and marginal domain within choreographic education. If the two types of failure are combined, the impossibility of dance writing's practical integra-tion thus takes the form of a trilemma: (1) in order for the activities of reading and writing to become inseparable from choreographic practice, the categorial divisions effected in the notation would have to be sufficiently close to elements in play within practice; (2) but for a real writing *tradition* to establish itself, the system would have to be sufficiently broad and open, in order to accommodate changing styles and genres while remaining relatively stable over time; (3) this "openness" of the system—a weaker term than "universality"—is only possible on condition of abandoning the categories local to the practice, which seems to contradict the first condition. Labanotation obeys conditions (2) and (3) to the exclusion of (1); Feuillet notation fulfills only (1) at the expense of (2) and (3). Such would be one, quasi-logical explanation for the impossibility of integrat-ing notational systems with dance practices.

It is, though, important to recognize that Labanotation also enjoyed a brief moment of integration. Mass dance and movement choirs (*Bewegungschöre*) in Germany in the 1920s, which sometimes brought together several thou-sand participants, would likely have been impossible to stage without notation being widely disseminated, making it possible to learn the dance at a distance.[9] Moreover, the system of movement analysis underlying Labanotation is not reducible to a mere descriptive device in Laban's work; he is concerned with a system of real human movement, the same system that is at issue in so-called modern or free dance that developed in the same period, and whose province is working beyond any code or established gestural vocabulary. "Modern" dance shared with Labanotation a common, universal space, which suddenly allowed the occurrence and recognition of ordinary movement, not drawn from exist-ing vocabularies and unprecedented in dance. In this sense, one might claim that notation's categories of thought were destined to become the categories of dance itself. Only Labanotation could rise to the challenge of this tabula rasa that became for dance the condition its modernity. In fact, the concepts of Labanotation were originally formed in line with this imperative: to be as much notational as choreographic. The notion of the *kinesphere*—the virtual sphere of possible movements of the limbs around the body—is as much a

---

9. "In conjunction with my friend Knust, I wrote the movement score of a festival play for a thousand performers, and sent the notation to sixty towns from which the performers at the festival meeting were drawn. As our scores had been studied by the sixty local groups, the whole thousand people were able to dance together at the first rehearsal, performing not only the main motives, but the whole rather elaborate choreography, lasting two hours, with very few mistakes or interruptions" (Laban 1956, 11).

condition of graphic mastery of space (from the kinesphere follows the analysis of space into twenty-seven fundamental directions resulting in twenty-seven corresponding signs) as an analytic support for improvisation and composition. But this original link between the two conceptual regimes, if indeed it ever existed, has been gradually eroded. Laban concepts have survived only through two completely disjoint means of preservation: through their deposit in what is implied by the notational code and through their veiled and distorting series of oral transmissions. One can certainly find today, in the work of particular choreographers and teachers, the residue of specific Laban concepts, but never in virtue of explicit links connecting those concepts back to Laban and which would give the notation system the obvious relevance to practice that it lacks.

Feuillet notation and Labanotation, therefore, fail in two different but symmetrical ways.[10] The consequences of this failure are not limited to the functional externality already discussed. At a deeper level, they threaten the very status of the choreographic work. The sporadic development of notation promised a radical shift, which would align choreographic works with the way musical and theatrical works typically operate, and would establish a principle of work identification independent of its material history of production and transmission. In short, notation made it possible to consider the choreographic work an ideal object that functions as a set of correct performance instances and thereby allows restaging and reconstructions outside of the linear series produced by oral transmission. Or, in other words (this time Nelson Goodman's), notation presaged the possibility of a shift from the autographic to the allographic.[11] Laban was particularly aware of these stakes and described them in terms of liberation from the relations of production. Notation thus heralds an end to the imperative of presence that weighs on the practice of dance, an end to the ties of intersubjective dependence that seem to be its foundation. To know how to read and to write is for dancers to liberate themselves from the contingent grip of the choreographer, and for the choreographer finally to create independently of the no less contingent presence of the dancers.[12] This emancipation motif

10. By failure, I do not mean that notation systems are incapable of describing what they set out to record: the Feuillet system and Labanotation describe what they notate perfectly well, the former confining itself to the baroque style otherwise known as "la belle danse," the latter accommodating the whole range of human body movement. I am concerned here, once again, with the historical (and probably conceptual) impossibility of their integration with practice.

11. For a discussion of these terms, see below, 197.

12. "The introduction of a dance notation system would mean a revolution in production and performance. Dancers would no longer be restricted to studying and performing their own inventions, or to relying on the imagination of a ballet master who happened to be at hand. Dancers could take their choice from the works of many gifted dance-authors, of whom they

is also implicit in Feuillet. As the subtitle of *Chorégraphie* suggests, notation means that "any person [. . .] may of himself easily learn all manner of Dances" (Feuillet 1706a).[13] This ambition is also evident in the simultaneous publication of collections of scores, for everyone to appropriate as he desired. However, the motif of emancipation through writing should be qualified. The use of notation to teach German choral dances in many ways marked the demise of practices of collective improvisation: originally based on the emergence of a communal dance form that developed through improvisation, the production of choral dances gradually became the mass performance of a transcendent text, imposed from the outside.[14] What is more, the establishment of Feuillet notation is inseparable from an attempt to codify and preserve a choreographic vocabulary. Pierre Beauchamp, who is usually considered the real inventor of the system published in *Chorégraphie*, recounts in his court case against Feuillet how Louis XIV personally entrusted him about thirty years before with inventing a form of writing for dance.[15] If these claims can be trusted, this would make the notational project roughly contemporaneous with Louis XIV's establishment in 1661 of the Académie Royale de la Danse, aimed at putting an end to the stylistic excesses of the dancing nobility.[16] The Académie was designed to subject the practice of dance to the control of eminent peers whose role was to codify the vocabulary and preserve it from all distortion. The graphic inscription of the code was conceived as one possible instrument of such control and thus appears eminently political. It suffices to recall that the *Lettres Patentes du Roi pour l'établissement d'une Académie Royale de la Danse* followed swiftly on the arrest and imprisonment of Nicolas Fouquet (France's superintendent of finances) after his fall from grace with Louis XIV. The Académie's founding

had no personal knowledge. Those who invent movement works which they are unable to or do not want to perform themselves could write them down and submit them to the judgment of the entire dancing world. The two professions viz. the dance-author and the dancer, would probably become separated" (Laban 1956, 14).

13. Translator's note: Weaver inserts a qualifier here, which marks an important difference between his presentation of the system as distinct from Feuillet's: the subtitle in full in Weaver's translation reads, "By which any Person, *who understands Dancing*, may of himself easily learn all manner of Dances" (my emphasis). See also Ralph (1985, 102–4).

14. On this issue, see Laure Guilbert (2000).

15. On the attribution of authorship of the Feuillet system to Beauchamp, see Laurenti (1991) and Jean-Marie Guilcher (1969). Beauchamp's authorship seems so generally accepted that Laban, for example, only ever refers to the system via a double attribution, Beauchamp-Feuillet (e.g., Laban 1956, 7).

16. On this issue, see the *Lettres patentes du roi pour l'établissement de l'Académie Royale de la Danse en la ville de Paris, mars 1661*, reproduced in Mark Franko (1993).

thus coincides with the moment when the young king took power into his own hands, assuming personal control of the monarchy. It is also notable that the Fête de Vaux-le-Vicomte both marked the downfall of Fouquet and appeared a high point of choreographic invention, including the performance of the first *comédie-ballet*, Molière's *Les Fâcheux*. The brilliance of the spectacle and the invention of new artistic configurations could no longer be the result of private initiatives and could only now flow from the state. Notation should be reinscribed in the context of this political monopolization of an art form and its rigid codification. The notion of dance's emancipation through writing is thus debatable in many respects. Or at least, that emancipation appears always capable of being reversed.

However one interprets the motif, the promise of change presaged by notation—emancipation from the relations of production and establishment of a true concept of the choreographic *work*—was never realized. The practice of dance remained bound up with presence, as demand or necessity. As a result, still today, choreography is not created on the page in the solitude of the study but directly on the individual bodies of selected performers working together in the collective space of the studio. Nor is it transmitted via the intermediary of a text that definitively fixes the work's criteria of identity and renders superfluous the indications of the original participants. Rather, dances are passed from one dancer to another, via personal contact, who "learns the role" from the previous performer. The ambivalence of the choreographic *work* derives from its striking dependence on the person. Neither autographic nor allographic, neither ephemeral improvisation nor ideal object, the choreographic work is repeatable from one night or one season to the next, its identity apparently preserved intact without being articulated via external means that transcend the embodied process, in a model or a text. The work certainly has an immanent generality that opens the space of repetition (in other words, the work rests on a distinction between essential and contingent properties); but neither that generality nor the distinction between essential and contingent properties exists outside of its embodiment by successive performers. The transcendent generality of the *class* of performances that are its members is thus contrasted with the immanent generality of the *series* in perpetual self-reproduction, a kind of generality that seems to exceed Goodman's distinction between the autographic and the allographic.[17] Thus the ambiguous status of the choreographic work,

17. A committed Goodmanian here might object that this notion of serial multiplication of artistic objects falls neatly under the same category as multiple autographic arts such as engraving and photography. I would respond that the serial repetition of choreographic works cannot be accommodated in the category of the autographic: it remains founded on a distinction between essential and contingent properties rather than being based on the mechanical

neither autographic nor allographic, is a direct consequence of the failure of notation, understood not as an incapacity to describe dance but as an incapacity to become integrated with practice.

My contention is that this failure of notation is no mere historical accident but the result of a fundamental conceptual tension. And rather than claiming, in the abstract terms I have tended to use thus far, that the supposed link between dance and presence nullifies every attempt at graphic inscription, I will argue that the difficulty consists in a more profound tension internal to the notational project. The argument about presence as it stands explains nothing and is insufficiently specific. What remains to be shown is how the imperative of presence is reflected at the level of notational discourse itself, and articulated therein as a contradiction. I will diagnose this contradiction in the way that the linguistic paradigm becomes a constant point of reference, such that *choreographic notation is said to stand to dance in the same relation as alphabetic writing stands to language.* I will maintain that this paradigm is essentially *dialectical.* It articulates two imperatives, the "alphabetic" (or analytic) and the "semantic" (or discursive), imperatives that risk exposure as completely contradictory when interpreted in domains outside of verbal language. The "alphabetic" imperative demands that manifest choreographic units be parsed into simple elements that are capable of recombination in characteristic ways. For this to be possible, dance movements must be treated as neutral, nonsignifying entities, similar to phonemes. By contrast, the "semantic" imperative requires that graphic inscription be more than a combination of signs which records elements that themselves do not signify: it requires that writing, over, above, and through the composition of phonemic elements, properly inscribe *discourse.* To obey this second imperative, choreographic notation must be considered like the writing of language as a "second-order symbolic system": that is, a system that records signs and not things, a system that doubles another which itself already signifies. The analogy with verbal language must thus be taken seriously, and the claim made that dance is a language in its own right, not merely obeying the alphabetic imperative but producing signification and articulating discourse. But this claim can apparently only be sustained by ignoring the alphabetic imperative, neutralizing elements of the language and treating them as pure things. In light of this difficulty, I will maintain that only the alphabetic imperative is indispensable to the establishment of a choreographic notation,

---

reproduction of the unique characteristics of a prototype. However, insofar as this division between properties remains inextricable from, and indeed incorporates, the material history of a work's lineage, it is also impossible to classify dance as allographic. In short, as I argued above, the choreographic work is neither autographic nor allographic, a point that I shall seek to further justify in the chapters to follow.

and that this imperative is, ultimately, dissociable from any reference to the verbal linguistic paradigm. The alphabet of verbal language is but one example among many of a symbol system based on parsing entities into simple elements and then recombining them in characteristic ways. It likely remains a privileged and singularly complex example because the semantic imperative also operates therein: in fact, the term "alphabet," rather than privileging either one of the two imperatives, refers to their problematic and unusual articulation,[18] though as suggested the alphabet remains but one example of a symbol system. Below, I will test my thesis about the necessary and sufficient character of the analytic imperative with reference to Feuillet notation.

Because only the analytic imperative is necessary to notation, I will maintain as a corollary that the paradigm of verbal language generally is most often referenced in contexts where the claims are asserted of the semantic imperative over the alphabetic. That is, such reference occurs as part of an effort to discredit a mode of writing that parses danced movement into abstract symbols but fails to grasp what that movement essentially signifies. To invoke the linguistic paradigm is most often a way of saying that notation succeeds in fixing an *alphabet* of movement, but which in the process is condemned to ignorance concerning the discourse it generates.[19]

This contradiction revealed in references to phonetic writing appears for the first time in an *external* critique, namely, Jean-Georges Noverre's argument against Feuillet notation, the key points of which depend upon the linguistic analogy. The contradiction appears a second time *internal* to notational discourse itself, at the center of Rudolf Laban's writing. Constantly referencing the linguistic paradigm as he does, Laban is forced to articulate *two* systems of notation: standard Labanotation, which obeys the analytic and descriptive

---

18. It is appropriate to highlight an ambiguity here. The analogy invoked (that "choreographic notation should be to dance what alphabetic writing is to language") can be read in two different ways. Either the term "alphabet" refers only to the analytic parsing of nonsignifying phonemes (this being what characterizes alphabets as distinct from ideogrammatic writing or syllabaries: see Havelock 1976). Or, "alphabet" designates globally the product of phonetic writing, which, by virtue of the double articulation phoneme/morpheme, is in fact a definitive inscription of verbal signification. In the first case, the analogy implies that choreographic notation is strictly indifferent to what the movements recorded signify. In the second, notation is obliged to allow meaning to be read off of the movement it inscribes. To clarify things, I will use "alphabet" in its sense of simple analytic parsing and use the term "linguistic paradigm" to mean the general imperative of marrying analysis and sense, phoneme and morpheme, an imperative that merely applies the double articulation characteristic of language to other domains.

19. In line with the previous note, it is entirely typical for an alphabet to be oblivious to the discourse it inscribes. It is simply our habituation to the linguistic paradigm, the double articulation uniting analysis and sense, that makes this dissociation appear strange.

imperative, and Effort notation, which seeks to accommodate the semantic and discursive, aiming finally to capture the *sense* of movement that escapes alphabetic parsing and is indexed to the unavoidable presence of an *expressive* singularity.

FEUILLET: FIGURE AND CHARACTER

Feuillet notation consists in the articulation of two heterogeneous symbol systems: those of *figure* and *character*. The very title of *Chorégraphie* (*Chorégraphie ou l'art de décrire la danse par caractères, figures et signes démonstratifs*) should not mislead: the third term *signes* (signs), which actually disappears when the title is reprised on page 1, is merely a general noun that subsumes the previous two terms.[20] The adjective *démonstratif* functions in distributive fashion, applying equally to figures and to characters in an essentially ambiguous usage. The *demonstrative* is both that which is represented directly in the iconic mode of the figure, and that which is inscribed in the symbolic and combinatorial representation of the character.

Figure is, in the first instance, the graphic representation of the course taken by the dancers (or the *tract*), and thus a signifier. But it is also the floor pattern traced onstage when the dancers follow that course, and hence a signified.[21] For the two to overlap, the space of the page must be a direct projection of the space of the room. This room has an "up," a "down," a "right." and a "left," and the same is true of the page, which renders the graphic figure a trace in miniature of the pathway or tract (see figures 6 and 7). It is important, then, when reading the score, to ensure that the book is always held in the same orientation: if it moves through even a quarter turn, its projective relation to the room is immediately disrupted.[22] The space of the page is thus referenced to

20. Translator's note: Weaver's translation omits this third term: *Orchesography, or the Art of Dancing by Characters and Demonstrative Figures* (Feuillet 1706a, title page).

21. "Figures are *Tracts* made by *Art*, on which the *Dancer* is to move" (Feuillet 1706a, 2, emphasis in original; see Feuillet 1700a, 2, for original French text). "The Line on which the Dances are described, I call the *Tract*. Which *Tract* serves for two Ends, the first to direct the *Steps* and *Positions*, and the other to represent the Figure of the Dance" (1706a, 4, emphasis in original; see Feuillet 1700a, 4, for original French text).

22. "You must understand, that each Page, on which the *Dance* is described, represents the *Dancing-Room*; and the four Sides of the Page, the four Sides of the *Room*, viz. the upper part of the Page, represents the upper end of the *Room*; the lower part, the lower end; the right side of the Page, the right side of the *Room*; and the left side, the left [...] You must observe always to hold the upper end of the Book against the upper end of the *Room*; and whether the *Dance* have any *Turning* in it or not, you must carefully avoid removing the Book from the Situation [...] When any *Steps* are made without *turning*, or in *turning* quite round,

the objective coordinates of the room, and not to the subjective position of the body as it orients itself in space. The notation inscribes an objective pathway—a *figure*—not a series of personal orientations (such as "go right," "turn left," and "move straight ahead"). As well as the skill needed to maintain the book in the correct orientation, reading and performing the movement thus implies a process of translation, similar to that required when orienting oneself from a map.[23] What is represented on the page only by its spatial results, by the pathway, must be translated into a series of subjectively oriented intentions. And since the room functions as the point of reference rather than the dancer's own body, what figures on the page as a movement forward might well in reality be a step back or a step to the side. This planimetric feature of notational representation makes it important to specify in more detail what in the *figure* is directly "figurative." The figure is clearly the image and direct projection of the floor pattern, but it is also an image that no one actually sees or otherwise experiences. Leaving aside for the moment the question of the subjective orientation of the dancers, it seems that what the spectators effectively *see* during the representation is neither the figure nor even the path but the temporal unfolding of a pathway. The *figure* is what captures this unfolding in the simultaneity of a graphic form—an *image*—which annihilates the temporal dimension. Moreover the *figure* is the projection of a nonexistent point of view, a point of view that belongs to no one and has become known since Desargues

then both sides of the Book must be held with both Hands; but in *turning* a quarter round, half round, or three quarters round, it will be necessary to take more Care, because it will be difficult to *turn*, unless the Book turns also; yet this must be absolutely avoided; for if the Book moves out of its Scituation [*sic*], it will be impossible to comprehend the *Steps* therein describ'd" (1706a., 33–35, emphasis in original; see Feuillet 1700a, 33–34, for original French text). Immediately following this passage, Feuillet supplies some rather complicated rules for turning without moving the book. Thus, to perform a quarter turn to the right, one should place the left hand on the upper edge of the book, and the right hand on the bottom edge. For a half turn, the left hand is placed on the right side, and the right hand on the left side, and so on.

23. On the relation between cartographic representation and subjective orientation, see for example Merleau-Ponty (1965 [1942]): "The difficulty of a pure description of the itinerary is of the same order as that of reading a map or orienting oneself on a plan [. . .] The purely visual sketch demands that we represent the itinerary for ourselves from a bird's eye view, from a point of view which has never been ours when we traversed it; it demands that we be capable of transcribing a kinetic melody into a visual diagram, of establishing relations of reciprocal correspondence and mutual expression between them" (117–18). Thanks to Maël Renouard for this reference, as well as for the invaluable information about projective geometry in the seventeenth century (on this issue, see Renouard 2001).

and Leibniz as the "geometral."[24] To see the figure actually being traced, one would need to place oneself directly above the dancers, exactly perpendicular to them, in the ideal and infinitely distant space of the geometral; in other words, at the point at infinity that is the meeting place of the orthogonal lines derived from the plan.[25]

That no one ever sees the figure does not, however, render it a purely artificial device or mere abstraction. The adoption of a planimetric form of representation corresponds with the principles of an actual choreographic tradition. Feuillet's *figure* is the distant echo of a regime of choreographic signification that reached its height around a hundred years earlier. At the turn of the sixteenth century, the central function of a ballet was to represent symbolic and geometric figures on the floor of the space. At that time, the audience was given leisure to decode these figures not from the frontal perspective familiar today but from raised galleries surrounding the room. Dance in this period was conceived as an immanent writing and graphic inscription of symbols. The most striking example is probably the *Ballet de Monseigneur le duc de Vendosme* (1610), which has remained famous for its representation of a "druidic alphabet" in which each choreographic figure constitutes a veritable scenic hieroglyph. This geometric, graphic function of the ballet retained its currency at least to some extent during the first half of the seventeenth century, until the gradual raising of the stage and frontal organization of the audience rendered impossible this kind of decoding.[26] By 1700, the figure had long ceased to be visible onstage, yet it still secretly determined the framework of the Feuillet notation system.

24. Translator's note: French mathematician Girard Desargues (1591–1661) is considered one of the founders of projective geometry and coined the term "geometral" to describe the viewpoint discussed here.

25. Noverre himself uses the term *géométral* in order to characterize the way Feuillet notation represents space (Noverre 1760, 382, 383). Translator's note: Beaumont translates the term *plan géométral* as "geometrical plan" and "ground plan" in the respective instances of its use by Noverre (Noverre 1930, 138).

26. On the "geometric" dance of the late sixteenth and early seventeenth centuries, then still termed "horizontal" dance, see McGowan (1963, chapter 2) and Franko (1993, chapter 1). Besides the *Ballet de Monseigneur le duc de Vendosme* already mentioned, typical examples include the *Ballet des polonais* (1573) and the *Ballet Comique de la Reine* (1581). On the disappearance of the geometric function of dance, see McGowan (1963): "This horizontal dance remained in fashion among the ballets given at the French Court for as long as performers were able to move down from the stage to dance in the room of the theater. It disappeared around 1640 when the stage was raised, rendering the geometry of the steps invisible to the spectators on the ground" (37).

It should be noted, however, that a strict equivalence between graphic figure and pathway followed by the dancers does not always obtain. The figure
recorded on the page must also, parallel to directly representing the path, show
the passage of time: bar lines placed at regular intervals on the tract mark a
correspondence with the bars in the musical score, such that there appears a
perfect equivalence between spatial displacement and the passage of time. This
equivalence is necessarily compromised when dancers no longer move *through*
space but dance on the spot. In this case, the graphic figure ceases temporarily
to function as a pathway and merely shows a succession of gestures in time:

> You must resolve in what part of the *Room* the *Dance* is to begin, and there
> place the beginning of the *Tract*; then trace out the *Figure*, and mark thereon
> the *Position*; then describe the *Steps*, as I have shown in the foregoing exam-
> ples [...] Altho' the *Tract* serves generally for the [*sic*] explaining the *Figure*
> of the Dance, yet it often happens that many *Steps* are to be perform'd in the
> same Place, and then (as I have shown before) the *Tract* is to have regard only
> to the *Steps*. This *Tract* is only a borrow'd *Tract*, and which may be drawn any
> way, as shall be most convenient. As for Example, from A to B, altho' the *Tract*
> is drawn out in length from A to B, the *Dancer* nevertheless removes not from
> A, which may also be well understood by the *Steps*, which are from A to B,
> which can only be perform'd in the same place. (Feuillet 1706a, 57–58)[27]

Steps must then be inscribed on this tract and general figure. The steps give the
pathway its real efficacy and temporalize the figure, the pathway itself being
what enables figure and steps to be articulated:

> The *Tract* serves for two Ends, *viz.* first, on which to describe the *Steps* and
> *Positions*; and secondly, for the Direction of the *Figure* of the *Dance*. (Feuillet
> 1706a, 53)[28]

27. See Feuillet (1700a, 103–4), for original French text. See also Feuillet (1706a, 53): "I shall
now add, that when in *Dancing*, several *Steps* are to be perform'd in the same place, the *Tract* is
then to be respected only as the Conductor of the *Step*, and not in Relation to the *Figure*; but
where the *Steps* move continually from one place to another, then the *Tract* is to be observ'd,
not only for the Description of the *Steps*, but also for the *Figure* of the *Dance*" (Feuillet 1700a,
85, for original French text). As regards the connection between the tract and the musical bar,
see Feuillet (1706a, 47): "The *Barrs* or *Measures* in *Dances*, must be mark'd in like manner with
those in *Musick*, viz. with little *Barrs* crossing the *Tract*, which are to agree with those of the
Tune" (Feuillet 1700, 87, for original French text). Translator's note: Weaver's translation alters
the original by omitting a qualifying phrase at the end of this passage: in Feuillet's text, the
little bars crossing the tract "représentent les mêmes barres qui tranchent les cinq règles de la
Musique, dont les entre-deux seront autant de mesures."

28. See Feuillet (1700a, 4), for original French text.

At first glance, the *step* appears like a figure or pathway in miniature, being the projection on the floor of the line traced by the foot during a transfer of weight. The step sign is thus governed by a mode of iconic representation, similar to that which characterizes the *figure*. At least, that is what is implied in the graphic nature of the step signs:

> A *Step* is known by the character following, *viz.* a black Spot [...], representing the *Position* of the *Foot*, the Line drawn from that Spot, [...] shewing the *Motion*, *Figure*, and *Largeness* of the *Step*, [...] and lastly, by a small side Stroke join'd to the End of the Line [...]. Altho' *Steps* made use of in Dancing, are almost innumerable, I shall nevertheless reduce them to five, *which serve to express the different Figures the Leg makes in moving.* These I shall call, a *straight plain Step*, an *open Step*, a *circular* or *round Step*, a *waving Step*, and a *beaten Step.* (Feuillet 1706a, 9, my emphasis)[29]

Thus, the straight plain step is represented by a straight line (vertical or horizontal, according to whether the step is forward, backward, or to the side). The open step is represented by a semicircle, the circular step by a kind of corkscrew line, the waving step by a zigzag line, and so on. Step signs are like small figures, accidentals qualifying the main figure, and likewise require to be read as images (see figure 8). However, the fact that they designate *categories* of step ("plain step," "open step," and so on) and not individual movements means that they already function as *characters*, in other words as signs that are syntactically (graphically) and semantically disjoint.[30] A straight line can be more or less straight, a curved line more or less curved, and will still designate in each case whatever is subsumed under the category "plain step" or "open step."

Despite these indications of an incipient character-based system, *step* signs still appear to function as global designations. They do little more than abbreviate verbal descriptions, in the manner of earlier systems for recording dance, as in the *Manuscrit des basses-danses de Marguerite d'Autriche*, for example, or the system proposed by André Lorin a few years before Feuillet.[31] Only at the level of accidentals on the step itself, that is, those small

---

29. See Feuillet (1700a, 9), for original French text.

30. This recalls two of the criteria proposed by Nelson Goodman (1976) in his theory of notation, and which he applies himself to the particular case of Labanotation.

31. The *basse danse* form was current from the beginning of the fifteenth century to the middle of the sixteenth century. It is based on five basic steps (*révérence, simple, double, branle,* and *reprise*), abbreviated to the following letters: R, s, d, b, r. This enabled the recording of dances simply by combining the letters. This notation system, which appears in the *Manuscrit des basses-danses de Marguerite d'Autriche* (1460, reproduced by the Library of Congress), also

additional signs that further specify it, do the analytic parsing and modus operandi of a character-based notation really emerge. The step-sign merely indicates a transfer of weight, but one that might be effected in a number of different ways. It could, for example, be (recalling the global designations of contemporary practice) a *jeté*, a *coupé*, a *contretemps*, a *pas de bourré*, or a *cabriole*. These are the "natural" units that notation parses into simpler elements that can be recombined as characters. These elements and the signs attributed make notation lose whatever iconic elements might still be evident in the way steps are represented:

> To a *Step* may be added these following Marks, *viz. Sinking, Rising, Springing* or *Bounds, Capers, Falling, Sliding, holding the Foot up, Pointing the Toes, placing the Heel, turning a quarter Turn, a half Turn, a three quarter Turn,* and a *whole Turn*. (Feuillet 1706a, 11)[32]

Sinking (*le plié*) is represented by a short diagonal line placed on the step sign ("a little stroke inclining towards the little black Head"); *rising* (*l'élévé*) by a straight line ("a little straight stroke upon the step"); *springing* (*le sauté*) by two straight lines; *capers* (*la cabriole*) by three straight lines (see figure 9), and so on. Moreover, these new signs show that the line representing the step is itself neither a simple nor a continuous element. It actually has three zones corresponding to the three moments of the step: a beginning (before the transfer of weight), a middle (during the transfer), and an end (after the transfer).[33] The meaning of the global sign will depend on whether the sink or spring occurs at the beginning or end of the line. A *contretemps* and a *jeté* (or *bound*) are composed of the same elementary signs (a step modified by a sink and a spring) but differ according to the moment (or place) where that modification is introduced. A *contretemps* is a step in which the jump is effected before the transfer, while in the *jeté* the jump occurs at the end. A simple displacement of the sign, then, can represent very elegantly and economically two steps with little in common in the everyday context of their performance.

This recomposition of "natural" units via their simple graphic signs has a twofold aim: to designate a particular step unequivocally by means of a single

appears in an anonymous fifteenth-century treatise, *L'Art et Instruction de bien dancer*. On Lorin's notation system, see Guilcher (1969).

32. See Feuillet (1700a, 11), for original French text.

33. "How to place the Marks in their proper Order. It is necessary first to know, that a Step has three Divisions, viz. a Beginning, Middle, and End" (Feuillet 1706a, 14; Feuillet 1700a, 13, for original French text).

sign and to elucidate its structure analytically. Its goal is not just to find an adequate abbreviation but really to bring to light, through the device of the sign, a kind of structural truth. This graphic cross-referencing of designation and analysis corresponds very closely with the project of the character-based notation system. The "Cartesian" spirit of Feuillet notation has often been noted, steeped as the system is in order and method.[34] Yet the connection with Leibniz seems to me much more pertinent, if only because of the strange alliance of the geometral with the character-based that can be read in Feuillet. More generally, in my view, the system invokes the global space of classical mathesis, which from Leibniz onward is also a mathesis of qualitative orders. Feuillet notation aims at discovering, by the graphic and analytical device of the sign, the real *nature* of choreographic entities; it seeks to bring to light the real structural affinities that organize and link steps, at a more profound level than that of their empirical grouping and routine combinations. It thus assumes implicitly the project of the classical episteme, as discussed by Michel Foucault:

> An arbitrary system of signs must permit the analysis of things into their simplest elements; it must be capable of decomposing them into their very origins; but it must also demonstrate how combinations of those elements are possible, and permit the ideal genesis of the complexity of things. [. . .] there exists a single, necessary arrangement running through the whole of the Classical episteme: the association of a universal calculus and a search for the elementary within a system that is artificial and is, for that very reason, able to make nature visible from its primary elements right to the simultaneity of all their possible combinations. In the Classical age, to make use of signs is [. . .] an attempt to discover the arbitrary language that will authorize the deployment of nature within its space, the final terms of its analysis and the laws of its composition. (1989 [1966], 68–69)[35]

This inscription of notation within the classical episteme is confirmed by the very particular status Feuillet accords the *table*. Before it makes possible the writing of dancing, notation must enable a reasoned classification of steps. Between Feuillet's account of the notation system and the collection of scores he supplies is placed a series of *tables* devoted to each of the most important step categories bequeathed by the choreographic tradition, and which aims to reorganize those steps in terms of their graphic truth, or, in other words, analytically. Thus, one finds a "Table of Courant Movements," a "Table of

---

34. See, for example, Laurenti (1991).

35. See Foucault (1966, 76–77), for original French text.

Half Coupees," a "Table of Coupees," a "Table of Bounds or Tacs," a "Table of composd Hops, or Contretemps," and so on. The tables are organized according to a principle of growing complexity. They begin with a basic step—a simple bound or contretemps—to which the gamut of its possible variations is progressively added by graphic combination. Affinities thus emerge that remain obscure within practice itself, and it even becomes possible to invent steps that are not in actual use. The essential link between mathesis and *taxonomia*, as described by Foucault (1989, 79–84),[36] is thereby here confirmed (see figures 11 and 12).

Feuillet notation thus responds well to the analytic imperative identified earlier. Parsing choreographic units into simple elements, it functions as a character-based system or as a kind of alphabet. But it can only do so in virtue of complete indifference to the semantic imperative: it remains an alphabet that records no actual *discourse*. The units of *la belle danse* are treated as mere things among other mere things, which do not signify and are capable of being broken down and recombined at will. It is not just a question of the analytic imperative being dissociable from the semantic (Feuillet does not once mention the linguistic paradigm that grounds their association) but more radically of the suspension of *meaning* being a condition of the very possibility of analysis. Thus is bracketed the whole network of correspondences and significations that made dance during the Renaissance, and still in the age of reason, a "mute rhetoric," or figured allegorical representation, or even a scenic inscription of the harmony of the spheres.[37] For Feuillet notation to become established, steps and gestures had in some sense to be neutralized, subtracted from all pretension to signify, and treated as mere things. A vocabulary of steps rather than a repertoire of meanings, a description of figures rather than the writing of a language, the Feuillet system appears as an alphabet without discourse. And around sixty years later, Noverre highlighted precisely this paradox when using the linguistic paradigm as the very agent of his critique.

36. See Foucault (1966, chapter 3, section VI): "'Mathesis' et 'Taxinomia,'" for original French text.

37. The phrase "mute rhetoric" is drawn from Lucien's *De Saltatione* and can be found in practically all dance treatises from Arbeau (1589; see also 1967) to Ménéstrier (1972 [1682]) and beyond. The cosmic significance of ballet is omnipresent in the Renaissance and still evident in classical age, for example, in Mersenne (1636), Traité des Chants, Proposition XXII: "I would say firstly that one can make ballets that will represent and teach Astronomy." This representational and didactic function of ballet moreover allows dance to be considered a truly universal language: "I would add that dances by which will be represented the sciences and the liberal Arts, will be as well received and understood by the Chinese and by all other nations as by the French, and consequently they will be able to function as a *common, natural and universal language*, by means of which commerce, mutual intelligences and reciprocal friendship might be established and maintained in the world" (160, my emphasis).

NOVERRE: LETTER AND SPEECH

Indeed, Noverre aims in his *Lettres sur la danse et sur les ballets* (1760) to establish a new order of choreographic signification, an order in which dance is indexed to the unmediated expression of the passions rather than the representation of figures and signs.[38] Recalling an expression used by de Louis de Cahusac (1754), he calls this new order *danse en action*:[39]

> Action, in relation to dancing, is the art of transferring our sentiments and passions to the souls of the spectators by means of the true expression of our movements, gestures and features. (Noverre 1930, 99)[40]

This *danse en action* can only be understood against a backdrop of radical dualism, opposing the mechanical and the expressive, the mute and the speaking, the physical and the mental:

> Dance properly so called confines itself to the mechanics of steps and arm movements; as a result, it can only be regarded as a profession in which success is measured solely by skill, agility, vigor, and the height of elevation of the dancer's *cabrioles*. But when pantomimic action is united with all of these mechanical movements, dance acquires a vividness which renders it interesting; it *speaks*, it *expresses*, it paints the passions and is thus worthy of being ranked in the class of imitative arts.[41]

38. Even during Noverre's own lifetime, there were several editions of his *Lettres sur la danse et sur les ballets*, originally published in 1760. The author significantly expanded and reworked the text throughout his career. In 1803, twenty new letters were added to the original fifteen to create a second volume (published as volume 2 of Noverre 1803). The final edition (Noverre 1807) revises the whole significantly, notably by changing the order of the letters and giving each a title. A reproduction of the 1760 and 1807 editions is accessible online via the Bibliothèque nationale de France and the website http://www.gallica.bnf.fr; a facsimile of the 1803 edition has also been recently published (Noverre 2012). The English translation by Cyril Beaumont (Noverre 1930) is focused on the fifteen letters of the 1760 edition but follows the text of 1803. Citations are from Beaumont's translation (Noverre 1930) except where otherwise specified.

39. On Cahusac's concept of *danse en action*, see Kintzler (1997a). Translator's note: No English translation of Cahusac's treatise has yet been published.

40. Noverre 1760, Letter X, 262; Noverre 1803, vol. 1, Letter X, 130; Noverre 1807, vol. 1, Letter XXVII, "De l'accord du Geste avec la Pensée et les Mouvements de l'Ame," 389.

41. Noverre 1803, vol. 2, Letter VII, 72; Noverre 1807, vol. 1, Letter IX, "Renaissance de l'art de la dance," 125. Translator's note: this passage does not appear in Beaumont and is translated here directly from the French text. The same applies to the following quotations, referenced in notes 42 and 43 below.

I will divide dance into two categories: the first is *mechanical dance or execution*; the second is *pantomimic dance or dance in action*.
The first only speaks to the eyes, charming them with the symmetry of
movements, with the brilliance of the steps and with musical variety; with
the body's elevation, self-assurance, firmness, the elegance of attitudes, the
nobility of positions, and the refined grace of the person. This only represents the *material* part of dance.

The second, called dance *in action*, is, if I dare express myself in this way,
the *soul* of the first; it gives the mechanical dance its life and expression, and
in seducing the eye it captivates the heart, and draws it into the most vivid
emotions. This is what makes art what it is.[42]

Dance is made to *speak* because previously it was *mute*.[43] As long as the sole preoccupation was combining *steps*, maintaining *positions*, and respecting the complexity of *figures*—as Feuillet instructed—dance remained trapped within the
purely mechanical, visually pleasing certainly but expressing nothing. *Meaning*
could only be bolted on from outside, by introducing a *livret* or dialogues:

It is only nowadays that the title of ballet has been applied to those figure
dances which should be called *divertissements*; in former times the name
of ballet was lavishly bestowed on all the splendid festivals given at the different courts of Europe. The examination I have made of all these festivals
has persuaded me that the title of ballet accorded them was a misnomer. I
have never see in them *danse d'action*; long recitatives were introduced in
order to acquaint the spectator with what the performance was intended to
convey—a very clear and convincing proof of their incompetence, as well
as of the complete insignificance and lack of expression in their movements
[...] In the reign of Louis XIV, recitatives, dialogues and monologues
equally served as an explanation of the dancing which could not yet speak
for itself. *Its feeble and inarticulate sounds* had need to be supported by music
and explained by poetry [...]. (Noverre 1930, 50–51)[44]

42. Noverre 1803, vol. 2, Letter XI, 106; Noverre 1807, vol. 1, Letter X, "Division de la
danse," 135.

43. "I taught mute dance to articulate and express the passions and affections of the soul"
(Noverre 1803, vol. 2, Letter VII, 71; Noverre 1807, vol. 1, Letter IX, "Renaissance de l'art de la
danse," 124).

44. Noverre 1760, Letter VII, 114–16; Noverre 1803, vol. 1, Letter VII, 58–59; Noverre 1807,
vol. 1, Letter XXI, "Défauts de nos premiers ballets," 264–65, my emphasis.

This characterization of the *ballet de cour* is reductive in a number of ways. The *ballet de cour* of Louis XIV aimed at *imitation* just as much as Noverre's *danse en action*. Ménestrier (1972[1682]) (for example) emphasizes continually that dance is an imitative art. It is simply that the very concept of imitation was revolutionized in the shift from Ménestrier to Noverre. If the *ballet de cour* could only imitate through the support of annexed representational elements such as costumes, masks, decor, and text, this was precisely because it did not seek to show either individuals or affect, but to produce symbolic figures, instantaneous *signs*, which spectators would take pleasure in decoding and understanding. Thus one could, without risking a failure of verisimilitude, dance the Wind, the Sun, Anger, Peace, or the movement of the Stars. This was inconceivable for Noverre. The court ballet was not concerned with expressive utterance, with emotion shown in its temporal development, but with an image offered as a snapshot to be decoded, as discussed very clearly by Cahusac in the critique he formulates of the *ballet de cour*:

> In the *grand ballet*, there is much movement but no action. Dance there can easily depict by means of costume, steps and attitudes national characters and mythological or historical personae; but the manner of its depiction is like ordinary painting which can only render a single moment, and theater is designed by its very nature to represent a succession of moments, from which is produced a living and unfolding picture which resembles human life. [...] The Furies in a specific *entrée*, for example, can probably by quick steps, hurried jumps and violent twists depict the anger which excites them, but this is only a general trait, an episodic brushstroke. The consequence was that one saw the Furies and nothing more.[45]

Thus, the *ballet de cour* either rests content with the pure, nonsignifying virtuosity of its steps, or is developed through heterogeneous signs in which the dance is only one of several elements. In neither case does dance *speak*. To

---

45. Cahusac (2004), part 2, book III, chapter 4, "Vices du grand ballet," 196–97 [translated here directly from the French]. The pictorial and instantaneous characteristic of choreographic signification is remarked upon already in Ménéstrier (1972). "The same persona should only appear once, or at least least only appear once in a given costume. This is because Ballet represents solely through figures and movements, and when a persona appears a second time, he expresses nothing new as regards the figure and the movements must be varied such that one can understand whatever he represents that is new. Tranlsation here is directly from the French" (141–42).

make dance speak, for Noverre, is to succeed in transfiguring its mechanical basis, presenting combinations of a kind that allow discourse miraculously to emerge. And here, once again, appears the metaphor of writing, the image of the alphabet and of language:

> I admire the skill of the human machine, I render justice to its strength and ease of movement, but it leaves me unmoved; it does not affect me or cause me any more sensation than this arrangement of the following words: *Fait . . . pas . . . le . . . la . . . honte . . . non . . . crime . . . et . . . l'échafaud*. But when these words are ordered by a poet they compose this beautiful line spoken by the Comte d'Essex:[46]
>   *Le crime fait la honte, et non pas l'échafaud.*
> It may be concluded from this comparison that dancing is possessed of all the advantages of a beautiful language, yet it is not sufficient to know the alphabet alone. But when a man of genius arranges the letters to form words and connects the words to form sentences, it will cease to be dumb; it will speak with both strength and energy; and then ballets will share with the best plays the merit of affecting and moving, and of making tears flow [. . .]. (Noverre 1930, 19–20)[47]

Steps are like nonsignifying letters of the alphabet, or like isolated words that must be appropriately combined according to formulae that would at last enable them to speak. These *letter* and *writing* metaphors are also to be found in Cahusac, used to the same end but taking various forms. Sometimes, the incompetent dancer is compared to the Chinese sage, who knows only isolated ideograms that he never articulates as discourse. This sage clearly has all the ingredients of knowledge at his disposal but in the form of absolute non-knowledge because those ingredients are rhapsodically dissipated and atomized. The purely mechanical dancer is in a similar predicament: he has the alphabet of movement at his fingertips but treats letters, absurdly, as ideograms because he knows nothing of language. Elsewhere this dancer is compared to the Master Writer, or the character type who shows exemplary mastery in the graphic writing of letters while completely failing to master discourse.[48]

46. Translator's note: Beaumont comments, "The crime causes the shame and not the scaffold. A celebrated passage from Act 4, Scene 3 of the *Comte d'Essex* (1678) by the playwright Thomas Corneille (1625–1709). The phrase is imitated from Tertullian—*martyrem fecit causa, non poena*" (Noverre 1930, 19n1).

47. Noverre 1760, Letter II, 28–29; Noverre 1803, vol. 1, Letter II, 15–16; Noverre 1807, vol. 1, Letter XVIII, "Règles à suivre dans la Composition des Ballets," 242.

48. "The person most respected in China is he who knows the largest quantity of words. Erudition in that country does not even touch things. A lettered man spends his life putting in

This writing metaphor is, however, misleading: it suggests that movement meaning might emerge as a result of the simple combination of nonsignifying elements, approximately in the manner of letters combined into words. In fact Noverre maintains the opposite: dance *signification* is radically different from its alphabet and only manifests at a different level to that of steps and figures. Alphabetic writing does not here function as a paradigm, properly speaking, but only as a critical metaphor. This metaphor enables the claim that a purely mechanical dance is just as absurd as mastery of an alphabet unaccompanied by linguistic competence. In reality, however, nothing in the choreographic alphabet and the combinations to which it gives rise allows meaning to emerge, so the disjunction is entirely to be expected. *Meaning* must emerge elsewhere, in a properly topological "elsewhere." The alphabet of movement is focused on the legs, in the succession of steps and figures. The locus of *meaning* however—through which dance becomes utterance and expression—is the arms and the face. Noverre states again and again that more attention should be paid to the arms and less value given to the legs:

> To hasten the progress of our art and bring it nearer the truth, we must sacrifice all our over-complicated steps; what is lost in regard to the legs will be gained in the arms [...] I ask for more variety and expression in the arms, I wish to see them speak with more energy; they express sentiment and voluptuousness, but this is not sufficient; they have yet to depict fury, jealousy, spite, inconstancy, grief, vengeance, irony, all the passions of man which, in harmony with the eyes, features and gestures, will make me understand nature's sentiments. (1930, 102–4)[49]

As for the face, the privileged locus of emotional expression, Noverre congratulates himself on having rendered it transparent by proscribing the use of masks:

> I had the courage to forbid the use of masks on the theater stage, and they now only appear in the ballroom. I always considered these wooden or wax

order in his head a huge number of isolated words, and the wise men of China declare that he is a fount of knowledge. I think of watching a man who has in his hand the key to the Temple of the Muses, and who spends his days and his all his skill turning that key over and over again in the lock without ever touching the spring. Such is our best dancer" (Cahusac 2004, 227; translated here directly from the French). "A Master Writer is an expert who teaches others how to form letters. A ballet master is an artist who shows others how to perform steps. The first is no more distant from what we call in literature a Writer than the second is from he who in the theater deserves to be called a dancer" (232).

49. Noverre 1760, Letter X, 270–6; Noverre 1803, vol. 1, Letter X, 135–38; Noverre 1807, vol. 1, Letter XXVII, "De l'accord du Geste avec la Pensée et les Mouvements de l'Ame," 394–97.

masks to be a thick and clumsy envelope, stifling the affections of the soul and preventing the external manifestation of the impressions imprinted on that soul.[50]

Meaning—this "elsewhere" of the step constituted by the movements of the arms and expressions of the face—falls into place with the establishment of a new concept of *gesture* and a new logic of *expression*.[51] The expressive gesture cannot be subject to any prior codification. There is no question here of a pre-existing choreographic unit that one could simply perform, but rather a focus on directly manifesting an individual, passionate interiority, which is expressed through subtle, infinitely varied movements:

> The *port de bras* must be as varied as the different sentiments which dancing can express; set rules become almost useless; they must be broken and set aside at each moment, or, by following them exactly, the *port de bras* will be opposed to the movements of the soul, which cannot be limited to a fixed number of gestures [...]
>
> Gesture is the countenance of the soul, its effect must be immediate and cannot fail to achieve its aim when it is true.
>
> Instructed in the fundamental principles of our art, let us follow the movements of our soul; it cannot betray us when it is subject to a lively feeling, and if at those moments it cause the arm to make such and such a gesture, this gesture is always just and correct and sure in its effect. The passions are the springs which actuate the machine; whatever movements result from it, they cannot fail to be expressive. After this, it cannot but be concluded that the sterile rules of a school must disappear from the *danse d'action* to give place to natural expression. (Noverre 1930, 100)[52]

The logic of gesture necessarily moves beyond the alphabet. It confronts us with the singularity of the dancing subject and the tautological truth of expression, such

50. Noverre 1803, vol. 2, Letter VIII, 84; Noverre 1807, vol. 1, letter VI "Des Spectacles anciens et surtout de la Pantomime," 96. Translator's note: passage not included in Beaumont's translation, and translated here directly from the French.

51. "Maîtres de ballet are persuaded that by gesture I understand the expressive movements of the arms, supported by striking and varied expressions of the features" (Noverre 1930, 101). See Noverre 1760, Letter X, 269; Noverre 1803, Letter X, 134 (a slightly different version of the same text); Noverre 1807, Letter XXVII, "De l'accord du Geste avec la Pensée et les Mouvements de l'Ame," 393.

52. Noverre 1760, Letter X, 264–66; Noverre 1803, Letter X, 131–32 (a slightly different version of the same text); Noverre 1807, Letter XXVII, "De l'accord du Geste avec la Pensée et les Mouvements de l'Ame," 390–91.

that the externality of the vocabulary vanishes. It brings us face to face with the continuity of signs: expressive symptoms are infinitely varied and cannot be categorized as discontinuous elements. The notions of "character" and "unit" thus also disappear. The logic of gesture implies the simultaneity of meaning and its utterance: there is no expression outside of an emotion experienced internally and lived in the present. This logic therefore also, lastly, returns us to the intimate connection between dancing and presence.

So, we are now well equipped to understand Noverre's case against Feuillet.[53] It can be summarized in a single phrase. Choreography "spells out dance." The letter about Feuillet's *chorégraphie* opens with a summary of principles, which simultaneously condemns the alphabet and the geometral:

> The tracks or figures of these dances were drawn, the steps were then indicated on the tracks by lines and conventional signs; the cadence or bar was marked by little transverse lines which divided the steps and fixed the time. The air to which the dance was composed was noted at the top of the page, so that eight bars of choreographic notation corresponded to eight bars of music. By means of this arrangement, one succeeded in *spelling out* the dance, provided that one took the precaution never to change the position of the book and to hold it always *in the same direction*. (Noverre 1930, 132, my emphasis)[54]

Notation only retains the alphabetic element of danced movement, capturing only what participates in the code's explicitness and the vocabulary's discontinuity: "This art [...] indicates with exactitude the movements of the *feet* only" (1930, 133, my emphasis).[55] The subtle movements of the arms, the *effacements* of the shoulders, the oppositions of the head, the expressions of the face, which are all essential elements of choreographic signification, can find no place in notation. The grain of notation is insufficiently fine to account for the very locus of expressivity. This is no mere contingent difficulty, which could be remedied by refining the system and rendering it more complex, but rather an essential impossibility resting on the dualism of the mechanical and the expressive. Notation assumes the mechanical and spells it out. Even if it

53. Noverre 1930, Letter XIII; Noverre 1760, Letter XIII; Noverre 1803, vol. 1, Letter XIII; Noverre 1807, vol. 1, Letter XXX, "De la Chorégraphie."

54. Noverre 1760, Letter XIII, 364; Noverre 1803, vol. 1, Letter XIII, 182; Noverre 1807, vol. 1, Letter XXX, "De la Chorégraphie," 451–52.

55. Noverre 1760, Letter XIII, 365; Noverre 1803, vol. 1, Letter XIII, 182; Noverre 1807, vol. 1, Letter XXX, "De la Chorégraphie," 452.

appears already to be outmoded at this level ("nowadays, the steps are complicated [. . .] it is then very difficult to note them in writing, and still more difficult to decipher them" [Noverre 1930, 133]) complementary signs can always
be added, by inventing graphic devices and making them more and more complex. But notation's irremediable impediment is signification as such, or the
kind of expression that escapes all codification and defies all categories, and
that needs to be fully and wholly realized to be conceivable at all. The essence
of dance is in the presence in action of an emotion being expressed, and *that*
can scarcely be recorded.

This is why Feuillet scores really function as *vestiges* or *traces* of a vanished
event, and not as a repertoire preserving the identity of works:

> Hoard as much as it pleases you of these feeble monuments to the glory of
> our celebrated dancers; I see in them, and there will only be in them, the
> first sketch or the first thought of their talents [. . .] I shall perceive only the
> remains and tracing of a movement of the feet which will be accompanied
> neither by the attitudes of the body nor the positions of the arms, nor the
> expression of the heads; in short, you offer me only [the imperfect *shadow*
> of superior mastery, and a mere *cold and speechless copy* of inimitable origi-
> nals]. (1930, 133)[56]

Thus the full arsenal of Plato's *Phaedrus* is recalled here: the metaphor of the
shadow and the light, of the copy and the original, of that which speaks and that
which remains mute. This imperative of the *living utterance*, of the necessary
presence of meaning to itself, must also be obeyed in the creation of dances:

> It is an error to believe that a capable *maître de ballet* can trace out and com-
> pose his work by his fireside. Those who labour thus will never achieve any-
> thing but miserable combinations. You do not make dancers move by writing
> in your study. The stage is the parnassus of ingenious composers; there, with-
> out seeking for them, they encounter a multitude of new things; there, every-
> thing is connected, everything is soulful, everything is drawn in lines of fire
> [. . .] The arrangement and development of a grand well-conceived ballet
> requires, Sir, knowledge, intelligence, taste, ingenuity, a delicate tact, a wise
> foresight and an all-seeing eye. And all these qualities are not acquired by
> the deciphering or notation of a dance by choreography; a single moment

---

56. Noverre 1760, Letter XIII, 367–68; Noverre 1803, vol. 1, Letter XIII, 183 (significantly different version of the text); Noverre 1807, vol. 1, Letter XXX, "De la Chorégraphie," 453. Translator's
note: The phrase in square brackets revises Beaumont's translation (based on Noverre 1803),
which reads "a canvas on which you have preserved some scattered lines by different masters."

determines the composition: the skill consists in seizing it and turning it to account. (1930, 139–40)[57]

Composing can only have meaning in the theater itself and in the simultaneous presence of the participants. This is because composition involves, above all, knowing how to turn to account a contingent present, a happy accident, an unforeseen moment, a *kairos*. Note that this logic of the choreographic *kairos* still governs modern dance at a deep level, including and perhaps especially its most "advanced" fringes: as in, for example, practices of instantaneous composition, site-specific work, and choreography that awaits and incorporates the accidental—in short, all those practices that in the name of *performance* voluntarily render dance indissociable from its inscription in the event.

Noverre, however, does not completely devalue the graphic inscription of dance. If the ideal of a repertoire of scores is given up, and they are considered simply as traces or archives, then improvements to the way dance is recorded can be envisaged. Critical of the article "Chorégraphie" written by Louis-Jacques Goussier for Diderot and d'Alembert's *Encyclopedia* (1751), Noverre suggests some positive changes. Goussier is content to describe the Beauchamp-Feuillet system in neutral terms and simply appends some plates drawn from Feuillet's book *Chorégraphie*. Noverre imagines a project of much greater breadth, based purely and simply on returning to pictorial representation and verbal description and thus implying a radical devaluation of the merits of planimetric and geometral representation. The ground plan, besides obliging the reader to turn about the book, only offers a bird's-eye view of the main dance figure. This bird's-eye view lets slip the reality of the representation, which can actually only be seen from the ground, from a frontal perspective, in elevation. In fact, this is no longer even a planimetric but rather a perspectival view. Hence Noverre suggests appending to what is recorded in the geometral plan a purely pictorial representation of the stage, an engraving that would allow the real image of figures, situations, characters, costumes, and expressions to be perceived. Noverre calls this pictorial representation a "plan in elevation," a somewhat inappropriate term but one intended to highlight the parallel with the "ground plan" or "geometral plan." And to this plan in elevation, which in fact offers a perspectival view, he suggests appending also verbal descriptions. In short, the working angles are multiplied, with all available means (notation, drawing, discourse) being used: not to fix work identity so that it can be passed on in the absence of its creators in the manner

---

57. Noverre 1760, Letter XIII, 387–91; Noverre 1803, vol. 1, Letter XIII, 192–94; Noverre 1807, vol. 1, Letter XXX, "De la Chorégraphie," 461–63.

authorized by the text but only for the sake of leaving an archive or trace of ineliminable presence for generations to come:

> Choreography would then become interesting. *Ground plan, plan in eleva-tion, a faithful description of these plans,* everything would be presented to the eye; the whole would explain the attitudes of the body, the expression of the heads, the contours of the arms, the position of the legs, the elegance of the dresses, the accuracy of the costumes—in fine, such a work, illustrated by the pencil and graver of two such illustrious artists,[58] would enable one to go to the fountainhead, and I should regard it as the *repository* of all that art can offer of enlightenment, interest and beauty. (1930, 138, my emphasis)[59]

From *repertoire* to *repository* (or *archive*)—such is the movement that Noverre makes notation undergo. And this is the direct consequence of the dialectical play of writing. As soon as notation is conceived as the writing of a language, it finds itself necessarily judged in terms of a pretension that it cannot fulfill. It is writing that says nothing, which can only inscribe the skeleton of an external meaning, and become the trace of a necessarily vanished *presence.*

LABAN: MOVEMENT AND EFFORT

Laban's standpoint can be deduced from the fact that he admires Feuillet and Noverre in equal measure.[60] The implication of this double heritage is a return of the linguistic paradigm, this time as an integral element of the theory: that is, the paradigm appears not as a spur to an external critique but as the metaphor of an imagined resolution. Linguistic writing reveals itself to be the miraculous concordance of analysis and meaning, or of the alphabet and utterance, a con-cordance that notation still lacks:

> A new and generally acceptable dance notation *comparable with the pho-netic alphabet* had to be built up. Pictures or diagrams of the external shapes of bodily positions and movements will not serve the ultimate purpose of notating the spiritual content of dances. (Laban 1956, 13, my emphasis)

58. Translator's note: The two artists mentioned earlier in this passage are the painter François Boucher (1703–70) and the engraver Charles Nicholas Cochin (1715–90).

59. Noverre 1760, Letter XIII, 383–34; Noverre 1803, vol. 1, Letter XIII, 190–91; Noverre 1807, vol. 1, Letter XXX, "De la Chorégraphie," 459–60.

60. See Laban (1948; 1956, 7–8).

Dance as a sequence of movement can be compared with *spoken language*. As words are built up of letters, so are movements built up of elements; as sentences are built up of words, so are dance-phrases built up of movements. (Laban 1948, 26, my emphasis)

Just as the *letters of the alphabet* are compounded into words, and the words arranged into sentences, so are the simple elements of motion compounded into more complex movements, and finally into phrases of dance. (42, my emphasis)

If dance is constituted like a language, made up of simple elements that become meaningful purely in virtue of their combination, notation can then assume the role of pure alphabet. And it can then also automatically be the transcription of discourse. This is the ideal that seems to govern Labanotation (or Kinetography Laban), a system geared toward the analysis of movement.[61] In accordance with the *kinesphere*, subjective space is divided into twenty-seven simple direction signs (twenty-six directions such as up, down, left, right, plus "place" or "center"), and the body conjointly is analyzed into its main parts corresponding to different columns in the score. This double analysis enables a purely symbolic representation of any body position, movement being understood as the implied transition from one position to another. Support signs meanwhile represent the transfer of weight and therefore traveling in space (see figures 13 and 14).

More precision is called for here, however. In fact, the system does not record positions so much as the transitions between them. This is only possible because the spatiality of the symbol is endowed with a purely temporal significance. Of course, the shape and color of the sign indicate the endpoint of the movement (the position), but its length (i.e., its temporal duration) together with the previous endpoint are what really describe the movement.

Thus, Labanotation abandons planimetric representation, breaking in this way with the procedures of Feuillet notation. The page is no longer a projection of the space, but only a projection of time. The score, which is read from bottom to top, deploys a sequence of gestures and displacements, the spatial character of which is accommodated only in symbolic and not iconic form. Moreover, this spatiality is not that determined by an external reference point but that which is oriented around the dancer's own body. A sequence of subjectively referenced motor instructions is recorded rather than the direct figuration of a pathway. Positions in objective space (that is, positions relative to an external reference point) are only readable as implied consequences (see

61. For a detailed exposition of Labanotation, see, for example, Challet-Haas (1999).

figures 15 and 16). Paradoxically, this notation system that appears to reflect space as it is lived—inscribing as it does the subjective orientations of the dancer's own body rather than her objective pathway in space—is also the least intuitive graphically, and the most distanced from our habits of projective reading. Space is represented here in a purely symbolic manner, the graphic spatiality of the page now only designating the passage of time. Feuillet notation articulated two heterogeneous systems: those of figure and character, or in other words of the iconic representation of the pathway and the symbolic representation of the steps. Labanotation is based on the analytic and combinatory power of purely abstract symbols. This is clearly a case, therefore, of a perfect alphabet, all the more complete because it seems capable of describing any type of movement.

A difficulty arises, however, and in fact it is the same difficulty as before. This is still an alphabet that *says* nothing.[62] It records the objective profile of movement, including lines, positions, and duration; it inscribes quantitative parameters such as speed, direction, amplitude; but it necessarily leaves out what might be called, roughly speaking, the *qualitative*, the subjective accompaniment of movement. Laban calls this accompaniment (which is clear to whoever can perceive the difference between the fall of a stone and that of a living being) expression, color, or *mood*: it is both affective tonality and the manifestation of a lived state. And it is *mood* in this sense that must ground choreographic meaning: "The sense of the phrases of movement can [. . .] be understood as the expression of definite action moods" (Laban 1948, 43). Mood—a qualitative, subjective profile of the movement that is the very principle of its "coloration"— is only partially concerned with the exteriority of positions and gestures. Of course, the simple spatial coordinates of Labanotation already have a qualitative dimension. Already implicit therein are weight and flow. There is, however, a remainder. Two movements identical from the spatiotemporal perspective are capable of several different colorations or *moods*:

> The moods or expressions of movement have a double source. It will be easily understood that a body and arm stretched high and wide has a different expression from that of a body huddled up on the floor. It would be wrong, however, to speak of definite moods expressed by positions, because the dancer can move into any position in very different ways [. . .] The expression of a movement depends therefore on several factors—space location, including shape, and dynamic content, including *effort*. (Laban 1948, 44, my emphasis)

---

62. On this issue, see above 172, n 18. It is entirely in keeping with the nature of an alphabet that it be oblivious to the meaning it inscribes. However, the linguistic paradigm, with its double articulation, gives the impression that meaning must ultimately be inscribed.

"Effort" here is a term unlike the others. It represents no less than the seed of an alternative notation system, the dream of a systematic analysis and combinatorial that would accommodate the phenomenological remainder of Labanotation. "Effort" designates the motor dimension of *mood*, a particular internal attitude in relation to movement, an attitude that is understood simultaneously as visible content; it is an "inside" directly exposed, or an expressive quality. This motor attitude called "Effort" is broken down by Laban into four factors: the movement's relation to weight, flow, time, and space:

> The components making up the different effort qualities result from an inner attitude (conscious or unconscious) towards the motion factors of Weight, Space, Time and Flow. (Laban 1980 [1950], 11)

A qualitative combinatorial can thereby be established. By introducing signs that are adequate to attitudes toward these four factors, the whole range of possible global attitudes can be engaged, such that every *effort* can have a specific graph and every graph allows a *structure* of effort to be read off it (see figure 17).[63] This combinatorial gives place to some basic types that Laban calls basic actions. These actions do not designate particular gestures but rather (again) qualities of movement: pressing (relation to weight, strong; relation to space, direct; relation to time, sustained); flicking (light, flexible, quick); punching or thrusting (quick, direct, strong); floating or flying (sustained, flexible, light); wringing (flexible, sustained, strong); dabbing (direct, quick, light); slashing (quick, strong, flexible); gliding (sustained, light, direct).[64]

This, then, is an alphabet of qualities and, indirectly, an alphabet of meaning. However, such an alphabet is only possible at the price of abandoning the notational imperative. Either these actions really function as discrete categories (in which case it should be possible to place every movement quality in one or another), or they merely represent markers in the infinite continuity of possible qualitative nuances (in which case the principle of syntactical and semantic disjointness at the root of notation is rendered null and void). In the first case, graphic signs only operate at the cost of doing violence to actual practice. In the second, they cease purely and simply to function as a notation system.[65] And

63. On Effort graphs, see Laban (1947); Laban (1948, 74–104); Laban (1980, 105–18).

64. Basic actions result from the combination of just three factors: weight, time, and space. Flow is essentially an accessory element.

65. On syntactic and semantic disjointness as criteria of notation, I refer the reader once again to Nelson Goodman's analysis (1976), chapters 4 and 5.

it is probably in line with this second perspective that one should read Effort notation. Effort is less a case of an alternative notation system that, relative to the same object, would describe what escapes Labanotation; it is more like an attempt to describe an entirely different object. With Effort, Laban seems to abandon the notational project in light of an analysis of the particular, in favor of elaborating tools capable of inscribing idiosyncratic motor activity. In this sense, generic categorization (in types of action verbs) are less important than in Labanotation. What matters above all are the infinite qualitative nuances engendered by these categories, the continuum of movement "colors" that alone allows the adequate description of the particular. This, once again, moves us outside of any notational project.

This failure to export combinatorial analysis to the domain of the qualitative and the expressive is probably a consequence of a more fundamental impossibility. The application of the linguistic model to notation cannot fulfill its promise. The miraculous articulation of analysis and of meaning, of alphabet and utterance, is only evident in language and in language alone, and in virtue of its double articulation. Effort notation seeks to reconquer expressivity and meaning, to occupy the territory in the name of which graphic inscription was condemned. But meaning is integral to Effort notation from the beginning, already contained in the very elements it defines. Meaning cannot be *engendered* by those elements, and this is precisely why this second system of analysis is no more meaningful than the first: it simply differs in terms of the object on which it focuses, which is now the qualitative and the expressive. And this object, moreover, obliges the system to function as a continuous classification rather than as a notation. The resonance of the alphabetic model at the heart of notational discourse is but a symptom of the truly choreographic dependence of meaning on presence: by such means, the possibility of an autonomization of meaning, of an absented meaning, is simultaneously imagined and obscured, along with the hope it entails of finally breaking the intimate connection of dancing with presence. It is a dream that can only, ultimately, attest to its own impossibility, dance slipping back into its habitual analphabetism and its unworking [*désoeuvrement*].

In summary, two factors would explain the nonintegration of notational systems with dance practice. The first, of a quasi-logical order, reveals a contradiction between the conditions of integration and the conditions of survival of a notational system across time. On this issue, I refer the reader back to the trilemma previously discussed. The second issue, with a more textual and dialectical flavor, is based on the omnipresence of the linguistic paradigm at the heart of notational discourse. This paradigm articulates two imperatives that, outside of verbal language, can only ever be contradictory: analytical parsing of complex phenomena on the one hand, and the inscription of signification on the other. Notation, in the very moment of breaking movement down, must account for the meaning of movement, which seems moreover only capable of being revealed through presence.

This thesis should, however, be qualified. For one thing, the two Laban "systems" can be kept separate, neither being necessary to the descriptive function of the other. Their juxtaposition reveals, perhaps, that the contradiction is not so much internal to the object of analysis (quantity as against quality, analysis as against meaning, etc.) as it is a product of an attempt to describe two different objects. Secondly, I have thus far proceeded as though the integration of notational categories with practice had been entirely ineffective, as if notation functioned only as an archivistic, external tool rather than in any sense a way of thinking internal to movement. This view is partly false. Alongside the fact that Labanotation (as well as Benesh) has enabled the reconstruction of numerous works of the past, it should be recognized that the pedagogical work associated with Laban's ideas has had an effect on the choreographic field (and I am thinking here particularly of the work of Jacqueline Challet-Haas at the Conservatoire National Supérieur de Musique et de Danse de Paris). I will offer a further illustration of this effect in a later chapter when discussing the work of the Quatuor Knust.[66]

66. See part III, chapter 4, 244–48.

Chapter 2

Identity: Two Regimes

I now need to examine in detail the identity of the choreographic work, which has the peculiarity of being unwritten yet repeatable. A theoretical framework and a minimal idea of what is more or less commonly understood by the term "work" are needed. I shall borrow these from Nelson Goodman (1976) and Gérard Genette (1997 [1994]). First, I explore Goodman's distinction between autographic and allographic works, as first elaborated in chapters 3 and 5 of *Languages of Art*, and subsequently developed in the article "On the Identity of Works of Art" (in Goodman 1984). This distinction enables two broad regimes of existence and identity to be delineated for art objects: that of the singular, material object (the painting or sculpture) and that of the ideal object in principle susceptible of multiple correct instantiations (the novel or symphony, for example).

THE GOODMAN MODEL: AUTOGRAPHIC AND ALLOGRAPHIC

Goodman draws his distinction on the basis of an apparently trivial fact: there are works that can be forged (more accurately, works for which the idea of forgery makes sense) and others for which forgery is impossible, even nonsensical. One can seek to forge a painting, producing a copy of the object and passing it off as the original. But such an attempt makes no sense in the case of a novel or a symphony. If I transcribe Proust's *À la recherche du temps perdu*, I will simply produce another correct copy of that work. If I transcribe the score of Beethoven's Ninth Symphony or perform it in concert, I will simply have produced one more copy of the score or a performance of the work, each equally correct. Of course, I can try to forge the *manuscript* of *À la recherche du temps perdu*, or the manuscript score of the Ninth Symphony, but then the forgery is of the manuscript as a singular material object, not of the work as such. So there are artworks for which forgery is possible and others for which it is nonsensical. Goodman chooses to call the former "autographic" and the latter "allographic."

Some conceptual elaboration of this empirical distinction is needed. Forgery is impossible in the case of allographic works because they depend on a distinction between constitutive properties, integral to the identity and definition of the work, and contingent properties, that is, features left to the decision of the performer or the person entrusted with instantiating the work (these properties being considered not features of the work as such but rather properties of one or other of its manifestations). À la recherche du temps perdu does not prescribe the font or type of paper that should be used when it is printed. Nor does it prescribe the speed or type of intonation appropriate to reading it aloud. The same, in large part, goes for musical works (or at least for a certain canonical type of musical work), which preserve their work identity (as defined by the score) independently of their multiple performances and interpretations. This division between constitutive and contingent properties renders identification of the work independent of the material history of production. When listening to a performance of Beethoven's Ninth Symphony, I have absolutely no need, in determining whether it really is the Ninth, to trace a kind of genealogy that would link this specific performance with Beethoven's own creation of the work. All I need to do is to assure myself that the collection of properties defined by the score is effectively instantiated in the performance. The identity of autographic works, by contrast, does not depend on a distinction between essential and contingent features, and so can only be determined by the work's material history of production. All the properties of the object (of a given painting or sculpture) are integral parts of what defines it. And because one cannot compile a finite list of the properties that define a material object, the work is ultimately only identifiable by reference to the singular history of its material genesis. If I know that the work in front of me really is Leonardo da Vinci's Mona Lisa and nothing else, this is not because it conforms to some inventory of its objective properties but because I believe that the object itself has a certain history (possibly as validated by art experts): this object was effectively produced about five centuries ago, by an individual named Leonardo da Vinci, and finally, after many travels, is now exhibited in this room of the Louvre where I can stand in front of it today. To emphasize the point: what allows one to identify the object is not a catalogue of essential properties but a certain genealogy by which the present object is connected to its specific historical origins.

To summarize, there are three criteria that allow one to distinguish between autographic and allographic works. (1) Is forgery of the object nonsensical? If so, the work is allographic; if not, autographic. (2) Does the work depend on a distinction between essential and contingent properties? If so, the work is allographic; if not, autographic. (3) Is the work's identity independent of its material history of production? If so, the work is allographic; if not, autographic. The three criteria appear linked and coextensive: a positive response to any of the three questions will automatically generate a positive response to the two others. This is something that I will question in what follows, as I seek to show the independence of criteria (2) and (3) in the case of the choreographic work: in other words, the work can depend on a distinction between essential and contingent properties without thereby being identifiable by purely external means, or independently of its history of production. This is the wedge I will try to drive into Goodman's theory. And the dissociation of criteria central to my thesis ultimately points up how oral transmission of works itself is structured: there is a generic or conceptual entity present, but it emerges only in the effective transfer from one body to another, in direct material descent from its source. Consequently, the choreographic work emerges as simultaneously autographic and allographic—or, perhaps more accurately, belongs to neither regime.

But before discussing the choreographic work specifically, I will make some further general observations. Firstly, autographic identity seems to go hand in hand with a purely numerical form of identity. The notion of authenticity only makes sense if it refers back to the singularity of an object understood materially. Even were a perfect copy of the object to exist, which reproduced all the properties integral to it, one would still draw a distinction (at least conceptually) between copy and original, because of attachment to numerical identity.[1] Some have objected to this fetishization of the singular object and have sought to account for work identity purely in the sense of specific (or qualitative) identity: if it were possible to produce an exact double, there would be no reason that was not commercial or fetishistic, to prefer the original to the copy.[2] But this passes over in silence the discrepancy between numerical and specific identity in the case of physical objects. A physical object can partially change its specific identity without thereby ceasing to be numerically the same. The work can suffer damage, lose its colors, get covered in black paint, lose its varnish, and so

---

1. To some extent, this is the claim Walter Benjamin makes in "The Work of Art in the Age of Mechanical Reproduction": "Even the most perfect reproduction of a work is lacking one element: its presence in time and space, its unique existence at the place where it happens to be" (1992, 214). Identity as defined by presence in time and space is ordinarily what is understood by numerical identity. What is more, the definition of the aura as "the present appearance of something distant" returns to the idea of a historical or genealogical foundation for identity. The problem is that Benjamin extends, inappropriately in my view, this aura of numerical identity distinctive of the autographic to all works of art. More accurately, the implicit horizon of this view being the work of plastic art, he says nothing about allographic works (like those of music or literature) whose distinction is precisely that of escaping the singularity of presence in time and space.

2. See, for example, Prieto (1992) and also Benjamin himself, although his argument is more complex.

on; it does not thereby cease to be numerically the *same* work.[3] Conversely, the identity of allographic works is purely specific. The work is defined by the set—determinate and finite—of properties that must be instantiated. This definition is perfectly strict. To change a single constitutive property of the work is not to change the work; it is in fact to perform a *different* work.

Secondly, the autographic-allographic contrast remains clearly distinct from certain other traditional oppositions that at first might appear similar: such as, for example, the contrast between one-stage and two-stage arts. No doubt the division between prescription and execution at the heart of the allographic regime is reminiscent of the category of *arts à deux temps*, or two-stage arts, previously proposed by Henri Gouhier (1989). However, there are two-stage arts also within the autographic regime (etching, photography and cast sculpture, for example). What is more, the identification of the two stages within the art form of literature (which is allographic) is somewhat problematic. In some respects, the literary work is finished with the completion of its manuscript, printing and publication relating more to the dissemination of the work than its realization, properly speaking. Nor is the autographic-allographic contrast coextensive with the distinction between arts producing unique objects and arts producing multiples. Of course, every allographic work is virtually multiple (its very ontological structure, which distinguishes essential from contingent properties, calls for multiplication); but this kind of multiplicity can remain virtual (in the case of an unpublished manuscript, for example). Conversely, the autographic regime is in no way identified with the production only of singular objects: consider, once again, the cases of photography, etching, or cast sculpture.[4]

Thirdly, the contrast between autographic and allographic does not identify art forms as such; it rather delineates two fundamentally distinct regimes of identity according to a line of demarcation that can divide a single particular art form internally. Thus it is incorrect to identify a given art *form* as "allographic" or "autographic" because the division can be evident even within that single art. Thus, music is mainly allographic in so-called classical practice but autographic when it comes to jazz improvisation, where the distinction between constitutive and contingent properties ceases to be pertinent. What defines a given improvisation by Coltrane is not just the rhythmic and melodic line that can be notated after the fact but equally the particular timbre of Coltrane's

---

3. An example here would be the celebrated case of Leonardo da Vinci's *The Last Supper*.

4. See Goodman: "Concerning the distinction between autographic and allographic arts or works [. . .], the first point is that this distinction does not coincide with that between singular and multiple arts; for some multiple arts, such as etching, are autographic" (1984, 139).

saxophone, the singular quality of his breathing, in short a whole collection of idiosyncratic properties that cannot be captured in the code of notation. And, beyond jazz, one might think of the recent evolution of pop music where studio recording has ceased to be the documentation of a singular performance and tends instead to identify the work as such. This signals a (re-)turn of musical practice in the direction of the autographic. The work no longer consists in the ideality of the melodic and rhythmic line that anybody might reperform but in the singular performance of the artist or the group as it is preserved—and in large part created—by the recording.[5]

Finally, aside from this recent evolution of musical practice, the contrast between autographic and allographic seems to imply for Goodman a kind of diachronic hypothesis. All the arts were once autographic, he claims, bound to the unrepeatable singularity of their products. But some, for practical reasons linked to the ephemeral and collective character of their works, progressively detached themselves from the autographic by establishing a notational code capable of "transcend[ing] the limitations of time and the individual":

> Initially, perhaps, all arts are autographic. Where the works are transitory, as in singing and reciting, or require many persons for their production, as in architecture and symphonic music, a notation may be devised in order to transcend the limitations of time and the individual. This involves establishing a distinction between the constitutive and the contingent properties of a work (and in the case of literature, texts have even supplanted oral performances as the primary aesthetic objects). Of course, the notation does not dictate the distinction arbitrarily, but must follow generally—even though it may amend—lines antecedently drawn up by the informal classification of performances into works and by practical decisions as to what is prescribed and what is optional. (Goodman 1976, 121)

There must be some practical reasons for an autographic art to become allographic: namely, works must be ephemeral or collectively produced, making the recourse to graphic artifice a necessity. Once fixed on paper, the work is liberated from time and person: it becomes allographic. But this transformation, though it appears legitimate from the pragmatic point of view, does not emerge ex nihilo. For a system of notation to become established, the art that it records must already have a "virtual" allographic basis; in other words, there must be a collection of distinctions and categories immanent in the practice that allow one to distinguish between constitutive and contingent, between repeatable and

---

5. On this issue, see Pouivet (2003).

singular features. Notation only follows—and possibly amends—these already trodden paths or informal classifications, the repertoires of entities (gestures, sounds, or words) that constitute a given practice. As I will explore in what follows, dance has a central place within Goodman's diachronic account and, indeed, appears to function as the perfect example of an art form arrested in its process of transformation from autographic to allographic. Dance does have a practical basis in a collection of gestural entities that are clearly identified and repeatable, but it has not validated and explicitly liberated this practical basis through the artifice of an external graphic code. Dance can, therefore, give the illusion of an allographic art without a notation. This is what Gérard Genette implies and what I will seek to deny, arguing that notation is a strict condition of the allographic.[6]

GÉRARD GENETTE'S CONTRIBUTION: TRANSCENDENCE AND PERFORMANCES

Gérard Genette makes a twofold contribution to Goodman's analysis. Firstly— and this is the general aim of the first volume of *The Work of Art* (1997)—he seeks to move beyond the Goodmanian contrast by drawing a further distinction between immanence and transcendence. The autographic-allographic contrast concerns artworks only in respect of their objects' mode of existence. Every work consists in an object that identifies it: if the work is autographic, this is a physical object or an event; if the work is allographic, the object is an ideal set of prescriptions that can ground multiple actualizations (in the form of physical objects or events). But the work's "objective" identity, its existence as object that Genette calls its "immanence," does not exhaust the question of the work's being. The work has a life that far exceeds the identity of its object. Genette calls this its "transcendence":

> The other mode of existence of works, which I have christened *transcen-*
> *dence*, encompasses all the extremely diverse and by no means mutually
> exclusive ways a work can obscure or else surpass the relation it maintains
> with the material or ideal object it basically "consists in"—all the cases in
> which "play" of one sort or another springs up between the work and its
> object of immanence. (1997, 161)

Genette details three forms of transcendence. The first is transcendence by *plurality of immanence*, evident in works with multiple versions or copies, but

6. See above, 210.

also translation, adaptation, and transposition; these are cases where there are several objects of immanence for a single work. The second is transcendence by *partiality of immanence*, as evident in lost or fragmentary works, as well as works that are manifested indirectly, only in secondary reproductions or by hearsay, for example; these are cases where there is a partial object for a single selfsame work. The third is transcendence by operal[7] *plurality of effect*, for example, when the history of the work's reception reveals several works—or readings of the work—for a single object; the limit case here is Borges's fictional example of Pierre Ménard's *Don Quixote*, in which two works share a single text. This account of the work's transcendence, aside from the way it nuances the widespread, restrictive focus on the work's "objective" existence, will play a crucial role in my argument. As we will see, the choreographic work finds no place within Genette's taxonomy except by cutting across the distinction between immanence and transcendence. As an iterated performance, although its repeatability does not depend on the anonymous and allographic generality of an external text, the choreographic work should be understood as autographic, made multiple by self-imitation.[8] But because it appears to me illegitimate to conceptualize iteration on the model of self-imitation (as I will explain below), I prefer the claim that the choreographic work is neither autographic nor allographic. I will thus argue that its mode of existence reveals the failure of Goodman's categories, and perhaps more generally of the concept of the *work* as such. In what follows, the cases of transcendence picked out by Genette will prove useful in thinking through more precisely how the choreographic work defies categorization in these terms: the idea of *plurality of immanence* will help describe the classical model of the work-with-multiple-versions;[9] his notion of *partiality of immanence* will help account for the survival of the work through its documentary traces;[10] and the idea of operal *plurality* will be useful in analyzing some contemporary modes of revival and restaging[11].

---

7. Translator's note: A neologism derived from "opus" and "operate" used by Genette and his translator, G. M. Goshgarian,. See Genette (1997, 20n40, and 256n42).

8. Or at least on the model of self-imitation: "Iterative performances thus tend to recall the practices of more or less free self-imitation that give rise to works with replicas. Like Chardin's *Saying Grace*, 'Gérard Philipe's Rodrigo' or 'Boulez's *Parsifal*' are works of plural immanence that do not necessarily set out (as *The Thinker* does) to attain the empirical indiscernibility of objects of immanence" (Genette 1997, 72).

9. See below, 215.

10. See below, 233.

11. See below, 301.

Genette's second contribution consists in an exhaustive empirical taxonomy of the autographic-allographic distinction, as part of the discussion of what he calls "immanence." Detailing and classifying a whole collection of art objects according to Goodman's contrast and its possible subclasses, he reveals the distinction's pertinence as well as its ultimate limits: this is the aim of the first part of Genette's book, entitled "The Regimes of Immanence." It is at these very limits of the autographic-allographic contrast that I will be working, specifically considering the cases discussed in Genette's chapter 5 titled "Performances." A work of performance[12] as a singular event clearly belongs to the category of the autographic (it is not completely nonsensical—although it is materially difficult—to try to forge such a work). But its categorization as such must be qualified according to two contrasts. One concerns the nature of performances as such and distinguishes between an improvisation and a work-performance. Either performance is independent of all already existing works and is thus called "improvisation." Or its task is to "create a manifestation, perceptible to the eye and/or ear, of already existing works of the allographic regime" (Genette 1997, 57). It is then described, variously depending on the context, as an execution, performance-interpretation, or staging. The fact that a performance actualizes an allographic work does not compromise its own autographic status. The identity of a given musical interpretation or a specific staging is entirely determined by reference to its history of production (which performers? when? where, and so on) and not by its instantiation of an inventory of identifiable essential properties. Moreover, it is possible to try to forge a performance-interpretation.

The other contrast concerns the principles of survival or multiplication of the singular and therefore ephemeral event that is any given performance. Genette distinguishes between recording and iteration or repetition:

> The two means by which a work of performance can, to a certain extent, escape from the temporal condition of an event, that is, from its ephemeral, one-time only character [are] reproduction by means of *recording*, and *repetition* [. . .]. (1997, 66)

Recording is just as relevant to improvisations as to performance-interpretations, to Coltrane's *My Favorite Things* as much as to Beethoven's *Hammerklavier Sonata* as interpreted by Pollini. By virtue of mechanical reproduction, the work of performance thus becomes a "multiple autographic object," comparable in its

---

12. I follow Genette in using "performance" in its most general sense of an action brought in the present before a public and susceptible of having an immediate aesthetic effect.

recorded form to the objects produced by photography, etching, or cast sculpture, except insofar as the status of the recording relative to the work remains more or less indeterminate. In the case of theater, opera, or dance, one would tend rather to consider recording on film as simply a documentary trace of the event. Framing effects entailed by even the simplest of recordings already determine a point of view in excess (or in contradiction) of the experience of watching the performance live. By contrast, and probably for opposite reasons (perceptually, the greater homogeneity of recording and source), the musical field more readily conceives of the record as an adequate manifestation of the original performance. It remains important, however, to distinguish between concert and studio recordings: the first is more clearly a case of documentation, whereas the second more clearly creates a work-as-recording. These nuances and mutations are no doubt a function of habits and conventions, yet they nonetheless have determinate implications for ontology. If a recording is merely a document, the work of performance becomes multiple only in virtue of an effect of transcendence. It is only through a partial and indirect manifestation that the event can survive and multiply. Conversely, if one considers recording to be the direct manifestation of the work (as the field of the contemporary recorded music industry mostly does), this implies an understanding of the object of immanence itself as multiple (just like the products of photography or etching). One could even say that performance thus ceases to constitute a work as such. The performance becomes merely the pretext for a recording that, with all the retouching and editing accompanying the process (sound engineering, multiple takes, montage, and so on), really brings the work into being.

I mentioned that the possibility of recording was as relevant to improvisations as to work-performances. This is not the case where repetition or iteration is concerned, at least according to Genette:

> In theory, an improvisatory performance does not lend itself to iteration of any kind. [...] The same cannot be said of performances of realization. An allographic work is susceptible of an indefinite number of good or bad *correct* performances (in compliance, that is, with the indications in the text or score), leaving aside the incorrect ones; furthermore, *a* performance, defined by its conformity to the text as well as its specific identity as performance, is always considered, by the conventions of the world of art, to be repeatable within the limits of that conformity and that identity. (1997, 69–70)

Work-performances, insofar as they are iterated, possess a specific identity, beyond the general framework fixed by the allographic work performed. A musical interpretation, the staging of a scene from an opera or a play, can be reperformed and remain more or less the same from one evening to the next, and this repeatability is founded not only on the identity of the allographic text. It depends on a set of choices or artistic properties that define the interpretation in question, and which can give rise to an iterative series:

> Thus one is entitled to consider an iterative series of performances (Pollini's *Hammerklavier*) as a subclass of what Goodman calls the "compliance class" constitutive of an allographic work (Beethoven's *Hammerklavier*). The term generally used to designate the stable identity of such a series [. . .] is *production*. (Genette 1997, 70)

That a given production (Boulez and Chéreau's *Ring*, for example, or Pollini's *Hammerklavier*) can have a specific identity (which is what opens the space of repetition), without however being susceptible of purely external re-production, forces us to consider a type of identity in between the autographic and the allographic.[13] The fact of iteration or repetition indicates at least the tacit existence of a distinction between constitutive and contingent properties. But because this distinction has not been fully articulated and remains in some ways trapped in the bodies of the original performers, it is insufficiently firm to constitute identity freed from the history of production. Hence these objects are typically designated by date and location: Boulez and Chéreau's *Ring* as performed at Bayreuth, 1976–80, for example. Genette interprets this mixed identity as a fact of transcendence. According to him, iteration should here be conceived on the model of self-imitation or works-with-replicas:

> Iterative performance [proceeds] from an endless effort of renewal: instinctive or deliberate faithfulness to an interpretative style constantly clashes, on the common basis of a text to be performed, with a legitimate desire to revitalize and improve. Iterative performances thus tend to recall the practices of more or less free self-imitation that gives rise to works with replicas. (Genette 1997, 72)

Considered in terms of this model, the fact of iteration thus transforms performance into a "work with plurality of immanence" (there are several distinct and concurrent objects instantiating a single work, as in Genette's first form of transcendence). I examine below the extent to which it is problematic to thus make iteration depend on a fact of transcendence.

---

13. "[We are entitled] to regard works of performance as capable of sustaining, by dint of reiteration, an intermediate mode of existence, located somewhere between the autographic and allographic regimes" (Genette 1997, 71).

More immediately, let me summarize what I have here sketched as a general theory of performance. (1) A performance is either an improvisation or the performance of an allographic work. As a physical event, it constitutes a unique autographic object. (2) A performance can only escape its status as a singular event via two routes, namely, recording or iteration. Recording can apply just as well to improvisations as to work-performances. Iteration is only possible for work-performances. (3) Via recording, the performance enables a "multiple autographic art" (on the model of photography and etching), and via iteration a "plural autographic art" (on the model of self-imitation and works with replicas).[14] (4) Point 3 above brings together two facts of transcendence: transcendence by indirect manifestation (a partial object for a single work, via recording), and transcendence by plurality of immanence (several objects for a single work, via iteration).[15] This can be expressed as in the table below:

		Immanence	Transcendence	
			Recording	Iteration
Works of performance	Improvisation	Unique autographic object	Multiple autographic object by indirect manifestation	Not applicable
	(Work) performance-execution	Unique autographic object	Multiple autographic object by indirect manifestation	Plural autographic object by self-imitation

It is now pertinent to examine how dance works resist this scheme. The first major reason they do so is the absence of notation in dance. Choreographic performances, even classical ones, are never quite performances of an already existing allographic work, in the sense that such a work does not exist. Thus the

14. Here it is a question of distinguishing between multiplicity and plurality. By "multiple," I mean a series of perceptually indiscernible objects that are equally valid instances of the same work. By "plural," I mean the coexistence of distinct and concurrent objects relative to one and the same work, whose identity is not externally inscribed.

15. "To sum up, and in broad outline: a performance is a physical event, and, as such, a unique autographic object; but, by way of recordings, it gives rise to a multiple autographic art, and, by way of iteration, to a plural autographic art. These two facts are also facts of transcendence, the first by way of indirect manifestation, the second by way of plural immanence" (Genette 1997, 72).

choreographic dimension of *Swan Lake* by Petipa and Ivanov, although it was textually inscribed in a score in the Stepanov system, has mostly been handed down only in an oral tradition.[16] And this predominance of oral transmission appears perfectly incompatible with the idea of the allographic. I will explain further below. For now, let me say simply that oral transmission restores a reference to the material history of the work's production that notation aimed to suppress. We are thereby obliged to question the strict division between improvisation, on the one hand, and performance of preexisting allographic works, on the other. The tradition and repertoire of classical ballet certainly seem founded on the idea of performing preexisting works, yet these works remain poorly identified, fluid, and subject to the vagaries of oral transmission and of the families of traditions that preserve them. We therefore have to understand the choreographic work not as a clear and distinct set of prescriptions but more as a framework for variation that fixes some features of identity and some limits, but cedes ground, via the vagaries of history and the fluidity of transmission, to myriad concurrent and equally legitimate "versions." This "frame-*work*" (*Swan Lake* by Petipa and Ivanov, *Giselle* by Coralli and Perrot), whose choreographic identity remains in large part inaccessible, gives rise to "versions," the only real manifestations of the work: Petipa and Ivanov's *Swan Lake* in a version by Gorsky, Sergeyev, or Bourmeister for example, or Coralli and Perrot's *Giselle* in a version by Lifar or Alonso.[17] These "versions" establish an absent text and fix the general identity of the choreography, giving rise to "productions" that actualize the work onstage. Productions also have a specific identity (particular decor, lighting, costumes, interpretative choices, and so on) and are in this respect like opera or theater productions—with one reservation that is important to emphasize: the claim that they execute a preexisting allographic work cannot be sustained without adopting a significantly enlarged conception of the allographic.

Choreographic works also resist Genette's scheme insofar as the distinction between the work and its execution is further problematized by works of contemporary dance. The notion of a "production" or "staging" depends on a conceptual distinction between two fields: those constitutive of the work (the literary text in the case of theater; the libretto and music in opera; and the

16. On the use of the Stepanov scores in the restaging of *Giselle* and *Swan Lake* by Nicholai Sergeyev (in 1924 and 1934), 218–20.

17. This model of the multiversion work is very evident within the classical repertoire and can be understood, in terms of Genette's vocabulary, as a case of transcendence by plurality of immanence, except that there is no primary object on the basis of which transcendence is deployed. There is only transcendence and only on the basis of transcendence is the illusion of an identifiable object (or an immanence) created.

choreographic "text," however vague and unarticulated it may be, and music of a ballet) and those that are contingent, or left to the discretion of the designer, lighting designer, or stager. I have shown how this distinction generally has no place in modern and contemporary dance.[18] The work of contemporary dance assimilates directly to the model of a production or a staging, except insofar as it is not a staging or a production of any preexisting work. This is a "production-work," with the same status as some productions within contemporary theater (such as those of Robert Wilson). This is the immanent writing for the stage imagined by Artaud. I can thus apply the ontological model described by Genette in the context of "productions." The latter can be repeated without difficulty from one evening to the next, but this power of iteration is not based on any external text: the founding ideality remains trapped in the very series of material executions. One might say, then, that the intermediary status (being neither autographic nor allographic) from which this model emerges applies directly to the choreographic *work* (or the contemporary theatrical work) and not just (as Genette argues) to "productions" or "performances of allographic works."

Moreover, it seems to me doubtful that only performance-executions can be the objects of iteration. Jazz improvisation offers many examples of "series of iterative performances." Coltrane's improvisations around *My Favorite Things* make manifest and repeat each evening, even in their variation, a kind of indeterminate identity that reduces to neither the theme of departure nor the simple melodic and rhythmic lines, notable after-the-fact and variable from one performance to another. It is one thing to recognize the indeterminacy of the identity relation linking each member of the series (the most appropriate model that springs to mind here is Wittgenstein's unfortunately much cited notion of family resemblance). It is quite another to deny this identity relation and argue that there is no iteration in this context. This issue arises again for works of contemporary dance, where what is presented as a kind of choreographic text often actually consists in an iterated improvisation.[19]

Finally, it is important to highlight an ambivalence as regards the very concept of the work. If the question of the work reduces to its identity conditions—to whatever allows us to say that it really is what it is—one seems obliged to argue that a singular event (an ephemeral improvisation or an irreducibly unique performance) is a work. That position is implicitly adopted by Genette. As a unique autographic object, a singular performance falls neatly into the categories of Goodman's ontology, and the simple deictic virtues of date, place, and proper

18. See above, 125–27.

19. See below, 273.

name are enough to ensure its identification. My position is slightly different in that I claim that the concept of the work is not restricted to the question of identification or the formal, taxonomical divisions that accompany it: the notion of the work always concerns in some way the question of its survival, the ambition of seeing the object or the experience survive the death of those who initiated it. This part of my book makes sense only in light of this question.

DANCE: AN ALLOGRAPHIC ART WITHOUT NOTATION?

It is clear that my argument rests on two premises. (1) *Dance does not really have a notation* or, more accurately, has never really integrated the possibility of writing into its actual practices. I hope I have demonstrated this sufficiently in the previous chapter. (2) *Notation is a strict condition of the allographic.* This is what I now need to demonstrate.

Goodman's diachronic hypothesis, articulated above, was called for specifically by the case of dance. From a pragmatic point of view, dance is an art form predisposed toward notation. Its works are ephemeral and most often collectively produced: in contrast to painting, which is durable and solitary, it qualifies on both counts. However—and it is this which makes the art form interesting to Goodman—dance has remained effectively lacking in notation:

> Since an art seems to be allographic just insofar as it is amenable to notation, the case of the dance is especially interesting. Here we have an art where the ways, and even the possibility, of developing an adequate notation are still matters of controversy. Is the search for a notation reasonable in the case of dance but not in the case of painting? [...] Amenability to notation depends upon a precedent practice that develops only if works of the art in question are commonly either ephemeral or not producible by one person. The dance, like the drama and symphonic and choral music, qualifies on both scores, while painting qualifies on neither. (Goodman 1976, 121–22)

Although pragmatically dance qualifies for notation, in fact notation is effectively still lacking. The diachronic hypothesis intervenes to account for this discrepancy. Dance has started down the path. It has defined a repertory of steps and gestures, a collection of identifiable and repeatable choreographic elements. But this incipient structuration has not yet been notationally validated.

So a domain's prestructuring within a practice is connected to the possibility of its notational validation. This raises the question of the relationship between notation and the allographic. To what extent is notation indispensable to the transformation from autographic to allographic? Could dance not economize on the graphic detour and rely solely on the categories already established in practice (steps, movement vocabularies, and repertories of movements that authorize iteration and thus allow the work to escape the strictly autographic)? In short, can an allographic art without notation not exist? Goodman appears perfectly adamant on this point, at least in *Languages of Art*:

> Definitive identification of works, fully freed from history of production, is achieved only when a notation is established. The allographic art has won its emancipation not by proclamation but by notation. (1976, 122)

If notation really does guarantee the allographic (of identification independent of the history of production), that means establishing a theory of notation strictly deduced from its primary function to nonambiguously identify works. This function is actually twofold. The score regulates the relation between the work and its performances in two directions: given a score of the work, the class of its correct performances can be unequivocally deduced; equally unequivocally, given a performance and a notational system, one can deduce the work's score:

> Not only must a score uniquely determine the class of performances belonging to the work, but the score (as a class of copies or inscriptions that so define the work) must be uniquely determined, given a performance and the notational system. (Goodman 1976, 129–30)[20]

From this primary function derives the relatively strict character of Goodman's theory of notation, which consists in five requirements that I will only mention here.[21] Whatever the nature of these criteria, I will note simply that notation remains in the 1968 text (2nd ed., 1976) a strict condition of the allographic. Goodman, however, reconsiders this claim in his later essay:

> While availability of a notation is usually what establishes an art as allographic, mere availability of a notation is neither a necessary nor a sufficient condition. What *is necessary* is that identification of the or an instance of a work be independent of the history of production; a notation as much codifies as creates such an independent criterion. (1984, 139)

---

20. The citation is from chapter 4, "The Theory of Notation," section 1, "The primary function." It is this "return" that distinguishes notational definition from other types of definition: "While a good definition always unequivocally determines what objects conform to it, a definition is seldom in turn uniquely determined by each of its instances. [...] No such latitude can be tolerated in the case of scores" (Goodman 1976, 129).

21. These requirements are syntactic disjointness, syntactic differentiation, unique determination, semantic disjointness, and semantic differentiation.

If Goodman provides an example of a nonsufficient notation (the rather tenuous case of a library-like system for numbering paintings), he nonetheless fails
to make explicit the potentially non-necessary character of notation. One waits
for an example of an allographic art lacking notation, but it does not come.
Genette, insisting on the prestructuration of the domain to which notation
is applied, uses exactly this passage in support of making notation's role less
important within the allographic regime:

> I would be inclined to say that a notation codifies *rather than* creates such
> a state of affairs, which, to repeat, defines the allographic regime, of which
> notation is both an effect and an instrument: when such circumstances (for
> example, the ephemeral nature of performances or the collective character
> of certain creations) impel an art to move toward the allographic regime,
> the invention and gradual refinement of a system like classical musical nota-
> tion cannot but promote and sustain this mode of existence. But *allographic*
> *regimes can arise and persist in the absence of such a notation, muddling*
> *through until something better comes along, as choreography did for centuries*
> before the recent invention of one or more notations deemed unambiguous.
> (1997, 79–80, my emphasis)

I wrote in the previous chapter of these recently invented notation systems,
which are actually all but unambiguous. Let us recall here simply that dance
again appears as an (apparently perfect) example of an art that lacks notation
but remains allographic. But this claim rests on precisely the point it needs to
demonstrate. We know that dance, in the way it is practiced, manages without
notation. But nothing indicates (except perhaps a spontaneous analogy with
those theatrical and musical works largely maintained by cultural institutions)
that this is a properly allographic art, one freed from identification by history
of production. The structuring of the domain into discrete elements—steps,
gestures, and so on—allows the transmission of practices but probably does
not in itself enable the persistence and independence of works. The notion of
"muddling through until something better comes along" implies much more
than a simple ontological approximation. In the field of ballet, it is at the root
of the quasi-complete disappearance of pre-nineteenth-century works and the
extremely patchy transmission of pre-twentieth-century works (only some
"classic" ballets, inscribed in the repertory of institutions, have come down to
us and, once again, in a very particular form that I will need to describe in more
detail in the following chapter).

Anxious to elucidate notation's basis in practice, Genette insists with
good reason on what might be called the *arche-writing* of practices,

on the classification of elements, on repertories of steps or gestures constitutive of a given practice. This arche-writing predetermines the graphic categories of notation and is effectively the germ of the allographic regime: by establishing general categories, it founds the possibility of iteration, wrenching the work from the singular event. Arche-writing can probably dispense with writing altogether and persist through simple oral transmission:

> To a layman, the movements of a dancer or matador can seem uncoordinated, random, and perfectly resistant to an analysis that would analyze them into contingent properties, on the one hand (characteristic either of the artist's style or of some particular feature of his performance), and properties constitutive of the passage he is executing on the other; but a connoisseur will recognize them as an entrechat, grand jeté, veronica, or final thrust *a recibir*, that is, as so many codified movements constitutive of the practice in question, and identifiable amid the chance events or special twists proper to this or that particular performance [...] As we have noted in passing, none of the operations I have just mentioned depends on the availability or utilization of a notation in the strict sense, which would presuppose artificial, sophisticated graphic conventions [...] the repertory of techniques proper to each practice can simply be described in words and *handed down by oral tradition*. (Genette 1997, 85–6, my emphasis)

But it is crucial to note that only the arche-writing ("the technical repertory characteristic of a practice") is transmitted and not works themselves. If oral tradition succeeds in ensuring the persistence of practices by transmitting their constitutive categories, it is not clear (and for obvious reasons relating to the limits of memory) whether that tradition alone can preserve the singular combinations of elements that constitute works. It is possible without a great deal of difficulty to learn and retain the whole constitutive vocabulary of the practice known as "classical ballet." But it is more difficult to preserve, by oral means alone, all of its operal combinations. In this respect, it is not surprising to see Genette assimilating dance to the art-without-works that is bullfighting. Bullfighting certainly transmits an arche-writing, a repertoire of gestures and moves; but it is not touched by the question of the work (or, more precisely, by the question of the work's iteration). Each fight presents a new and singular combination, drawn of course from the common repertoire of moves, but varying according to accidents of presence, the singular qualities of the bull, and the inspiration of the moment. A bullfight remains a unique autographic object, similar in this regard to improvisations and indifferent to the question of its iteration. And it is striking to see how Genette's argument aims to show the possibility of allographic structuration independent of notational artifice but leads, ultimately, to an art whose "works" (if this is the appropriate term) are purely autographic.[22]

The position that I will take in this regard is decidedly the inverse of Genette's. I will maintain that only the preservation of the work through writing allows it to be freed from its material history of production. A practice can be structured in an essentially allographic fashion, organized around a repertoire of ideal elements that are easily repeatable and identifiable. But nonetheless a further step is necessary for works to become completely allographic. This step is preservation in writing, through inscription.

Choreographic works, therefore, are not allographic: their identity cannot be liberated in an external and indefinitely available ideality. But neither are they autographic: as soon as they are repeated and transmitted, they escape from the pure singularity of the perceptible event. This status as neither allographic nor autographic is the very mark of their specificity. Reflecting the absence of the work even within a body of works, this status might be described as an *unworking* of choreography.

22. Once again, the fact that Genette can call a bullfight a "work" confirms that he considers the work as such separately from the question of its persistence. To articulate this using the categories I have outlined: the work is retained only as a public object (whether as a thing or an event) but not as a persistent object. On my view, these two dimensions are not dissociable and together constitute the concept of the work.

Chapter 3

Oral Identities: Passing Dance On, Making Versions

As we have seen, dance is typically preserved and passed on via oral transmission and person-to-person transfer. A proper analysis of the various means of transmission would far exceed my focus here. What does it mean to pass on or hand down a dance? What is it to wrench a dance from the body to which it first belonged? And what does it mean to see that dance revived on another body, appearing at once the same and different? And, finally, is there such a thing as a dance that is *not* idiosyncratic, that escapes the idiolect of the individual body?

You show me a movement, I perform it. That already implies several processes of translation, if only at the level of the always complex action of face-to-face demonstration, where your right systematically corresponds to my left. Perhaps I need to put myself behind you, at your back, where the face of the movement is hidden, although we are oriented on the same coordinates. Perhaps we need to refer to a third party, that enigmatic mirror that reflects both our images, reversed in equal measure. But when you show me a movement, you are not *just* showing. And, in any case, you may be growing older and demonstration proving more difficult. You mainly talk. You give indications, which allow me to correct my movement. In the process, I navigate between the image and the concept, between imitating your person and understanding categorially that which abstracts itself from what you do. I isolate and invent an unwritten text that extracts itself from your body. I treat you like a score, which does not exist. And yet we well know that everything hinges on what exceeds the score, on the singular image and gesture, on the transfer of affect, and on this intertwining of our bodies' experience.

All transmission involves establishing (whether by presupposition or invention) some conventions that allow recognition of the same within difference,

or the isolation of invariants enabling the repetition of a gesture in two different bodies. Genette calls this operation "allographic reduction" and, notably, he
illustrates the nature of the process with reference to an example of (minimal)
gestural transmission. I raise my arm and ask you to copy me. But what does
it mean to *copy* what I do? I raised my right arm. Does that mean that you
should lift your left, the one that corresponds when we stand face to face face?
Or should you raise your right arm, because that matches what my body itself
is doing? That question settled, to what extent should you imitate the action of
my arm? Was my arm straight or bent? Somewhere between the two? And *how*
did I raise it? Sharply? Softly? Did I initiate the movement with the wrist or with
the elbow? Or perhaps the shoulder blade? And so on and so forth (see Genette
1997, 82–83).

As these apparently trivial questions ramify, it quickly becomes clear that
all gestural transmission implies a reduction of singularity. In other words,
a set of ideal elements must be identified at some level to sort the essential from the contingent. This set may already be present as an established
framework for transmission. Above, I called such a framework choreographic *arche-writing*: a repertoire of gestural entities, known and shared
by all, that can form the basis for passing on a dance. Classical ballet and
so-called traditional dances have this kind of framework. But in other contexts, it is lacking: the movement itself is developed outside of preestablished
codes and vocabularies. The process of transmission then involves inventing
those generalities and that vocabulary, identifying ex post facto what was
initially produced in the proximity of the self to itself and the immediacy
of sense experience. This, broadly speaking, is the situation of modern and
contemporary dance.

Here I consider the means of oral transmission only in terms of what they
imply for the survival and status of works. It would be a whole other project to
explore what is at stake ideologically and pedagogically when these means are
employed.

THE PARADOX OF THE REPERTOIRE: THE FRAME-*WORK*

One obvious consequence of dance relying on oral transmission is the disappearance of very many works. Practically all eighteenth-century ballets have
been lost,[1] and the 160 ballets composed by Noverre during his career are
known only through their titles and texts, which give only a partial idea of
their choreography. The transmission of nineteenth- and twentieth-century

---

1. Excepting those works from 1700 to 1750 recorded in Feuillet notation. See above, 165–66.

works, meanwhile, has been very patchy and distorted. Where the survival of works depends on the memory of the creators and original participants, those works will die unless there is a real desire to reactivate that memory and an institutional framework that values the preservation of works. This kind of framework is a recent phenomenon in dance, even in the institutions devoted to classical ballet. Right up to the beginning (even the middle) of the twentieth century, the notion of the fixed repertoire remained largely alien to the choreographic field. Choreographic institutions still appear founded more on the principle of continuous creation and novelty that is constantly refreshed, in keeping with the spirit of the dance conceived as *divertissement*.

This belies the mantra constantly repeated at the Paris Opéra, which claims it as a place of memory and continuous preservation from its founding to the present day.[2] In fact, the history of this institution, from the point of view of the persistence of works, is riddled with lacunae and forgetfulness. By 1950, the Opéra had forgotten the core works of its own Romantic repertoire (*La Sylphide, Paquita,* and *Le Corsaire,* for example) and was largely ignorant of the grand classical Russian ballets of the late nineteenth century, which only really became part of its portfolio in the 1960s.[3]

As regards Romantic works, *La Sylphide*[4] disappeared from the Opéra's repertoire as early as 1866, despite the fact that this ballet made Marie Taglioni a living legend and fascinated a whole generation of intellectuals in the 1830s. The work "survived" in Denmark, however, with a different musical score and different choreography devised by August Bournonville in 1836; the ballet in this form has been handed down within the continuous tradition of the Royal Danish Ballet.[5] In short, oral tradition purely and simply forgot Filippo Taglioni's *La Sylphide.* It was only thanks to Pierre Lacotte's documentary research and

---

2. See, for example, the words of Martine Kahane, former director of the cultural service of the Paris Opéra: "In 1669, Louis XIV founded the Académie Royale de Musique et de Danse [. . .] The repertoire of the Opéra was thus born three centuries ago. Since then, it has grown with each season, been lost, then rediscovered again, following a kind of pendulum movement." See the text "De quelques facteurs d'un repertoire official," *Marsyas,* no. 25 (March 1993).

3. Thus, Petipa and Ivanov's *Swan Lake* (1895) only "entered" the Paris Opéra in 1960 (in Bourmeister's version). It was not until the 1980s, and the impetus given by its director Rudolf Nureyev to the construction of the academic repertoire, that the Paris Opéra acquired versions of *Don Quixote* (1869), *La Bayadère* (1877), *The Sleeping Beauty* (1890), *Nutcracker* (1892), and *Raymonda* (1898).

4. Created in 1832 at the Paris Opéra, with choreography by Filippo Taglioni, music by Jean Schneitzhoeffer and libretto by Adolphe Nourrit.

5. *Sylfiden* (1836), with music by Løvenskjold, choreography and libretto by Bournonville.

work of historical reconstruction that the "original version" of the ballet could be presented in 1971 and reintegrated into the repertoire of the Opéra in 1972.[6]

Giselle, created in 1841 at the Paris Opéra,[7] had disappeared from the repertoire by 1868 and might have suffered a similar fate to *La Sylphide* had the ballet not been "appropriated" by the Russian tradition. The work toured on all the big European stages in the 1840s, and Marius Petipa helped to restage it in St. Petersburg. He developed his own "version" in 1884, which henceforth would serve as the reference point for the tradition. France only rediscovered the ballet through this Russian filter, first in 1910 in Michel Fokine's version for Diaghilev's Ballets Russes, and then in Nicholai Sergeyev's restaging for the Paris Opéra in 1924. These two versions take Petipa's choreography as their basis, the first deriving from the oral tradition and the second from the Stepanov scores written a little after Petipa's heyday. These early twentieth-century Russian versions still provide the basic materials for today's collection of productions called *Giselle*. This has not prevented multiple other, subsequent versions being developed from the same base. Thus, as early as 1932, Serge Lifar reviewed and adapted the choreography, giving the prince a more central role. Lifar's version was supplanted, within the Paris Opéra, by Alicia Alonso's version of 1972. This was itself replaced in 1991 with a version by Patrice Bart and Eugène Poliakov, which is still performed today.

Moreover, the Russian tradition and Marius Petipa's restaging work are not just important in the case of *Giselle* but also in how subsequent works by Joseph Mazilier, such as *Paquita*[8] or *Le Corsaire*,[9] have come down to us. *Paquita* had disappeared from the repertoire by 1851 and owes its survival to a version developed by Petipa in St. Petersburg in 1881. This version served as a point of reference, which enabled the reintroduction of the ballet to the Paris Opéra in 1980, in the restaging by Oleg Vinogradov.

6. The first version, starring Ghislaine Thesmard and Michaël Denard, was produced for television, following which a stage version was integrated into the repertoire of the Paris Opéra in 1972. On the use of documentary sources in "reconstructions," see below, 234.

7. Choreography by Jean Coralli and Jules Perrot, music by Adolphe Adam and Norbert Burgmüller, and a libretto by Théophile Gautier, Jules-Henry Vernoy de Saint-Georges, and Jean Coralli.

8. Created in 1846 at the Paris Opéra, with choreography by Joseph Mazilier, music by Édouard Deldevez, and libretto by Paul Foucher.

9. Created in 1856 at the Paris Opéra, with choreography by Joseph Mazilier, music by Adolpe Adam, and libretto by Jules-Henry Vernoy de Saint-Georges. Note that Petipa's final version of this ballet added pieces by three further composers (Leo Délibes, Riccardo Drigo, and Cesare Pugni) to the "original" music.

The Opéra's Romantic repertoire has therefore only survived thanks to Petipa's restagings and adaptations in St. Petersburg, which themselves only returned to Western Europe at the beginning of the twentieth century, via the Ballets Russes on the one hand, and Sergeyev on the other—sufficient evidence to disprove the frankly misleading picture of the Opéra as the conservator that, by virtue of a continuous tradition, has enabled the memory of these works to be preserved.

The case of the French Romantic repertoire and the various historico-geographical transfers that enabled its survival, then, lead me to examine conditions of the persistence of works within the institution of ballet. I have frequently invoked the concept of "version," and, effectively, the entire edifice depends upon it. Reference to the original choreographer is certainly always maintained (*Giselle* by Perrot and Coralli, *Swan Lake* by Petipa and Ivanov). But the choreography slips out of memory and is not lodged in any text that guarantees its identity, so it can only be actualized within different theaters in the form of a "version," under-signed by the restager or the ballet master. Such ballets are systematically credited in terms of a double signature, the formulation of which varies: "*Giselle* by Coralli and Perrot, in a version by Lifar"; "*Swan Lake*, choreographed and staged by Vladimir Bourmeister, after Petipa and Ivanov"; "*Giselle*, choreography after Jean Coralli and Jules Perrot, restaged and adapted by Patrice Bart and Eugène Poliakov"; or "*Swan Lake*, choreographed and staged by Rudolph Nureyev, after Petipa and Ivanov."

To analyze the notion of the work-with-multiple-versions, I will here take the example of *Swan Lake* by Petipa and Ivanov and permit myself to pose a few apparently simple questions. Firstly, when exactly was it created? Should the reply be "January 1895, the date of the premiere at the Maryinsky Theatre in St. Petersburg"? This is hardly clear-cut, since this "work" was already a restaging or recreation of a ballet created in 1877 at the Bolshoi by Julius Reisinger, restaged and adapted three years later by Joseph Hansen. Should one say, despite the changes to the choreography between 1877 and 1895, that at least Tchaikovsky's music and the story as written in the libretto remain stable? This is not the case either, because Petipa asked Tchaikovsky to rework the score and himself rewrote the libretto with Ivanov. Hence this ballet, the very emblem of the classical repertoire, remains indeterminate as regards at least its date, its authors, and its identity. And this constitutive vagueness, partly linked to the very structures governing production within the classical tradition, is reproduced directly in the modalities of its transmission. If the Petipa-Ivanov version of 1895 immediately became the point of reference for future productions, even this version only survived through constant readaptation and geographical dispersal. Alexander Gorsky's 1901 version for the Bolshoi is certainly situated within the continuity of an oral genealogy and tradition. But this is not really the case with Fokine's version for Diaghilev's Ballets Russes (London, 1911, with Nijinsky in the role of Siegfried), which shortened the ballet to two acts. The Nikolai Sergeyev version for the Vic-Wells Ballet in London (1934), a product of the oral tradition and the Stepanov scores, was the first complete instance of the work in Western Europe. Lifar presented extracts from the work in 1936 at the Paris Opéra, but it was not until Bourmeister's 1960 version (stemming from the Russian oral tradition) that *Swan Lake* was finally presented in its complete form in Paris. Subsequently there have been further notable versions, including Nureyev's 1964 production for the Vienna Opera, Eric Bruhn's in Toronto in 1967, or Baryshnikov's in Washington in 1981. A new Nureyev version (1984) entered the repertoire of the Paris Opéra in 1986, such that the Opéra today still has two versions of "*Swan Lake* by Petipa and Ivanov," given alternately (the Bourmeister and Nureyev versions, respectively).[10] The Parisian public was recently invited to experience *Swan Lake*'s plurality of immanence when in December 2005 two versions of the ballet were being performed concurrently (one by the Paris Opéra, the other by the Maryinsky Theatre, drawing on the Russian oral tradition), in addition to two contemporary reinterpretations: one by the British choreographer Matthew Bourne at the Théâtre Mogador, and the other by Pina Bausch's former dramaturg, Raimund Hoghe, at the Théâtre de la Bastille.[11]

Drawing on the examples just given, it is important to distinguish between a "version" and a "reinterpretation." To enable performance, a "version" establishes a choreographic text that the vagaries of memory and oral transfer have left incomplete. It does not signal itself as such, but nonetheless is always "undersigned" by the name of the restager, of the ballet master, or of the choreographer associated with the company. Such is the case with all of the examples that I have so far considered in detail. A "reinterpretation," meanwhile, is signed by a choreographic author and establishes a new work in its own right. Such is the case with Mats Ek's *Giselle* or *Swan Lake*, where the only invariant feature as regards the original ballets is the music, and where the narrative schema itself is radically subverted in favor of a different reading—a broadly psychoanalytic one in these particular cases. Contemporary reinterpretations of the classical repertory are a very common feature of the choreography made during the second half of the twentieth century: there are innumerable

---

10. Thus, during the 1989–90 season, Nureyev's version was given, while in 1991–92 the Bourmeister version was staged, offering a strange experience of the plural immanence of the work across just two performance seasons.

11. On this group of "versions" and "reinterpretations" given concurrently in Paris in December 2005, see the special issue on *Swan Lake* of the magazine *Danser*, no. 249 (December 2005).

examples.[12] But because they are signed by a choreographic author and enjoy status as works in their own right, they fall outside the model of the work-with-versions that I am trying to delineate: that of the classical ballet that persists through the multiplication of its versions, all equally legitimate and all equally referencing an original work.[13]

This model of the work-with-versions clearly shows a twofold transcendence. On the one hand, there is transcendence by partiality of immanence: the choreographic text is missing, given over to the oral tradition and its lapses of memory. Besides, this text was probably flexible even at the moment of its inception, as Balanchine suggests with regard to Petipa;[14] it was constantly re-elaborated in the course of different seasons and productions. On the other hand, there is here transcendence by plurality of immanence, which typically structures the work-with-versions: given the absence of the original choreographic text, the different versions, realizations or "readings" of the missing text, will multiply, responding to the global demands of performance and filling in the gaps for presentation on the stage. The identity of the classical choreographic work is therefore doubly and structurally transcendent: its immanence is plural, precisely because from the beginning it is incomplete and partial. More radically still, one could say that there is no immanence of the classical choreographic work. The different objects that present themselves as such and which are signed, for example, by Perrot or by Petipa, rest only on facts of transcendence. An empty reference to the name of the author is certainly maintained—a commitment as symbolic as it is commercial—but everyone well knows that no one knows the original choreography.

This possibility of classical works persisting depends ultimately on a double condition. Firstly, it is paradoxically the indifference to the work, or more precisely the indifference to authorial authority, which enables the survival of the object. It is because the work is now only a vague structure, a general framework for successive versions or continual, licit variations, that it can ultimately

12. See also, for example, Maguy Marin's *Cendrillon [Cinderella]* (1985) and *Coppélia* (1993), or Angelin Preljocaj's *Noces* (1989), *Roméo et Juliette* (1990), and *Le Spectre de la Rose* (1993).

13. Thus, one of the essential functions of dance dictionaries is to provide a long list of each work's different versions, sometimes betraying conceptual hesitation over whether these qualify as "versions," "stagings," or "reinterpretations." In this regard, the most exhaustive, but also the least clear, dictionary seems to me to be the *International Encyclopedia of Dance* edited by Selma Jeanne Cohen (1998). By contrast, Philippe Le Moal's *Dictionnaire de la Danse* draws a clear distinction between version and reinterpretation.

14. "It would be fruitless to try to reconstitute with archaeological precision an 'original' that Petipa himself changed from one season to another"; Balanchine cited in the French edition of Petipa's *Mémoires* (Petipa 1990).

persist. This is the very logic of variation that, through constantly readapting the missing choreographic text, perpetuates a certain identificatory framework, a certain general idea perhaps of *Giselle* by Coralli and Perrot. In a kind of paradox, it appears therefore that indifference to the work and to the author, issuing directly from the model of the *divertissement*, is the condition of the repertoire within the domain of classical ballet. It is because no one cares about the work that it stays alive, abandoning an identity that it never had.

Secondly, the condition of this kind of transmission is the preexistence of an experiential framework and fixed, widely shared lexicon. For the oral tradition to function, an arche-writing must already be present that is common to everyone. Such is the case with classical ballet vocabulary and technique that, even while they apparently obliterate the historicity of ballet's objects, authorizes their transmission.

This double condition of the classical repertoire (the indifference to authorial authority and a preexisting framework of experience as well as a common lexicon) is, as we shall see, explicitly rejected by modern and contemporary dance.

IDIOSYNCRASY'S IMPASSES: THE CORPOREAL WORK

Two modern figures seem to me to exemplify this shift and the difficulties it implies as regards transmission of works: they are Isadora Duncan and Mary Wigman.

The "free dance" invented by Duncan depended on a close concatenation of work and dancing subject, of the choreographic object and the dancing body that inhabited it. Abandoning the codes of academic technique implies, in order to avoid the experience of mere emptiness, that the subject return to herself. It implies an exploration and simultaneous exposition of whatever constitutes the individual as an irreplaceable singularity. Hence Duncan's works almost all took the form of solos: a few years after Loïe Fuller and in reaction against ballet, Duncan reinstituted the form of the "dance concert" or "choreographic recital," in which the lone individual showed her *own* body and her *own* dances to the public. In the moment of performance, such ownership implies a complete lack of differentiation between the object and the person, between what is danced and he or she who dances it. At least, that was the perception in Duncan's own time. It was Isadora who one came to watch, such that the body of Isadora became constitutive of the work itself, in accord with a purely autographic—even *auratic*—identity regime.[15]

This principle of singularity was combined with a commitment to improvisation, a further consequence of rejecting all preexisting codes. Abolishing all

15. I refer here to Rebecca Schneider's general analysis of the choreographic solo entitled "Unbecoming Solo," in Rousier (2002). The text is adapted and developed in English in

preestablished vocabularies can only infect the movement with a fundamental contingency: there is no longer any reason to do one thing rather than another. This contingency, and the emptiness of the subject confronted with herself, cannot be redeemed, or rendered full again, except by virtue of an enhanced attention to the present as such, a sensitivity to what here and now has the allure of corporeal necessity. In Duncan's practice, contingency was redeemed, and attention paid to what appeared necessary in the current moment, via the intermediary of music. For Duncan, dance was always transitive: one danced *a* piece of music. Or, more precisely, danced movement was only ever the projection, here and now, of musical listening, each time singular, each time unique.[16]

This double model of the solo that is improvised (although in this case it was structured by certain motifs and musically guided) entails the impossibility of iteration and indeed of transmission. The work, to the extent of its authorial signature and corporeal anchoring, becomes a strict singularity. If transmission and teaching were integral parts of Duncan's project, these never happened through artistic work-objects being repeated or brought together in a repertoire. What was transmitted emerged rather from an aesthetics, even an ethics, of the body and movement; it did not come from a body of work(s), understood as a collection of stable objects isolated from the body that nourished them and alone guaranteed them. It is appropriate, therefore, to follow the work of Laetitia Doat (2006) in claiming that there is no Duncan oeuvre. Or, more precisely: there is an oeuvre only in retrospect, when schools are established and a practice is handed down, when practice must be fixed as an object, although it was only ever constituted by movement and attention to the present.

Mary Wigman radicalized these two characteristics of solo dance and improvisation, both of which appear to exclude the idea of a *work*. Nowhere was the critique of all anterior tradition as strong as it was in Wigman's discourse. Wigman established the tradition of the tabula rasa: in other words, she inaugurated a modern tradition that sees itself as a complete *absence* of tradition

---

Schneider's essay "Solo Solo Solo" in Butt (2005): "In solo performance as it developed in the latter half of the twentieth century, the single body increasingly performed in a piece authored and/or choreographed and/or staged and/or designed by that single body [...] The Solo Artist *making* art became, then, the auratic object itself. The artist stepped (or danced) into the place of the object" (32–33). I have, however, one qualm concerning this reference to Walter Benjamin. The aura of the work of art for Benjamin attaches only to the present manifestation of something distant, which is probably not the case (as I have suggested) where the aura of the performance event is concerned, which reduces completely to the simple disappearance of its present.

16. This account of Duncan's idea of improvisation should be further nuanced: one should speak rather of a free development of corporeal motifs that are set in advance and modulated according to the character of musical listening.

and that dreams of the perpetually new body, returned to the simple bareness of its present: "I have always been a fanatic of the present," says Wigman, "in love with the moment" (1966, 8). Truly unprecedented movement can spring only from the intimacy of the corporeal now. This is movement that has never been seen or coded before yet is physically necessary. The exploration of singularity enables truly new movement to appear as corporeal necessity. Such was the meaning of improvisation for Wigman, as she freed herself from all musical diktats. The present silence of the body allowed the affective power of what was internally necessary to be prolonged.

One might say, indeed, that this dance was a product of possession, in the double sense of that which *takes over* and that which *belongs to* the dancer. And if the movement was the product of possession, one can well understand how it was impossible to share: the dancer could not without suffering let herself be dispossessed of what miraculously took hold; she could not pass that movement on to the interminable drift of history and intersubjectivity. Once again, Mary Wigman was above all a soloist and an improviser.[17] Denial of the passage of time was internal to her project. Or perhaps it was rather an expression of desire for a present that would constantly begin again. The work would only count at the very moment of the experience that nourished it. And there was no work beyond that present experience, always different and always singular, by which the own body's self-identity could simultaneously find itself and be lost. Only a constantly renewed relationship to the present could prevent movement from sinking into reification, such that for Wigman "there are no ready-made modern dance works which can be rehearsed and performed" (Wigman in Sorrell 1975, 113). That meant, in terms of transmission, that "after me, all will be swept away!"[18] To re-emphasize, Wigman schools have never tried to pass on *works* but rather tools for exploring corporeal singularity. If there is pedagogy here, it is certainly not oriented toward the survival of work-objects but more toward the transmission of processes enabling the subject to produce in her own terms, according to the idiosyncrasy of her corporeal "I." And, to short-circuit history, we thus rejoin a certain model of production characteristic of the 1980s—what one might term, company "immersion." In other words, an author-choreographer establishes and extends in the form of an idiolect his own, singular corporeality. This distinctive idiom, which both inscribes his self and guarantees his authorial signature, is passed on to his

17. She created seventy solos as compared to only twenty group works. As with Duncan, but even more acutely, the question arises of the link between improvisation and composition: how can the lightning flash of the present be transformed into a stable, repeatable object? See below, 273.

18. "Après moi, le deluge!": Wigman cited in Jacqueline Robinson's preface to French edition of Wigman (1990).

dancers.[19] Generally, this happens via the mechanism of the daily class and a form of unconscious mimicry that, despite the particularity of all the individuals concerned, appears to transform them into the same bodily "clay," allowing all to develop the same general habitus of posture and movement. In short, it generates a sort of common body, something real but nonetheless difficult to pin down, whose establishment is part and parcel of the company structure and the quotidian encounters it implies, in which the dancers are immersed. And this "common body" seems, even more effectively than writing, to guarantee the identity of the choreographic work. It is thus possible to understand how difficult it is to pass works on from one company to another, from those immersed in one idiom to those immersed in another, from one body of tacit corporeal knowledge to another. The identity of the work therefore rests not so much on a collection of objective motor parameters as on the collective bodily history of the company, which creates its distinctive idiom. Or, perhaps, it depends on an arche-writing, which is common to the group, yet so tacit and so intimate that it cannot be transmitted beyond.

One consequence is the well-known fact that it is very rare for contemporary works to be shared beyond the companies that originally created them. And it is this fact—and the impossibility it implies—that I will now explore.

ORAL MUTATIONS: THE HANDED-DOWN WORK

A major choreographer of the 1980s, Dominique Bagouet died on December 9, 1992, after sixteen years of making choreography with the company that bore his name. Six months later, in July 1993, his company decided to disband. But in the intervening time between his death and the company's dissolution, a new kind of organization was invented in the Carnets Bagouet, a collective of former company dancers, who would work to hand down Bagouet's choreography. They present a unique example in the world of French contemporary dance of works being transmitted from one company context to other dancers.

Nonetheless, at the outset, the Carnets Bagouet still seemed to be built on the model (discussed above) of the *corporeal work*. There were no *carnets*—or notebooks—in the material sense of the term, and contrary to what was often assumed at the time. There were no notes or scores sufficiently clear to guarantee in the choreographer's absence the perpetuity of these works. At least in their choreographic dimension, the works seemed to survive only in the corporeal

---

19. On this issue, see Derrida on the nature of the idiomatic as "a property that one cannot appropriate; it signs you without belonging to you" (1995 [1992], 119).

memory of the dancers. As Catherine Legrand remarked, the term "carnet" should not be understood to refer to anything beyond the actual bodies of the original performers.[20] But what does it mean for the body to be a "notebook"? Or, better, what could an incarnate "carnet" possibly be? The notebook generally is actually always midway between the body and ideality, between the singularity of the autograph and the universality of the shared code. Someone else can certainly try to read my notebooks, but not without some prior, quite laborious effort at decoding, and not without exposing himself to inevitable errors of interpretation. Only the original writer seems capable of accessing the writing of a notebook, the writing itself being intimate, or idiographic, one might say. Hence, to call the bodies of the performers "notebooks" was, from the outset, to highlight and reveal the ambiguous status of the corporeal source at the heart of practices of oral transmission; the ambivalence of that which is destined for another and yet does not seem capable of being read by anyone but oneself. All the work of the Carnets Bagouet consisted of trying to decipher the notebook that was the body of the performer. They tried to extract from the idiosyncrasy of personal history and the autograph some "score" that might be shared.

It is also clear that a gap had already opened up in the model of the *corporeal work* at the time when the works in question were made: a gap created by the distance established between choreographer and dancer, writing and interpretation. Perhaps the dissociation between work and body, between writing and interpretation, remained merely virtual and latent while the company still existed:[21] pieces were described as "Catherine's solo" or "Fabrice's solo," and so on. All the work of passing on these pieces thenceforth consisted in making this dissociation explicit, isolating identity parameters that would enable detachment of the dance from its original body. The task was to make "Catherine's solo" as arranged by Dominique into an autonomous object, without an established owner (except Bagouet as choreographic author), not in order to render the object corporeally anonymous but rather to demand of each restaging that it become the site of a singular appropriation, an act of *performance interpretation*.

20. She made this claim in the context of the *État des lieux* symposium, October 2003, at Magrin, marking ten years of activity on the part of the Carnets Bagouet and bringing together Anne Abeille, Christian Bourigault, Claire Chancé, Sylvie Giron, Olivia Grandville, Isabelle Launay, Catherine Legrand, Anne-Karine Lescop, Alain Michard, Dominique Noël, Laurent Pichaud, Frédéric Pouillaude, Fabrice Ramalingom, Jean Rochereau, and Michèle Rust (Archives of the Carnets Bagouet).

21. In this era, dancers certainly learned other performers' roles, but more according to the logic of a familial, quotidian immersion in the company; this general complicity with the work and the distinctive corporeality of Bagouet's choreography rendered superfluous a clear articulation of the conditions of transmission.

As Isabelle Launay notes, perhaps it is only at the moment of being passed or handed down that the work is able to prove itself as a work, as an autonomous object subject to various interpretations and reinterpretations:

> A return to the work of Bagouet assumed that it was now possible to conceive of "Bagouet's work" as distinct from "Dominique's dance." Without this assumption, it would not be a question of *handing down* the choreography so much as a kind of semiconscious initiation into *dances* which were not *roles*. (2007, 54)

> It is in the act of transmission itself that the written work is discovered and is objectified as such, that the dancers become effectively interpreters of that work, in other words *conscious of what it is they do*. (73)

How is this move from "dance" to "work," from the status of "dancer" to that of "interpreter" effected? By triangulating the relation, inserting a third term between the choreographer and the dancer, as between the dancer and "her" dance. This third term is indeterminate and belongs properly to no one: it is the choreographic as such, choreographic writing or, perhaps, a kind of score that does not necessarily have to be written down. This triangulation becomes possible after the fact only because it was present from the beginning, because the mediation of writing and the choreographic was already implicitly floating between the choreographer and the dancer. A counterexample supports this view: that of *F. et stein*, the only solo created by Dominique Bagouet on himself,[22] the restaging of which appeared strictly impossible to the members of the Carnets Bagouet. It was not just that an oral transmission of this work had become impossible (because of the death of the performer); rather, the very project of restaging appeared aesthetically (even morally) incongruous or inappropriate because the concatenation between work and body, between choreographer and performer, seemed here to have been explicitly intended by Bagouet. The work could dissociate itself from the body only on the condition that it was, at some level, already thus dissociated, which seemed manifestly not the case with *F. et stein*. At least this was the substance of the response to Christian Bourigault (former company dancer and former member of the Carnets) when he announced his desire to revive this solo. Bourigault retorted that he understood this revival specifically as an attempt to validate *a work*, extracting its text from the singular body of Dominique. If this extraction could not be effected

---

22. Created in 1983 at Villeneuve-lez-Avignon. For a description and aesthetic analysis of the collection of pieces by Dominique Bagouet that I discuss here, see the remarkable monograph by Isabelle Ginot (1999).

via oral transmission, perhaps video documentation and the testimony of the original collaborators could be used, even if that meant moving beyond the strictly oral framework to which the Carnets had committed themselves.[23]

Even if the conditions of oral transmission are fulfilled, however (including, importantly, the condition that there be surviving witnesses), what is specific about the means of transmission devised by the Carnets Bagouet? How does this differ from a mere reactivation of the framework by which classical ballets are typically handed down? The first difference with classical ballet is the fact that, in the contemporary case, transmission cannot rely on a self-evident vocabulary, shared by all. If the modern or contemporary choreographer really does invent his own lexicon of movement and his own corporeality, the transmission of his works then implies that a new framework for articulating and categorizing that lexicon must also be established. The second difference—which is perhaps merely the flip side of the first—is that this individual lexicon only has meaning when embodied by dancers whose corporeality has been molded in a specific way, which includes embodying a general collection of postural and motor principles, over and above the vocabulary, color, or signature of the choreographed movement as such. Here once again the issue of "immersion" and slow impregnation with a choreographic idiom arises, something that the usual temporal and financial conditions of restaging rarely favor. This was noticeably the case when *So Schnell* was taught to the Paris Opéra in 1998: the demand for a long period of corporeal habituation imposed by the Carnets Bagouet[24] was directly in conflict with the usual process for mounting revivals at the Opéra.[25] From this experience and its contradictions emerged the need to identify and explicitly articulate the shared corporeality

23. This interpretation/revival of *F. et stein* by Christian Bourigault was performed in 2000, outside of the Carnets Bagouet structure, under the title *F. et stein. Ré-interprétation*, the Carnets having refused to allow the original title to be retained. For a summary of the debate, see the transcription of the symposium "État des lieux," Archives Carnets Bagouet, from which I cite the following comment by Christian Bourigault: "My aim in reviving this work was to make it a complete choreographic work, which could be passed on to another performer. And the fact of its transmission would make it a choreographic work, with an author and a performer." The revival of *F. et stein* by Christian Bourigault seems ultimately to rest on a double, heterogeneous principle of identity or authenticity: on the one hand, the video documentation served as a basis from which to learn the solo (according to a model that I will explore in chapter 4 below); on the other hand, the fact of Bourigault's having himself been a performer with Bagouet, his immersion in the idiom of the company, which to some degree legitimated or counterbalanced the exteriority of the learning process.

24. Matthieu Doze and Olivia Grandville, in this context, who were in charge of the project.

25. Although in possession of a contract specifying exclusive performance rights to this work for six years, the Paris Opéra never restaged *So Schnell* after the first series of performances, the

that constituted the distinctive artistic signature of Bagouet's work, but which exceeded all predefined vocabulary. How it should be identified was one of the key issues discussed in the *États des lieux* symposium held in 2003 in Magrin. Another solution would have been to put this requirement to one side and allow the confrontion between Bagouet's choreographic writing and the other corporealities of contemporary performers, opening a space of interpretation in the encounter between choreographic writing and the singular, present bodies of the dancers. That was the approach taken by Fabrice Ramalingom in his revival of *Meublé sommairement* in 2000.[26]

The third way in which the approach of the Carnets differs from the classical framework is the manner in which certain Bagouet works depend less on choreographic text and more on the process that brings them into being. I am thinking particularly of *Jours étranges*,[27] the very substance of which was the outcome of a long process of improvisation on the part of the performers. A piece such as this, when transmitted to the Dance Theatre of Ireland in 1998, involved devising other transfer strategies, notably a practice of retracing the process of improvisation. Finally, more generally, it seems that the contrast with the classical tradition also emerges in the relativization or distancing of oral sources. Transmission here is less a site on which the person who knows the work unilaterally hands it down to the person who does not; it is more like a space where, ex post facto, the very identity or absent body of the work is created in the intertwining of different bodies' experience. In other words, and following Isabelle Launay once again, transmission consists in a present elaboration of the choreographic archive and not in the fixation of the identity of its origin:

> It was not a question of abandoning the logic of the oral tradition, but rather of bringing an internal critique to oral memory, to the genealogical handing down from body to body, such that this process might free itself from the ideology of direct descent, reinventing in some way the source or the material to be worked and thus problematizing the point fixed as its origin. (2007, 76)

directors having refused the working conditions imposed by the Carnets Bagouet for future revivals. As a result, *So Schnell* was not seen onstage again until 2007, after the expiration of the Opéra contract, when it was performed by the Geneva Opéra.

26. For a detailed analysis of this revival and the issues it raised as regards the idea of interpretation, see Isabelle Launay (2002).

27. Created in December 1990, this piece is the last or penultimate work by Bagouet, depending on whether or not one considers the second version of *So Schnell* (October 1992) to be a new work. On this issue, see Ginot (1999).

This process of revival is not without its problems, however, notably in the context of stage performance. Is there not a risk, in the moment of performance, that the show is perceived by the public (and perhaps to an even greater extent by the programmers) not as a present actualization of the work of Bagouet but as a simple repetition, identical to an original performance that is known to have proved its worth? Is there not a risk that the signature of the "Carnets Bagouet" is obscured by the very memory of the "Compagnie Bagouet," as if by retaining the initials "C.B." all is left intact, as if no distance or rupture has in fact been introduced by time, history, and death? In one way, the methodology of the first Carnets Bagouet revivals seemed to encourage this view. The rules were simple and threefold: (1) each revival would require the presence of two project directors (one man and one woman), the dual leadership being implicitly intended to prevent any personal artistic appropriation of the project and to avoid all effects of individual signature; (2) during the process of learning the work, as many of the original performers as possible would be involved, clearly establishing the primacy of corporeal memory as source material; (3) finally, there would be supplementary recourse to the largest possible number of documentary and video sources. These three rules (despite their possible internal contradictions) all seem to manifest a desire to let the work efface the restager, as if the revival is a transparent process whereby interpretation becomes simply a neutral medium for actualization and presentation. In this respect, the revival of *Meublé sommairement* by Fabrice Ramalingom in 2000 marked a break in the history of the Carnets Bagouet, which in any case was characterized by a number of internal tensions. In Ramalingom's project, in contrast to the double leadership of revivals up until this point, a single individual assumed full responsibility and credit for the restaging. Participation of the original performers was limited, and, finally, there was no recourse to video, in an effort not to crush the possibility of a new interpretation under the weight of the recorded image. The course taken by the transmission in this case was also more tortuous than previously.[28] It was effected less through direct demonstration of gestures than through a prior series of workshops and improvisation sessions designed to generate the movement itself. From this point on, the restager ceased to be a mere memorial deposit (in any case, his role had never been limited to this) and became the real artistic cosignatory of the interpretation. Contemporary dance lacks the relevant terms to designate such a role. Aligning with theater or film, one might talk of a "director" (*metteur en scène*), even a "director of dancers" in the same way as one speaks in French of the "direction d'acteurs." Otherwise, this attempt to rediscover a choreographic writing determined by

28. On this, see Launay (2002).

other bodily means than those initially pursued is reminiscent of the model Genette describes in terms of operal plurality, using Borges's imaginary case of *Don Quixote* by Pierre Ménard. There, two radically distinct writing processes, separated by the simple fact of their historical distance, produce one and the same text—and yet, following the paradoxical line of argument implied in Borges, two distinct works. I will return below to this model of operal plurality: a repetition of the same that simultaneously reveals the impossibility of strict identity.

This tendency to highlight the artistic signature of the restager, then, borrows from the theater the notion of stage direction (*mise en scène*) that is atypical of contemporary dance. The tendency was also present in the project to transmit *Jours étranges* and *So Schnell*, led by Olivia Grandville, to the Geneva Ballet in 2007. On this occasion, there was a clear desire to dissociate the choreographic text not only from its original bodies but also from its other constitutive theatrical parameters (lighting, decor, and costumes, or what one might call its scenography in a very broad sense), which would be entrusted to new collaborators. In a project of this kind, the only invariant of the work is the choreographic text, and (as in theater) its identity enables a multitude of productions and interpretations to be developed.[29]

Finally, the Carnets Bagouet experimented with another kind of dissociation: that between the work and dance. For the tenth anniversary of Bagouet's death, Jean-Paul Montanari, director of the Montpellier Danse festival, commissioned from the Carnets a tribute performance, which gave rise in 2002 to the project entitled *Matière première [Primary material]*: this was not the revival of a work in its integrity, according to all its scenic and dramaturgical parameters, but a series of *solos* extracted from their original contexts, showcasing the work of the performer as much as the choreographic material, moving beyond any operal proposition. As a consequence, one is tempted to ask—and perhaps this was the question underlying the project—whether these dances really need the work in order to survive. Can the dances extract themselves from their contexts and persist on their own, as they pass from one performer to another?[30] But there is an inevitable tension between the autonomy of individual dances and the global demands of production for the stage: this reappears here in that *Matière première* was itself presented as a "complete" stage show, perhaps even

29. In the event, the directors of the Geneva Ballet rejected the idea of a new "staging" of *So Schnell*, and the revival was presented as an identical reperformance of the work created by other dancers in former times.

30. It is in this mode that the greater part of the classical repertoire survives: in the form of variations (in the sense of solos) handed down from one generation to the next (mostly for competitions) and extracts of works that are rarely danced in their entirety.

as a *work*, with its own premiere and its tour. There are numerous, problematic implications: what was conceived as an evening for performers or as a recital of dances became—because of the very structures of production—a work carrying the authorial signature of the Carnets Bagouet, despite the members renouncing choreographic intention or, at least, all presumption that they were themselves authors. The global demands of stage production long precluded the very possibility of the choreographic work. But here, in a strange reversal, these demands reasserted themselves to prevent the possibility of a "concert of dances" (a mere performance of works or preexisting fragments thereof) in the name of the choreographic work for the stage.

I will introduce one final nuance here. Until now, I have written as though concern with documentary traces was foreign to the Carnets Bagouet, as if the body-to-body transmission of dances was all that mattered to them. This is partly false. One of the first projects of the Carnets was to reperform *So Schnell* and *Necessito* in 1993 for video capture, and to this day films of practically all of Bagouet's works exist and are housed at the Centre National de la Cinématographie. What is more, the considerable archival work effected by Anne Abeille, coordinator of the Carnets Bagouet, should be emphasized. One consequence was the company archives being made available to researchers, via the Institut Mémoire de l'Édition Contemporaine (the Institute for Contemporary Publishing Archives). Another was the creation of a Carnets Bagouet website that constitutes a formidable documentary resource.[31] More generally, this material concern with the archive suggests two things: firstly, a relativization of corporeal source materials (insofar as the documentary archive often reveals and palliates lapses in embodied memory);[32] and, secondly, the need after thirteen years of oral transmission to store what the body remembers in inscriptions external to the subject, finally lightening the burden of memory by giving it up to the dissemination of the trace.

The play of the trace and its various manifestations are explored in the next chapter.

31. http://www.lescarnetsbagouet.org.

32. On this issue, see the film by Marie-Hélène Rebois, *Ribatz, ribatz! ou le grain du temps* (2003), which charts the work undertaken by the former dancers of *Ribatz, ribatz!* (1976) to remember this piece, and the upheaval caused by the discovery, during the process, of a series of photographs that contradicted on several points what the dancers remembered.

Chapter 4

The Supporting Trace: Images and Scores

So dance *passes* (down/on). It moves from one present body to another, from an old body to a body full of youthful promise. It thus follows the normal cycle of the generations and is structured by the logic of the oral tradition. However, in this passage from life to death—the very principle governing oral transmission—the *trace* always already lingers. The trace is dead, so surpasses and survives the living. It remains in the form of fragments of pottery, inscriptions, photos, films, and also scores. The work effaces itself from the unstable memory of subjects and comes to rest in the materiality of a few objects. Present incumbents must reactivate these objects, trying to fill in the cracks of memory and the gaps between generations.

The function of museums and libraries is to preserve these trace-objects and make them accessible. There is significant research to do analyzing the role of such institutions within the choreographic field and explaining the likely particularity of the dance archive. Here I will mention only the importance for our own time of the project begun by Rolf de Maré during the 1930s and called the Archives Internationales de la Danse (AID). The patron and director of the Ballets Suédois sought to establish a collection of historical, ethnological, and aesthetic documents relating to choreographic practices.[1] The Paris Opéra's library-museum draws a significant portion of its dance collection from the AID,[2] and an institution like the recently created Centre National de la Danse in Pantin appears partly inspired also by de Maré's Archives. Here, though, I must put to one side the general question of the dance archive and its institutional management to focus solely on the different types of restaging, revival, and reconstruction[3] that it makes possible.

1. See Baxmann, Rousier, and Veroli (2006).

2. See Auclair in Baxmann, Rousier, and Veroli (2006).

3. The use of these terms is quite fluid. Usually, the term "reconstruction" implies that continuity of oral memory and transmission has been broken, and the project must rely solely on the

THE RESTAGER AS ARCHAEOLOGIST: THE ARCHIVE-WORK

What should be done with so-called lost ballets? Indeed, what does it mean for a ballet to be "lost"? Perhaps a ballet is lost when it is no longer danced. Or perhaps when it has disappeared from body memory because the last surviving performers have forgotten it or because they themselves have died. Maybe it remains only in the form of a few press cuttings or etchings like the *Journal Amusant* clippings about *Viviane*.[4] Arguably, the mere survival of a title within collective memory means the work continues to exist, in some sense: phantom-like existence this may be, but not a state of complete *non*-existence. To recall Gérard Genette's terminology, this would be an instance of transcendence in which immanence tends asymptotically toward zero, though it never quite arrives there. And if this fading state of the work suffices for its existence, nothing then precludes someone seeking out a more consistent set of traces that might enable the ballet's rebirth.

Pierre Lacotte's research on Filippo Taglioni's *La Sylphide* was motivated by this kind of project. Recall that this ballet, created at the Paris Opéra in 1832 with music by Schneitzhoeffer, had disappeared from the repertoire by the 1860s; only Bournonville's *La Sylphide*, with a different musical score and a different libretto, was preserved by oral tradition. Hence Lacotte's ambition of seeing the original version (which had fascinated Europe in 1830) live once more:

> Fascinated by this work that disappeared more than a century ago, I dreamed of one day restaging *La Sylphide* and enabling this masterpiece to live again. The work must have possessed magical power to have cast the spell it did on the whole of Europe.[5]

Lacotte's research only really started to bear fruit in 1968 with the discovery of the will of Marie Taglioni's granddaughter, which revealed the several individuals who owned portions of her grandmother's archives. Lacotte could then begin accumulating documentation:

> Gradually, through my inquiries, I found contemporary reviews from every country where Taglioni's *La Sylphide* was performed. Some of these (particularly in England) must have been written by former dancers as the description

work's external traces. "Revival," meanwhile, suggests a production based on a living memory and the continuity of the company. "Restaging" sits somewhere between the other two terms.

4. See Appendix, fig. 4 and 5.

5. Pierre Lacotte, "A la recherche du ballet perdu ... ," in the programme of *La Sylphide*, Paris Opéra, 1990–91 season, p. 25.

of the steps was very precise. I also found Filippo Taglioni's correspondence with other artists and collaborators, his personal notes. I managed to get my hands on the drawings and notes penned by the choreographer, his class note-books and the music he used during dance lessons. Finally, I discovered the score (the violin *conducteur*) which had belonged to Taglioni himself: under the musical stave, some steps were described in minute detail, as was the stag-ing. Of course, I also consulted the archives of the Bibliothèque de l'Opéra de Paris, which holds the detailed inventory of costumes and models designed by Ciceri. I could also read the testimonies of dancers who worked in Russia with the choreographer when he presented *La Sylphide* in St. Petersburg.[6]

The restager, then, is confronted with very disparate source materials: newspa-per reviews, collaborators' correspondence, the choreographer's drawings and plans, an annotated musical score, class notebooks, models of the scenography, and personal accounts by the original participants. Add to these an element of oral transmission, in this case thanks to Pierre Lacotte's teachers Egorova and Zambelli:

> Madame Lubov Egorova (who had worked with Christian Johannsen, one of the last men to partner Marie Taglioni) and Mlle Zambelli also taught me what had been handed down to them by tradition.[7]

In this last statement appears the recurring motif of classical ballet transmis-sion or, rather, the motif of recurrence itself understood as a principle of trans-mission: in other words, the importance of having access to the last person who saw the person who saw the person, and so on.

On the basis of these disparate traces (oral, written, pictorial, descriptive, anec-dotal, unofficial, and so on), the restager uses all available means to try to recom-pose the work as a whole. Yet it is not clear that the archive can fill all gaps in memory: the very principle of the trace incorporates vacancy and absence. There will always be scraps of choreography missing. Restaging is a process of muddling through with the materials at hand (although this idea of what a restaging should be is itself merely a contingent one). To express the thought more elegantly, the restager "composes in the style of" the choreographer or work in question:

> For four years, I searched everywhere that I might find the missing pieces to complete the jigsaw. Sometimes I was obliged—like an archaeologist—to

6. Lacotte, "A la recherche du ballet perdu . . . ," 25–26.

7. Lacotte, "A la recherche du ballet perdu . . . ," 26.

recompose by creating transitions "in the appropriate style" to connect up the existing elements.[8]

Lacotte's claim here is problematic, given that the archaeologist, when reconstituting a damaged object, ultimately makes explicit the distinction between the original fragments and those (modern) elements that have been filled in, whose function is solely to enable the object to be presented as it might have been. Yet drawing this specifically archaeological distinction is clearly impossible in performance (although this might be merely a question of convention), which is always presented as an undifferentiated global entity.[9] The Carnets Bagouet challenged the idea that it should be with *Ribatz, Ribatz!*, where the aim was to push the archaeological model to its limit, daring to show the gaps in memory and the impotence of the trace—to recognize that for particular passages of music nothing was now known of the movement and, since no document could compensate this absence, the performers should just stop dancing. The economy of performance and the structures of production (whether they be classical or contemporary) make it manifestly impossible to present a work in this fragmentary way, even though it is the only form adequate to its temporal structure.

The difficulty of gaps in memory and documentation is compounded by the problem of identifying the "original version." Which version should be retained when a ballet is reconstructed? Perhaps the answer usually given is the version performed at the premiere. But this generally does not set the standard of the work. This issue did not really arise in the case of *La Sylphide*, which disappeared quite quickly from the repertoire and whose leading role remained the prerogative of Marie Taglioni. It was significant, however, in the reconstruction of *Giselle*, which knew many versions and successive additions in the course of its dissemination. Pierre Lacotte was thus obliged to invent in the contemporary moment of performance a kind of temporal patchwork, mixing different moments or versions of the work according to their weight within the tradition but never explicitly articulating their historical heterogeneity (see Pastori 1987, 79–90).

Finally, if Pierre Lacotte's work was based on a patient perusal of the archive (that is, of the traces left by dance outside of dance itself), it also depended, albeit marginally, on the notation systems of the nineteenth century. I am thinking

8. Lacotte, "A la recherche du ballet perdu . . . ," 26.

9. Indeed, Pierre Lacotte himself comments on this: "There are two methods of reconstituting [. . .] The archaeologist's, who leaves the traces he has exhumed in their original state, and that which consists in breathing fresh life into the finds. I have chosen the second" (cited by Jean-Pierre Pastori, 1987, 25).

here particularly of the fact that Lacotte deciphered scores in the Saint-Léon system to reconstruct *La Vivandière*.[10] Note, however, that the score was treated here as one archival document among others and not as a work-identifying text.

The mode of analysis just described can also be applied to the choreographic repertory of the twentieth century, as shown by the reconstruction work of Kenneth Archer and Millicent Hodson (1994). Their main claim to fame has been the reconstruction of Vaslav Nijinsky's *Le Sacre du Printemps*[11] for the Joffrey Ballet in 1987. No recording of the work was available, and oral memory had been lost. In some respects, the approach they adopted toward reconstruction was similar to Pierre Lacotte's for the nineteenth-century repertory: it involved a comparable accumulation of disparate source materials, documenting the context, reception, and scenography of the work, as well as the choreographic practices of its time. In short, once again, all available means were used to try to reconstitute a ballet thought to be lost, and the process was again described in terms of the metaphor of the jigsaw puzzle already invoked by Lacotte:

> When reconstructing a ballet, we are grateful for every bit of information found. And, as the pieces fall into place, we experience the pleasure of compulsive puzzle-solvers. (Archer and Hodson 1994, 109)

In a more sensitive manner than Lacotte, however, Archer and Hodson attempted as far as possible to organize their source material hierarchically, since different documents sometimes proved mutually contradictory. Thus, in the case of *Le Sacre du Printemps*, two different annotated musical scores presented marginal notes on the choreography—one set of annotations was by Stravinsky, the other by Marie Rambert, Nijinsky's choreographic assistant on *Sacre*. Where the scores conflicted, Archer and Hodson elected to treat Rambert's score as authoritative by virtue of its greater proximity to the choreographer.[12]

The issue of the "archival gap" arises again here, of course. What to do when none of the traces documents a particular passage of choreography within the overall work, whose surviving framework is essentially musical? What should the dancers do on a particular section of the music whose choreography has

---

10. *La Vivandière*, choreographed by Arthur Saint-Léon in 1844. Reconstructed by Pierre Lacotte in 1976. On the use of Saint-Léon scores, see Pastori (1987, 89–90). On the Saint-Léon notation system, see Saint-Léon's *Stenochoreography* (1992 [1852]).

11. Premiered at the Théâtre des Champs-Élysées, Paris, in 1913.

12. "But there are moments when conflicting evidence presents itself. Our method on these occasions is to re-evaluate the sources and place them in a hierarchical order. We ask which document or documentor has the greatest authority and use the information accordingly" (Archer and Hosdon 1994, 109).

clearly disappeared? On these questions, Archer and Hodson responded similarly to Lacotte: thanks to immersion in the work's context and style, they could
"fill" the gaps in the "spirit" or "style" of the choreographer (Archer and Hodson
1994, 105). And the problem of what is meant by the "original version" was
also raised here, as in the case of Balanchine's *Cotillon* (1932), reconstructed
by Hodson and Archer for the Joffrey Ballet in 1988. Three versions were available to the restagers, corresponding to the three generations of dancers who
had performed the work: first in Europe, then in the United States during the
Great Depression, and finally once again in the United States after the Second
World War. Faced with this multiplicity of versions (this time in the context of
a single company and a single choreographer), reconstruction seems capable of
producing only a strange blend. There was little trace of the first version of the
"Destiny pas de deux," so the restagers decided to focus on the second version,
excluding the third on the grounds that it was too distant from the original.
A similar difficulty was evident when restaging another Balanchine work, *La
Chatte*"[13] three successive versions of the solo were performed; the restagers
retained the third because Balanchine himself seems to have preferred it.[14]

The methodology of archival restaging—whether applied to nineteenth- or
twentieth-century works—reiterates Noverre's thesis on documentation. As
soon as the work ceases to be experienced in the vivid present of performance,
it becomes identified with a collection of disparate external traces. A choreographic score, envisaged on the model of musical notation, can then only
count as one trace among others, and not as the authoritative means of work-
identification. Contextual and stylistic documentation, giving information as
regards costumes, scenography, the historical period, relevant choreographic
practices, and so on, matters as much as a univocal definition of the movement.
And that was just what Noverre imagined when he envisaged replacing Feuillet
notation with other kinds of documentation.[15]

THE POWER OF FILM: THE EVENT-WORK

The advent of modern techniques of mechanical reproduction may appear to
have rendered the foregoing discussion obsolete. To what extent does film—and

13. Created in 1927 and restaged for the Grands Ballets Canadiens in 1991 by Hodson and
Archer.

14. On this question of choosing an "original version" and its reconstruction ex post facto, see
Archer and Hodson (1994, 104–5).

15. See above, 189–90.

perhaps particularly video—today constitute a perfectly sufficient means of identifying the choreographic work?

Film really does signal a definitive, quasi-ontological break in the history of traces of danced movement. Like photography, film escapes the traditionally mediated character of the choreographic archive. It is not like a review or an etching. In film, the trace is not mediated by a subject who describes or who pictures the dance. Rather, it offers a mechanical impression based on a real causal relation: the image before me shows for sure that a body was once present and left its imprint on the celluloid.[16] Moreover, while assuming the (causal or physical) reality effect typical of photography, film escapes the fixity of the image: movement, and not the static pose, imprints itself. And so film seems capable of becoming the privileged medium through which choreographic works survive.

As is well known, the birth of the cinematograph has its roots at a time when photography intersects with the scientific investigation of the movement of living beings.[17] However, the filming of danced movement is a relatively late development, at least in the domain of theatrical dance. Only a few snippets of film survive from the 1920s and 1930s and have become quasi-legendary: for example, Pavlova's *Dying Swan* (filmed in 1925),[18] Mary Wigman's *Hexentanz* (filmed in 1930), and three solos by Valeska Gert (filmed in 1925). By contrast, there is no surviving footage of Nijinsky, Diaghilev having always opposed the idea of his star dancer being filmed. The status of these first dance films, the nature of the soloist's body imprinted upon them, and the manner in which they disclose what often remains hidden when the work is experienced onstage (the wide angle, the face, and so on) are all important topics to investigate. An interesting aspect of such research would be the crossover between silent film, dance, and cabaret in the 1920s.[19] This, of course, extends far beyond my concern here, and I will focus for the moment more narrowly on examining the uses of film and video as possible instances of preservation and/or identification of works.

The first question to ask is why the development of film recording did not provoke a revolution in dance of the kind effected by sound recording in music. The record did not just radically transform listening practices (in particular making possible repeated listening of the same piece); it also modified musical production as such. For example, jazz was born more or less at the

16. On the causal reality of the photographic image, see Roland Barthes (1982 [1980]).

17. I am thinking here of the work of Étienne-Jules Marey.

18. Produced in Hollywood by Douglas Fairbanks Studios. Thanks to Cyril Lot for the reference.

19. For example, the choreographic force of the first films of Ernst Lubitsch or Buster Keaton, who both drew from the wellsprings of cabaret and music hall.

same time as sound recording developed or at least became widespread. And if jazz was indissociably connected to the emergence of the record, it was also the record that liberated jazz from the concept of the work, understood as repeatable and capable of being preserved. While "classical" music (or, more precisely, Western music with a written tradition) fuses composition and preservation in the moment of writing and postpones the moment of performance, jazz by contrast links performance and composition in the moment of improvisation, leaving the task of preservation to recording. Within jazz practices, the record is the irreplaceable means of transmission and tradition, short-circuiting the opposition between written and oral cultures. Similarly, the whole domain of pop music is inconceivable without the possibility of recording. As I noted above, the record here ceases to be merely documentation or capture *of* the work and becomes the work as such. So why not imagine a similar transformation in dance, stemming from the development of film recording? By analogy with jazz, it is possible to conceive of dance performances being routinely captured on film, liberating practice from the double bind of work-repetition and preservation. And by analogy with pop music, it is equally possible to imagine a choreographic work entirely identified with its recording (the dance film). Yet this double possibility has in fact only been realized in quite marginal contexts, and for reasons which I think are both cultural and ontological.

Firstly, supply of choreographic material on VHS and DVD markets is virtually nonexistent, the prime movers within the economy of the culture industries having probably surmised that demand is very low. There are often only three or four DVDs for sale on the "Dance" shelf of the average FNAC (a chain of music and book stores across France); these are typically recordings of ballets from the classic repertoire, often bought as Christmas gifts for young girls. Other recordings, whether they be documented performances or true dance films, generally do not make it onto the open market. Films documenting performance often have no legal status and are passed on the sly between interested parties. Dance films, governed by authors' rights and copyright law, are mostly only available for consultation in the big regional and national media libraries.[20] The dance lover might dream of building a true choreographic video collection, like the music lover's record collection, but in fact this proves neither possible nor legal.

Secondly, there may be a firm (quasi-ontological) distinction to be drawn between image and sound reproduction. Let alone the editing techniques that

20. For example, the Cinémathèque de la Danse (CND) or the "Images de la Culture" collection at the Centre National de la Cinématographie.

are proper to the medium, the film image is always reproduced from a certain point of view and within a certain frame. This double filter is probably also evident in sound reproduction but is much less significant in that domain. As a consequence, when I listen to a record, I can have the feeling that I am accessing a reality similar to that of the original performance. This is never the case with dance performance documented on film. The difference perhaps explains the relative lack of enthusiasm for dance on film.

Clearly, however, video plays an important role in everyday dance practice and in the life of dance companies (notably helping performers to learn their roles), where it functions as an *aide-mémoire*, even as a means of work-identification. Indeed, the use of video is ubiquitous today, though it is a relatively recent phenomenon dating back to the end of the 1970s. This raises the question of what exactly is identified by the video trace; or, more precisely, of the extent to which video traces can really function as identifying. It is important to remember that video does not document the work as such but only one of its instances (its performance on a given evening, on a given date, on a particular tour, and so on). That instance may not be the best performance, but it nonetheless comes to stand as the embodiment of the work's features for subsequent revivals. Moreover, the possibility of restaging a work from a single video recording implies that the dancer is capable of treating the image as a quasi-score, disengaging from the body of the original performer the choreographic text which she herself must embody. To recall Goodman's categories, she must mentally transform an analog into a digital system.

Let me take a brief detour through these categories of Goodman's, which enable me to justify and better articulate the distinction between video and score. For Goodman, a system is considered analog if it is syntactically and semantically *dense*, in other words, if the slightest perceptible difference can be considered relevant and significant. Within an analog system, between two perfectly similar marks, there will always be the possibility of imagining a third; in other words, the system is infinitely divisible. A nongraduated watch provides an example. As Goodman notes, an analog system is the very antithesis of a notational system that must, by contrast, be wholly digital. A system is digital when it is syntactically and semantically discontinuous and differentiated or, in other words, articulate. Between even the two closest marks, there is no conceivable third mark, and each mark corresponds to a discontinuous entity. A graduated watch offers one example (provided one accepts that the position of the hand between two marks is not relevant to reading the time), a machine for counting coins another (Goodman 1976, 159–61).

Once the terms have been defined, it is clear that the "analog" has little to do with analogy or resemblance, and that the "digital" is not particularly concerned with digits.[21] The distinction depends ultimately on the contrast between density ("any difference in perceptible material should be judged relevant and significant") and articulation ("there are non-relevant differences and only some are pertinent to reading"). And, more generally still, the continuity-discontinuity opposition is key to the contrast between analog and digital. The paradox of this model is that it obliges us to think of digital (or notational) repetition as prior to analog reproduction (photo, film, video, and so on). In the present context, this means that the theater event must have first discovered how to repeat and identify itself conceptually, via articulate systems (whether written or otherwise), before being reproduced mechanically through analog systems.

In addition to framing and editing problems, video documentation still presents a global image, which is syntactically and semantically dense, even saturated, and where the slightest perceptible feature can be held to be definitive of the work. That is why I claimed that the possibility of restaging from video already implies a reading that abstracts and filters, sorting essential from contingent properties. The score, by contrast, depends on a prior rarefaction of the perceptible, on the imposition of discontinuities, which do not admit the possibility of a third term between two others. Labanotation's establishment of directional signs would be an example of this.[22] At some point, one must stop breaking down the continuum and make the decision that there will be no third term between two given directions. As a consequence, the score presents a motor schema or idealization, which leaves the question of its embodiment indeterminate and opens de facto the space of interpretation. This cannot be the case with video, unless one assumes that the dancer has the capacity to read and abstract from the recording, as previously discussed.

I will also make a brief digression at this point to note my disagreement with Bernard Stiegler's argument (1998 [1994], 2004, 2009 [1996], 2011 [2001]). Steigler conceives the emergence of analog reproduction (photography, film, and video) in the lineage of a continuous, developing externalization of memory; this process, he thinks, takes the form of strict codification and exact reproduction and is the driving force of Western civilization. In my view, this schema tends to minimize (if not abolish) the distinction between the digital and the analog, the discontinuous and the continuous, the articulate and the saturated. In the transition from alphabetical and notational writing to simple mechanical

---

21. "Plainly, a digital system has nothing special to do with digitals, or an analog system with analogy" (Goodman 1976, 160).

22. Moreover, Goodman bases his claims about Labanotation as a notational system on the example of its directional signs: see Goodman (1976, 211–18).

reproduction of the visually or aurally perceptible, there is a qualitative shift that should not be ignored. The position of the reading subject is also at stake here. In the one case (that of photography, film, or audio recording), an image, a body, or a sound imposes itself upon me, and I can only have a purely passive relation to it. In the other case (that of writing or the score), I am concerned purely with an abstract schema that is also a condition of my freedom. And probably Stiegler's lack of differentiation between the analog and the digital is linked to the weakness of the definitions on which his argument depends,[23] a weakness that I think renders questionable also his political claims, though the stakes of the latter are high.

This digression perhaps helps to better explain how the term "digital revolution" is currently understood. Because the digital, according to Goodman's definition, has almost always been present (alphabetical writing is a digital system, being articulate and discontinuous), new information technologies should be understood not as providing access to the digital but rather as attempting to fuse the digital with the analog, the score with the perceptible, or the concept with the image. That fusion realized by new technology is very evident in dance, in the form of two types of system: *Lifeforms* software and motion capture. In the one case, a program is available that has already integrated a certain number of motor categories and capabilities of the human body. It can then be used to compose dance directly on the computer, in the way it was composed on paper in the seventeenth century, except that now abstract composition immediately gives rise to a visual representation of movement. This is what *Lifeforms*—the software used by Merce Cunningham for a number of years[24]—does. In the second case, initial digital recording of a particular dancer's singular movements becomes a pure algorithm that can find expression in a completely different perceptible form. That is what motion capture systems—initially developed for the film and video game industries, and recently applied also in the choreographic field—do.[25] *Lifeforms* starts from a categorial and analytic system that can immediately produce images, as anticipated by Cunningham when he posed the following question: "Why not design a notation for dance that is immediately visual?" (Cunningham 1968, cited by deLahunta 2001). Motion

23. See Stiegler: "A signal is analogic when its form is proportionally analogous to what it signals, and digital when its encoding bears no isomorphic relation to what it encodes" (2009 [1996], 124).

24. For a discussion of the *Lifeforms* software, see Menicacci and Quinz (2001).

25. Scott deLahunta's essay "Coreografie in bit e byte: Motion capture, animazione et software per la danza" examines the different digital motion capture systems and their uses in dance: see deLahunta(2001). See also below, 271.

capture starts from the perceptible and the singular, which is translated digitally to become a manipulable set of concepts, and which could ultimately be transformed into a Laban score.

However, both systems impose a significant material as well as financial burden, so there is little prospect of their replacing good old video as a way of preserving works, at least in the short term. They only seem to find a real use at another level of experiment, in relation to intermodal perception and *biofeedback*.[26] Once again, then, the opposition between image and score, between the perceptual and the conceptual, rears its head. At the beginning of part III, I argued that notation has only been weakly integrated with choreographic practice, although I have still here noted several singular instances of scores being used within contemporary reconstructions. My analysis must now turn to these instances of score use.

THE SCORE, ONCE AGAIN: THE SIGN-WORK

I began this part of my book with a study of two notation systems: Feuillet's"Choreography" and Labanotation. I will also end with a discussion of these two systems, not with a view to revealing the structure and ideologies implicitly governing them but in order to describe how they are currently used as a way of perpetuating works.

Francine Lancelot's untiring research into Feuillet notation showed how patient decoding could lead to the reconstruction of dances.[27] This was the aim of her company, Ris et Danceries, founded in 1980. But Feuillet documentation itself remains very partial. Although there are collections of scores for several of Pécour's choreographies, the system is designed for the contemporary reader, indicating only the movement for the legs and not the positions of the torso or arms.[28] Another accessible source—Pierre Rameau's (1725) treatise—enables arm movements to be added to what is described in Feuillet notation. But Rameau's treatise only records "town dances" or "ball dances" and not dance works. The reconstruction practice of Ris et Danceries oscillated between these two sources, alongside a number of others that can be studied by perusing Francine Lancelot's archives recently deposited at the Centre

---

26. See below, 271.

27. On the late Francine Lancelot, see Catherine Kintzler's tribute (accessible online at www. mezetulle.net), as well as Françoise Dartois-Lapeyre's article "Francine Lancelot, the Passion of Dance and of Research" in the proceedings of the European Association of Dance Historians International Cultural Exchange Conference, Stockholm 2006, 69–77.

28. This, moreover, was one of the key points of critique in Noverre's evaluation of the system, alongside his attachment to presence.

National de la Danse. The company engaged in both historical research and artistic creation, hence the heterogeneous character of its productions. The latter can be grouped into three categories: (1) strict reconstructions, where the choreography is attributed to an original author;[29] (2) creations "in period style," authored by Francine Lancelot herself (for example, the solo *Bach suite* created for Rudolf Nureyev in 1984, or *Quelques pas graves de Baptiste* for the Paris Opéra in 1985); and (3) choreography for opera, restaged "in period style" but without a score playing an identifying role (for example, the production of Jean-Baptiste Lully's *Atys* in 1986, in collaboration with William Christie and Jean-Marie Villégier).

This fluctuation between research, creation, and reconstruction is also evident elsewhere than in Francine Lancelot's unique approach and is probably a function of the particular nature of baroque source materials. The Feuillet system is characterized by definitional weakness, and it lacks determination for readers external to the practice it describes. This is merely the flip side of its remarkable degree of integration with the dance of its time. Projecting onto paper the dance of his own period, Feuillet could leave some things unsaid, letting some blanks be implicitly filled in by the conventions that everyone knew. Three centuries after these conventions have faded, any attempt at reconstruction depends simultaneously on archival research (which is in principle never-ending) and, necessarily, on a degree of choreographic invention (since to maintain performance continuity, archival gaps must be filled).

Where Labanotation is concerned, the score really can aspire to a work-identifying function. In this regard, the work of Ann Hutchinson-Guest (which has been essential to Labanotation's own transmission and to historical research)[30] in my view reveals a use of notation that is quite problematic for the reconstruction of dance works. Hutchinson-Guest's most significant reconstruction, produced in collaboration with Claudia Jeschke, was of Nijinsky's *L'après-midi d'un faune*[31] for London's Royal Ballet in 2001. This was based on a prior decoding of Nijinsky's original score, written in 1915, and its translation into Labanotation (Hutchinson-Guest and Jeschke 1991). According to Hutchinson-Guest, Nijinsky invented his own, idiosyncratic notation system, which she herself spent years deciphering. In fact, the process was somewhat more straightforward than

29. As in *Bal à la cour de Louis XIV* (1981), with choreography by Pécour, reconstructed by Francine Lancelot with *mise en scène* by François Raffinot (for the 1987 version).

30. Hutchinson-Guest (1961; 1989).

31. *L'après-midi d'un faune* was premiered on May 29, 1912, at the Théâtre du Châtelet in Paris, with choreography by Nijinsky, music by Debussy, and scenario by Cocteau.

this suggests: Nijinsky's system is in some respects merely a more complex adaptation of the Stepanov system taught in Russia.[32] In any case, there is a film that records the work of transmission and reconstruction with London's Royal Ballet, and bears the rather striking title *Histoires de danse (1). Les origines. Ann Hutchinson-Guest et le Faune de Nijinski.*[33] This film shows, probably unintentionally, how Ann Hutchinson-Guest reinscribes notation-use within the strictly oral framework of the classical tradition. The score is not treated as a shared means of work-identification, on which the group of dancers work together but rather as the document that guarantees the authority of those who know over those ignorant of how to read it. What the film ultimately reveals is the very absence of the score in the studio, and the preference for simple demonstration of the movement to be performed. Ann Hutchinson-Guest's own body is presented as having in some way absorbed, after years of decoding and reading, the choreographic identity of *Faune*, and this (singular and mortal) body once again functions as the medium of transmission. But the double power of the score—freedom from the individual performer, buttressed by the precision of writing—thus evaporates. The dancers remain entirely dependent on the body of Ann Hutchinson-Guest, and (because they can never be *her* body) their dependence paradoxically opens a space of vagueness and approximation. That space is then immediately occupied by the bodily habitus of classical technique, inappropriate to this particular dance.

It is possible to use scores very differently, as the work of the Quatuor Albrecht Knust has shown.[34] The Quatuor's first project, entitled *Les danses de papier* [*Paper dances*] (1994), took up two pieces by Kurt Jooss and three by

32. These claims are based on personal communications from Jacqueline Challet-Haas and Dominique Brun. For Nijinsky's views on choreographic notation, see the letter he wrote to Reynaldo Hahn: "I work, I compose new dances and perfect the system of dance notation that I have invented over the past few years. I am happy to have discovered this form of notation, which has been sought after for centuries, because I think and am sure you will agree, my dear friend, that this notation is indispensable to the development of the art of dance. It is a simple and logical means of noting down movements. In a word, this system will perform for dance artists the same service as musical notes do for musicians" (cited in the program for the Quatuor Knust production, ". . . *d'un faune*" (*éclats*), 2000).

33. Or, *Histories of Dance (1). The Origins: Ann Hutchinson-Guest and Nijinsky's Faune*, documentary directed by Dieter Schneider, 2001.

34. The Quatuor Knust was formed in 1993 by the dancers and notators Dominique Brun, Anne Collod, Simon Hecquet, and Christophe Wavelet. Its name pays homage to Laban's disciple and collaborator Albrecht Knust, who further developed the system of which Laban laid the foundations. This developed system finds a definitive form in Knust's *Dictionary of Kinetography Laban* (1979).

Doris Humphrey, each recorded in Labanotation.[35] The aim of these revivals was, through the abstraction of notation, to try to dissociate choreographic composition from its traditional mode of person-to-person, oral transmission, even though that might leave the group open to reproach on the grounds of stylistic infidelity. The approach also sought to highlight those corporeal spaces left vacant by writing—the gaps in the score, in some sense—and which could only be filled by aesthetic choices.

Paradoxically, the Quatuor's second project moved away from Labanotation and worked in the very margins of the score. This was the revival or recreation of Yvonne Rainer's *Continuous Project/Altered Daily* and Steve Paxton's *Satisfyin' Lover* in 1996. Each of these emblematic works of American choreographic postmodernism rests on a collection of verbal task prescriptions, and their scores thus appear the dance equivalent of Cage's and Stockhausen's verbal scores in the field of music.

Finally, the Quatuor's third and last project was "... *d'un faune*" *(éclats)* ["... *of a faune*" *(fragments)*] in 2000. This reread the score of Nijinsky's *L'après-midi d'un faune* via the Labanotation translation produced by Ann Hutchinson-Guest and Claudia Jeschke in 1991, even while problematizing the work's past reception and present memory. I will return later to the historico-aesthetic stakes of this production.[36] For now, I want to limit my focus to an analysis of the score's potential, retaining this exemplary case study of Nijinsky's *Faune* by discussing a subsequent project of Dominique Brun, former member of the Quatuor Knust, which was dissolved in 2003. Brun continued work on the Laban score for *Faune* and began to make a documentary film offering a global interpretation of the work on the basis solely of its notational trace, studied together with the dancers. I was able to attend the shoot, and something essential seemed at stake in the process, something that troubled or perhaps counterbalanced the starting point of the project. Admittedly, restaging from notation is mostly the exception within the choreographic field. However, what I saw offered a concrete illustration of what the potential of notation in dance might be. In the case of *Faune*, notation endowed the work with an unprecedented readability as writing;[37] it enabled a detached articulation of the lines

---

35. Namely, Kurt Jooss's trio *Storenfried* and duet *Märzlied*, both created in 1953 following Jooss's return to Essen; and Doris Humphrey's *Two Ecstatic Themes (Circular Descent; Pointed Ascent)* (1931), *The Call: Breath of Fire* (a 1929 solo), and *Invention* (a 1930 trio).

36. See below, 301. See also the interview with the members of the Quatuor Knust in the magazine *ArtPress*, "Médium Danse," no. 23, pp. 16–25.

37. Unprecedented in that this degree of readability was evident in neither the orally transmitted version performed at the Paris Opéra (which entered the repertoire in 1976) nor Ann Hutchinson-Guest's score-based version.

and embodied polyphonies generally left (in the case of the young nymphs) to the approximations of the corps de ballet; and it simultaneously gave the viewer, through the abstract medium of the notational scheme, the singular body of the performer.[38] In short, the score here offered something like a fully allographic structuration of the work.[39]

- You contradict yourself once again. You begin by refuting writing and end with its glorification. What's the meaning of this?
- I could clarify by saying two things. First, my conclusion here is merely a hapax legomenon, and it confirms by its very status what I said earlier. Second, the contradiction that you highlight is integral to writing itself.
- What?
- To be clear: graphic writing merely prolongs an initial movement to stabilize presence, known (according to the jargon) as arche-writing. This returns us to what is typically known in everyday dance practice as "technique" or "vocabulary." This is the substratum of writing, or its premise, which I now need to examine in more detail.

38. On the issues raised by score reading in dance, illustrated with respect to Nijiinsky's *Faune*, see the very interesting article by Dominique Brun, "Le trait et le retrait," *Quant à la danse*, February 2006, no. 3, pp. 34–39.

39. Dominique Brun's film was released with the title *Le Faune—un film ou la fabrique de l'archive* [*Faune—a film, or the archive factory*] (Paris: CNDP, 2007).

PART IV

A Technique With No Object

I made, and went on making for several years, the fundamental mistake
of thinking that there is technique only when there is an instrument.
I had to go back to ancient notions, to the Platonic position on technique,
for Plato spoke of a technique of music and in particular of a technique of
dance, and extend these notions.

MARCEL MAUSS
Techniques of the Body

Prior to the issue of the work and its survival (but perhaps also representing
a kind of fallback position), there is the question of practices and whether/
how they are transmitted. The durability of practices is a condition of the work,
in the sense that everything cannot be learned from scratch each time a work
is made or reperformed. Unless transmitting a work is to become a process of
continually and profoundly re-forming the subjectivities involved, a common
framework of experience must be assumed: there must be a shared space of
nomination and categorization on which to base the process of passing on the
dance. This durability of practices also represents a kind of fallback position
for dance, a default solution to the problem of the work: works are lost because
they are not externalized in objective, shared traces; yet oral transmission
seems nonetheless sufficient to enable the framework to survive, enabling
continuity of the categorial, motor space around which a given dance practice
is organized. We glimpsed that framework or space earlier in the idea of *arche-
writing*. The establishment of a practice preexists and conditions graphic writing
or notation but also (as we have seen) sometimes resists it. Practices anticipate
and compete with the conceptual gesture of graphic writing: they divide and
refine the sensory continuum into a collection of stable and repeatable entities;
they isolate idealities that permit one to recognize *the same* in what is *different*,

and create motor categories that are shared according to the generality of the concept rather than belonging to any single individual. In line with common usage, I will employ the term "dance *techniques*" to mean these forms of arche-writing, insofar as they form identifiable and coherent wholes.

I must qualify my claims here from the start, however. First of all, the idea of technique as "default" solution is likely to seem incongruous to the dancer. What the logic of my argument presents as ultimately a fallback position relative to the work is, in the context of everyday practice, the vivid and immediate core of dance. Alongside or beyond choreographic works, the ordinary space of the studio, class, or workshop is the primary milieu of the dancer: halfway between private and public domains, the studio is the space where dance techniques are invented and transmitted (very often) independently of any project of work creation. Indeed, a history of the dance studio might be written that leaves to one side the history of mere choreographic works and takes as its focus everyday technique practice (including its processes of warming up, training, and workshopping), examining also the evolution of that practice over the long term. Second, the model of *arche-writing* here discovers its limits. The idea of technique as common framework of nomination and categorization—as transparent lexicon shared by all—probably only holds for a certain type of dance technique. Perhaps it only accounts for a very partial dimension of what one ordinarily understands a dance technique to be. The difficulty of transmitting contemporary dance works obliged me to emphasize the importance of the implicit construction of a common body or corporeality, born of immersion within a given company context. This tacit postural and dynamic code, which signifies a particular (shared) mode of action, is an essential facet of technique, alongside its repertoire of gestures and movements. And this dimension is evident in ballet too: even if ballet *vocabulary* remains practically unchanged since the beginning of the twentieth century, the ways in which the vocabulary is performed or embodied have been profoundly transformed, partly in line with morphological shifts (I am thinking, for example, of the height of leg extensions, inconceivable at the beginning of the twentieth century, or of the way *petite batterie* has slowed down to accommodate the increased height of jumps). It is not clear that this facet of technique (the "ways of doing" that are learned implicitly through imitation and training) can be properly conceptualized on the model of arche-writing and transparent, shared ideality.

Finally, I must examine how improvisation to some extent moves beyond technique. Improvisation appears to be based on the aim of relinquishing control and abandoning oneself to the spontaneity and intuition of the moment, in opposition to preplanning and prior intention. And yet there are "improvisation techniques" that can be learned and transmitted, even schools or styles of improvisation. My task, then, is to explore how far improvisation subverts or not the concept of technique, and whether it can be integrated with a work-making or compositional project without contradiction. That is the focus of my final chapter, entitled "Intending the Unintentional, Repeating the Unrepeatable," which brings us back to the question of the work as it is problematized by today's contemporary dance. This will then enable me to move toward my first conclusion.

Chapter 1

What Is a Dance Technique?

Practitioners often use the term "dance techniques" and in its plural form. The term "ballet technique" is employed to mean a codified form of Western ballet practice, which was established in France in the middle of the eighteenth century, underwent numerous historical and geographical transfers (notably between France and Russia), and resulted in the kind of dance that can now be seen on certain evenings at the Paris Opéra. But equally, in the field of modern dance, there is talk of "Graham technique," "Limon technique," or "Cunningham technique" (for example). In this terminology, the name of a choreographer and founder of a school singles out and refers to the technique in question. I will return in what follows to this feature of modern dance, which binds an established school, style, or (as I use the term here) technique to the name of its founder. This phenomenon is much less common in classical ballet, where "subtechniques" or specific modes of technical training are rather designated by proper name (like the "Cecchetti method" devised in the early twentieth century, or the "Vaganova method" from the interwar years).

Nonetheless, the term "technique" generally refers to a systematic collection of gestures, which are codified, repeatable, and transmissible. A technique is thus like a verbal language or a scale of distinct musical notes (for example, the chromatic scale of Western music, with twelve pitches separated by intervals of a semitone). It consists of a repertoire of identified gestural entities and, in this sense, depends on a prior process of selection and imposition of discontinuities. Within the infinite continuum of possible bodily movements, only some elements are isolated and recognized as part of the technique. A gestural practice is collectively organized around these elements and persists through dissemination. In other words, a "dance technique" depends on a collection of discontinuous ideal gestural entities, such as the *développé à la seconde*, the *entrechat quatre* or *six*, the Cunningham curve, or the Graham contraction. These ideal entities enable the observer immediately to recognize sameness in difference: whether you or I do a *développé à la seconde*, the same movement is recognizable however well or idiosyncratically it is performed. Of course, there are limits to the range of possible variation: you might know very well what a *développé à la seconde* is and intend to do one, but if you cannot lift your leg to the appropriate height, I might struggle to accept that this is indeed what you are doing.

This apparently trivial observation leads me to define another use of the term "technique" to refer not to a determinate gestural system made up of ideal abstract entities but rather to the singular competence of a given individual within that system. The term is used in this way when a dancer is said to have "good" technique, to be an accomplished technician, and so on. Or it might be said of someone, for example, that she may not have great technique, but she has exceptional stage presence. Here, the term "technique" designates the individual's capacity to embody—in the fabric of her muscles, nerves, tendons, even her skeleton—the movement elements that are part of the system. It refers to the dancer's capacity to transform these gestural entities into true bodily schemata that, through training and habituation, become purely automatic. With this second use of the term, a gap opens, characteristic of technique as distinct from science: the gap between theoretical knowledge and ability. The dancer does not become capable of embodying the relevant gestural entities by reading Agrippina Vaganova's (1953 [1948]) treatise, or even the tract by Cyril W. Beaumont and Stanislas Idzilkowski (1922) that develops the principles of the Cecchetti method. This apparently trivial fact points up a constitutive dimension of technique: technique is present when the ability to do no longer follows automatically from the fact of knowing. This is made clear by Immanuel Kant in §43 of the *Critique of the Power of Judgment*, where he defines "art in general" by contrast with theoretical knowledge:

> Art as a skill of human beings is also distinguished from science (to be able from to know), as a practical faculty is distinguished from a theoretical one, as technique is distinguished from theory (as the art of surveying is distinguished from geometry). And thus that which one can do as soon as one knows what should be done is not exactly called art. Only that which one does not immediately have the skill to do even if one knows it completely belongs to that extent to art. Camper describes quite precisely how the best shoe must be made, but he certainly was not able to make one. (2000, 183)

In this passage, Kant characterizes technique in terms of a negative qualification: there is "technique" (or "art" in Kantian terminology) as soon as one is no longer capable of doing something merely because one knows what to do. This gap between knowledge and competence exists because, ultimately, the body itself is in play in technical activity. The body presents resistance and needs to be trained and accustomed to certain gestures, to develop a knack (as craftspeople might say). The body must appropriate certain sensorimotor schemata such that they become stable, repeatable, and transmissible constants. Thus dance seems perfectly to exemplify this characterization of "technique" in terms of the gap between the body and mere knowing.

Applied to dance, then, the term "technique" can be understood to mean essentially two things: (1) an articulated gestural system, made up of discrete entities which can be named and transmitted; and (2) the singular competence that an individual can have within a given system. The gap between these two senses of the term corresponds precisely to the disjuncture between knowledge and ability that is the very hallmark of corporeal mediation. The body must appropriate the technique's gestural entities and itself become like an articulate tool. That is more or less what is generally understood by "learning to dance" or "learning a dance technique."

This distinction and the accompanying characterization of technique should be further qualified, however. For one thing, reducing dance technique to just a repertoire of postures and gestures perhaps caricatures the phenomenon. More specifically, movement as such and the different ways of engaging with it are obscured. Both Duncan and Cunningham (to choose two quite disparate examples) reuse several elements of classical vocabulary (the attitude, the arabesque, turns, and so on); but clearly a Duncan attitude has nothing much to do with a classical one, while a Cunningham turn implies a completely different corporeal and physical engagement to the classical pirouette. In short, aside from the nameable movement elements, steps, and poses, there is a whole field of "ways of doing" or "ways of being," as significant as it is difficult to articulate. There is a general corporeal mode associated with classical ballet that forms a constant postural and dynamic basis but is not reducible to the vocabulary of identifiable steps and gestures. I am thinking, for example, of the placement of the pelvis, the projection outward from the sternum, and even the carriage of the head induced by this projection, always slightly above the horizontal line. Equally, one might think in dynamic rather than postural terms of the way phrases are accentuated, or of how the relationship to gravity is managed in a manner particular to classical ballet. And if there is a specifically classical corporeality (whose history might be written), there is also a Duncan or a Cunningham corporeality. These singular corporealities cut across the postural and the dynamic. They give movement a specificity independently of, or alongside, its particular vocabulary. The imitative practices of the daily class and training are typically what transmit and establish these corporeal regimes.[1]

---

1. Earlier, I wrote of "immersion" within a company idiom.

One of the tasks of dance research today, in fact, is to identify these corpore-alities from within their implicit practice and to try to define and characterize them in words.

This means that my distinction between the ideal and the body, between the abstract repertoire of gestures and the individual's singular capacity to embody them, becomes porous. In between the ideality of vocabulary and concrete indi-vidual performance are modes of doing and being. These modes are not purely idiosyncratic but are rather shaped by shared experience of apprenticeship and training. Although it may be implicit and difficult to articulate, there is still an ideal dimension to these corporeal modes. They affect each movement element and each singular performance yet are irreducible to any single individual. This is a kind of ideality that really issues from the body and is still trapped therein. It is not the ideality of the figure or the step that the body realizes but rather a general mode of being and of doing that can be passed on and shared, even as it marks the body's singularity. From this perspective, the in-between phe-nomena that I am trying to describe might be the choreographic equivalent of what is called literary style, but broadened to a whole community of dancers or performers.

With this qualification, I return to my simple model to ask how pertinent it really is to apply the notion of technique to the dance domain. A single phrase summarizes why one might object to the notion's application here: namely, dance is a *technique without object*. And three distinct lines of argument that I will now consider help to clarify just how dance lacks an object and hence why it eludes conceptualization in terms of technique.

First of all, the lack of object implies that there is no strict or determinate finality at stake here. All technique appears subordinate to the realization of a particular end that endows it with meaning and gives it a raison d'être. Navigation techniques, for example, developed alongside techniques of naval construction to allow two coastal locations to be connected via the quickest and most reliable maritime route. The technique's orientation toward particular ends frames and justifies the means employed. Since Max Weber, this phenom-enon has often been called "instrumental rationality" (*Zweckrationalität*). To return to the case of dance, however (and perhaps the same applies to all the arts), it proves difficult to assign a determinate end to danced movement that might enable evaluation of the means employed. In other words, dance appears fundamentally contingent, since its movement is divorced from any identifiable teleological structure. There is no particular reason to dance. Or rather, if some-times a reason can be identified (like suing for mercy from the gods, making it rain, entering a trance state, or simply seducing a sexual partner), it rarely func-tions to determine precisely the nature of the gestures made: at some basic level, there is no reason to perform one set of movements rather than another. This contingent quality of danced movement—its lack of object—can be counterbalanced (as I will mention only in passing) by two phenomena. One is the traditional code that endows movement with a kind of necessity by limiting what counts as an acceptable gesture to those selected and transmitted by the tradition: typically, this is what happens in "traditional" or "folk" dance but also in classical ballet. The other is a distinctively modern phenomenon and depends on improvisation: truly compelling, basic movement is thought to emerge only in the subject's improvisations, as her presence to herself and to the moment allows the individual to elude the arbitrary diktats of intentional projects.[2]

Secondly, dance lacks an object in the sense of lacking a product or not being a form of production. Dance does not produce "things." Neither does music or acting. These are practices that produce events rather than things. So this absence of product, if not of an object per se (since I will not dwell on the complex ontological question of whether an event is or is not an object), clashes with intuitions about the poietic or productive dimension of technique. Technical man is above all *Homo faber*, that is, man as producer of artifacts, who transforms the external world through his work. As a consequence, the unproductive techniques (or techniques of the event) characteristic of dance, music, and acting remain very difficult to consider in terms of technicity.

Thirdly and finally (and this is probably a feature specific to dance), the idea that dance lacks an object also suggests an absence of tools or instruments. In contrast with music, there is no instrument for dancing. Of course this claim warrants immediate qualification, since although there is not instrument in the strict sense, there are still objects occasionally or even structurally employed in dances. Costume, for example, generally configures certain possibilities and impossibilities for the body in movement, and perhaps more broadly determines a particular body state. Likewise, the invention of pointe shoes in classical ballet radically transformed female classical technique, as is well known. Equally, the veils and fans of Kabuki dances, or the sticks and swords in the warrior dances described by Curt Sachs, spring to mind. In short, it would be possible to write an organology of these instruments, or conduct a historical and ethnological inquiry into the various objects that sometimes or structurally accompany dance, and into the uses that are made of them. Yet an organology

2. Perhaps this distinction between two ways of counteracting contingency (via the code or through improvisation) is too sharply drawn. For one thing, improvisation must aim at establishing a new code, or risk finding itself trapped within a preexisting idiom (as it does, for example, in the work of Odile Duboc). On this issue, see below, 273. Besides the dichotomy of code versus improvisation, there is also a more general necessity that compels danced movement in the form of the particular "artistic project," whereby a collection of ideological, social, or subjective determining factors appear to make certain types of movement inevitable. In this respect, the "free dance" of Duncan springs to mind, though it is only one of several possible examples.

of this kind would always remain marginal or beside the point of the practice as such. These various objects never determine gesture in as strict or articulated a manner as a musical instrument does the range of sound. An instrument's very materiality—the solidity of its wood, its copper, or its strings—inscribes the scales of notes that allow a given musical practice to be collectively organized and transmitted. This is not the case in dance, where the equivalents of scales of notes are ideal motor principles and repertoires of gestural entities, which are not themselves inscribed in the body's structure. I will soon need to explore the consequences of technique's immanence in the body, of dance's lack of object understood as an absence of instrumental mediation. In its materiality and solidity, the instrument is an object in which memory is housed and relayed. Dance lacks such objects, with the consequence that its transmission and historical consciousness are much more tenuous.

First, however, I will try to respond to the threefold objection outlined above by answering three questions: (1) What can a technique be that serves no explicit end? (2) What can a technique be that produces no-thing? (3) What can a technique be that does not pass (or barely passes) via the mediation of tools or instruments? In short, what can a technique be when it has no object?

Chapter 2

Technique or Language:
An Analogical Impasse

Here I will take a historical and textual detour to discuss Marcel Mauss's paper "Techniques of the Body" (1934; reprinted in Mauss 2006). This enables me to address only the second and third objections to applying the notion of technique in the dance domain. It does not permit me to address the first, since Mauss conceives of technique as linked to realizing an end conceived as such by the subject. In his paper, Mauss starts from experience—indeed, he begins with a biographical anecdote—of the historical and sociocultural relativity of bodily practices. He notices that in 1934 people are not learning to swim in the way he learned in his youth. He also observes how, during the First World War, English and Australian solders did not march in the same way as French soldiers. What he discovers through these diverse experiences is that the apparently spontaneous and natural use of the body is actually already framed and conditioned by the social. Mauss decides to call this socially learned and constructed use of the body a "technique of the body":

> By this expression I mean the ways in which from society to society men know how to use their bodies. (2006, 78)

By thus introducing the term "technique" to describe practices that concern only posture and gesture, without producing an object and without the mediation of an instrument, Mauss is very conscious of violating the sociologically accepted usage of the concept of technique:

> I made, and went on making for several years, the fundamental mistake of thinking that there is technique only when there is an instrument. I had to go back to ancient notions, to the Platonic position on technique, for Plato

spoke of a technique of music and in particular of a technique of dance, and extend these notions. (81–82)

The notion of a "technique of the body" here comes to question the very concept of technique, at least as employed in sociology, as the use of an instrument with the aim of modifying the external world. Instead, the idea of a technique of the body recognizes the totality of bodily aptitudes and capacities of all members of a group as imposed from outside by social authority. And, in fact, Mauss emphatically insists on the idea of transmission and traditional learning in the delineation of his concept. He still perceives a problem here, however, in that the idea of the bodily act transmitted and founded by social tradition seems to encompass much more than the simple notion of technique can bear. To further delineate the concept, he needs a supplementary notion to act as a foil, namely, that of the ritual act. Through the contrast between rite and technique the phenomena described by Mauss can be unified:

> I saw how everything could be described, but not how it could be organised;
> I did not know what name, what title to give it all. It was very simple, I just
> had to refer to the division of traditional actions into techniques and rites,
> which I believe to be well founded. All these modes of action were tech-
> niques, the techniques of the body. [. . .]
>   I call technique an action which is effective and traditional (and you will
> see that in this it is no different from a magical, religious or symbolic action).
> It has to be *effective* and *traditional*. There is no technique and no transmis-
> sion in the absence of tradition. This above all is what distinguishes man
> from the animals: the transmission of his techniques and very probably their
> oral transmission. [. . .] But what is the difference between the effective
> traditional action of religion, the symbolic or juridical effective traditional
> action, the actions of life in common, moral actions on the one hand and the
> traditional actions of technique on the other? It is that the latter are felt by
> the author as *actions of a mechanical, physical or physicochemical order* and
> that they are pursued with that aim in view. (2006, 82–83)

This distinction between technique and ritual, between the mechanical and the symbolic, remains problematic, especially when applying the concept of technique of the body to dance. Dance remains (at least ethnologically) indissociable from ritual: at the very least, technique and ritual are very often imbricated. Besides, Mauss himself recognizes that the distinction between rite and technique, between the symbolic and the mechanical, is purely operational and methodological. He insists that most often social agents themselves experience these two dimensions as completely intertwined. Nonetheless, it remains very restrictive to qualify the notion of technique by simple contrast with that of rite, and to associate the technique of the body with a purely mechanical, physical, or physico-chemical order (to take up Mauss's terminology). This makes its application to dance quite problematic. And this is probably why subsequent work in the anthropology of dance, notably the research developed in the Anglo-American context in the 1960s and 1970s, turns away from the concept of technique in favor of a different model: that of language and structural linguistics.

But before I examine this type of research that analyzes different dance techniques on the model of language, I should pause to consider the historical context of Mauss's paper. The paper is roughly contemporaneous with the 1930 publication of Curt Sachs's magnum opus *World History of the Dance* [*Eine Weltgeschichte des Tanzes*], which was translated into English in 1937 and French in 1938. However problematic this book might be in its methodological and axiological premises, it nonetheless remains a founding text of the anthropology of dance. Mauss, moreover, makes reference to Sachs in his paper, and his comments are full of admiration. Mauss's essay is also contemporaneous with the series of lecture-demonstrations organized by the Archives Internationales de la Danse (AID)[1] from March to May 1935 under the general title "La technique de la danse." In this series, representatives of the most significant choreographic schools or trends of the interwar period were invited to demonstrate the particularities of their own techniques and teaching practices. The special issue of the *Revue des Archives Internationales de la Danse* dated November 1, 1935, gives a description of each intervention, as well as a long retrospective commentary by Paul Bellugue.[2]

Sachs's book, Mauss's paper, and the series of lecture demonstrations organized by the AID are united not merely by the coincidence of place and date but by a thematic that is truly characteristic of the period. In this quasi episteme, the anthropological, historical, and aesthetic investigation of movement seems unable to do without the idea of the "dance technique." Indeed, the origin of this idea in its modern form might even be traceable to the 1930s.

Paul Bellugue's commentary in the special issue of the *Revue des Archives Internationales de la Danse* already suggests vacillation between the technical and linguistic paradigms, however. At first, Bellugue seems to endorse the distinction that served as my point of departure in defining the notion of choreographic

---

1. On the aims and history of the Archives Internationales de la Danse, see above, 233, as well as the collection of articles and texts published by the Centre National de la Danse (Baxmann, Rousier, and Veroli 2006).

2. For a detailed analysis of this series of lecture demonstrations and of the commentary of Paul Bellugue, see the article by Franz Anton Cramer, "Dire la danse: les conferences-démonstrations et le discours sur la technique et le movement," in Baxmann, Rousier, and Veroli (2006).

technique, namely, that between body and ideality, between physical mastery and repertoire of gestural entities. He describes this distinction in terms of an opposition between *skill* and *technique*:

> Thus, dance technique is: "the collection of *ideal* procedures employed to express an emotion through gestures organized spatially and rhythmically," whereas skill is: "the collection of *material* procedures employed to express an emotion by a gesture organized spatially and rhythmically."
>
> Technique enables conception, skill execution.
>
> Once these points have been clarified, we can see that, generally during the lecture-demonstrations, skill was being discussed much more often than technique. (Bellugue 1935, 38)

Putting to one side the definition of dance (as "the expression of emotion through gestures organized spatially and rhythmically"), I will focus on the distinction between *skill* and *technique*, between body and ideality, which matches my own characterization of the notion of a dance technique. And here it seems that the disappointment Bellugue expresses ("people have mostly spoken about skill and but little about technique") is not unconnected to the fact that the distinction is excessively schematic. If there is ideality (of *technique* in Bellugue's sense), this is always a function of bodily practices themselves. It emerges *from* the ways of doing that specify a given technique, in short, from what Bellugue calls "skill." And if the ideality of technique derives from skill, it seems obvious that the lecture-demonstrations would focus on the latter. Nor is it surprising that, disappointed by the lectures of "skilled practitioners," Bellugue's commentary turns implicitly toward another paradigm, even more focused on ideality, claiming: "Dance, in its most advanced stage of evolution, is a form of language" (39). This paradigm of shared and tradition-based language, which Bellugue sometimes also calls "style," breaks down when confronted by modern trends, by the multiplication of styles and individual ways of doing, in short by modern dancers' idiomatic practices:

> Faced with the diversity of modern trends, we have a right to ask if there is today a particular dance style?
>
> If we accept that there is no dance without style, that is without a defined, permanent and transmissible choreographic form, one can say that aside from ancient and exotic dances, *there is currently no Dance only a collection of dancers*. One should not in fact confuse style and aesthetic. Thus Duncanesque and expressionist movements correspond to an aesthetic but do not result in a style. Their artistic principle would oppose this because it

aims at giving each individual the means of singularly expressing his ephemeral personality. A style is a social phenomenon *like a language*. It has its grammar and syntax, in other words a system of conventions accepted by all. A style is a collective, and from a certain point of view anonymous, work. (41, my emphasis)

If dance only attains its "most advanced stage of evolution" by becoming "a form of language," then to characterize language as an anonymous and collective system of "conventions accepted by all" is to bring us paradoxically back to "traditional" or "folk" dance. And it is precisely within the field of anthropology of dance that the linguistic model became, from the 1960s onward, ubiquitous.

The concept of bodily technique developed by Mauss has the disadvantage of minimizing the symbolic dimension of gesture in favor of its mere physical efficacy. By contrast, postwar anthropological research—particularly in Anglo-American and Hungarian contexts—adopts the scientific paradigm of structural linguistics, making the analogy with language the founding principle of its approach. This is clear in the introduction by Georgiana Wierre-Gore and Andrée Grau to a collection of essays on the anthropology of dance published by the Centre National de la Danse (Grau and Wierre-Gore 2005, 19–23). In that volume, Adrienne Kaeppler's essay seems to me to exemplify this application of the linguistic model to dance.[3] In the same way as a language can be broken down into phonemes and morphemes, into minimal phonic elements and minimal meaningful units, so a given dance can be broken down into *kinemes* (minimal motor elements recognized as discrete by the agents within a system) and *morphokinemes* (*morphokines* or *choremes* depending on the author), in other words into the smallest meaningful gestural units:

The two basic units of linguistic analysis are phonemes and morphemes. A structural analysis of dance distinguishes movement analogues of phonemes and morphemes—i.e., *kinemes* and *morphokines*. [...] Kinemes are units treated as comparable to phonemes; that is, they are elements selected from all possible human movements and positions and are recognized as significant by people of a given dance tradition. Kinemes are those actions and positions which, *although having no meaning in themselves*, are the basic

3. The French title of the essay is "Méthode et théorie pour l'analyse structurale de la danse, avec une analyse de la danse des îles Tonga," a translation by I. Leymarie of Kaeppler's "Method and Theory in Analyzing Dance Structures with an Analysis of Tongan Dance," originally published in *Ethnomusicology* 16, no. 2 (1972). Quotations here are from the 1972 version.

units from which all dance of a given tradition is built. (Kaeppler 1972, 174, my emphasis)[4]

The second level of structural organization of dance movement is here termed the morphokinemic level and is analogous to the morpheme level in language structure. A morphokine can be defined as "*the smallest unit that has meaning* in the structure of the movement system." (185, my emphasis)

This research model has proved its analytical power in breaking down movement (Kaeppler's analysis of Tongan dance is exemplary), but it nonetheless still confronts a fundamental difficulty. The process of breaking a language down into phonemes and morphemes is supported by the linguistic fact of *double articulation*: that is, the simple combination of nonsignifying units (phonemes) produces signification (morphemes). But it is very difficult to discern in dance movement any equivalent of linguistic double articulation. Of course, there are the equivalents of phonemes, or minimal motor units that make up a gestural repertoire for agents. But identifying something that would be the equivalent of a morpheme remains very difficult. The morphokines or choremes that structural anthropology usually treats as equivalent are actually just more complex combinations of kinemes, which do not make the real qualitative leap that would enable passage from the nonsignifying to the signifying.[5] This difficulty is always there in analysis based on the linguistic analogy. In fact, I already highlighted the problem in my commentary on Noverre's writings.[6] Choreographic signification is not based on a simple combination of nonsignifying units, on a sequence of atomized steps that by some miracle suddenly says something. It

---

4. It is important to note that this kind of analysis is also based on the linguistic distinction between the "phonetic" (the general study of the sounds produced in natural languages) and the "phonemic" (the study of the distinct characters within a given language). The analysis seeks to pass from an "etic" description (that is, one from the outside, from the point of view of the analyst) to an "emic" description (from the inside, from the point of view of the indigenous agent): "The concept of 'emes' is basic here and can best be illustrated with phonetics and phonemics. When describing languages, linguists first of all take down in phonetic notation all the sounds they hear—just as a dancer might take down in a kinetic notation (such as Labanotation) all of the movements they see. A linguist then subjects his phonetic notation to 'emic' analysis to obtain an inventory of the significant movements which I have termed kinemes" (Kaeppler 1972, 174).

5. The Portuguese philosopher José Gil develops a similar analysis in his 2004 book, where he writes of the *quasi articulation* of dance. My own view is that there is clearly a first-level articulation in dances (there are discrete units that are identifiable and repeatable) but no second-level articulation that would be equivalent to the qualitative leap produced in language by the morpheme.

6. See above, 185.

always occurs both alongside and beyond the combination of kinemes: insofar as a singular body embodies the movement, signification is already present in the slightest step; but it is also understood and enriched when one grasps the global (artistic, social, or religious) context that governs its appearance.

To summarize the respective difficulties of these two models (technical and linguistic), each ultimately stumbles over the question of signification. The technical model merely sets that question aside, minimizing the symbolic dimension of gesture. The linguistic model, meanwhile, aligns gestural signification too closely with the phenomena of language and the conceptual. Its failure is probably inevitable, since the very question of gestural signification is difficult to frame outside of the linguistic analogy and requires an alternative of this kind. However, the two models still have one key element in common: both highlight how the motor categories and ideal gestural entities that constitute and collectively organize a given dance practice are transmitted by tradition. In the next chapter, I focus once more on the conditions of that process of transmission.

Chapter 3

Lack of Tools as Loss of Memory

I base my discussion here on Bernard Stiegler's analysis in *Technics and Time* (1998),[1] where he argues that every technique externalized in material objects simultaneously exteriorizes memory.[2] Every object produced or used by a technique both houses and relays the memory of the living actions and gestures that produced or used it. Not every technique is a mnemotechnique like writing or mechanical recording; but every technique involves a process of memory insofar as it passes via object mediation. Stiegler calls this process of exteriorizing memory a form of "tertiary retention," invoking the vocabulary used by Husserl in *The Phenomenology of Internal Time-Consciousness* (1964). "Primary retention" corresponds to what is ordinarily considered immediate memory, which assures the continuity of consciousness: when I talk to you, I remember that I have just begun my phrase with the expression "when I talk to you." "Secondary retention" corresponds to episodic memory: I remember that, when I was six, my parents gave me a very beautiful red bike. According to Stiegler, any memory exteriorized in objects is a form of "tertiary retention," whether or not these objects are specifically geared toward preserving memory: thus not just books, scores, or recordings but also tools, machines, and instruments, fulfill a memorial function.

Musical organology offers an excellent example of this idea of "tertiary retention." Of course, the instrument's material structure does not completely

---

1. First published in French as *La technique et le temps* in three volumes (Paris: Galilée): vol. 1, *La faute d'Épiméthée* (1994); vol. 2, *La disorientation* (1996); and vol. 3, *Le temps du cinema et la question du mal-étre* (2001). All volumes exist also in English translation: vol. 1, *The Fault of Epimetheus* (1998); vol. 2, *Disorientation* (2009); and vol. 3, *Cinematic Time and the Question of Malaise* (2011).

2. The work of Stiegler is rooted in that of André Leroy-Gourhan (1993; first published in French in 1964–65), who was an active member of the AID and gave two lectures for the organization in 1939: "La danse classique japonaise" and "La danse classique modern." See Baxmann, Rousier, and Veroli (2006, 232).

determine its use, and when an old musical instrument is discovered, one still has to reconstruct how it might have been played. This is the task of archaeological research on musical instruments.[3] Yet often the very materiality of the instrument inscribes the categorial and perceptual distinctions around which a given musical practice is organized (notably scales of distinct notes). The instrument thereby already offers a material condensation of practices and theories of sound,[4] such that it relays the memory of the practice by way of "tertiary retention" (to take up Stiegler's own terminology).[5] The instrument also thereby enables music to become conscious of its own historicity (here I concur with Bernard Sève's 2013 analysis). Because instruments have survived, the issue of "period" or "historically informed" performance can arise, notably in the reconstruction of baroque music. Rediscovered instruments enable an awareness of the radical disjunction between contemporary performance styles and our notions of what period performance might have been. Conversely, it is largely due to the way the *instrumentarium* has been technically and technologically transformed that music is aware of its own historicity.[6] Instrumental mediation appears to enable both transmission (or recall) and historical consciousness.

Returning now to the case of dance, we can pose the following question: What could a technique be whose transmission is never mediated by objects? In other words, what is a technique deprived of tertiary retention, whose perceptual and conceptual categories remain immanent in the bodies of practitioners? What could a technique be that never finds a home except in living bodies, in bodies that are mortal precisely because they are alive? What is the significance of technique's immanence in the living body for the transmission and historicity of dance?

Such immanence must imply a structural weakness of dance technique. Either this weakness is counterbalanced by a strong framework of tradition, as in the case of classical ballet and the pedagogical mechanisms that ensure its survival. Or it is accepted as such, entailing a constant renewal of technique, as

3. On this issue, see Bruneau and Planchet (1992): an archaeology of the visual presents "the product in the effective absence of production tools," while the archaeology of the musical presents "production tools in the effective absence of the product": "in the first case, we ask how the thing was made, and in the second how it worked" (55). Thanks to Bernard Sève for drawing my attention to this important article.

4. For illustration of this thesis, see Schnaeffer (1936), as well as his essay published in 1998, which qualifies the thesis in certain respects. The fact that Curt Sachs, founder of dance anthropology, also founded the discipline of musical organology is also relevant here (see Sachs 1940).

5. Steigler applied the concept of tertiary retention directly to musical organology in a paper given at the Cité de la Musique in the series "Leçons magistrales" (April 6, 2004).

6. See the chapter titled "La question de l'authenticité" in Sève (2002), as well as Sève (2013).

appears to be the case with modern and contemporary dance. As Paul Bellugue (1935) noted, there are as many techniques as there are choreographers. Hence it becomes easier to understand why modern techniques often adopt the proper names of their founders. More radically still, one might claim that there are as many techniques as there are dancers. This claim leads to the question of improvisation and obliges an analysis of the idea of a purely idiosyncratic vocabulary and technique. It also implies interrogating the conditions under which such techniques are transmitted. What part of "movement research on oneself" can be disseminated to others? What kind of ethos or mode of being is shared in lieu of steps and poses? I will take up these questions in the next chapter.

Whatever the answers, the same issue of obliterating historicity arises in both classical and contemporary dance contexts: ballet posits an eternal present in a tradition that never reveals its sources or transformations; contemporary dance is constantly reinventing itself from scratch. In both cases—and precisely because these techniques are not exteriorized in material traces—historicity is obscured. In other words, presence once again saturates movement.

Clearly, I should qualify this thesis, and I will make three observations. First, it is only a contingent fact that pedagogical structures almost always work to conceal their own sources. The body of the teacher, the master or the workshop leader (however he or she is designated) becomes the immediate and all-encompassing point of reference for the student. In the vast majority of cases, the sources of the exercises and structures are never named or historicized. This has the effect of making the class or workshop appear to unfold in a present without history, indeed in a fantasy of the body's pure presence to itself and to others. There are a few exceptions, however, which complicate the picture. For example, the ballet classes of Wilfride Piollet at the Conservatoire National Supérieur de Musique in Paris offer technique teaching based both on her own experience as an *étoile* at the Paris Opéra and on her reading of Arthur Saint-Léon's nineteenth-century dance treatises (Piollet 2005). In the field of contemporary dance, Dominique Brun makes the effort in her classes (no doubt encouraged by her training in Labanotation) always to cite the historical sources of the exercises she sets. These two examples, however, are quite isolated. Typical pedagogical practice consists in presenting one's body to the other as an object that is simply there, in the here and now; that is, as an object without history even though it is of course entirely historically constructed. This blindness of dance toward it own history might be modified by a simple modification of teaching practices to make oral transmission less opaque with regard to its own sources.[7]

7. For example, there is no need to so clearly demarcate courses in the history of dance and technique classes, as is currently the case in training programs for the Diplôme d'État de professeur de danse (the French state diploma for teachers of dance).

Secondly, it is possible that dance does have a less marginal organology or technology than I have thus far suggested. Loïe Fuller's performances, for example, fascinated her late nineteenth-century audience primarily by virtue of their technological innovations in costume and lighting. These enabled her to experiment with creating a new kind of stage space. The massive tunic extended by poles became a true instrument in this dance artist's practice. The costume had its own constraints and possibilities, which Fuller played as one might play a piano or a trumpet, that play forming the basis for her *Serpentine Dance* and *The Lily*.[8] And the optical structures employed in the practice of "the fairy of electricity," as Fuller was known, enabled a new kind of stage experiment that was the essence of her innovations in performance. These technical innovations—which it is tempting to describe as organological—were much imitated, to the point where Loïe Fuller was obliged to lodge several patents on her inventions with the Ministry of Commerce and Industry.[9] Indeed, her intellectual property was only recognized in respect of technical innovation, since it was never legally acknowledged from the artistic point of view.[10] This idea of an organological extension of the dancing body might also be developed with reference to Oskar Schlemmer's works for the Bauhaus, notably his *Triadic Ballet* and his series of object-dances *(Stick-dance, Hoop-dance, Glass-dance* and *Metal-dance)*.[11] Here, the object became as much as a way of constructing a geometrical schema of the human body—what Schlemmer calls a *Kunstfigur*—as an instrumental centering or amplification of movement.[12] Finally, the central role of the objects (sticks, chairs, balls, scarfs, and so on) in the pedagogical and choreographic work of Dominique Dupuy springs to mind.[13] Yet still it remains unclear whether this marginal organology has any role in preserving memory. No doubt sticks and hoops determine a structure of possibilities and impossibilities for movement that enable one more easily to retrace the embodiment of works (as in Gerhard Bohner's reconstruction of Schlemmer's *Stick Dance*,

---

8. For a detailed account of these two dances, see Giovanni Lista (1994).

9. Patents were lodged on January 13, 1893, with the Intellectual Property Division of the French Ministry of Commerce and Industry: one for a "new dress design specifically for theatrical dance" and another for a "new type of optical illusion in staging specifically designed for theatrical dance" (Lista 1994, 651).

10. On the failure of Fuller's lawsuits for copyright infringement, see Lista (1994, 104–6).

11. *Das Triadische Ballet* was first performed in Stuttgart, September 20, 1922. *Stäbetanz (Stick-dance)* and *Reinfentanz (Hoop-dance)* were created at Dessau in 1927. Glastanz (*Glass-dance*) and *Metaltanz (Metal-dance)* were created at Dessau in 1928.

12. See Rousier (2001), as well as the collection of texts by Schlemmer (1978).

13. See Dupuy and Dupuy (2001) and Bernard (2001, 235–45).

for example).[14] However, the dependence of these objects—which I hesitate to call instruments—on their handling renders unstable any memory they house and, in many respects, thwarts the idea of "tertiary retention." Perhaps it is only when digital technologies are applied in dance that the body's technological equipment can really function as a memory support and tool for preservation.

I have already considered digital technologies in my discussion of the trace, examining their fusion of image and score.[15] Now I need to explore their role as technological prosthetics and perceptual apparatuses. Aside from their minimal role in preserving dance (with video being likely to remain for the foreseeable future the cheapest and most efficient way of recording works), systems of digital motion capture[16] seem to have found their real use in the movement and choreographic domains through what has been termed *biofeedback*, that is:

> The use of a motion sensor placed on a person to capture data that is then processed by a computer to create a sonic or visual representation of his movement and inform him about certain features of that movement of which he would be otherwise unaware. (Godard and Kuypers 2006, 74)

The different dance experiments with motion capture were summarized by Armando Menicacci and Emanuele Quinz during the Monaco Dance Forum in 2004 (see Menicacci and Quinz 2006). As they show, this type of body equipment is primarily a way of amplifying perception, and not a memory support. Currently, these new technologies are mainly used in dance in the following way: they make the subject aware of features of her movement of which she otherwise, in the immediate sensation of moving, remains unconscious; the micromovements captured are transformed via digital technology into auditory and visual sensations, in an artificially constructed process of intermodal perception. From this perspective, the technological apparatus appears simply an external amplification of what one ordinarily understands by "technique" in dance, and not a radical transformation of its relationship to memory.

14. See Rousier (2001, illustrations, p. ix).

15. See above, 243–44.

16. There are currently three main types of motion capture system in use: (1) electromechanical systems, in which an exoskeleton is strapped to the performer (with sensors in each of its joints to record the movements made), the weight of the apparatus limiting the performer's movement possibilities; (2) optical systems, in which the movements of reflective dots worn by the performer are recorded by several video cameras and the data triangulated to create a three-dimensional reconstruction; and (3) magnetic systems where the performer wears magnetic receivers that affect the surrounding magnetic field, as in the *Startracker* system. Thanks to Armando Menicacci for his very helpful advice.

This leads me to my third and final observation. A technique of the body—whether it be ballet technique, contemporary technique, or somatic practice—is already a perceptual apparatus in spite of its lack of instrument. This renders my notion of a dance "without tools" more tenuous. Learning is already a perceptual tool. Through training and habituation, perceptual thresholds are refined and new perceptual discriminations can be made. External apparatuses—whether they be mere sticks or unwieldy digital sensors—merely extend this process of perceptual refinement, already a proper part of developing an embodied dance technique. This leads me to argue, ultimately, that it is not even the lack of object or technology in dance that induces a failure of memory. From the point of view of practice, even when objects and instruments abound, preservation and memory are not the concern, so much as the present refinement of sensation. Objects, digital tools, sensors, and cameras may proliferate, but sensory presence still remains the primary material of choreographic work.

Chapter 4

Intending the Unintentional, Repeating the Unrepeatable

So far, I have explored two dimensions of the notion of technique: technique as bodily mastery, or corporeal appropriation of idealities; and technique as arche-writing, understood as the lexical and categorial substrate underpinning both composition and graphic notation as forms of choreographic writing. I now want to question and qualify this twofold definition of technique by considering contemporary improvisation practices. I need to render dialectical the very idea of "bodily mastery," since the space of improvisation only opens (at least from the utopian perspective) once the intentional project is abandoned. I also need to question the notion of the choreographic work, understood merely as a combination of pregiven choreographic entities (steps, poses, and so on). In short, I will examine here the contemporary relationships between improvisation and composition, precisely insofar as these apparently distort how we conventionally conceive of both the work and technique.

Let me first establish schematically a standard model for these relationships. *Improvisation* is often conceived as the first stage of creation, the moment of free research in the studio, which is supposed to enable the emergence of truly new, unprecedented, noncodified, and unidentified movement. *Composition*, in turn, is conceived as the second stage of creation, the moment of writing and fixation, which guarantees that the movement emerging in improvisation can acquire a certain stability and repeatability. This fixation of movement is a necessary condition of its negotiation in the form of a *work*—an object that escapes pure eventfulness and can repeat itself, more or less identically, from one evening to the next. This model of the relationship between improvisation and composition largely governed the production of choreographic works in the 1980s and 1990s[1] but is currently in major crisis. That crisis is probably more than mere fashion generated

---

1. This model, evident in French contemporary dance of the last twenty years, is also part of a long tradition that reaches back to the 1910s and 1920s and the practices of Dalcroze, Wigman,

by the tyrannical and rampant impulse to renew choreographic form, to innovate or be different for the sake of it. I see here something more profound, namely, the result of an internal contradiction. On the one hand, the production of rich, interesting, or innovative movement is said to be possible only under the auspices of unintentional, unpremeditated, indeed *improvised* movement. On the other, such movement seems capable of acquiring form as a work only when its principal characteristics are denied and it becomes fixed in a predetermining text. The form of the finished object, through its modes of construction and givenness, thus ends up denying its own conditions of emergence and possibility. The title of this chapter, "Intending the Unintentional, Repeating the Unrepeatable," seeks to capture that contradiction in the form of a double paradox. "Intending the unintentional" designates the first stage of creation that improvisation represents, a stage that is already paradoxical in itself: unintentional (or at least unpremeditated)[2] production of movement remains subordinate to a perfectly intentional and deliberate artistic project, whose aim is to produce the unintentional intentionally. But this first paradox remains minor until doubled by a second, which creates the true contradiction by supposedly stabilizing improvised movement in a composed work. "Repeating the unrepeatable" designates this second stage of composition and defines the whole enterprise as self-contradictory. In composition, we try to transform the apparently unrepeatable—that which depends on the unique event and on singular experience—into a repeatable object. Contemporary choreography proposes very diverse ways of resolving this contradiction. All are based, however, on a deliberate blurring of the distinction between improvisation and composition, and on a radical rethinking of the idea of "choreographic writing" [*écriture chorégraphique*].[3]

   It is not a given that a moment of improvisation precedes composition. Classical ballet does perfectly well without one, for example. And a number of

and Laban, transmitted via Hanya Holm to American modern dance. And when I write of "French contemporary dance of the 1980s," this should be understood as a retrospective, schematic characterization that merely reflects some contemporary consequences in the field of dance. A detailed history of the period remains to be written, which would understand it in broader terms than those of its present effects.

2. The unpremeditated is probably not the same as the unintentional, although it might be its minimal condition, making it a short step from one to the other. Making improvisation the first stage of creation already renounces an inherent voluntarism that would seek to control every part of the project's realization. It also gives fortuitous movement a kind of necessity that exceeds the projections of the subject.

3. "Writing" here does not mean graphic notation but rather functions as a synonym for "composition." Dances are "written" when they are sufficiently established and fixed to be reiterated and reidentified from one evening to the next. This double notion of "fixation" and "identification" is what is today being radically transformed through the idea of "choreographic writing."

choreographers, including some contemporary artists, seem to accord improvisation a very minor role in their artistic process. Thus for Cunningham the
subversion of writing depends not on vague trust in the subject's spontaneity
but rather on the purely impersonal principle of Chance: throwing dice just
before the dancers enter the stage to determine the order in which movement
sequences are performed. More recently, there have been many contemporary
works wholly written in advance, set before the first day of rehearsal. For example, Bagouet's *Déserts d'amour* was written graphically even before the dancers
became involved.

If improvisation is not necessary to the process of creation, why do artists
typically resort to it? I will argue that improvisation functions to confer a kind
of necessity on danced movement that it lacks by definition. Recall that dancing
appears to consist above all in moving *for nothing*. When I dance, I disengage
from the world of work and practical tasks, isolating my gesture from any practical end that could orient or determine it. There are probably general reasons
to want to move *for no purpose* (to expend excessive energy, for example, or to
take a break from heteronomous action). But within the general horizon of this
lack of purpose, there is no particular reason to want to move this way rather
than that, to prefer this particular gesture over another. Any practical end that
might determine the nature of the gesture is absent here, with the consequence
that the production of movement is affected by a fundamental *contingency*. The
conventional response to such contingency is to resort to a *code*: producing
movement thus becomes a process of selecting and combining, from within
a *finite* vocabulary, a certain number of permissible entities. So-called traditional dances, as well as classical ballet, depend on this kind of model, which
denies contingency through distinguishing what is permitted or precluded by
the vocabulary in question. But contemporary dance is precisely a form that
implies working beyond codes and established traditions. Contingency must,
then, make a violent return. Why prefer this movement over that, once there is
no vocabulary to predetermine the subject's choices? I argue that improvisation
is a distinctively contemporary process that compensates the absence of code
and immanently reabsorbs the contingency of movement. The urgency of the
situation—of having to generate movement in real time—lends movement a
necessity that far exceeds subjective choice and judgment's prevarications, yet
without closing it down via external code or conventions.

Usually, recourse to improvisation is justified in terms of a rejection of vocabulary and code.[4] My own thesis takes up this idea, even while expanding it.

---

4. We need once more to distinguish between discourse and practice. Often presented as a
form of liberation from codes, improvisation gets rapidly absorbed into other kinds of codified
practice, generally linked to the style of the teacher or the choreographer.

Rejection of the code is less the explicit aim than a constraint that radicalizes contingency and obliges the dancer to invent new ways to resolve it. It is no longer a question of working (or not) at one remove from vocabulary (which is already excluded in principle), but rather of conferring on the free-floating, noncodified movement of contemporary dance a kind of necessity that conforms to its new regime. Only at this level, I argue, is there a need for improvisation. If rejection of codes is made the explicit and primary aim of improvised movement, we would be led to construct a partial and unsatisfying image of the process. According to that image, to begin with improvisation would be essentially to return to the singularity of the dancing subject, and thus erase the sedimentations of movement inscribed by tradition. Improvisation would thus represent a space of freedom, beyond all vocabulary, in which subjectivity could give itself free rein with no frame or constraint, and the subject could discover herself in the intimacy of a gesture that is truly hers. This is an image of an essentially *solo* improvisation. Mary Wigman's expressionism, itself a product of improvisation practices at Hellerau, presents a striking example. For Wigman, improvisation was above all a practice and experimentation on *oneself*, which brought to light the deep self beyond the externality of vocabulary and convention. To improvise prior to composing thus becomes a process of rediscovering the immanent ground of subjectivity by virtue of which one can exclude the code.

But relying in this way on the subject's spontaneity—on what emerges immediately, without premeditation or judgment, from mere proximity to oneself—risks empty repetition and uninterrupted reiteration of those conventional figures and schema that appear most reassuring and natural. Starting from oneself, as both point of departure and horizon, runs the risk precisely of never going beyond oneself and remaining entrenched there, hence the risk of being caught up again in convention and vocabulary. "Spontaneity" perhaps consists simply in forgetting self-determinations, in a fantasy of virginity whereby the dominion of the code is believed to have evaporated, when in fact it merely operates at a more intimate and resonant level. If the body's return to itself is really to herald liberation, then a supplementary determination is needed. I hypothesize that this supplement involves placing intentional decision-making outside the circuit; only the intervention of some *necessity* external to choice can simultaneously challenge the code and reabsorb contingency.

The partial character of my first image of representation already signals how improvisation is rarely confined to this pure modality of the subject's free return to itself. Given the constraints it imposes, improvisation might even be a prime haunting of that return. Improvisation usually has a *framework*, if only in virtue of the space in which it is performed and the presence of other dancers (where there are such). Both function as *constraints*, simultaneously retracting and extending the field of possibilities. Features of the space (its height, breadth, depth, or the presence of columns, absence of windows, and so on) obviously dictate what is and is not possible: but they also establish, through their concrete specificity, a whole sphere of virtual actions that pure subjectivity could not have invented on its own. Other dancers, through the physical actions they perform in relation to my body as well as by their presence at a distance, have the same effect: they limit abstract possibility but establish concrete virtualities. The improviser's role then consists in seizing these virtualities as they present themselves, neither before nor after that precise moment. The framework thus functions as both constraint and kairos. But we have thus far only considered this framework as *pregiven*. It can also be *constructed* or made more effective by making its parameters more precise. We can give ourselves some *rules of the game*, which prestructure the improvisation. We might even set the core choreographic material. Such rules (and American dance practices of the 1960s and 1970s present many examples) are more like the simple elements of a game structure than principles that cannot be flouted, however. It is not so much conformity to rules as the *play* of the structure which prevails, even when going against the framework. Improvisation is usually practiced over an extended period, such that the structure can evolve from the inside and be transformed into something other than the mechanical actualization of external rules. An unforeseen reality can thereby emerge, which remains inextricable from the constraining *framework* that it both extends and denies.

That second image of improvisation as what I will call "framed" improvisation partially confirms the hypothesis I advanced on the subject of solo improvisation. The *framework*, whether it is *given* (through the determinations of space and other dancers' presence) or *constructed* (in the structure and its rules), allows movement to escape from the *contingency* of the intentional project and endows it with a kind of *necessity* that does not derive entirely from the choices of the subject. A constraint is above all expected to allow an *elusive* movement, an *unintentional* result, or an *accident* to happen—all things (or rather events) that the subject cannot generate intentionally but that follow rather from the objective (although unforeseen) play of the *framework*. The code is probably also thereby challenged, but in a different way. From the start, the constraint places us at one remove from intentional positioning. It is no longer a question of taking part in, repeating, or challenging a vocabulary but simply of allowing what follows from the framework and its play to happen. The code, then, is not rejected so much as simply dissolved. Consequently, the end that we attribute to improvisation (reabsorbing movement's contingency by bypassing the intentional project) does not fundamentally question my first image of improvisation but simply obliges us to interpret it differently.

It seems indeed that intention can be bypassed in two contrasting ways: by the subject becoming absorbed in herself, such that her action becomes the simple correlate of internal sensations that are indifferent to all externality; or by an extreme openness to the environment, which makes each gesture a kind of pure reflex action. The first is linked to the idea of solo improvisation, which it reinterprets in line with the ideas of sleepwalking and ecstasy that we already explored in the work of Valéry and Straus. It shows how the unintentional, *elusive* movement can still happen despite the subject's solitude and indifference to the frame, or perhaps specifically *because* of these factors: by foreclosure and self-engulfment, since the body that we assume is returned to itself is actually anything but master of its own action. Following its own affects and the internal logic of kinesthesis, the body plays a game that is both intimate and alienated, with consciousness at best a spectator. Listening intimately to itself, the body simultaneously renounces all intentional projection, or any intention that exceeds the body's own logic. The idea of sleepwalking furnishes the operational metaphor that enables this state to be conceptualized. In itself, corporeal immanence is connected to an inevitable abdication of the will. Lluis Ayet's work, particularly his *Si la pièce est trop courte, nous y rajouterons un rêve* [*If the piece is too short, we'll add a dream*],[5] is a good example of this connection. Conceived as an extended form of hypnotic trance, dance improvisation here functions as the choreographic equivalent of the surrealists' automatic writing. The movement here can be specified as *unintentional* and depends entirely on the subject's absorption within itself, a state so effectively described by Valéry. Eyes closed, the dancers seem indifferent to any external world, being completely focused on the internal logic of their bodies and physical states, as if driven by a necessity that is both internal and foreign, imperious and hidden. To improvise alone and for oneself is never a case of trying to restore mastery and ownership of one's own body (like the pilot in a vessel) but rather of allowing oneself to be dispossessed, in the hope that what transpires could never have been produced within the limits of the will and the intentional project. In other words, this is a case of *intending the unintentional*.

Meanwhile, openness to environmental stimulation—the second way to bypass intention—corresponds to the image of *structured* improvisation (*structured* by possible rules as well as awareness of the space and others in it). Steve Paxton's Contact Improvisation presents a striking example of a practice that accords such force to the external environment. Based on the interaction between bodies and the sharing of weight between partners, this practice produces a kind of movement that results directly from weight transfer and can no

---

5. Created in Montpellier, July 2001.

longer be attributed to a particular subject. I cannot even properly be described as *acted upon* by the other, because the other is no more the author of the action than I am. When I lose my balance, I initiate a new action, but in response to the moment rather than premeditated intention, and thus the interaction begins again. A whole dialectic of *availability* is implied by this kind of movement. If my partner is to act on me as something other than a dead weight, I must remain available to him; yet intentional postural control must simultaneously be relaxed (or my partner will not be able to act, only struggle against me); nor does my body abandon itself to the purely mechanical physicality of weight (or my partner will end up manipulating my "dead" body). This tension between relaxation and poise, between abandonment and receptivity, is precisely what constitutes this state of availability. It enables the subject to avoid self-focused, intentional muscular contraction *and* transformation into pure object. Indeed, the idea of the "unintentional" or "involuntary" that I am proposing does not demand that one become *thing*, like a mere toy batted about by mechanical forces. The constraint is not expected to function like brute necessity but rather as a way of establishing concrete virtualities, which the dancer perceives and actualizes in the moment, aside from any external aim. This kind of unintentional behavior does not come naturally. One still has to make oneself *available*, in other words (in a certain sense) *intend* to make oneself available.

The dialectic of availability can be extended to less directly physical forms of interaction. The other dancer's presence and action at a distance in themselves exert a constraint. They establish a concrete situation in relation to which I cannot just do *anything* (any structural rules merely radicalize such constraint by overdetermining it). Availability consists, then, in inventing for each transformation of the situation (which in principle is constantly changing) an *appropriate* response: a response born not of abstract, individual desire but rather generated by what is happening here and now, and nowhere else. One might object here that the "appropriate response" remains intentional, that it fully depends on intentional decision-making, and that this is why it can be described as "appropriate" or otherwise. After all, I used the term "kairos" earlier, apparently making improvisation a specific case within a general theory of decision-making. Yet my reply here would be that the appropriate response, or reaction to the situation, is at the very least unpremeditated—the very logic of the kairos means that it cannot be grasped in outward projection. And from the unpremeditated to the unintentional there is, perhaps, but a short step; or perhaps it is merely a question of degree.[6] At a deeper level, it is important

---

6. At what moment, within what time frame, does an action cease to be reflex and become a real decision? This is hardly obvious, even from the legal point of view, where it nonetheless remains crucial to drawing the distinction.

to recognize how the "appropriate response" of dance improvisation is foreign to the general structure of action, understood as the realization of global and predefined goals. It is also thereby distinct from the strategic logic of the kairos: in contrast to practical action, appropriate improvisational responses are not governed by the subjective horizon of a unifying project, by the direct and linear structure of a goal, which would reduce the surrounding circumstances to the status of mere occasions for actualization. Rather, they stem directly from the situation itself, like immanent responses. The contradiction highlighted in the objection to my view, then, seems to be there in the phenomenon itself and in the dialectical logic of availability: by renouncing individual and intentional aims, abandoning oneself to the situation, one becomes capable of making good decisions that respond effectively to the requirements of the moment—and to those requirements alone.

This contrast between two images of improvisation—through which I am trying to distinguish two possible modes (sleepwalking mode and availability mode)—is probably too starkly drawn. Empirically, neither is experienced purely. In the sleepwalking mode of solo improvisation, there is always a vague awareness of the external environment that can occasionally serve as stimulus. And, reciprocally, reflexive availability cannot completely annul consciousness of one's own body and the internal logic of kinesthesis. My distinction between these two images, then, is largely ideal. But as distinct as they are in their ideal forms, they still share a common trait, a sort of indispensable condition of possibility: the present as the environment of being, and openness to the singularity of the moment as the principle of their exercise. If the products of improvisation emerge from this kind of environment and openness, the second stage of creation—composition—returns as a kind of impossibility. What sense could there be in trying to fix as repeatable what appears entirely incapable of being detached from the moment of its production?

Two connected concepts dictate the need for composition: the work and the author. For movement to become *work* it must first establish itself as repeatable, escape the pure eventfulness in which it is given, and persist identically across a series of evenings and tours. Repeatability implies fixation and identification. An ideal object, functioning like a class of occurrences, can be substituted for the singular movement of improvisation. Typically, this object is called a "choreographic phrase." The processes that generate the phrase are themselves called "writing" and ultimately depend on the "chore-grapher." The operation of writing also entails the responsibility of an *author*. To compose is not just to fix but also to choose and to modify. Not everything produced in improvisation is good. There remains a need to edit and refine improvised material. And an overall structure also needs to be determined to encompass and organize that material, such that choice and responsibility (although eliminated from the details) again come to govern the whole, according to the demands of *authorship*.

Through this double impetus toward fixation and selection (toward work and author), composition contravenes the primary aims of improvisation. By treating movement like a generality that is indifferent to its conditions of actualization, composition detaches improvisation from the openness to the moment that alone seems to make it possible. And by selecting the "best" moments, composition re-establishes a structure of choice and responsibility in that place where the work process unfolds below the level of subjective decision-making. In both cases, movement is disconnected from the network of (internal and external) constraints that made improvisation the way for dance to escape the contingency of the intentional project. Composition thus denies the conditions of emergence of its own material.

In the face of this contradiction, two solutions are possible. The first consists in globally challenging the distinction between improvisation and composition. Improvisation can then be reconceived as *instantaneous composition* (as in the work of Mark Tompkins) or *composition in real time* (as in the work of João Fiadeiro). The first characteristic of composition (fixation and repeatability) is radically overturned: when the work is immediate and invents itself with the event, instantaneous composition does not expect fixation. It suffices in itself and, in the immediacy of the situations it engenders, does not aspire to repeatability at all. The second characteristic of composition (choice and responsibility) is partially retained, however. In this form of improvisation that aspires to the work and the finished show, "composition" comes to mean lucid consciousness of what is shown and an element of responsibility associated with it. In contrast to traditional composition, however, this responsibility is not localized within a single subject (an author) but involves the whole group of participants, each taking responsibility (in real time and in front of an audience) for the collection of choices and abstentions. This instantaneous and collective choreographic writing, which developed out of postmodern American dance, resolves the tension between composition and improvisation by maintaining a radical faithfulness to the moment. It partially maintains the demands of authorship (although they are diluted in the collective) and willingly renounces the demands of the *work*— at least if the work is understood as stable, repeatable object.[7]

The second solution maintains the demands of the work. It preserves the binary between improvisation and composition and aims simply to extend the function of writing, so that it becomes embedded in each reiteration of the unforeseen and the new. Writing no longer consists in fixing a singular

7. On the practice of instantaneous composition, see the Autumn/Winter edition of *Nouvelles de Danse*, 1997: "On the Edge/Créateurs de l'imprévu," particularly the texts by Mark Tompkins.

movement that the performer actualizes as a whole but rather in establishing
an open structure that can be re-experienced with each occurrence. It is not a
case, then, of composition falling back on improvisation but rather of opening
writing up, injecting it with fluidity, and blurring the distinction between the
two processes. This new form of composition can take two forms: *structure-*
[dispositif] writing or *material- [matière]* writing. In the former case, an overall
structure is set, rather than determinate pathways or actions: general principles
come to govern the movements and the interactions of the dancers but without
determining their effective actualization. The result is that, each evening, the
movement is both the same and different: it is engendered by the same principles but without being a reiteration of any prototypical realization. This practice
of structure-writing was also a product of American postmodern dance and is
the compositional achievement of structured improvisation. The work of Gilles
Jobin[8] would be a good example, albeit in a deliberately rigidified form.

But aside from the global functioning of the work, the gesture itself can be
the focus of an open form of writing that sets *material* for performance rather
than *phrases*. Composing a movement phrase usually involves fixing the physical pathway of a gesture and establishing it as an abstract ideal, susceptible of
many realizations. Material-writing merely determines the general parameters
of the gesture's identity (a particular kinesthetic theme, rhythmical structure,
imaginative accompaniment, and so on) but without fixing its form. The dance
can then be repeated independently of any reference to a primary realization.
This is not a case of reproducing an effective trace but rather reactivating (in
a different way each time) the core experience highlighted in improvisation.
Material-writing consists, then, in generating a kind of choreographic ideality from improvised elements—a general scheme that retains only the gesture's
eidetic and experiential core, and is susceptible of very diverse actualizations.
The open ideality of *material* is opposed to the abstract ideality of the movement *phrase*. The latter allows only interchangeable instances, whereas the
former posits an identity for dance at a deeper level than that of its image, welcoming diverse realizations even as it demands greater fidelity as regards kinesthetic experience. Experience is repeated, not form. And the repetition implies
identifying the experience sufficiently clearly in advance. Material-writing—a
renewed form of composition—consists precisely in this *identification* of the
product of improvisation.[9]

8. *The Mobius Strip* (Paris, 2001) and *Under Construction* (Berlin, 2002).

9. "Material" is a richly ambiguous term in contemporary dance. It refers simultaneously to
the brute product of improvisation (*material* waiting to be formed) and an ideal object of
composition—*material* that, like a musical theme, opens a space of variation and secondary
improvisations.

Based on the singular experience of the dancing subject, *material* represents the compositional achievement of solo improvisation. The work of Mathilde Monnier offers a striking example. Indeed, her work *Multi-materials*[10] is actually about the close link between the subject and choreographic material, that same theme re-emerging clearly in *Déroutes*.[11] Here, the individual is identified by her own material, which is not reproduced mechanically but put back in play and re-embodied each time. The dancer does not merely reiterate an externally fixed form—each performance is different. But because she attempts to experience once more what she experienced in improvisation and identified through choreographic writing, nor does the dancer simply improvise—each performance is the same, the same experience being repeated in its very difference.

Open choreographic writing, whether of material or structure, attempts to restore on the basis of repetition itself those phenomena that dictated the turn to improvisation—availability in the moment and the necessary force of the event. More specifically, such writing aims to be faithful to those phenomena. And thus it aims to *repeat the unrepeatable*.

From the technical substrate and arche-writing of movement, we thus return—via the question of improvisation—to the present status of the work in contemporary dance. In the attempt to describe what "contemporary" means here, I will propose a first conclusion to the argument of this book.

10. Created in Montpellier, June 2002.

11. Created in Paris, December 2002.

Conclusion (1)

Reflect and Repeat

Cracking pecans doesn't entail any particular artistry, none whatsoever, hence nobody would be so daring as to gather up an audience and then for his performance that he would shell a pound of pecans. But, all the same, if one were to do just this and if one's performance were to be a great success, well then, obviously it couldn't possibly simply be a matter of cracking nuts! Or maybe it does have something to do with nut-cracking but it suddenly has become apparent that there's more to cracking nuts than meets the eye, that we've been overlooking something because we just happen to be so good at it and that only now its innermost essence has been put up on display whereby it is even quite conceivable that this might be a distinct advantage and quite useful, namely that the artist performing such a feat isn't really all that good at cracking nuts to begin with.

FRANZ KAFKA
Josephine the Songstress, or the Mouse Folk

Section 1

Stage and Contemporaneity

The contemporary is perhaps displayed, even *staged*. Maybe the contemporary (choreographic?) stage can be read as somehow representing the spirit of our times, our own era. A defining feature of human time is its tendency to represent itself, depicting its own image, even performing itself onstage. Those products traditionally called "works of art" are the favored medium of this self-representation. This would suggest that any discussion of dance and the contemporary need merely decode dance works and their stage environment to reveal something like an image of the times, the figure of *our* time.

This is precisely the path I will *not* take here. There are two reasons for this. First (and here I advance a hypothesis that far exceeds my topic) what is currently understood by the empty term "contemporary" may be nothing more than an assertion of the impossibility of epochal representation. We no longer believe in a unified epoch that is our own, or in the possibility of a unifying representation of our era. Several different, ideologically various, terms are used to describe this condition: "the end of master narratives," "the end of utopias," "the death of art," "postmodernity," "the end of avant-gardes," "the end of history," and so on. Such laments—the diverse forms of elegiac discourse—perhaps reveal something better defined than we believe it to be: what is lost is not history as such and in general but rather the capacity of the contemporary moment, of "our" time, to represent itself and grasp itself as a single epoch. Within this context, the role of art—or rather a certain diagnostic evaluation of its condition—becomes predictably crucial. As a traditional means of epochal figuration and the representation of historical periods, art should logically find itself at the center of the crisis. Experiencing its first end in Hegel's grand onto-theological narrative, the ghost of art survived its secularization for some time. It took on other tasks and found an alterative, atheist teleology in modernist discourse and the image of the avant-garde—a teleology that could guarantee its historico-political function and epochal responsibility. But this alternative did not last long: today, the ghost of art is well and truly dead not because it achieved its mission but rather because any teleological structure that could give it a role has evaporated. Art has entered what Yves Michaud (2003) calls a gaseous state [*régime gazeux*]: liberated from any responsibility, art floats among infinite possibilities; it is driven only by the games of institutional recognition, novelty, and empty subversion, which is immediately reabsorbed and recycled by the market and the State. Art has lost all capacity to depict an image of our times. It remains content (just like any other economic sector) with playing its own social game—neither more nor less.

The term "contemporary" would thus signify both the general incapacity of our time to understand and imagine itself as an epoch, and the local embodiment of that incapacity, maybe even its cause: namely, a crisis in artistic production or, at least, its transformation under a new paradigm so unprecedented that art cannot currently be conceptualized except in terms of what it now lacks. This means that it would indeed be absurd to expect art—or indeed dance—to follow the mandate of epochal representation that the very term "contemporary" seems doubly to disown. This is the first reason to reject the path mapped out at the start of this conclusion—a reason that is actually both external and insufficient.

In fact, escaping the logic of periodization is not so straightforward. Our era's incapacity to understand itself still appears as an epochal characteristic. A temporal, homogeneous, and unified (albeit negative) image or our times still underpins the contemporary impossibility of constructing "an" era that is "ours." The defining characteristic of our times would be that they are neither a single era nor properly ours. But this characteristic (as a defining characteristic) still allows talk of "an" era, attributed to us, even though the "us" here merely states its own impossibility. The term "contemporary," in its nominal and unifying form, is the very emblem of this contradiction. "Contemporary" is a residual term that simultaneously dreams and annuls the possibility of unification as zeitgeist: the zeitgeist is annulled even as the empty space of its content is preserved. Of course we no longer believe in the idea of a unified, shared epoch, in the idea of a substantial community in time. But the form of our disbelief remains a way of subscribing to that idea. Whatever we may say, therefore, we remain believers.

But then epochal figuration must itself, in some way, still be operating. And, indeed, it is difficult to deny how perfectly the new regime of art is matched to the contemporary impossibility of self-representation. The fact that the adjective "contemporary" can be used to describe both the era and its artistic products posits just such a match, understood as a residual and negative form of positive figuration. The epoch or spirit of the times is still negatively represented by contemporary art's incapacity to give form to the times. This makes my refusal to read dance works in terms of what they say about our times seem even more naive. Although a positive reading of art's epochal figuration would be obsolete, a negative route remains available in two guises. One might, for example, seek to show, from the inside, that contemporary (or maybe "post-modern") art has taken on the essential task of representing the impossibility of representation—of presenting the unpresentable itself, and thereby also in the process representing our times. As Lyotard himself recognized, such nega-tive representation remains in keeping with modernism and the logic inter-nal to artistic process.[1] Conversely, one might simply bring to light, from an external perspective, a straightforward renunciation of art—the abandonment · or evaporation of its historical task—and then treat that renunciation itself as the symptom (or accessory artistic image) of our times: art still, then, repre-sents the era but only as external symptom, not through the negative interiority of the symbol. This is the cultural and sociological route whereby the general theme of the "end of art" or the "end of art's myth" (and so on) is inevitably linked to the brute exposition of how it functions socially and economically. The work of Arthur Danto (1997), Natalie Heinich (1998), or Yves Michaud (1997; 2003) would, in their different ways, be the milestones on this second, "external" path.

I could attempt to apply this idea of negative figuration to the choreographic field. I could show how dance is also (especially in its non-iconic use of the body) an experience of the unpresentable, a presentation of unpresentability. Conversely, I could take the deflationary path and show that the choreographic "field" itself is the site where art becomes uncoupled from responsibility, released into insignificant eclecticism and singularity—in short, that the social game of empty subversion and recognition is as much in play in dance as any-where else. I will not go down this route, however, for the second of the two reasons I mentioned: because we would not thereby learn anything that we did not already know, or at least nothing particular to dance. This approach would remain external to the object in hand, merely applying to it a network of con-cepts and problematics derived from a whole other field, namely, that of the visual arts and literature. We might understand something about dance by tak-ing this approach, but only about that element which participates in the general regime of the art of our time. The specificity of dance's participation would be left unexamined. That is why I propose a different strategy, which (for the time being at least) pretends ignorance of all of the above arguments.

---

1. "A work can become modern only if it is first postmodern. Thus understood, postmodern-ism is not modernism at its end, but in a nascent state and this state is recurrent [...] The postmodern would be that which in the modern invokes the unpresentable in presentation itself" (Lyotard 1992 [1988], 13–15).

Leaving aside the question of epochal figuration, I start from a particular internal connection between dance and *contemporaneity*. By "contemporaneity" I do not intend here a historical period or epoch but rather a specific structure of temporality: namely, *neutral simultaneity* and *contingent coexistence*. In its most general sense (and without trying to name a specific era), the "contemporary" is *everything that coexists*, everything that belongs to the same time. This coexistence need not be based on shared traits or identities, on some form of substantial commonality. Things, people, and events simply coexist—full stop. There is no prior justification. As I said, simultaneity is *neutral* and coexistence *contingent*. But, at the same time, precisely because it enables coexistent entities to be collected together under a single term (the "period," the "era," the "contemporary"), contemporaneity seems to imply going beyond contingency. Simultaneity must at some point become self-conscious and establish real commonality. An identity, reason, or content is needed to explain the *fact* of coexistence and ensure that it derives from a truly *common* present. Contemporaneity should, therefore, be understood as neutral simultaneity marked as insufficient and aspiring to the unity of substantial commonality. I will argue that dance, as *scenic event*, is directly exercised by this structure. Its *works* exist only on the *stage*, which (as I hope to show) is quite simply a structure of contemporaneity. Then, I return to the idea of the "contemporary" itself and explore a specific transformation of the choreographic field over the last ten years. I will argue that this transformation can only really be understood in reference to the *contemporaneity* of the stage, which it self-consciously and radically questions, in the form of the reflexive labor of performance.

I begin with a simple—although apparently exorbitant—axiom: *there is properly speaking only contemporary dance*. Obviously, I am not claiming that the genre of "contemporary dance" represents the endpoint of choreographic history, or the moment of assumption where movement experience is revealed in its ultimate figure of truth. Rather, I want to draw attention to a simple fact: namely, that dance has only ever been given from *presence* to *presence*, in that space of simultaneity with oneself and with others known as the *stage*, which has all the features of a structure of contemporaneity. It might be objected, of course, that the *stage* is hardly necessary to experience dance. One can perfectly well dance for oneself, without addressing anyone else. And even if someone else is present, often she is also dancing—entirely participant, not seated observer. This is true. But it is also true that dance can only constitute and display itself *as work* via the structure of the stage. As long as dance remains closed in on itself, folded into the intimate experience of gesture, nothing emerges that assumes objective shape (except when an inappropriate, voyeuristic gaze transforms into spectacle something that was not at all made to be seen). Only through intentional address and explicit sharing between agents and viewers does a third object emerge, opening the possibility of a *work*. And here I am concerned with dance as art, as a mode of production and presentation of objects in which doers and non-doers meet—so I continue without scruple this reduction of dance to the stage.

Through this reduction, the link between dance and the contemporary is affirmed once again. The solipsistic experience of movement is not at all concerned with contemporaneity. It does occur in a time of *presence*, but that presence folds back on itself, without any dialectical connections, creating a perfect sphere of pure auto-affection. Deploying in and for itself the flow of its own kinesthetic sensations, the dancing body's temporality is merely an eternal present that absents all possible coexistence. Dancing within a group apparently alters nothing in this respect. The global subject is simply placed at one remove: the subject's experience remains solipsistic even within the group, as she participates in a fused, nondialectical form of shared experience.[2] For contemporaneity to be properly experienced, coexistence must not be reabsorbed immediately in a fusion with no outside. There must be a hiatus and the division introduced by the *stage*.

I will, then, reduce dance to the stage and treat the latter as the emblem of a possible link between dance and contemporaneity. But recall that we still do not know what the stage is and how it functions. So I will endeavor to describe both in (very) pseudo-phenomenological vein.

People inhabit a space, brought together in indifferent multiplicity and for no other reason than simply being there. They form a sort of localized crowd. They do nothing, or not very much, or not really. They are expecting some event. Others, facing them (or behind, alongside, or even in among them—it makes no difference), make something happen, make something materialize, ultimately in the form of nothing but still in a sufficiently clear way to distinguish themselves from the crowd and transform the rest (the crowd) into an *audience*. Perhaps we move too fast here in calling them an "audience." Perhaps that term merely conceals the phenomenon underpinning it. All we know for the moment is that on one side, people expect but do nothing, while on the other side, people act, make things happen, and move (or not). Above all, we know that these two things must happen *at the same time*, in a kind of coexistence that we can for the moment describe as *contingent*. Neither doers nor non-doers have any real reason to be there, still less a reason to be *together*. A given event—the event in whose name the *stage* is delimited—opens a space of coexistence, establishing a "we" of simultaneity. But this "we"

2. This needs considerable qualification, given that contemporary choreographic creation is largely oriented toward a search for forms of community that do not involve such fusion. On this issue, see Mathilde Monnier's *Les lieux de là* (1999), which was a kind of catalyst for this strand of dance endeavor.

has for the moment no content other than expectation and its mechanical satisfaction, such that nothing is really done. Expectation cannot be satisfied by the bare event, by what happens here and now, whose sole merit is its haecceity. Some supplement is needed. Presence alone is not enough, given that we are already inherently immersed in it: what is given over there on the stage appears authentic and firsthand, inducing in everyone present the lucid consciousness that it will never be repeated identically anywhere else, and thereby decorating itself with aura. But we know that such presence is manufactured, that as such the aura is automatically induced by the idleness [*désoeuvrement*] of the crowd and the vacancy of its time. That is inevitable: an ineliminable condition, which can even produce a degree of pleasure. Yet something else is required. We expect the coexistence of the doers and the non-doers, in their togetherness, to escape ultimately the pure foundational absence in which it originates and to be re-established around some "common" ground. We expect that Truth and Presence (a supplement of presence, or rather its transubstantiation in the shift from "p" to "P") redeem in some way the initial contingency and transform it into an assertion of community, a present that is really shared. The applause that concludes the event is like a late signal of this hope, its final, disappointing substitute.

The stage is simply an intensified and complexified structure of contemporaneity. Coexistence is given there folded in two, complicated by the idleness [*désoeuvrement*] of some and the intentional address of others. Contingency is thematized here from the very beginning—it is *for* itself and no longer simply *in* itself.

This is all well and good, but how does it *directly* concern dance? The structure of the stage seems to apply just as much in the case of theater and the concert. Yet there is a difference. The choreographic work (in contrast to the musical or theatrical work) subsists only on the *stage* itself, such that access necessarily implies participation in the way it is given in *presence*. There are two reasons for this. Firstly, the choreographic work does not make a particular element of the performance into its condition of identity. While the identity of an opera or a play is defined by a single artistic field, enabling it to generate diverse interpretations and productions, the dance spectacle retains without hierarchization the heterogeneity of its spectacular elements. Everything participates in the definition of the work, including those elements that are apparently secondary, namely, scenography, costumes, or lighting.[3]

Secondly, if the work can be said to be defined purely by the identity of its choreographic text, that text remains ambiguous, poorly established, and very

---

3. See above, 125–26.

frequently oral in character. Few dancers and choreographers know how to read or write a choreographic score. Notation, when it happens (infrequently), often functions more like a mechanism for external preservation (through *archival* fixing) than like a principle of identification that would enable restaging beyond person-to-person transmission (a corpus). Notation has never really integrated itself with practice, so the shift to the allographic it heralded (enabling the work to abstract itself from local conditions of production and transmission) remained unrealized. Works continued to be transmitted in largely oral fashion, from body to body, from presence to presence. Without the reproduction in absentia that the text permits, dance remains linked to a horizon of generalized presence. And one result is that, yet again, its givenness remains bound to contemporaneity.[4]

The 1980s in France seemed to forget this dependence—or at least to bracket it, unquestioningly. The work was first and foremost defined as *indifferent repeatability*. The pieces making up the repertoire of dance companies sought independence from their local conditions of actualization and unstintingly supported a varied calendar of evening performances and tours. These were "all-terrain" works, in a sense, which experimented with denying their eventful mode of givenness and with abstracting themselves from it. Performed here one evening, there the next, in this or that theater—it remained demonstrably the *same* work. The consequence of bracketing the *fact* of performance was a failure to question its very *form*. The structure of the stage and its parameters were treated as self-evident—as inescapable, unquestioned medium. What was still known at the time as a *spectacle de danse* [dance *show* or *spectacle*] seemed perfectly natural. The essence of *performance*—to do something in real time in front of people who do nothing—was not conceived as posing any particular difficulties.

The transformation that I mentioned earlier can be dated to the middle of the 1990s and should be understood as diametrically opposed to the above state of affairs. Variously described by the critics in ways that reduced it to the status of local avant-garde ("the New French scene," "young dance," and so on),[5] this new wave represented more than mere fashion or a passing tendency, however one judges it artistically. It heralded a radical change of regime in relation to the production of works. In fact, this change has already happened. For anyone who wants to work in dance today, there are some things that are impossible,

4. See above, 163.

5. Without seeking to compile a catalog, I will mention a few of the artists involved: Alain Buffard, Jérôme Bel, Boris Charmatz, Emmanuelle Huynh, Xavier Le Roy, Alain Michard, Laurent Pichaud, and Loïc Touzé.

things that one can quite simply no longer do—or, at least, no longer do with the same naiveté.

What are the features of this shift? For clarity of analysis, I will isolate five, which can be summarized in a single phrase: "the *reflexive* labor of performance." The transformation is structurally linked to another, although it might seem diametrically opposed. In the interests of parallelism, I will call this "the *memorial* labor of the work."

Section 2

The Reflexive Labor of Performance

The first feature of the transformation described above consists in the dissolution of stable companies. Temporary and local coalitions took the place of stable teams of salaried collaborators (what used to be called "companies). These coalitions brought together around a defined project a group of individuals with their own independent artistic careers. The coalition model is both liberal and libertarian, in linking labor to the temporary mission and the circumscribed consent of the participants. Yet its presence in dance is not merely a response to economic pressures, as the dissolution of Mathilde Monnier's company in 1999 indicates. This was not driven by real financial necessity (the company was well known and in receipt of funding as a Centre Chorégraphique National) but rather responded to the state of impasse generated by salaried employment within a company (what Monnier calls "family neurosis") and to an acute consciousness that the reciprocal engagement of dancer and choreographer did not reach beyond mutual investment in particular projects. Precarity of labor thus became an internal artistic norm. The absence of permanent (or at least long-term) contracts for performers was no longer deplored; such contracts were shunned for reasons internal to artistic production. The regime of freelance work was no longer a poor substitute for coveted salaried employment; it became the social manifestation and indispensable accompaniment of dance artists' acceptance and embodiment of economic liberalism. Boris Charmatz articulates the shift in exemplary fashion, defining freelancing as "accepting and embodying (social) precarity for the benefit of (artistic) exchange" (Charmatz and Launay 2003, 139). The critical bite of his phrase resides in the play of the parentheses: if one omits "(artistic)," the phrase looks like just the sort of statement that might be made by any business association.[1] This transformation of

1. On the transformations of the performing arts within economic liberalism, see the remarkable analysis by Pierre-Michel Menger (2002), who examines artists' employment in relation to the growing precarity of labor within the "ordinary" economy more generally.

labor practices has implications for the concept of the *work*. It tends to weaken two connected components of that concept: the notions of *author* and *repertoire*. The work ceases to be a product created and owned by a choreographer and becomes the local and temporary result of a coalition that is equally local and temporary: "Some artists consented to work together for a given time, and here is the result. . . ."[2] The notion of repertoire disappears within this model, since the work struggles to persist beyond the coalition that enables it. Works become part of a repertoire only when identified solely by the signature of an author and when a stable company linked to the name of that choreographer exists to actualize them. I interpret this general shift in choreographic labor (which is also a transformation in the nature of the work) as a realization of the necessarily local and temporary character of *performance*, and also as highlighting its inescapable *contemporaneity*, obscured by the structures of "company" and "repertoire."

The second trait consists in integrating works with their economic context of production and dissemination. The financial parameters of creation are treated as real, constitutive features, and not as secondary or contingent elements over which one should draw a discreet veil. The work is variously adapted to the locations and institutions that host and finance it. This abandons the universal image of the "all-terrain" work abstracted from its material conditions of production, an image that reigned through the 1980s. In economic terms, the transformation involves blurring the distinction between production and distribution. In production, partners give money for a new work to be created. In distribution, they simply purchase a ready-made piece that can then be actualized onstage. But today, each instance of distribution (each performance of the work) is expected to also be an instance of production (of recreation). Emmanuelle Huynh's *Bords* offers the perfect example of this fusion. The piece metamorphoses in each of its actualizations and is only sold on the express condition that a period of creation is involved in each distribution. Here again, performance is expected to live up to its inevitable *contemporaneity*.

The third trait depends on a transformation of the concept of choreographic "writing" (not graphic notation but *composition*: that is, the collection of processes that allow a choreographic objected to be identified and fixed as a stable and repeatable entity). Choreographic writing now no longer involves fixing a determinate gestural trace that can be actualized mechanically by the performer

2. A paradigmatic example of this model is Alain Buffard's project for Montpellier-Danse 2003, *Mauvais genre*, which was canceled because of an artists' strike. This was supposed to bring together about thirty dancer-choreographers, all of whom were already well known as artists in their own right: Régine Chopinot, Xavier Le Roy, Mathilde Monnier, Rachid Ouramdane, Mark Tompkins, and so on.

from one evening to the next; rather, it involves creating open structures that demand to be re-experienced and revisited in different ways each time the piece is performed. The openness of writing thus implies an element of improvisation embedded in each realization, such that the scenic event is no longer mechanical actualization but becomes partial recreation. *Material*-writing, which merely determines the general parameters of a movement's identity without fixing its form, is one possible mode of this new form of writing. Although this approach is widely used today, Mathilde Monnier's work presents paradigm examples: particularly *Multi-materials* and *Déroutes*. In this transformation of writing too, the work is aligned with the inevitable eventfulness of its mode of givenness.[3]

The fourth trait consists in a loss of clarity about what constitutes the medium of "dance." In the 1980s, there was a fair degree of consensus about the identity of dance. Despite the diversity of styles, there was clear, constitutive, and unchallenged demarcation between dance and "pedestrian" or everyday movement. That is no longer the case. Anything can now be dance, including (perhaps especially) the most banal gesture, absent movement, or even immobility. In thus questioning the identity of the choreographic, artists explicitly recall American postmodern dance of the 1960s and 1970s.[4] There is a key difference, however. American postmodern dance understood itself a way of analytically questioning the essence of dance ("What is dance?"), through eidetic variation and the testing of limits ("How far can I go without ceasing to produce dance?"). But the French new wave seems rather to displace the question, concerning itself with the essence of *performance* ("Is there always *event* when I do something—or not—in front of someone who does nothing?") and only reinterrogating the dance medium through this questioning of performance. Emmanuelle Huynh's *Mua* (1998) offers a case in point. This is a solo entirely composed of immobility, silence, and darkness. Only through questioning the parameters of spectacle more generally does dance begin to question itself.

This means that my fifth trait—reflexively rendering the medium of spectacle opaque—is actually a function of the fourth. Dance artists in the 1980s worked with an essentially naive attitude to spectacle, treating it as an inevitable, neutral, and transparent medium for dance.[5] Via this medium, choreographic "worlds"

---

3. See above, 282–83.

4. On the link between the French new wave and American postmodern dance, see Luccioni's preface to the French translation of Banes (2002 [1987], 10) ("A mirror held up to contemporary French dance").

5. I should immediately qualify this claim. I was not present (or at least not of an age to be able to go to the theater) during this period. The meaning of the term "French dance of the 1980s" ultimately depends more on its present effects and its retrospective image than on the historical reality of its practices. A proper description and analysis of the latter are long overdue.

could be directly exhibited in a distant and autonomous way, unaffected by performer-viewer relations and indifferent to the manner of their givenness. Spectacle merely offered a window on those worlds, without modifying them in the least. Memorable works were produced under this paradigm, such as Maguy Marin's *May B.* (1980), which presents a closed Beckettian universe that straightforwardly presents itself to the viewer, without the mode of that presentation being thematized at all. That kind of approach has now become impossible. Today's dance is governed by the axiom that performance is necessarily self-reflexive. Spectacle cannot escape its essential duplicity unless it thematizes onstage its own operations, unless it becomes its own object. Beyond reflexivity of the medium of spectacle, no salvation! The most striking examples of this imperative are Jérôme Bel's works, whose titles (*The Last Performance, The Show Must Go On*, etc.) explicitly comment on themselves. These five traits of the recent transformation of choreography can be summarized by the single phrase "reflexive labor of performance." The eventfulness of performance is explicitly at stake here, to the point where it becomes integral to the concept of the work (points 1, 2, and 3). Presentation via spectacle becomes its own object and enables internal challenges to the work (points 4 and 5). My own move is to push the argument further, relating this transformation to the dialectical *contemporaneity* of the stage: the shift in practice both highlights that contemporaneity and puts it radically in play.

One might well wonder about the historical status of this transformation. I claimed at the beginning of this conclusion that questions of periodization, of the spirit of the times, could be set aside. In a fitting return, I now seem trapped by my own premise. Yet here again, I would offer an answer in negative mode. I would argue that this transformation exceeds the language we ordinarily use to conceptualize the historicity of the arts. It is neither *modern* nor *postmodern*. It does not involve a modernist progression of art toward the core of its own medium: *dance* as such is not the explicit object of reflection but rather *performance*, which is only contingently linked to dance and not an essential feature (it would suffice that notation become customary for dance's dependence on performance to be significantly weakened). Moreover, the transformation merely reiterates and foregrounds a prior transformation (that of American postmodern dance), such that its repetition ruptures the idea of progress through successive rejections, an idea central to the logic of modernism. But then this new dance is not *postmodern* either. Repetition here has a real internal consistency, which prevents it from tipping into a straightforward eclecticism of "returns to. . . ." It also thereby escapes the pure evaporation of historicity that postmodernity assumes. And the American postmodern dance that is repeated was in itself anything but postmodern, the historical labels applied to dance being out of kilter as regards their artistic content. Indeed, at the risk of paradox,

I would argue that "modern" dance (Laban, Wigman, Graham, and so on) is actually *classical*: it is wholly governed by the expressivity of a subject-creator. Equally, American "postmodern" dance is *modern*: it progresses toward an elucidation of its own being, by testing its limits and bypassing its conventional forms.[6] The transformation in French dance, meanwhile, is neither modern nor postmodern. It is *contemporary*, in an extra- or parahistorical sense. It seeks to envisage the necessary *contemporaneity* of performance (contingent rather than intrinsic to dance); it aims to reflect within works themselves on what it means to reveal the contingent coexistence of doers and non-doers. This connects up two themes: *presence* (the necessary eventfulness of what can only be given in action) and *contingency* (the dialectical insufficiency of neutral simultaneity), both themes that the transformation I have identified tries to raise to self-consciousness. The work is no longer abstracted from the eventfulness of its givenness, and contingency reflects on itself via forms of reduction that are essentially disappointing or even absent (non-events, invisible dances, immobile movements all feature, deliberately frustrating expectations). Something like an immanent definition of performance is thereby offered to us: performance is something that is only possible in *presence*, and on condition of its *failure*.

6. Here I draw on Sally Banes (1987): "Historical modern dance was never really *modernist*. Often, it has been precisely in the arena of post-modern dance that issues of modernism in the other arts have arisen: the acknowledgment of the medium's materials, the revealing of dance's essential qualities as an art form, the separation of formal elements, the abstraction of forms, and the elimination of external references as subjects. Thus in many respects it is post-modern dance that functions as *modernist* art [...] since "modern" in dance did not mean modernist, to be anti-modern dance was not at all to be anti-modernist. In fact, quite the opposite" (xiv–xv).

Section 3

The Memorial Labor of the Work

In the previous section, we saw how contemporary choreography reflects on the essence of the stage and its contemporaneity, in the very moment of performance itself. In parallel, a renewed consciousness of historicity and memory is also evident, complementing rather than opposing the transformations outlined. In the contemporary moment that I am trying to describe, there is a desire to wrench dance from its subjective absence of history, from its fixation in the perennial routines of tradition, as well as from its imprisonment in the bare present of experience. Dance-making seeks to *produce* [*mettre en scène*] its own history and memory, no longer relegating both to the externality of the written biographical or historical account. In short, present work becomes the primary interpreter of the memory of past works. Here I will explore some examples illustrating this new relation between choreographic works and their own history.

Quatuor Knust's project "... *d'un faune*" (*éclats*) (2000)[1] was probably the first to embody this transformation of the French choreographic field (or at least the first to embody it so vividly). Following its revivals from the score of selected key works of modern choreography,[2] the Quatuor attempted to decipher Nijinsky's score for *L'après-midi d'un faune*,[3] compiled two years after the work's premiere and translated into Labanotation by Ann Hutchinson-Guest and Claudia Jeschke in 1991. But beyond deciphering the notation, they also

1. "... *d'un faune*" (*éclats*), premiered in December 2000, conceived and performed by the Quatuor Albrecht Knust (Dominique Brun, Anne Collod, Simon Hecquet. and Christophe Wavelet), after works by Nijinsky, Mallarmé, and Debussy.

2. *Les danses de papier* (*recreation de danses de Doris Humphrey et Kurt Jooss*), 1994; the recreation of *Continuous Project / Altered Daily* by Yvonne Rainer of *Satisfyin' Lover* by Steve Paxton, 1996. On this issue, see above, 246–47.

3. *L'après-midi d'une faune*, premiered on May 29, 1912, at the Théâtre du Châtelet, with choreography by Nijinsky, music by Debussy, and plan by Cocteau.

offered an interrogation of the work as such through two different processes. On the one hand, they asked what it was about the work that made (and continues to make) it such an event for choreographic modernity. This implied research into *historical documentation* (concerning the context and the genesis of the work) as well as *psychic recollection* ("what remains, for me as a contemporary dancer, of this legendary *Faune* of 1912 that I never saw? What memory traces has it left in my body, without my knowing it?"). On the other hand, they treated the score not as guarantor or guardian of authenticity but rather as a supporting framework opening a space of interpretation and variation. Given this two-stranded process, the show called ". . . *d'un faune*" *(éclats)* can hardly be considered a "reconstitution" of Nijinsky's work. Rather, it is a production that combines dance history and remembering (through the historical documents read by the dancers, stories from their own memories, and so on) with a play on the parameters that the score leaves open (variation in number of dancers, several performers simultaneously dancing the role of the Faune, inversion of gender roles, and so on).[4] In 2000, ". . . *d'un faune*" *(éclats)* articulated a need for choreographic practices to reflect on (and reinvest current works with a clearer sense of) their relation to past works, while also prizing open the join between dances and bodies (ultimately in accord with the score's abstraction) so that those dances could be shared with other bodies and opened to new interpretations.[5]

This last point allows a glimpse of another kind of "revisiting" or "rereading"—not of *works* anymore but of *dances*. We can aim to appropriate a particular dance without thereby seeking to reperform the work in its entirely or revive the whole stage and musical apparatus that accompanied it. We can extract dances from their operal contexts of origin and attempt to reperform them for their own sake.[6] The status of the present body on the stage is then at issue, along with its potential to stage its own phantom, displaying the vestiges of movement that it tries to inhabit without ever quite succeeding, showing somehow in presence itself the absent original body. I base my discussion here on two clearly contrasting examples: *Phasmes* by Latifa Laâbissi (2003) and *Visitations* by Julia Cima (2005).

---

4. The gender inversion (where the faune is danced by a woman and the main nymph by a man) can also be justified historically on the grounds that in 1921 Bronislava Nijinska, Nijinsky's sister, herself danced the role of the faune (personal communication with Dominique Brun).

5. See, once again, the film by Dominique Brun, *Le faune—Un film ou la fabrique de l'archive* (CNDP, 2007), for more information on the current extensions of this project.

6. I already explored the possible dissociation of dance from work in the case of the Carnets Bagouet's *Matière première*. The dissociations tends to become problematic or porous in the case of solo works where the body of the performer and choreographer are no longer one. And it is precisely such solos that are the sample "revivals" mainly discussed in the paragraphs that follow.

Laâbissi's *Phasmes* revisits solos by Valeska Gert,[7] Mary Wigman,[8] and Dore Hoyer[9] via film sources. Despite differences in dates and movement approaches between these three choreographers, there is undeniable thematic, stylistic, and geographical unity revealed in this "revival." This is an exploration of German expressionism in its different forms, and hence also of our present relation to these foundational movements, to this dance of expression that was a pillar of choreographic modernity. That relation itself is displayed (and questioned) by the scenic structure adopted. The film sources are not erased but permanently present in their projection onstage. The relation between the two bodies is itself visible here: one appears in the live moment of performance, the other is reproduced mechanically on screen, yet each ultimately contaminates the other in a strange absent presence or phantom apparition. Hence the title: *Phasmes*, which denotes both a kind of self-camouflaging insect [*phasmid*] (the body of Latifa Laâbissi?) but also references the Greek word *phasma* or ghostly apparition (the bodies of Gert, Wigman, and Hoyer?). It seems as though no imitative revival is possible without absence being manifest at its very core—in this particular case, in the form of ghosts.[10]

The approach of Julia Cima in *Visitations* (2005) is very different:

Visitations is above all a dancer's project. It is a program of solos which for the most part do not belong to me and that I am appropriating.[11]

There is no thematic or stylistic unity here. Among the different solos revived (which are mostly extracted from longer works, even from group pieces), we jump from one to another without apparent connection: from a Butoh solo from Tatsumi Hijikata's *Hôsôtan* (1972) to a Cunningham dance from *Fractions* (1977), via Catherine Legrand's solo in Bagouet's *Le crawl de Lucien* and dances by Isadora and Lisa Duncan as well as Valeska Gert, to finally conclude with the solo of the "Chosen One" from Nijinsky's *Sacre du printemps* (1913). The heterogeneity of dances and bodies is apparently never problematized, at least

7. *Der Tod, Kupplerin*, and *Die Canaille*, filmed in 1925. On the life and work of Valeska Gert, see her autobiography (Gert 1989 [1968]).

8. *Hexentanz*, created in 1926, filmed in 1930.

9. *Angst*, created in 1962 and filmed for television in 1967.

10. On this imbrication of the mimetic and the spectral in the term "phasme," see Didi-Huberman (1998).

11. Julia Cima in the printed program for *Visitations*, September 22–27, 2005, Paris, Théâtre de la cité internationale.

in what is shown onstage. Ultimately, we are always focused on the singular body of Julia Cima, which "flattens" in the present of the performance any historical or aesthetic unevenness between the appropriated dances. What is more, although Julia Cima works mainly from film sources, the film's status as a means of dance preservation and identification is never questioned or thematized. The source of the work, and its potentially fragmentary or partial character, is once again hidden or erased. Julia Cima's present body imposes itself upon us, and we have to trust her, take her word for it. Although the project asks some valuable questions about the possibility of a pure performance by the dancer (the choreographic equivalent of the recital in music), it remains problematic in terms of what is not thought through, and its absence of reflection on the specificity of the choreography work, memory, and revival.

Other recent creations have explored a more distant or distanced relation to works of the past, via homage or citation. I will cite just a few titles in this regard: the series of *Hommages* by Mark Tompkins, which were less about returning to works or past dances than to selected iconic figures (Vaslav Nijinsky, Valeska Gert, Josephine Baker, and Harry Shepard);[12] Marco Berrettini's *No paraderan* (2004), which cited *Parade* (1917) by Cocteau and Massine, and reiterated a similar self-referentiality with regard to the scenic apparatus; and finally Rachid Ouramdane's *Les morts pudiques* (2003), which partly revisited the music and themes of Roland Petit's famous ballet *Jeune homme et la mort* (1946), which was supposed to have been called *La mort et le jeune homme* until Petit refused.

It is also with the memory of *Jeune homme et la mort* that I will conclude by discussing Olga de Soto's work *Histoire(s)* (2004). Commissioned by Lisbon's Culturgest, who asked the choreographer to produce a piece in homage to *Jeune homme et la mort*, de Soto elected to focus on the memories of spectators present at the premiere on June 25, 1946, at the Théâtre des Champs-Élysées—a quasi-legendary performance by Jean Babilée and Natalie Philippart. She went looking for surviving audience members and produced eight filmed interviews that were the focus and frame of the show called *Histoire(s)*. De Soto herself described the result, which was halfway between film and performance, as "documentary video-performance."

What was most immediately striking about the spectator testimonies was the very fragmentary and partial character of those memories as the interviewees tried to reconstruct their experience some sixty years later. The story of the

---

12. The *Hommages* series comprised four solos: *La valse de Vaslav: Hommage à Vaslav Nijinksi* (1989); *Icons: Hommage à Valeska Gert* (1998); *Under My Skin: Hommage à Joséphine Baker* (1996); *Witness: Hommage à Harry Shepard* (1992). For a detailed analysis of the series, presented together in 2002, see Ginot (2002).

ballet was largely forgotten, along with the appearance of death. A few striking moments lingered (Babilée's *cabriole* jump from the table to the ground, the final hanging), together with images of the scenography. Listening to the testimonies, we became aware of how memory primarily reveals the power of forgetting.

Yet in the filmed interviews themselves—those old and wrinkled faces of interviewees who, at the end of the Second World War, were young men and women—the striking presence-absence of recollection was revealed. Their gaze was entirely absorbed by an internal search for a far-off stage, no longer with their own audience in the present of the film or the performance. They were trying to be *there*, in that other time that we could not have known. But the absence of gaze was paradoxically the only appropriate way to reveal the presence of memory, its phantom or remainder. Only by showing the hollows and the gaps of intimate memory could the fragile (surviving, but rapidly disappearing) presence of that event of June 25, 1946, appear.

Finally, Olga de Soto's labor oriented the present work not toward the past work's agents or creators but toward their witnesses, in a manner simultaneously more specific and more vague. The aesthetics of reception was applied in "the memorial labor of the work."[13] This allows us perhaps to grasp the most vivid yet evanescent, most real yet ghostly, dimension of what can be termed the choreographic work's "survival." In a form of extreme transcendence,[14] the work is identified with the collection of (multiple, heterogeneous, and partial) memories of its event. It thus accepts its own mortality, even while entrusting to other works its potential (though still temporary) continued existence.

- But if the staged work itself reflects on its own essence and takes charge of its own memory, diffracted by the distance between bodies and history, why do we need you?
- You may well ask.
- Does this mean that your own interrogation merely reflects the transformations you are trying to discern?
- Certainly. But when did philosophy ever pretend anything else? Reflect on our times, only our time. In the best possible way.

13. See Palazzo (2005)

14. In Genette's sense of this term.

Conclusion (2)

Gesture and Trace

On the chain of supplements, it was difficult to separate writing from onanism [...] In both cases, the possibility of auto-affection manifests itself as such: it leaves a trace of itself in the world.

JACQUES DERRIDA
Of Grammatology

Cover your tracks.

BERTHOLD BRECHT
A Reader for Those Who Live in Cities

To conclude, I want to propose two distinctions that could form the basis for a classification of the various art forms. There are, it seems to me, two essential features that define the concept of the *work*: the work is an object that is both *public* and *durable*. I applied this definition to the field of choreography in parts II and III, thereby assuming that, in dance, the object's durability is logically subordinate to its publicity: the work first needs to be displayed in public (in a spectacle or show) in order for the question of durability to even arise. This was implied by the order in which I treated the two topics. Despite the relatively formal character of my two-part definition (in which the notion of the work of art is dissociated from notions of beauty or aesthetic value), it seems to me appropriate as a minimal definition of the work: all works, if they really do fall under the concept of the work, must fulfill the twin conditions of publicity and durability. Evidently, these come in degrees: an object can be more or less public or private, and more or less resistant or fragile in relation to the ravages of time. But in order for us to speak of a work, these two features must be minimally present in the object. From here, I want to introduce my second distinction by arguing that the logical subordination of durability to publicity applies only to one group of art forms, what I will call "arts of movement." Other arts have an exactly converse structure: the conditions of durability are the *very medium* of their operation, and publicity is relegated to a process of generating merely external, secondary work-instances. I will call these other art forms "arts of trace." In other words, the distinction between publicity and durability is a resistant polarity for the work, through which each artistic practice is open to two possible modes of hierarchization: a regime of movement (which is public) or a regime of the trace (which is durable).

This is a conceptual chiasmus. In the "arts of movement," the first and necessary stage is one of making-public (publicity), while techniques of inscription (durability) are the proper medium of the "arts of trace." Equally, durability is only a secondary issue for the arts of movement, while the arts of trace relegate the process of making public to external instances. In what follows, I develop and explore this chiasmus in greater detail.

The first thing to say is that there is probably only really art of movement. Realizing any work of art implies minimal participation of the body, even though that participation is sometimes confined to mere graphic inscription. The work must be externalized. And, given our humanity, the medium of externalization still remains the body. Yet we can distinguish between two types of movement: those whose function is specifically to leave traces (the movements of the writer, the painter, the sculptor, the engraver, the photographer and the filmmaker) and those that seem to suffice in themselves, despite possible mediation by instruments (the movements and vocal gestures of the singer, actor, and dancer, and the movements of the instrumental musician). Ultimately this is the distinction implied when I use the terms "arts of trace" and "arts of movement." My distinction should then probably be reread as contrasting the "arts (of movement) of trace" and the "arts of movement (without trace)."

Secondly, I need to say more about the chiasmus itself. By "arts of trace," I mean any art that makes inscription (in its most general sense) its very medium: like literature, painting, sculpture, engraving, architecture, photography, and film. Despite their variety, each of these art forms uses a specific technique or technology of memorial inscription for its own artistic ends. The artist's gesture here consists in inscribing a trace for posterity. The process of making the artwork public becomes a second stage, delegated to others or to institutions: publishing houses, museums, exhibitions, tours, buildings, and so on.[1] These modes of publicity or disclosure have their own histories that are, in many respects, linked to the problem of artistic autonomy discussed in part II, where the object seemed to discover its properly aesthetic function only by escaping the double bind of ritual and entertainment [*divertissement*]. Think, for example, of the invention of the museum as institution at the end of the eighteenth century, and the numerous studies of this process. The museum wrenched the object from its original (mostly ritual) context and opened an aesthetically homogeneous public space for its contemplation, in which the object's original (practical or symbolic) functions were ultimately erased.[2]

Conversely, by "arts of movement," I mean those artistic practices where movements of the body do not produce traces directly: essentially, theater, music, and dance—in other words, all of the performing arts. These arts make public display their first stage and relegate preservation to a secondary stage. In the case of dance, we saw how the institution of the spectacle was an ambivalent site of disclosure, in which the art object's autonomy was caught between the spectacle's functions as community ritual and mere entertainment. We saw how late the concept of *the work* became established in dance, at least from the point of view of its publicity or disclosure.[3] We also explored the difficulties dance faced because the question of its preservation was secondary: in the oral tradition, the work becomes merely a framework for a series of legitimate, permissible variations, while dance traces and the choreographic archive have a mediated character that frustrates attempts at restaging.[4] Perhaps new technologies of capture will alter this state of affairs, although I doubt it, at least from the perspective of my concerns in this book: specialists in these new technologies themselves admit that they are unlikely to replace video as a means of dance preservation.

Moreover, these two issues (the promotion of dance to the status of work within the public space of the stage and the conditions of the choreographic work's preservation) are probably connected. In the West, the ideological primacy of the arts of trace seems to have put pressure on the promotion of

1. The case of architecture is problematic: because of the distinction between architectural plan and actual building, architectural works seem to oscillate between durability and publicity; yet these two features are also fused in the building itself, with the monument standing as both *public* and *durable* object.

2. See Malraux's famous analysis in *Museum without Walls* [*Le musée imaginaire*] (1967 [1947]) and the more recent work by Jean-Louis Déotte (1993, 1994).

3. See above, 93.

4. See above, 215 and 233.

dance to work-status. The absence of the work, abstractly manifest in philosophers' writings on dance, perhaps merely reflects an assumption that works exist only in stable and perennially accessible mode, in the regime of the library or museum. The axiological primacy of the trace probably explains why music and theater—that I insist should be treated as arts of movement—progressively aligned their modes of production with the arts of trace. In Aristotle's *Poetics*, the theatrical work already seems to have become primarily a business of reading and writing. And Western "classical" music was oriented around its system of notation from the end of the fifteenth century onward. The integration of this system was such that music too became a practice of reading and writing. Undoubtedly, the model of the artwork as object, inherently fixed and owned by an author, has exerted axiological and aesthetic pressure, a pressure also felt in dance. Both Feuillet and Laban aimed to achieve institutional recognition for choreographic objects by inscribing them.[5] Yet, as I have tried to show, the possibility of inscription remained occasional and marginal in dance. Consequently, within what I have termed the "arts of movement," only dance has retained the strict order of priority that subordinates preservation to publicity. And that, in turn, brings us back to the notion of *unworking*.

Before I further examine that notion, however, I will make two further comments. First, my conceptual chiasmus, which relates two features of the work (publicity and durability) to two types of artistic practice (arts of movement and arts of trace), seems to enable a critical rereading of Nelson Goodman's work. Goodman in fact only classifies different arts of trace: the autographic (singular and material) and the allographic (ideal and conceptual). He is unable to conceptualize work identity outside of the field of the trace, since he considers the dimension of publicity (the public event) to be entirely secondary. He does appear to be aware of the problem: the work does not function as such because it is written or identified; rather, its publicity or disclosure enables it to function as a work. Goodman calls this "implementation" (1984, 142–45), which encompasses all processes external to the object as such which allow it to function as a work (the institutions of the museum, publishing house, theater, concert hall, publicity posters, and so on). The wedge that I am trying to drive into Goodman's thesis, drawing on experience of dance, involves identifying the hierarchy that he takes as given (the trace comes first, then the work is made public): there are art forms whose primary and essential stage is not the trace, but which prioritize the apparently second stage that Goodman calls "implementation" (what I term "publicity"). Blind to the possibility of such art forms,

5. See above, 163.

Goodman ultimately merely extends the axiological primacy of the arts of trace within Western art.

Second, my contrast between arts of movement and arts of trace requires some qualification if its significance is to become clear. More specifically, the contrast's importance is fully revealed only when we reconsider and again invert the polarity through a detailed examination of the corporeality of the writer's, painter's, or sculptor's movements, and when we examine those features of a dancer's present movement that are based on memory trace or survival (what Georges Didi-Huberman [2002] calls *survivance*). I will postpone investigation along these lines until future research.

I now need to offer a philosophical redefinition of the concept of *unworking*. This has emerged as our defining notion at four moments in this book. First, we moved from the *absence of the work*, abstractly brought to light in philosophers' writings, to *unworking* as a concrete process operating within choreographic works themselves (providing the link between parts I and II). Second, *unworking* was a way to conceptualize the very late operal, aesthetic, and legal recognition of dance within the wider contexts of the performing arts (the key concern of part II). Third, the notion of *unworking* was used to describe the limit case that dance represents within Goodman's taxonomy which, I claimed, ultimately only classifies arts of trace: dance eludes the autographic-allographic distinction precisely because it seems to know nothing of the *graph* (as discussed in part III). And finally—from the perspective of the work persisting through the perpetuations of techniques—the objectless state of dance (its lack of end, product, or instrument) became the core of the very idea of *unworking* (in part IV). There is no reason to dance, nor any object produced or used through dancing. This is the *unworking* that dominates the final sections of the book.

In conclusion, perhaps some comment on the sources and anchors of the notion of *unworking* is important. How, for example, does my notion of *unworking* relate to the arguments of Jean-Luc Nancy and his *unworked* or *inoperative community* [*Communauté désoeuvrée*] (1991 [1986])? The political implications of *choreographic unworking* still need thinking through, in a process that could follow Nancy's lead (without dogmatically deferring to his position). For the moment, my argument remains rooted in the sources of the concept, namely, the claims of Bataille, Foucault, and Blanchot.[6] Choreographic *unworking* ultimately only manifests the power of powerlessness itself—the paradoxical efficacy of the void that we are, inevitably permeated by what has been so aptly described as "negativity without employ."

6. Bataille (2011 [1961], 111–13); Foucault (2001 [1961], 273); Blanchot (1993 [1969]).

Appendix of Illustrations

Figure 1 *Viviane*, Poster 276 (Chéret), Bibliothèque de l'Opéra de Paris, BnF.

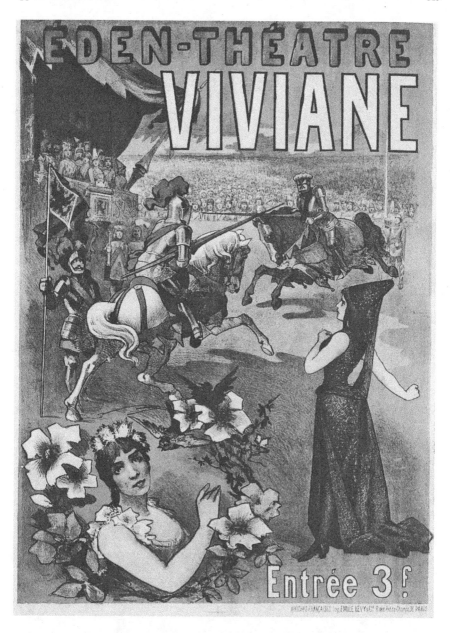

Figure 2 *Viviane*, Poster 277, Bibliothèque de l'Opéra de Paris, BnF.

Figure 3 *Viviane*, The tournament from Act III, *Le monde illustré*, Bibliothèque de l'Opéra de Paris, BnF.

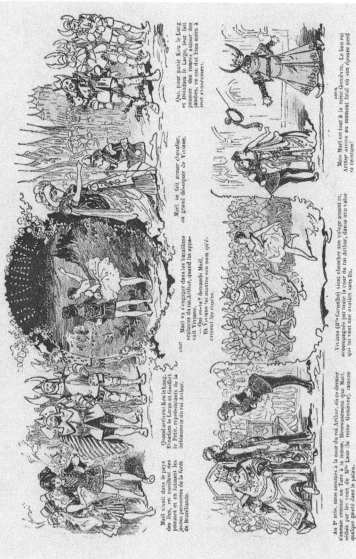

Figure 4 "A l'Eden - V·viane" by Henriot, *Le journal amusant*, BnF.

Figure 5 "A l'Eden - Viviane", by Henriot, *Le journal amusant*, BnF.

LA DANCE.

DE LA SALLE OU THEATRE.

L A Salle ou Theatre eſt le lieu où l'on dance, que je repreſente par un eſpece de quarré plus long que large , comme marque la figure A B C D, dont le haut ſera A B , le bas ſera C D , le côté droit ſera B D , & le côté gauche ſera A C.

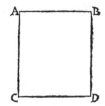

De la preſence du Corps.

L A preſence du Corps eſt quand le devant du Corps eſt vis-à-vis l'un des quatre côtez de la Salle, que je repreſente par la figure F G H I, dont F G marque les deux côtez du corps , H marque le devant, & I marque le derriere.

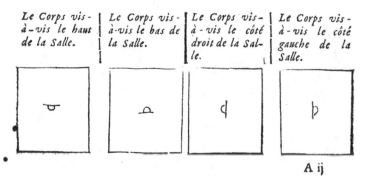

Le Corps vis-à-vis le haut de la Salle. | Le Corps vis-à-vis le bas de la Salle. | Le Corps vis-à-vis le côté droit de la Salle. | Le Corps vis-à-vis le côté gauche de la Salle.

A ij

Figure 6 The "Stage or Dancing-Room" and the presence, from *Chorégraphie ou l'art de décrire la dance par caractères et signes démonstratifs* by Raoul Auger Feuillet, Paris, Brunet, 1700, BnF. See Feuillet (1706a), 3, for John Weaver's English translation.

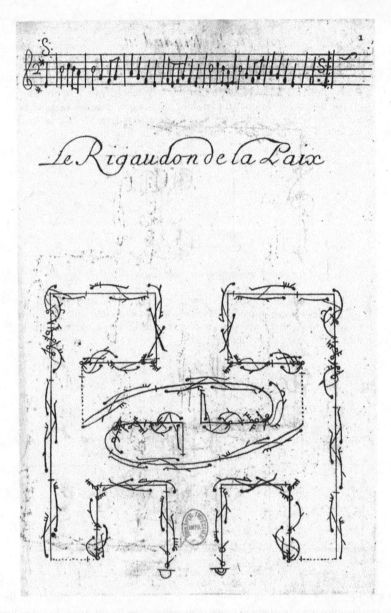

Figure 7 *Le rigaudon de la paix*, a sample score from *Chorégraphie ou l'art de décrire la dance par caractères, figures et signes démonstratifs* by Raoul Auger Feuillet, Paris, Brunet, 1700, BnF.

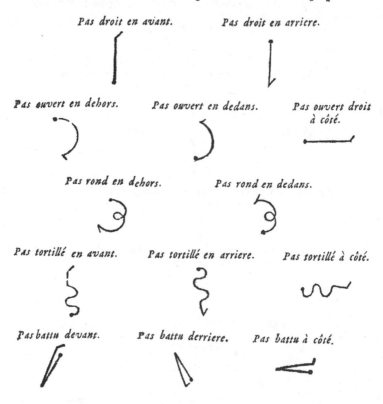

10   L'ART DE DE'CRIRE
On remarquera que le Pas qui eſt du côté droit dans l'exemple cy-de-
vant ſe fait du pied droit , celuy qui eſt à gauche ſe fait du pied gauche.

Demonſtration de tous les Pas qui viennent d'être expliquez.

Pas droit en avant.   Pas droit en arriere.

Pas ouvert en dehors.   Pas ouvert en dedans.   Pas ouvert droit
                                                           à côté.

Pas rond en dehors.   Pas rond en dedans.

Pas tortillé en avant.   Pas tortillé en arriere.   Pas tortillé à côté.

Pas battu devant.   Pas battu derriere.   Pas battu à côté.

On ſe reſſouviendra que j'ay repreſenté le pied dans la demy Poſi-
tion à la page 6. par un o , & une petite queuë ſortante de l'o , au lieu
qu'au Pas je le repreſente par un petit renvers joint à ſon extremité,
comme il eſt démonſtré dans tous les Pas cy-deſſus.

Figure 8 Taxonomy of steps from *Chorégraphie ou l'art de décrire la dance par caractères,
figures et signes démonstratifs* by Raoul Auger Feuillet, Paris, Brunet, 1700, BnF. See
Feuillet (1706a), 10, for John Weaver's English translation.

LA DANCE.   11

Les Pas peuvent être accompagnez des Signes ſuivans , comme Plié ,
Elevé , Sauté , Cabriollé , Tombé , Gliſſé, avoir le pied en l'Air , poſer
la Pointe du pied, poſer le Talon , tourné un quart de Tour , tourné
un demy Tour , tourné trois quarts de Tour , & tourné le Tour entier.

Le ſigne de Plier eſt quand ſur un Pas il y a un petit tiret panché
du côté de la petite tête noire.

Pas [*plié.*

Le ſigne d'Elever , eſt quand ſur un Pas il y a un petit cran tout droit.

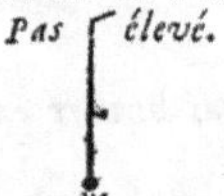

Pas [*élevé.*

Le ſigne de Sauter , eſt lors qu'il y en a deux.

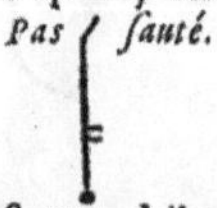

Pas / *ſauté.*

Le ſigne de Cabrioller , eſt quand il y en a trois.

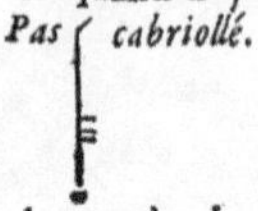

Pas (*cabriollé.*

Le ſigne de Tomber , eſt lors qu'au bout d'un cran il y a un petit
tiret allant vers ce qui repreſente le pied.

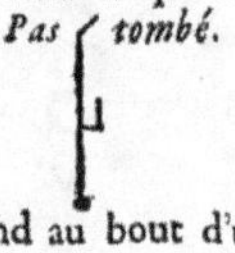

Pas (*tombé.*

Le ſigne Gliſſé , eſt quand au bout d'un cran il y a une petite barre
en longueur du Pas.

Pas [*gliſſé.*

B ij

Figure 9 Step modifications, from *Chorégraphie ou l'art de décrire la dance par caractères,*
figures et signes démonstratifs by Raoul Auger Feuillet, Paris, Brunet, 1700, BnF. See
Feuillet (1706a), 11, for John Weaver's English translation.

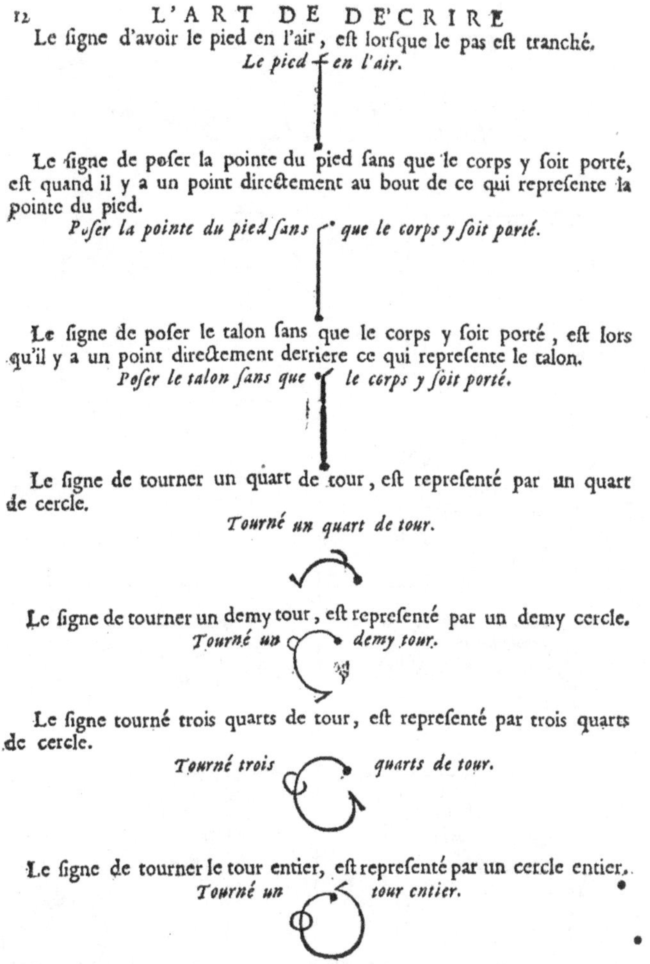

12   L'ART DE DE'CRIRE

Le ſigne d'avoir le pied en l'air, eſt lorſque le pas eſt tranché.

Le pied ┼ *en l'air.*

Le ſigne de poſer la pointe du pied ſans que le corps y ſoit porté, eſt quand il y a un point directement au bout de ce qui repreſente la pointe du pied.

Poſer la pointe du pied ſans ⌐ *que le corps y ſoit porté.*

Le ſigne de poſer le talon ſans que le corps y ſoit porté, eſt lors qu'il y a un point directement derriere ce qui repreſente le talon.

Poſer le talon ſans que ⌐ *le corps y ſoit porté.*

Le ſigne de tourner un quart de tour, eſt repreſenté par un quart de cercle.

Tourné un quart de tour.

Le ſigne de tourner un demy tour, eſt repreſenté par un demy cercle.

Tourné un ⌒ *demy tour.*

Le ſigne tourné trois quarts de tour, eſt repreſenté par trois quarts de cercle.

Tourné trois ⌒ *quarts de tour.*

Le ſigne de tourner le tour entier, eſt repreſenté par un cercle entier.

Tourné un ⌒ *tour entier.*

Figure 10 Further step modifications from Chorégraphie ou l'art de décrire la dance par caractères, figures et signes démonstratifs by Raoul Auger Feuillet, Paris, Brunet, 1700, BnF. See Feuillet (1706a), 13, for John Weaver's English translation.

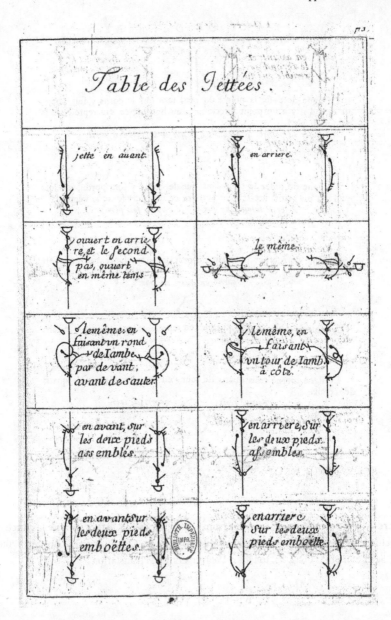

Figure 11 Table of *jetés* [*bounds*], from *Chorégraphie ou l'art de décrire la dance par caractères, figures et signes démonstratifs* by Raoul Auger Feuillet, Paris, Brunet, 1700, BnF. See Feuillet (1706a) for Weaver's translation.

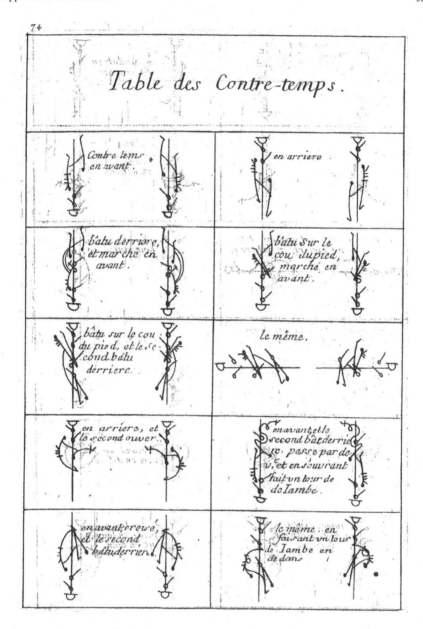

Figure 12 Table of *contretemps*, from *Chorégraphie ou l'art de décrire la dance par caractères, figures et signes démonstratifs* by Raoul Auger Feuillet, Paris, Brunet, 1700, BnF. See Feuillet (1706a) for John Weaver's English translation.

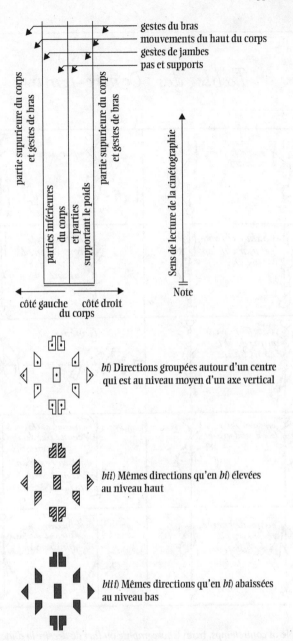

Figure 13 Basic principles of Labanotation, from Jacqueline Challet-Haas's French translation of Laban's *The Mastery of Movement* [*La maîtrise du mouvement*], Arles: Actes Sud, 1994.

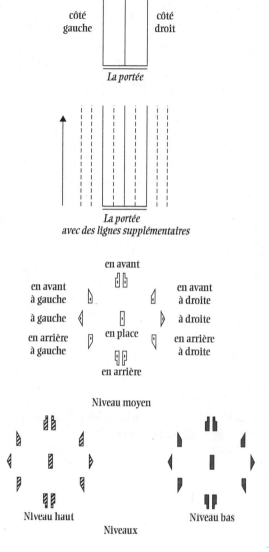

Figure 14 Basic principles of Labanotation, from *Grammaire de la notation Laban*, by Jacqueline Challet-Haas, Pantin: CND, 1999.

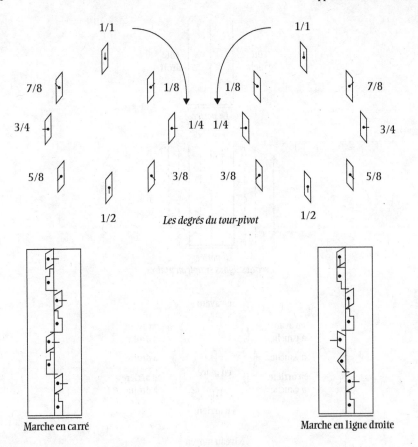

Figure 15 Rotation and walking in Labanotation, from *Grammaire de la notation Laban* by Jacqueline Challet-Haas, Pantin: CND, 1999.

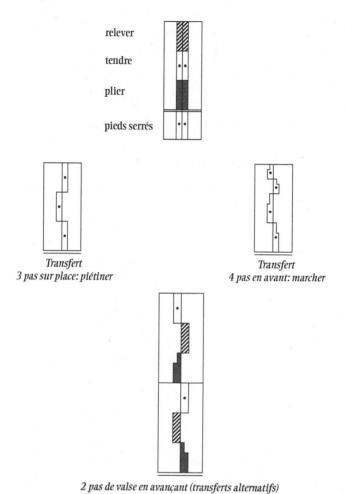

relever

tendre

plier

pieds serrés

Transfert
3 pas sur place: piétiner

Transfert
4 pas en avant: marcher

2 pas de valse en avançant (transferts alternatifs)

Figure 16 Weight transfers in Labanotation, from *Grammaire de la notation Laban* by Jacqueline Challet-Haas, Pantin: CND, 1999.

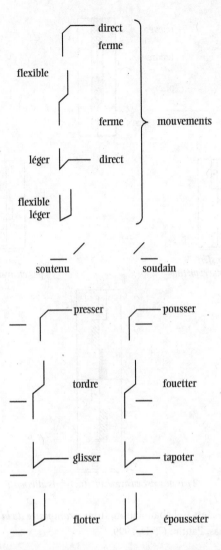

Figure 17 Basic principles of the Effort graphs system, from Jacqueline Challet-Haas's French translation of Laban's *Modern Educational Dance* [*La danse moderne éducative*], Bruxelles:Complexe-CND, 2003.

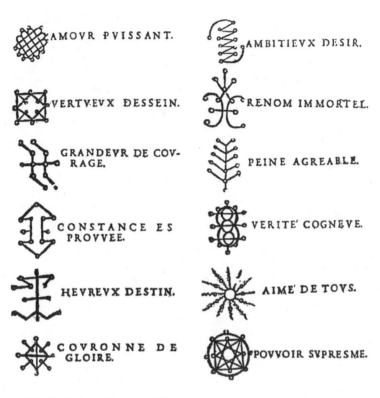

Figure 18 The "alphabet of the Druids", from the libretto of the *Ballet de Monseigneur le duc de Vendosme* (1610).

Bibliography and References

Apostolidès, Jean-Marie. 1981. *Le roi-machine: Spectacle et politique au temps de Louis XIV*, Paris: Éditions de Minuit.

Arbeau, Thoinot. 1967 [1589]. *Orchesography* [*Orchésographie et traicté en forme de dialogue, par lequel toutes personnes peuvent facilement apprendre et practiquer l'honneste exercice des dances*]. Trans. Mary Stewart Evans. New York: Dover.

Archer, Kenneth, and Millicent Hodson. 1994. "Ballets Lost and Found: Restoring the Twentieth-Century Repertoire." In *Dance History: An Introduction*, edited by Janet Adshead-Lansdale and June Layson, 98–116. London: Routledge.

Arendt, Hannah. 1998 [1958]. *The Human Condition*. Chicago: University of Chicago Press.

Aristotle. 1980. *La Poétique*. Trans. Roselyne Dupont-Roc and Jean Lallot. Paris: Seuil.

———. 1987a. *The Poetics of Aristotle*. Trans. Stephen Halliwell. Chapel Hill: University of North Carolina Press.

———. 1987b. *Poetics, with the Tractatus Coislinianus, Reconstruction of Poetics II, and the Fragments of the On Poets*. Trans. Richard Janko. Indianapolis: Hackett.

Artaud, Antonin. 1970 [1938]. *Theatre and Its Double* [*Le théatre et son double*]. Trans. Victor Corti. London: Calder and Boyars.

———. 1971. *Collected Works*. Vol 2. Trans. Victor Corti. London: Calder and Boyars.

———. 1974. *Collected Works*. Vol. 4. Trans. Victor Corti. London: Calder and Boyars.

Badiou, Alain. 2005 [1998]. *A Handbook of Inaesthetics* [*Petit manuel d'inésthétique*]. Trans. Alberto Toscano. Stanford, CA: Stanford University Press.

Banes, Sally. 1987. *Terpsichore in Sneakers: Post-modern Dance*. Rev. ed. Middletown, CT: Wesleyan University Press.

———. 1989. "Terpsichore in Combat Boots: Reply to Susan Manning. *TDR: The Drama Review* 33:2, 13–15.

———. 2002 [1987]. *Terpsichore en baskets: Post-modern dance* [*Terpsichore in sneakers: Post-modern dance*]. Trans. Denise Luccioni. Pantin: CND.

Barbaras, Renaud. 1998. "Sentir et faire: La phenomenology et l'unité de l'ésthétique." In *Phénoménologie et esthétique*, edited by Éliane Escoubas, 21–40. Fougères: Encre Marine

Barthes, Roland. 1982 [1980]. *Camera Lucida: Reflections on Photography* [*La chambre claire*]. London: Vintage.

——. 1991 [1982]. *The Responsibility of Forms: Critical Essays on Music, Art, and Representation* [*L'obvie et l'obtus*]. Trans. Richard Howard. Berkeley: University of California Press.

Bataille, Georges. 1985 [1933]. "The Notion of Expenditure." *Visions of Excess: Selected Writings 1927–1939*. Ed. Allan Stoekl. Trans. Allan Stoekl with Carl R. Lovitt and Donald M. Leslie Jnr. Minneapolis: Minneapolis University Press.

——. 1988 [1967]. *The Accursed Share: An Essay on General Economy*. Vol. 1, *Consumption* [*La part maudite*]. Trans. Robert Hurley. New York: Zone.

——. 2011 [1961]. *Guilty = Le coupable* [*Le coupable*]. Trans. Stuart Kendall. Albany, NY: SUNY Press.

Batteux, Charles. 2015 [1746]. *The Fine Arts Reduced to a Single Principle* [*Les beaux arts reduits à un même principe*]. Trans. James O. Young. Oxford: Oxford University Press.

Baxmann, Inge, Claire Rousier, and Patrizia Veroli, eds. 2006. *Les archives internationales de la danse, 1931–1952*. Pantin: CND.

Beaujoyeulx, Balthazar de. 1982 [1582]. *Le balet comique by Balthazar de Beaujoyeulx, 1581: A facsimile*. Binghamton, NY: Center of Medieval and Early Renaissance Studies.

Beaumont, Cyril W., and Stanislas Idzilkowski. 1922. *A Manual of the Theory and Practice of Classical Theatrical Dancing*, London: Beaumont.

Bellugue, Paul. 1935. "La technique de la danse," *Revue des Archives Internationales de la Danse*, special issue, November 1: 38–42.

Benjamin, Walter. 1992. *Illuminations*. Trans. Harry Zohn. London: Fontana.

Bergson, Henri. 2007 [1919]. *Mind-energy* [*L'Énergie spirituelle*]. Trans. H. Wildon Carr. Basingstoke: Palgrave Macmillan.

Bernard, Michel. 2001. *De la création chorégraphique*. Pantin: CND.

Berthoz, Alain. 2000 [1997]. *The Brain's Sense of Movement* [*Le sens du movement*]. Trans. Giselle Weiss. Cambridge, MA: Harvard University Press.

Berthoz, Alain, and Gérard Jorland, eds. 2004. *L'empathie*. Paris: Odile Jacob.

Blanchot, Maurice. 1993 [1969]. *The Infinite Conversation* [*L'entretien infini*]. Trans. Susan Hanson. Minneapolis: University of Minnesota Press.

Bruneau, P., and J.-Y. Planchet. 1992. "Music and Archaeology." *Ramage* Vol. 10: 31–56.

Bücher, Karl. 1896. *Arbeit und Rythmus*. Leipzig: Reinicke.

Cahusac, Louis de. 2004 [1754]. *La danse ancienne et moderne, ou Traité historique de la danse*. Paris: Desjonquières-CND.

Challet-Haas, Jacqueline. 1999. *Grammaire de la notation Laban*. Pantin: Centre national de la danse.

Charmatz, Boris, and Isabelle Launay. 2003. *Entretenir: A propos d'une danse contemporaine*. Paris: Les Presses du Réel—CND.

Christout, Marie-Françoise. 1967. *Le ballet de cour de Louis XIV, 1643–1672*. Paris: Picard.

Cocteau, Jean, Serge Lifar, and Paul Valéry. 1943. *Serge Lifar à l'Opéra*. Paris: Thibault de Champrosay.

Cœuroy, André. 1921. "Wagner et la danse." *Revue Musicale*, December 1, 111–17.

Cohen, Selma Jeanne, ed. 1998. *International Encyclopedia of Dance*. New York: Oxford University Press.

Condillac, Etienne Bonnot de. 2001 [1746]. *An Essay on the Origin of Human Knowledge* [*Essai sur l'origine des connaissances humaines*]. Trans. Hans Aarsleff. Cambridge: Cambridge University Press.

Danto, Arthur C. 1997. *After the End of Art: Contemporary Art and the Pale of History.* Princeton, NJ: Princeton University Press.

Davies, David. 2011. *Philosophy of the Performing Arts.* Malden: Wiley-Blackwell.

deLahunta, Scott. 2001. "Coreografie in bit e byte: motion capture, animazione e software per la danza." In *La scena digitale: Nuovi media per la danza*, edited by A. Menicacci and E. Quinz, 83–100. Venice: Marsilio.

Deleuze, Giles, and Félix Guattari. 2004 [1980]. *A Thousand Plateaus: Capitalism and Schizophrenia* [*Mille Plateaux: Capitalisme et schizophrénie*]. London: Continuum.

Déotte, Jean-Louis. 1993. *Le musée, l'origine de l'ésthétique.* Paris: L'Harmattan.

———. 1994. *Oubliez! Les ruines, l'Europe, le musée.* Paris: L'Harmattan.

Derrida, Jacques. 1976 [1967]. *Of Grammatology* [*De le grammatologie*]. Trans. Gayatri Spivak. Baltimore: Johns Hopkins University Press.

———. 1981 [1972]. *Dissemination* [*La dissemination*]. Trans. Barbara Johnson. London: Athlone Press.

———. 1995 [1992]. *Points … Interviews, 1974–1994* [*Points de suspension*]. Ed. Elisabeth Weber. Trans. Peggy Kamuf et al. Stanford, CA: Stanford University Press.

———. 2001 [1967]. *Writing and Difference* [*L'Écriture et la différence*]. Trans. Alan Bass. London: Routledge.

———. 2011 [1967]. *Voice and Phenomenon: Introduction to the Problem of the Sign in Husserl's Phenomenology* [*La Voix et le phénomène: Introduction au problème du signe dans la phénoménologie de Husserl*]. Trans. Leonard Lawlor. Evanston, IL: Northwestern University Press.

Didi-Huberman, Georges. 1998. *Phasmes: Essais sur l'apparition.* Paris: Minuit.

———. 2002. *L'image survivante: Histoire de l'art et temps des fantômes selon Aby Warburg.* Paris: Editions de Minuit.

Doat, Laetitia. 2006. "La figure isadorienne au regard de la transmission." Unpublished masters thesis. Université Paris 8/Département Danse.

Dubos, Jean Baptiste. 1748 [1733]. *Critical Reflections on Poetry, Painting and Music, with an Inquiry into the Rise and Progress of the Theatrical Entertainments of the Ancients* [*Réflexions critiques sur la poésie et la peinture*]. Trans. Thomas Nugent. London: John Nourse.

Duncan, Isadora. 1969 [1928]. *The Art of the Dance.* Ed. Sheldon Cheney. New York: Theatre Arts Books.

Dupont, Florence. 1986. *L'acteur-roi, ou, le théâtre dans la Rome antique.* Paris: Les Belles Lettres.

———. 2007. *Aristote ou le vampire du théâtre occidental.* Paris: Aubier.

Dupuy, Françoise, and Dupuy, Dominique. 2001. *Une danse à l'oeuvre.* Pantin: CND.

Escoubas, Eliane. 1986. *Imago mundi: Topologie de l'art.* Paris: Galilée.

Ferrero, Guillaume. 1896. "Les formes primitives du travail." *Revue Scientifique*, March 14, Vol. 5, no 11331-335.

Feuillet, Raoul Auger. 1700a. *Chorégraphie ou l'art de décrire la dance par caractères, figures et signes démonstratifs, avec lesquels on apprend facilement de soi-même toutes sortes de dances.* Paris: Brunet. Reprinted by Hildesheim, New York: G. Olms, 1979.

——. 1700b. *Receuil de danses composés par M. Pécour et mises sur le papier par M. Feuillet.* Paris, Brunet. Reprinted in the Olms facsimile of *Chorégraphie*, 1979.

——. 1706a. *Orchesography, or the Art of Dancing, by Characters and Demonstrative Figures.* Trans. John Weaver. London. Reprinted in facsimile by Gregg International and Dance Horizons, 1971.

——. 1706b. *Recueil de contredances mises en choregraphie d'une manière si aisée que toutes personnes peuvent facilement les apprendre.* Paris.

Foucault, Michel. 1989 [1966]. *The Order of Things: An Archaeology of the Human Sciences [Les mots et les choses].* London: Routledge.

——. 2001 [1961]. *Madness and Civilization: A History of Insanity in the Age of Reason [Histoire de la folie à l'âge classique].* Trans. Richard Howard. London: Routledge.

Franko, Mark. 1993. *Dance as Text: Ideologies of the Baroque Body.* Cambridge: Cambridge University Press.

——. 2002. *The Work of Dance: Labor, Movement, and Identity in the 1930s.* Middletown, CT: Wesleyan University Press.

Genette, Gerard. 1997 [1994]. *The Work of Art: Immanence and Transcendence.* Trans. G. M. Goshgarian. Ithaca, NY: Cornell University Press.

Gert, Valeska. 1989 [1968]. *Ich bin eine Hexe: Kaleidoskop meines Lebens.* Munich: Knaur.

Gil, José. 2004. *Movimento total: O corpo e a dança.* São Pãolo: Iluminuras.

Ginot, Isabelle. 1999. *Dominique Bagouet: un labyrinthe dansé.* Paris: CND.

——. 2002. "Livin's Deadly: A propos de *Hommages* de Mark Tompkins." *ArtPress* special issue « Médium Danse », no 23, 56–59.

Godard, Hubert, and Patricia Kuypers. 2006. "Des trous noirs: Un entretien avec Hubert Godard." *Nouvelles de Danse* no 53, 76–95.

Goll, Yvan. 1989 [1929]. *Sodome et Berlin.* Strasbourg: Circé.

Goodman, Nelson. 1976. *Languages of Art: An Approach to a Theory of Symbols.* Indianapolis: Hackett.

——. 1984. *Of Mind and Other Matters.* Cambridge, MA: Harvard University Press.

Gouhier, Henri. 1989. *Le théâtre et les arts à deux temps.* Paris: Flammarion.

Grau, Andrée, and Georgina Wierre-Gore, eds. 2005. *Anthropologie de la danse: Genèse et construction d'une discipline.* Pantin: Centre National de Danse.

Guilbert, Laure. 2000. *Danser avec le IIIe Reich: Les danseurs allemands sous le nazisme.* Brussels: Complexe.

Guilcher, Jean-Michel. 1963. *La tradition populaire de danse en Basse-Bretagne.* Paris: Mouton.

——. 1969. "André Lorin et l'invention de l'écriture chorégraphique." *Revue d'Histoire du Théâtre* 3: 256–64.

Guest, Ivor. 2006. *The Paris Opéra Ballet.* Alton: Dance Books.

Hanslick, Eduard. 1986 [1854]. *On the Musically Beautiful: A Contribution towards the Revision of the Aesthetics of Music [Vom Musikalisch-Schönen].* Trans. Geoffrey Payzant. Indianapolis: Hackett.

Havelock, Eric. 1976. *Origins of Western Literacy.* Toronto: Ontario Institute for Studies in Education.

Hegel, Georg Willhelm Friedrich. 1975. *Aesthetics: Lectures on Fine Art* [*Vorlesung über Ästhetik*]. Trans. T. M. Knox. Oxford: Clarendon Press.

Heidegger, Martin. 1962. *Being and Time* [*Sein und Zeit*]. Trans. John Macquarie and Edward Robinson. Oxford: Blackwell.

Heinich, Natalie. 1998. *Le triple jeu de l'art contemporain.* Paris: Minuit.

Henry, Michel. 1975 [1965]. *Philosophy and Phenomenology of the Body* [*Philosophie et phénoménologie du corps*]. Trans. G. Etzkorn. Leiden: Martinus Nijhoff.

Hodgson, John, and Valerie Preston-Dunlop. 1990. *Rudolf Laban: An Introduction to His Life and Influence.* Plymouth: Northcote.

Husserl, Edmund. 1964. *The Phenomenology of Internal Time-Consciousness* [*Zur Phänomenology des inneren Zeitbewusstseins*]. Ed. Martin Heidegger. Trans. James Spencer Churchill. The Hague: Martinus Nijhoff.

———. 1989. *Ideas Pertaining to a Pure Phenomenology and to a Phenomenological Philosophy* [*Ideen zu einer reinen Phänomenologie und phänomenolo-gischen Philosophie*]. Book II. Trans. Richard Rojcewicz and André Schuwer. Dordrecht: Kluwer Academic.

———. 2001 [1900/1901]. *Logical investigations* [*Logische Untersuchungen*]. Trans. J. N. Findlay. London: Routledge.

Hutchinson-Guest, Ann. 1961. *Labanotation.* Norfolk, VA: New Directions.

———. 1989. *Choreo-graphics: A Comparison of Dance Notation Systems from the Fifteenth-Century to the Present.* New York: Gordon and Breach.

Hutchinson-Guest, Ann, and Claudia Jeschke. 1991. *Nijinsky's Faune Restored: A Study of Vaslav Nijinsky's 1915 Dance Score, L'Après-midi d'un faune, and His Dance Notation System.* Philadelphia: Gordon and Breach.

Ildefonse, Frédérique. 2004. "Ta skhèmata tès lexeôs", in *Skhèma/Figura chez les Anciens. Rhétorique, philosophie, littérature, études de littérature anci*enne, edited by M. S. Celentano, P. Chiron and M.-P. Noël, 143–157. Paris: Rue d'Ulm.

Jaques-Dalcroze, Emile. 1967 [1921]. *Rhythm, Music and Education.* Trans. Harold F. Rubinstein. New York: G. P. Putnam's Sons.

Jankélévitch, Vladimir. 1979. *Liszt et la rhapsodie.* Vol. 1. Paris: Plon.

Jeannerod, Marc. 1997. *The Cognitive Neuroscience of Action.* Oxford: Blackwell.

Jeanmaire, Henri. 1951. *Dionysos: Histoire du culte de Bacchus.* Paris: Payot.

Kaeppler, Adrienne. 1972. "Method and Theory in Analyzing Dance Structures with an Analysis of Tongan Dance." *Ethnomusicology* 16:2, 173 217.

Kant, Immanuel. 2000 [1790]. *Critique of the Power of Judgment* [*Kritik der Urteilskraft*]. Trans. Paul Guyer and Eric Matthews. Cambridge: Cambridge University Press.

Kant, Marion, and Lilian Karina. 2003 [1996]. *Hitler's Dancers: German Modern Dance and the Third Reich.* Trans. Jonathan Steinberg. New York: Berghahn.

Kintzler, Catherine. 1997a. "La danse, modèle d'intelligibilité dans l'opéra français de l'âge classique." In *La pensée de la danse à l'âge classique: écriture, lexique et poétique,* edited by Catherine Kintzler, 71-81. Villeneuve d'Ascq/Université Lille III: Maison de la recherche.

———, ed. (1997b) *La pensée de la danse à l'âge classique: écriture, lexique et poétique,* Villeneuve d'Ascq/Université Lille III: Maison de la recherche.

Knust, Albrecht. 1979. *The Dictionary of Kinetography Laban.* Plymouth: MacDonald and Evans.

Laban, Rudolf von. 1926 *Choreographie*. Iena: Eugen Diederich Verlag.

———. 1928. *Schrifttanz: Methodik, Orthographie, Erläuterungen*. Vienna, Universal Edition.

———. 1947. *Effort*. In collaboration with F. C. Lawrence. Manchester: Lawrence & Co.

———. 1948. *Modern Educational Dance*. London: MacDonald and Evans.

———. 1951. "What Has Led You to Study Movement? Answered by Rudolf Laban." *News Sheet* of the Laban Art of Movement Guild, no.7, unpaginated.

———. 1956. *Principles of Dance and Movement Notation*. London: MacDonald and Evans.

———. 1975. *A Life for Dance: Reminiscences*. London: Macdonald and Evans.

———. 1980 [1950]. *The Mastery of Movement on the Stage*. London: MacDonald and Evans. 4th edition, revised and enlarged by Lisa Ullman.

Lacoue-Labarthe, Philippe. 1994 [1991]. *Musica Ficta: Figures of Wagner* [*Musica Ficta: Figures de Wagner*]. Trans. Felicia McCarren. Stanford, CA: Stanford University Press.

Lancelot, Francine, ed. 1996. *La belle dance: Catalogue raisonné fait en l'An 1995*. Paris: Van Dieren.

———. 2000. *Les sociétés de farandole en Languedoc et Provence*. Le Mans, Arès: Recherche ethnologique en Sarthe.

Larousse, Pierre, ed. 1866–77. *Grand dictionnaire universel du XIXᵉ siècle*. Paris: Administration du grand Dictionnaire universel.

Launay, Isabelle. 1997 *A la recherche d'une danse moderne*. Paris: Chiron.

———. 1999. « La danse moderne "mise au pas" ? », *Mobile*1, 73-106, « Danse et utopie », Paris: L'Harmattan,

———. 2002. "Les Carnets Bagouet: Sur le recommencement de *Meublé sommairement*." *Art Press*, no 23, "Médium Danse."

Launay, Isabelle, ed. 2007. *Les Carnets Bagouet: La passe d'une oeuvre*. Besançon: Les Solitaires Intempestifs.

Laurenti, Huguette. 1973. *Paul Valéry et le théâtre*. Paris: Gallimard.

Laurenti, Jean-Noël. 1991. "La pensée de Feuillet." In *Danses tracés*, edited by Laurence Louppe, 107–132. Paris: Dis Voir.

Leiris, Michel. 1958. *La possession et ses aspects théâtraux chez les Ethiopiens de Gondar*. Paris: Plon.

Le Moal, Philippe, ed. 1999. *Dictionnaire de la danse*. Paris: Larousse.

Lepecki, André. 2004. "Inscribing Dance". In *Of the Presence of the Body*, edited by André Lepecki, 124–39. Middletown, CT: Wesleyan University Press.

———. 2006. *Exhausting Dance: Performance and the Politics of Movement*. New York: Routledge.

Leroi-Gourhan, André. 1993 [1964]. *Gesture and speech* [*La geste et la parole, T.1 Technique et langage*]. Trans. Anna Bostock Berger. Cambridge, MA: MIT Press.

Levinson, André. 1927. *Paul Valéry, philosophe de la danse*. Paris: La Tour d'Ivoire.

———. 1933. *Les visages de la danse*. Paris: Grasset.

Lifar, Serge. 1946. *Pensées sur la danse*. Paris: Bordas.

Lista, Giovanni. 1994. *Loïe Fuller: Danseuse de la belle époque*. Paris: Stock.

Louppe, Laurence. 2010 [1997]. *The Poetics of Contemporary Dance* [*Poétique de la danse contemporaine*]. Trans. Sally Gardner. Alton: Dance Books.

Lucian. 1936. *The Dance*. Trans. A. M. Harmon. In *The Works of Lucian*. Vol. 5, 209–89. Cambridge, MA: Harvard University Press.

Lyotard, Jean-François. 1992 [1988]. *The Postmodern Explained: Correspondence 1982–1985 [Le postmoderne expliqué aux enfants]*. Trans. Don Barry, Bernadette Maher, Julian Pefanis, Virginia Spate, and Morgan Thomas. Minneapolis: University of Minnesota Press.

Madinier, Gabriel. 1938. *Conscience et movement: Essai sur les rapports de la conscience à l'effort moteur dans la philosophie française de Condillac à Bergson*. Paris: Alcan.

Maletic, Vera. 1987. *Space, Body, Expression: The Development of Rudolf Laban's Movement and Dance Concepts*. Berlin: Mouton de Gruyter.

Mallarmé, Stéphane. 1998–2003. *Oeuvres complètes*. Vols. 1 and 2. Ed. Bertrand Marchal. Paris: Gallimard (Bibliothèque de la Pléiade).

———. 2001. *Mallarmé in Prose*. Ed. Mary Ann Caws. Trans. Jill Anderson, Malcolm Bowie, Mary Ann Caws, Rosemary Lloyd, Richard Sieburth, and Patricia Terry. New York: New Directions.

———. 2004. *Mallarmé on fashion: A translation of the fashion magazine*, La dernière mode. Trans. P.N. Furbank and Alex Cain. Oxford: Berg.

———. 2007 [1897]. *Divagations*. Trans. Barbara Johnson. Cambridge, MA: Harvard University Press/Belknap Press.

Malraux, André. 1967 [1947]. *Museum without Walls [Le musée imaginaire]*. Trans. Stuart Gilbert and Francis Price. London: Secker and Warburg.

Manning, Susan. 1988. "Modernist Dogma and Postmodern Rhetoric: A Response to Sally Banes' *Terpsichore in Sneakers*." *TDR: The Drama Review* 32:4, 32–39.

———. 1989. "Terpsichore in Combat Boots: Reply to Sally Banes." *TDR: The Drama Review* 33:2, 15–16

———. 1993. *Ecstasy and the Demon: Feminism and Nationalism in the Dances of Mary Wigman*. Berkeley: University of California Press.

Martin, John. 1965a [1939]. *Introduction to the Dance*. New York: Dance Horizons.

———. 1965b [1933]. *The Modern Dance*. New York: Dance Horizons.

Martino, Ernesto de. 1966. *La terre du remords*. Paris: Gallimard.

Mauss, Marcel. 2006. *Techniques, Technology and Civilization*. Ed. Nathan Schlanger. New York: Durkheim Press/Berghahn Books.

McFee, Graham. 2011. *The Philosophical Aesthetics of Dance: Identity, Performance and Understanding*. Alton (UK): Dance Books.

McGowan, Margaret. 1963. *L'art du ballet de cour en France, 1581–1643*. Paris: CNRS Editions. Reprinted 1978.

Ménestrier, Claude-François. 1972 [1682]. *Des ballets anciens et modernes selon les règles du théâtre*. Geneva: Minkhoff.

Menger, Pierre-Michel. 2002. *Portrait de l'artiste en travailleur: Métamorphoses du capitalisme*. Paris: Seuil.

Menicacci, Armando, and Quinz, Emmanuele, eds. 2001. *La scena digitale: Nuovi media per la danza*. Venice: Marsilio.

———. 2006. "Étendre la perception ? Biofeedback et transferts intermodaux en danse", *Nouvelles de danse*, no 53, 76–95, March.

Merleau-Ponty, Maurice. 1964 [1960]. *Signs [Signes]*. Trans. Richard C. McCleary. Evanston: Northwestern University Press.

———. 1965 [1942]. *The Structure of Behaviour [La structure du comportement]*. Trans. Alden L. Fisher. London: Methuen.

Mersenne, Marin. 1636. *Harmonie universelle*. Paris: Cramoisy.

———. 1957. *Harmonie Universelle: The Books on Instruments*. Trans. Roger E. Chapman. The Hague: Martinus Nijhoff.

Michaud, Yves. 1997. *La crise de l'art contemporain*. Paris: PUF.

———. 2003. *L'art à l'état gazeux: essai sur le triomphe de l'esthétisme*. Paris: Stock.

Nancy, Jean-Luc. 1991 [1986]. *The Inoperative Community [La communauté désoeuvrée]*. Trans. Peter Connor, Lisa Garbus, Michael Holland, and Simona Sawhney. Minneapolis: University of Minnesota Press.

———. 1996 [1994]. *The Muses [Les Muses]*. Trans. Peggy Kamuf. Stanford, CA: Stanford University Press.

Nietzsche, Friedrich. 1967 [1872]. *The Birth of Tragedy and the Case of Wagner [Die Geburt der Tragödie aus dem Geiste der Musik]*. Trans. Walter Kaufmann. New York: Random House.

———. 1968 [1883–91]. *Thus Spoke Zarathustra [Also sprach Zarathustra]*. Trans. Walter Kaufmann. In *The Portable Nietzsche*. New York: Viking Press.

———. 1974 [1882]. *The Gay Science, with a Prelude of Rhymes and an Appendix of Songs [Die frölicke Wissenschaft]*. Trans. Walter Kaufmann. New York: Random House.

Noverre, Jean-Georges. 1760. *Lettres sur la danse, et sur les ballets*. Stuttgart and Lyon: Delaroche.

———. 1803. *Lettres sur la danse, sur les ballets et sur les arts*. Saint Petersburg: Schnoor.

———. 1807. *Lettres sur les arts imitateurs en général et sur la danse en particulier*. Paris: Collin.

———. 1930. *Letters on Dancing and Ballets*. Trans. Cyril W. Beaumont. London: C..W. Beaumont. Reprinted by Dance Books, Alton, 2004.

——— 2012. *Lettres sur la danse, sur les ballets et sur les arts*. Ed. Flavia Pappacena. Lucca: Libreria Musicale Italiana.

Palazzo, Claudia. 2005. "Corps à corps avec l'histoire: *Histoire(s)* d'Olga de Soto, 2004." *Vertigo*, special issue "Danses," October, 49–50.

Pastori, Jean-Pierre. 1987. *Pierre Lacotte: Tradition*. Lausanne: Favre.

Pautrat, Bernard. 1971. *Versions du soleil*. Paris: Seuil.

Petipa, Marius. 1990 *Mémoires*. Trans. Galia Ackerman and Pierre Lorrain. Arles: Actes Sud.

Petit, Jean-Luc, ed. 1997. *Les neurosciences et la philosophie de l'action*. Paris: Vrin.

Phelan, Peggy. 1993. *Unmarked : The Politics of Performance*. New York: Routledge.

Piollet, Wilfride. 2005. *Rendez-vous sur les barres flexibles*. Paris: Sens & Tonka.

Plato. 1960. *The Laws*. Trans. A. E. Taylor. London: J. M. Dent and Sons.

———. 1972 [1952]. *Plato's Phaedrus*. Trans. Reginald Hackforth. Cambridge: Cambridge University Press.

———. 1999. *The Symposium*. Trans. Christopher Gill. London: Penguin.

Plotinus. 1917–30. *The Enneads*. Trans. Stephen MacKenna and B. S. Page. London: Medici Society.

Plutarch. 1961. *Moralia*. Vol. 9, *Table-talk, Books 7–9. Dialogue on Love*. Trans. Edwin L. Minar, F. H. Sandbach, and W. C. Helmbold. Cambridge, MA: Harvard University Press.

Pouillaude, Frédéric. 2007. "*Scène* and Contemporaneity." Trans. Noémie Solomon. *TDR: The Drama Review*, 51:2, 124–35.

Pouivet, Roger. 2003. *L'oeuvre d'art à l'époque de sa mondialisation: Un essai d'ontologie de l'art de masse*. Brussels: La lettre volée.

Preston-Dunlop, Valerie. 1998. *Rudolf Laban: An Extraordinary Life*. London: Dance Books.

Prieto, Luis J. 1992. "Le mythe de l'original." In *Esthetique et poétique*, edited by Gérard Genette, 131–56. Paris: Seuil.

Prunières, Henri. 1914. *Le ballet de cour en France avant Benserade et Lully*. Paris: H. Laurens.

Pure, Michel de. 1668. *Idées des spectacles anciens et nouveaux*. Paris: Brunet.

Rabinbach, Anson. 1990. *The Human Motor: Energy, Fatigue, and the Origins of Modernity*. Berkeley: University of California Press.

Ralph, Richard. 1985. *The Life and Works of John Weaver: An Account of His Life, Writings and Theatrical Productions, with an Annotated Reprint of His Complete Publications*. London: Dance Books.

Rameau, Pierre. 1725. *Abrégé de la nouvelle méthode pour écrire toutes sortes de danses de ville*. Paris.

Rancière, Jacques. 2009 [2004]. *Aesthetics and Its Discontents [Malaise dans l'esthétique]*. Trans. Steven Corcoran. Cambridge: Polity Press.

———. 2011 [1996]. *Mallarmé and the Politics of the Siren [Mallarmé: La politique de la sirène]*. Trans. Steven Corcoran. London: Continuum.

Renouard, Maël. 2001. "Le point de vue de Sirius et la cartographie du visible." In *Historicité et spatialité, Le problem de l'espace dans la pensée contemporaine*, edited by Jocelyn Benoist and Fabio Merlini, 203–20. Paris: Vrin.

Ricœur, Paul. 1984 [1983]. *Time and Narrative*. Vol. 1 [*Temps et récit, t.1*]. Trans. Kathleen McLaughlin and David Pellauer. Chicago: University of Chicago Press.

Rizzolatti, Giacomo, Luciano Fadiga, Vittorio Gallese, and Leonardo Fogassi. 1996. "Premotor Cortex and the Recognition of Motor Actions." *Cognitive Brain Research* 3, 131–41.

Rouget, Gilbert. 1985 [1980]. *Music and Trance: A Theory of the Relations between Music and Possession [La musique et la transe]*. Trans. Brunhilde Biebuyck. Chicago: University of Chicago Press.

Rousier, Claire, ed. 2001. *Oskar Schlemmer: l'homme et la figure d'art*. Pantin. CND.

———. 2002. *La danse en solo: Une figure singulière de la modernité*. Pantin: CND.

Rousseau, Jean-Jacques. 2004 [1758]. *Letter to d'Alembert and Writings for the Theater*. Trans. and ed. Allan Bloom, Charles Butterworth, and Christopher Kelly. Hanover, NH: University Press of New England.

Sachs, Curt. 1937 [1933]. *World History of the Dance [Eine Weltgeschichte des Tanzes]*. Trans. Bessie Schönberg. New York: Norton.

———. 1940. *The History of Musical Instruments*. New York: Norton.

Saint-Léon, Arthur. 1992 [1852]. *Stenochoreography, or the Art of Writing Dancing Swiftly [La sténochorégraphie, ou l'art d'écrire promptement la danse]*. Trans. Raymond Lister. Cambridge: R. Lister.

Schaeffner, André. 1936. *Origine des instruments de musique*. Paris: Payot.

———. 1947. *Le pré-théâtre*. Paris: Polyphonie.

——. 1998. "Instruments de musique et musique des instruments." In *Variations sur la musique*. Paris: Fayard, 100–123.

Schelling, Friedrich Wilhelm Joseph von. 1845 [1812]. *The Philosophy of Art: An Oration on the Relation between the Plastic Arts and Nature* [*Ueber das Verhältniss der bildenden Künste zu der Natur*]. Trans. A. Johnson. London: John Chapman.

Scherer, Jacques. 1957. *Le "Livre" de Mallarmé: Premières recherches sur des documents inédits*. Paris: Gallimard.

Schlemmer, Oskar. 1978. *Art et abstraction*. Trans. É. Michaud. Lausanne: L'âge d'homme.

Schloezer, Boris de. 1921. « Danse et psychologie. Considérations sur la danse classique ». *Revue musicale*, special issue, 118–25 Paris: NRF.

——. 1979 [1947]. *Introduction à Jean Sebastien Bach*. Paris: Gallimard.

Schneider, Rebecca. 2005. "Solo Solo Solo." In *After Criticism: New Responses to Art and Performance*, edited by Gavin Butt, 23–47. Malden, MA: Blackwell.

——. 2011. *Performing remains: Art and War in Times of Theatrical Reenactment*. New York: Routledge.

Séchan, Louis. 1930. *La danse grecque antique*. Paris: E. de Broccard.

Sève, Bernard. 1998. "Ce que la musique nous apprend sur la notion de forme." *Philosophie* 59, 50-68.

——. 2002. *L'altération musicale*. Paris: Seuil.

——. 2013. *L'instrument de musique: Une étude philosophique*. Paris: Seuil.

Sorell, Walter, ed. 1975. *The Mary Wigman Book: Her Writings*. Middletown, CT: Wesleyan University Press.

Stiegler, Bernard. 1998 [1994]. *Technics and Time*. Vol. 1, *The Fault of Epimetheus* [*La technique et le temps, T.1 La faute d'Épiméthée*]. Trans. Richard Beardsworth and George Collins. Stanford, CA: Stanford University Press.

——. 2004. *De la misère symbolique*. Vol. 1, *L'époque hyper-industrielle*. Paris: Galilée.

——. 2009 [1996]. *Technics and Time*. Vol. 2, *Disorientation* [*La technique et le temps, T.2 La désorientation*]. Trans. Stephen Baker. Stanford, CA: Stanford University Press.

——. 2011 [2001]. *Technics and Time*. Vol. 3, *Cinematic Time and the Question of Malaise* [*La technique et le temps, T. 3 Le temps du cinéma et la question du mal-être*]. Trans. Stephen Barker. Stanford, CA: Stanford University Press.

Straus, Erwin W. 1963 [1935]. *The Primary World of Senses: A Vindication of Sensory Experience* [*Vom Sinn der Sinne*]. Trans. Jacob Needleman. Glencoe, IL, and London: Free Press of Glencoe/Collier-Macmillan.

——. 1966. *Phenomenological Psychology: The Selected Papers of Erwin W. Straus*. Trans. Erling Eng. London: Tavistock.

Tomlinson, Kellom. 1735. *The Art of Dancing Explained by Reading and Figures; whereby the manner of performing the steps is made easy by a new and familiar method*. London.

Valéry, Paul. 1951. *Lettres à quelqu'un*. Paris: Gallimard.

——. 1954. "Poetry and Abstract Thought." *Kenyon Review* 16:2, 208–33.

——. 1957. *The Collected Works of Paul Valéry*. Vol. 4, *Dialogues*. Ed. Jackson Matthews. Trans. William McCausland Stewart. London: Routledge and Kegan Paul.

——. 1960a. *The Collected Works of Paul Valéry*. Vol. 12, *Degas, Manet, Morisot*. Ed. Paul Jackson. Trans. David Paul. London: Routledge and Kegan Paul.

——. 1960b. *The Collected Works of Paul Valéry*. Vol. 3, *Plays*. Ed. Jackson Matthews. Trans. David Paul and Robert Fitzgerald. London: Routledge and Kegan Paul.

————. 1964. *The Collected Works of Paul Valéry*. Vol. 13, *Aesthetics*. Ed. Jackson Matthews. Trans. Ralph Mannheim. London: Routledge and Kegan Paul.

————. 1977. *Cahiers 2*. Paris: Gallimard.

————. 2000–2010. *Cahiers/Notebooks*. Vols. 1–5. Ed. Brian Stimpson, Paul Gifford, and Robert Pickering. Frankfurt: Peter Lang.

Vaganova, Agrippina. 1953 [1948]. *Basic Principles of Classical Ballet: Russian Ballet Technique*. 2nd ed. Trans. Anatole Chujoy. Ed. Peggy van Praagh. London: A. & C. Black.

Wagner, Richard. 1993 [1849]. "The Art-Work of the Future." In *The Art-Work of the Future and Other Works*. Trans. by William Ashton Ellis. Lincoln: University of Nebraska Press, 69–214.

Warburton, William. 1737–41. *The Divine Legation of Moses Demonstrated on the Principles of a Religious Deist*. 2 vols. London: Fletcher Gyles.

Wigman, Mary. 1966 [1963]. *The Language of Dance* [*Die Sprache des Tanzes*]. Trans. Walter Sorrell. London: Macdonald Evans.

————. 1990 [1963]. *Le langage de la danse* [*Die Sprache des Tanzes*]. Trans. Jacqueline Robinson. Paris: Chiron.

Xenophon. 2013. *The Symposium*. Trans. Donald F. Jackson. Lewiston, ME: Edwin Mellen Press.

Yates, Frances A. 1988 [1947]. *The French Academies of the Sixteenth Century*. London: Routledge.

Index